A Sociolinguistic History of British English Lexicography

A Sociolinguistic History of British English Lexicography traces the evolution of British English dictionaries from their earliest roots to the end of the 20th century by adopting both sociolinguistic and lexicographical perspectives. It attempts to break out of the limits of the dictionary-ontology paradigm and set British English dictionary-making and research against a broader background of socio-cultural observations, thus relating the development of English lexicography to changes in English, accomplishments in English linguistics, social and cultural progress, and advances in science and technology.

It unfolds a vivid, coherent and complete picture of how English dictionary-making developed from its archetype to the prescriptive, the historical, the descriptive and finally to the cognitive model, how it interrelates to the course of the development of a nation's culture and the historical growth of its lexicographical culture, as well as how English lexicography spreads from British English to other major regional varieties through inheritance, innovation and self-perfection.

This volume will be of interest to students and academics of English lexicography, English linguistics and world English lexicography.

Heming Yong is currently a professor and President of Guangdong University of Finance, China, with a doctoral degree from Macquarie University and titles of The New Century Extraordinary Talent by China's Ministry of Education, Outstanding Expert for Special Government Allowances by China's State Council, Honorary Professor from Murdoch University and the International Achievement Alumni Award for Distinguished Service from Macquarie University. He was a visiting fellow at the University of Oxford and the University of Massachusetts and worked as Velux Visiting Professor at Aarhus University, Denmark. His areas of study include diachronic lexicography, communicative lexicography and translation studies.

Jing Peng is currently an associate professor of Guangdong University of Finance and Economics, with a master's degree from Southampton University, UK. Her academic interests cover diachronic lexicography, communicative lexicography and business English studies.

A Sociolinguistic History of British English Lexicography

Heming Yong and Jing Peng

LONDON AND NEW YORK

First published 2022
by Routledge
2 Park Square, Milton Park, Abingdon, Oxon OX14 4RN

and by Routledge
605 Third Avenue, New York, NY 10158

Routledge is an imprint of the Taylor & Francis Group, an informa business

© 2022 Heming Yong and Jing Peng

The right of Heming Yong and Jing Peng to be identified as authors of this work has been asserted by them in accordance with sections 77 and 78 of the Copyright, Designs and Patents Act 1988.

All rights reserved. No part of this book may be reprinted or reproduced or utilised in any form or by any electronic, mechanical, or other means, now known or hereafter invented, including photocopying and recording, or in any information storage or retrieval system, without permission in writing from the publishers.

Trademark notice: Product or corporate names may be trademarks or registered trademarks, and are used only for identification and explanation without intent to infringe.

British Library Cataloguing-in-Publication Data
A catalogue record for this book is available from the British Library

Library of Congress Cataloging-in-Publication Data
Names: Yong, Heming, author. | Peng, Jing, author.
Title: A sociolinguistic history of British English lexicography / Heming Yong and Jing Peng.
Description: London ; New York : Routledge, 2021. | Includes bibliographical references and index.
Identifiers: LCCN 2021009886 | ISBN 9781032024677 (hardback) | ISBN 9781032024684 (paperback) | ISBN 9781003183471 (ebook)
Subjects: LCSH: English language—Great Britain—Lexicography—History. | Encyclopedias and dictionaries—Great Britain—History and criticism.
Classification: LCC PE1611 .Y57 2021 | DDC 423.028—dc23
LC record available at https://lccn.loc.gov/2021009886

ISBN: 978-1-032-02467-7 (hbk)
ISBN: 978-1-032-02468-4 (pbk)
ISBN: 978-1-003-18347-1 (ebk)

Typeset in Sabon
by Apex CoVantage, LLC

Contents

Introduction 1
0.1 Latin beginnings and paradigms of British English lexicography 1
0.2 Deficiencies in previous diachronic studies in British English lexicography 4
0.3 Methodology, approaches and historical segmentation 6

1 The Latin roots in English dictionaries and the inception of English lexicographical culture 10
1.1 The origin and development of the English language – from Old English to Middle English 10
1.2 The socio-cultural background of the UK prior to the 16th century 13
1.3 The tradition of Latin lexicography and the earliest beginnings of English lexicographical culture 18
1.4 The Latin roots of English glossaries and bilingual dictionaries prior to the 16th century 20
1.5 The characteristics and academic value of English glossaries and dictionaries prior to the 16th century 27

2 The early development of English bilingual lexicography and its deviation from Latin traditions 31
2.1 The socio-political background for the development of English bilingual lexicography in the 16th century 31
2.2 The linguistic and cultural background for the development of English bilingual lexicography in the 16th century 35

vi *Contents*

2.3 *The 16th-century English bilingual dictionary-making and its gradual sublation of Latin traditions 40*

2.4 *The design features and academic value of English bilingual dictionaries in the 16th century 48*

3 **The bourgeoning of the English monolingual dictionary paradigm and the extension of bilingual dictionary traditions in the 17th century**   52

3.1 *The socio-political background for the development of English lexicography in the 17th century 52*

3.2 *The linguistic and cultural background for the development of English lexicography in the 17th century 57*

3.3 *The making of the first English monolingual dictionary and its inheritance of European lexicographical traits 60*

3.4 *Robert Cawdrey and the first English monolingual dictionary 64*

3.5 *The development of English monolingual lexicography and the fading of English hard-word traditions 66*

3.6 *The continuation of English bilingual lexicographical traditions and innovations in bilingual dictionary compiling techniques 73*

3.7 *The academic and social values of English dictionaries in the 17th century 77*

4 **The termination of hard-word traditions in English lexicography and its pursuit of prescriptivism**   82

4.1 *The socio-cultural background for the shaping of British English lexicography in the 18th century 83*

4.2 *The codification of the English language and the establishment of prescriptive traditions 87*

4.3 *Samuel Johnson and his monumental* Dictionary of the English Language *93*

4.4 *Other major English monolingual dictionaries in the 18th century and their adherence to prescriptivism 101*

4.5 *The extension and emergence of other types of English dictionaries in the 18th century 112*

4.6 *The humanistic and academic values of English dictionaries in the 18th century 117*

Contents vii

5   The European philological traditions and the creation of
     the diachronic dictionary paradigm in the 19th century   124
     5.1 *The socio-cultural background for the development of*
         British English lexicography in the 19th century 125
     5.2 *The English and linguistic background for the*
         evolution of British English lexicography in the 19th
         century 130
     5.3 *The tradition of European philology and the theoretical*
         conceptualization of New English Dictionary on
         Historical Principles *133*
     5.4 The Oxford English Dictionary – *an epic of*
         inheritance, innovation and perseverance 139
     5.5 *The traditional inheritance and theoretical innovation*
         of other major British English dictionaries in the 19th
         century 146
     5.6 *The humanistic and academic values of British English*
         dictionaries in the 19th century 155

6   The transformation of lexicographical traditions and
     the prosperity of British English lexicography   160
     6.1 *The social and technological background for the*
         prosperity of British English lexicography in the 20th
         century 161
     6.2 *The linguistic and academic background for the*
         prosperity of British English lexicography in the
         20th century 166
     6.3 *The continuing development and prosperity*
         of British philological dictionaries in the 20th
         century 173
     6.4 *The emergence and thriving development of British*
         learner's dictionaries 180
     6.5 *The digitalization of printed dictionaries and the*
         booming growth of British electronic and online
         dictionaries 182
     6.6 *The tradition of phonetic transcription and the making*
         of British pronouncing dictionaries in the
         20th century 184
     6.7 *The changed attitude towards dialectal words and the*
         making of British dialect dictionaries in the
         20th century 185

viii   *Contents*

6.8   *The extension of slang lexicography and the compilation of British slang dictionaries in the 20th century 187*

6.9   *The continuation of the etymological tradition and usage criticism and the making of British dictionaries of etymology and usage in the 20th century 190*

6.10 *The studies in synonymous relations and the making of British thesauruses in the 20th century 195*

6.11 *The expansion of lexicographical functions and the making of British encyclopaedic dictionaries in the 20th century 199*

6.12 *The socio-cultural changes and the compilation of British dictionaries of new words 200*

6.13 *The enhancement of reference function and the making of British quotation dictionaries 201*

7   **English lexicography – accomplishments, developments and prospects**   203

7.1   *Linguistic theories in the 20th century and the diversified development of English dictionary paradigms 204*

7.2   *Theoretical innovations and developments in 20th-century English lexicography 213*

7.3   *The prospect of English lexicography in the 21st century 225*

Bibliography   229
Major referenced websites 241
Index   243

Introduction

Modern English dictionaries have their direct and remotest sources in the glossaries compiled in Britain between the 7th and 8th centuries, and those glossaries created the precedent of arranging entries on the alphabetical and topical bases, which, together with the annotative modes of defining words, became the archetype of English dictionary compilation.

0.1 Latin beginnings and paradigms of British English lexicography

Starting from its inception, British English lexicography has undergone four distinctive paradigms of dictionary production. Its earliest theoretical roots grew out of Latin grammar and traditions of making Latin glossaries and dictionaries. Its first systematically established approach is prescriptivism, which is grounded on the assumption that, like all other things, language use should be conducted in the "correct" way. Classic linguists claim that rules should be made for the best or the "most correct" use of language. Prescriptive grammar is based on their views of the best language usage rather than on the description of actual language use. It adopts such criteria as purity, logic and historical and literary superiority to pass judgment upon the best language use and make norms for it. Any deviation from or violation of language norms is treated as language decay and corruption and should be avoided, purified and put right in the light of logic and literary supremacy, just to prevent linguistic pollution and decay. Signs of prescriptivism in early English dictionary compilation were the manifestation of Latin lexicographical traditions, which continued to exert gradual yet visible impacts upon the shaping of the prescriptive paradigm of English lexicography. Prescriptivism became firmly established with the publication of Samuel Johnson's (1709–1784) *A Dictionary of the English Language* (1755).

Towards the late part of the 18th century, historical comparative linguistics, which had its roots in European philology, came into vogue in the linguistic circles of Germany, Austria, Hungary and the Scandinavian region. Through its evolution in the 19th and the early 20th centuries, a

2 Introduction

set of historical linguistic principles and methods were developed, and they started to be employed in English dictionary-making. The ideas of comparison and internal reconstruction, together with the explorations in word origins from phonological, morphological and semantic aspects and in the tracing of etymologies and the compilation of etymological dictionaries, inspired theoretical thinking and methodological construction. Those inspirations developed over time into the historical paradigm for English lexicography, which adopts historical principles and comparative approaches as its basic methodology, with focus on the evolution and representation of words of the same language source over different periods of time with a view to reconstructing the pronunciation, spelling, morphology, syntax and sense relations of words from the perspective of language development and exploring the evolutional traces of words and diachronic relatedness of linguistic variations in the light of historical literature and linguistic data. The making of *The Oxford English Dictionary* (hereinafter abbreviated as *OED*) is a good example of consistent, comprehensive, systematic and scientific implementation of the historical principles and an unparalleled signifier of their firm establishment in English lexicography and adequate application of the historical paradigm to English dictionary-making.

From the late 19th to the early 20th centuries, the conceptualization of linguistics underwent radical changes in approaches and dimensions, marking a significant transformation in methodology from prescriptivism to descriptivism. Language description, which developed on the basis of structuralism, was widely recognized as the mainstream approach of the 20th-century linguistic research, and descriptivism became the dominating school of linguistics in the century. It has exerted profound and extensive impacts upon language study and dictionary compilation in terms of notions, principles, methods and theoretical generalization. Compilers who were accustomed to designing dictionary policies from prescriptive dimensions started to adapt themselves to changes in the trends of linguistic study and turn their dictionaries into language recorders and describers rather than authorities and arbitrators.

This transformation stems chiefly from the following core notions of descriptivism: all languages are socially conventionalized systems rather than systems formed through natural laws; the primary step for language research is observing what really happens when native speakers use the language and making a faithful record of how it is actually used; all languages are dynamic instead of static and are in constant change as long as they are in use by their speakers. Therefore, the so-called rules are merely an agreement concerning their current use, and all language use is relative and not absolute. The judgment on whether language use is right or not can only be based on the actual use of language, not on the rules laid down by authorities.

These notions, which are the guidelines Philip Babcock Gove (1902–1972) and his team adopted in shaping their monumental work *Webster's*

Third New International Dictionary of the English Language, Unabridged (commonly known as *Webster's Third*, or *W3*, 1961), have become the theoretical foundation for the descriptive paradigm of English lexicography. Ever since, the descriptive paradigm has been dominating English dictionary-making and research. Descriptivism has played a leading role in the development of English lexicography and has become one of the fundamental principles of modern lexicography. The seeds of descriptivism are deeply sowed in the minds of present-day linguists and lexicographers, thanks to Gove's innovative efforts in *Webster's Third*.

Traditionally, all lexicographically related activities and issues were basically conjured up by compilers. They would be organized and resolved in the light of subjective judgments without taking into account dictionary design, function, compilation and use from both compilers' and users' perspective and adopting empirical approaches. Consequently, dictionary compilation was separated from dictionary use and language cognition. That situation was changed by another significant transformation and shift of focuses in English lexicography from compilers and dictionaries proper to users and user behaviour, which was marked by the ground-breaking publication of *Longman Dictionary of Contemporary English* (hereinafter abbreviated as *LDCE*) in 1978. Users' behaviours of language cognition and lexical information retrieval are of immediate relevance and essence to cognitivism in lexicography. Learners' dictionaries, with their origins from the early 20th century and in the wake of *LDCE*, started to mushroom in different forms and in close succession. Their thriving and prosperity pushed dictionary-making and research into the era of cognitivism and brought about the perfect integration of dictionary-making with language research, cognitive science, language pedagogy, electronic technology etc.

Dictionary users are the best critics. They give life to dictionaries and extend it into eternality. User needs and language cognition are of vital significance to dictionary design and compilation. Dictionary compilation and research are bound to be seriously defective without taking the user perspective into consideration. Owing to the enormous success of *LDCE* on the market worldwide, learners dictionaries, which made their debut in the early 20th century, developed with increasingly strong momentum, ushering in an era of cognitivism characterized by unique focuses on users in dictionary compilation and research and an era of seamless integration of dictionary design and dictionary use, dictionary function and language cognition and dictionary-making and electronic technology.

The cognitive paradigm of English lexicography is a natural outcome of integrated developments in theorization of cognitive science, cognitive linguistics, lexicography and foreign language pedagogy. It is based on such cognitive linguistic notions: language is not a self-contained vacuum system, linguistic competence is part of human cognitive capabilities and language description must draw inferences from cognitive processes; linguistic structure has something to do with the conceptual structure, knowledge

4 *Introduction*

structure, discourse function and practical experience of the humanity and uses them as motivation to frame; syntax is not a self-perfecting system and is intertwined with vocabulary and semantics – vocabulary, morphology and syntax are continuums constituting a semiotic body; semantics is not merely objective truth conditions but is closely associated with the subjective mind and the infinite knowledge system of humankind; dictionary-making and use are socio-cultural activities that highlight the natural process of linguistic cognition and the mental representation of vocabulary acquisition.

In practice, the cognitive paradigm of English lexicography starts from the links and processes of users' linguistic cognition. It adopts cognitive approaches and examines such dimensions as formal structure, categorical structure, valence structure and distributional structure to expound headwords in the dictionary and how they are acquired by users. It attempts to decipher the flow-process diagram of cognition, explore the lexical mental representation of potential dictionary users, the cognitive process of dictionary consultation, the needs and skills of information look-up, the learning strategies of dictionary use etc. so as to enhance the efficiency of lexical acquisition. All this entails the shift in dictionary-making from compiler-centred to user-centred, from decoding-focused to encoding-focused and from consultative look-up to productive association. *WordNet*, which is produced by Princeton University and available at wordnet.princeton.edu, brings the cognitive paradigm into a new phase of dictionary-making and marks the culmination and climax of the compilation of dictionaries on cognitive principles.

0.2 Deficiencies in previous diachronic studies in British English lexicography

A general review of diachronic studies on British English lexicography demonstrates some obvious drawbacks.

First, British lexicographical culture may be traced back to the Anglo-Saxon times, and British English dictionary compilation, in the strict sense, took place around 400 years ago. However, the existing diachronic researches in British English lexicography can hardly be considered comprehensive or systematic, for they are mostly limited to individual lexicographical works of ancient times and make light of or simply neglect contemporary works, thus lacking in historical continuity and short of subject coverage. They fail to fully demonstrate the evolutional characteristics and regularities of British English lexicography over different periods of time and provide a complete panorama of how it has evolved from the remote times to the present day.

Second, thanks to the in-depth research findings in dictionary user cognition and the perfect combination of dictionary compilation and electronic technology, fundamental changes have taken place in dictionary functions and typology since the first half of the 20th century. Works on diachronic

Introduction 5

lexicography must explore such changes and reflect lexicographical transformations thus caused. Functionally, previous researches tend to focus on the language functions, especially definitions, of English dictionaries and neglect their social and cultural functions. They fail to look at the development of British English lexicography from the integrated dimensions of compilers, dictionaries themselves and users. Typologically, they tend to regard English monolingual dictionaries as their sole object of study, pay limited attention to English bilingual learners and encyclopaedic dictionaries and give almost no consideration to other types like electronic and specialized dictionaries. Any serious work on the history of English lexicography without covering major dictionary types is doomed to be incomplete and should be discounted.

Third, "dictionaries are the product of the evolution of human civilization and the development of human society. The needs from society and culture are the catalyst for the inception and development of lexicography" (Yong and Peng, 2008). Lexicographical culture is an essential part of national culture, and from the development of dictionaries can be reflected the historical traces of advancements in civilization and the ups and downs of a nation. Owing to the prolonged influence of ontological studies of language, previous studies are to a great extent defective in methodology, as they are mainly confined to dictionaries proper and tend to be compiler-centric. They fail to conduct socio-cultural analyses of the development of British English lexicography from interdisciplinary perspectives, resulting in their separation from the socio-cultural context without which British English lexicography could never emerge and evolve. Diachronic studies in British English lexicography must be conducted from societal, cultural and interdisciplinary dimensions, without which they could not reveal the basic traits and regularities of English dictionary development. In addition, the comparative approach must be adopted to set the historical picture of British English lexicography against a larger scene of the history of world lexicography, particularly setting it against the European cultural background so as to highlight the uniqueness of diachronic lexicography of British English.

Finally, previous researches fail to make historical segments of the development of British English lexicography and eventually incorporate them into a coherent unified framework of theoretical generalization. Generally, they follow a well-beaten path: subsequent to a brief survey of the development of ancient wordbooks, the whole text is almost exclusively devoted to the evaluation of specific and representative lexicographical works. More emphasis is laid on the parts than on the whole, on the isolated analysis of cases than on systematic generalization and on accumulation of practical experiences than on formulation of lexicographical theories. No attempt has been made to historically segment the development of British English lexicography on the basis of distinctive features of different periods and establish a theoretically coherent framework incorporating all the findings concerning the holistic history of British English lexicography. It must be

6 *Introduction*

noted that individual case studies and analytical evaluations of ancient dictionaries are necessary and fundamental, but their separate treatment will reduce and even impair the continuity of history, the relatedness of theory and the integrity of research.

0.3 Methodology, approaches and historical segmentation

Since its earliest beginnings, British English lexicography has been developing for over 1,200 years. A sound framework that incorporates all its theories and practices should be established to reflect the trajectory of its whole evolution. Only when all the findings and accomplishments are collated, evaluated, analysed and integrated can we embrace the whole picture of the history of British English lexicography and put them under one umbrella. Only then can we further portray the evolutional trajectory and patterns of the development of British English lexicography against the background of the socio-cultural development in the UK and against an even larger European socio-cultural scene.

> The basic methodology in the study of the history of lexicography should be a combination of sequence, evaluation, and generalization, following the diachronic sequence as the main thread of inquiry and exploration, making objective assessment of major lexicographical works, formulating theoretical generalizations, and eventually establishing a coherent framework to incorporate all the findings of such research.
>
> (Yong and Peng, 2008:7–8)

This general methodology also applies to the study of the history of British English lexicography. Diachronically, focus must not be given to only the ancient period, leaving modern and contemporary periods untouched or little discussed. The ancient, modern and contemporary periods should all be treated in good proportions to cover all major works and periods.

First, typologically, consideration should be given not only to monolingual dictionaries but bilingual (multilingual) and encyclopaedic dictionaries, learners dictionaries, electronic dictionaries, specialized dictionaries and other types as well, certainly with more prominence being given to monolingual language dictionaries. An appropriate balance should be kept between the ancient heritage and modern and contemporary innovations. Emphasis should be given not only to the evaluation and analysis of representative dictionaries but also to the historical continuity, the systematicity of theoretical investigation and the comprehensiveness and unity of diachronic explorations. Only by so doing can we present a coherent historical picture of British English lexicography, covering its development from ancient times to the present day and from monolingual types to all other major types.

Second, diachronic studies of British English lexicography should not be confined within the limits of the traditional dictionary-ontology paradigm.

Introduction 7

The two interwoven threads of socio-cultural evolution and English lexicographical development in Britain will have to run in parallel throughout the diachronic research of British English lexicography so as to set relevant studies against Britain's grand socio-cultural background and relate the historical development of British English lexicography from the sociolinguistic perspective to language evolution, language education, social reform, civilization advancement, national rise and fall, religious transmission, scientific and technological progress etc. Prominence must be given to the interactive relationships between socio-cultural advancement and dictionary production and development and between socio-cultural demands and dictionary compilation and use. Meanwhile, comparison should be made to put the historical development of British English lexicography under the general context of world lexicographical culture to highlight the features and regularities of the historical trajectory of the development of British English lexicography.

Third, the practice of separate case study and isolated theoretical generalization must be reviewed and refined in the whole trajectory of the evolution of British English lexicography so that lexicographical products and culture can be approached, evaluated and elevated under a more consistent, coherent, integrated and interrelated framework. "The practical implication and historical value of specific dictionaries will be better appreciated when they are taken into the picture of the whole historical process in which they have evolved and developed". "In so doing, the diachronic inheritance in history, the systematic formulation in theory, and the integration of sequence, evaluation, and generalization will become conspicuous throughout the presentation" (Yong and Peng, 2008:9). As English has become a medium of international communication, the development of British English lexicography must be examined and analysed against the broad background of the advancement of civilization in the English-speaking world and the evolution of world lexicography so as to pinpoint the unique status and national traits of British English lexicography in world dictionary families.

Fourth, lexicography has been traditionally discussed from a single perspective, i.e. the compiler's perspective. That single-perspective mode in the study of lexicographical development must be re-evaluated and modified. The communicative theory of lexicography (Yong and Peng, 2007) can thus be adopted to

> establish a theoretical model for the study of lexicography: integrating the compiler, the dictionary, and the user into a trinity so that the dictionaries and their development can be examined from a threefold perspective — the dictionary, its compilation, and its use. Such an approach can help free us from the confinements of the conventional practice of looking at dictionaries only from the perspective of dictionary itself.
>
> (Yong and Peng, 2008:9)

8 *Introduction*

and create natural associations between user demand and dictionary compilation, between user study and dictionary use and between dictionary use and language pedagogy. Eventually a unified research framework consisting of three different but interdependent standpoints, i.e. from the position of compiler, from the position of user and from the position of dictionary context, is called forth to observe and analyse the evolution of British English lexicography.

Finally,

> the segmentation of historical periods is considered one of the most fundamental theoretical issues in the study of the history of lexicography in any language and it is essential that the division of the history of the development of lexicography into periods is made upon a scientific, distinctive, and objective basis.
>
> (Yong and Peng, 2008:10)

Breakthroughs will have to be made in the traditional practice of focusing on case studies of individual works and the parts of the history and making light of theoretical systematization so as to incorporate findings in separate studies, particularly in analytical studies of individual cases and specific parts, into a clear, comprehensive and coherent framework that fits in with the evolutional patterns and the entire trajectory of the history of British English lexicography. Such attempts have not been made so far in previous studies.

A scientific and feasible way to divide history into periods will help readers to gain a better understanding of how English lexicography has evolved from one phase to another in the British and the general European cultural setting, how they distinguish themselves via distinctive features and how various phases are interrelated to demonstrate the trajectory of their development, thus portraying a complete picture of the history of British English lexicography. The historical segmentation of British English lexicography will have to be approached from both diachronic and synchronic perspectives, taking into account the entire progress over different periods and the distinctive features at given points of time and pinpointing material differences and distinctive features in different phases, particularly those great-leap-forward accomplishments in the theory and practice of English dictionary-making.

English dictionary-making can trace its earliest beginnings to the Anglo-Saxon period and has lasted for about 1,200 years, even counting from *The Leiden Glossary*, which is based on an Anglo-Saxon exemplar and was prepared around 800 AD. Through refining the findings in English lexicographical research, exploring the regularities and distinctive features in English lexicographical evolution and examining different views in relevant discussions, we arrive at a five-period segmentation, following the basic theoretical line of dictionary paradigm evolution in English lexicography:

Introduction 9

the pioneering and foundation-laying period (prior to the 16th century), the period of Latin traditions (the 16th century), the prescriptive period (the 17th and 18th centuries), the historical period (the 19th century) and the descriptive and cognitive period (the 20th century and beyond). These periods are distinctive in features but evolutionarily interrelated, as history always progresses in an accumulative fashion, drawing on achievements from previous periods.

The pioneering and foundation-laying period is typically marked by the making of glossaries or *glossae collectae* that explain words and expressions from texts used in the classroom. The period of Latin traditions is chiefly featured by the making of Latin-English and English-Latin bilingual dictionaries that capitalized on Latin traditional heritage. The prescriptive period started with the appearance of the first English monolingual dictionary and reached its climax with the publication of Johnson's dictionary in 1755, characterized by its deviation from Latin norms and its adherence to prescriptive principles for linguistic codification and purity in terms of pronunciation, orthography and grammar. The historical period showed its early signs in the conceptual preparation and configuration of *OED* and was conspicuously marked by its more sophisticated functional design and splendid printed publication. The historical dictionary paradigm employed historical linguistics and historical comparative linguistics as its theoretical underpinning and the historical comparative approach to trace word origins in pronunciation, form and meaning. The descriptive and cognitive period, highlighted by *Webster's Third* and *LDCE*, adopts descriptivism as the dominating principle to guide dictionary compilation, coupled with the spirit of learners dictionaries that originated in the early 20th century, from which the cognitive ideas of userism were derived. Only by such historical segmentations can they be pieced together to form a complete historical trajectory of British English lexicography.

After over 1,500 years of evolution, English has become a truly globalized language. Thanks to its rapid expansion into the international community in the past centuries and the strengthened status in the international arena today, English dictionaries have consolidated their ever-increasing influences upon both theory and practice of world lexicography. In less than 500 years, English dictionaries have completed their travels from prescriptivism to historicism, to descriptivism and then to cognitivism, which amply demonstrate the social, cultural and interdisciplinary nature of dictionary research; the inheritance, interactivity and integrality between language and dictionary, dictionary and social communities and dictionaries and culture; and the organic association between user demand and dictionary-making, user research and dictionary use and dictionary use and language pedagogy. All this combines to present the evolutional paths of English dictionary paradigms, which are coherent, complete and in conformity with the true images of the development of British English lexicography up to the present times.

1 The Latin roots in English dictionaries and the inception of English lexicographical culture

Owing to its surprisingly rapid growth over different periods of time, particularly subsequent to the Industrial Revolution, Britain turned itself from an isolated island nation to the northwest of European continent into a magnificent empire that dominated territories over 140 times larger than itself for around 300 years. For almost 200 years, it remained the world's first super power from the 18th century to the early 20th century and exerted such long-term unparalleled impacts upon political, economic, cultural, scientific and military aspects of world life. The magic rise of America in the New World enabled it to share and eventually supersede Britain's leading role in the international arena after the Second World War.

The continuous strengthening of power and prosperity of America and Britain over the past centuries has endowed English with its international prestige and its unshakable status as an effective medium of international communication and has transformed it into the world's genuinely globalized language for international trade and commerce and for transmission and communication in science and technology. It has also given English lexicography the cutting edge in both theoretical and practical explorations. English lexicography boasts a history of over 1,200 years, counting approximately from the appearance of *The Leiden Glossary*, but it has its deep roots in the Latin language and the making of Latin glossaries and dictionaries as well as Old English and the making of Old English glossaries and wordbooks.

1.1 The origin and development of the English language – from Old English to Middle English

English, which has its deepest roots in Anglo-Frisian dialects spoken by the Germanic peoples of Northern Europe from the mid-5th to the 7th centuries, was developed from Old English and spread far and wide with the gradual shaping of the sun-never-setting British empire, initially through territorial expansion and colonization, and in modern times through reinforcement and consolidation of Britain and America's international importance in political, economic, cultural and military arenas.

The Latin roots in English dictionaries 11

As a modern international language, English has reached out to different parts of the world, unprecedented and unparalleled in the scope of its use, in the areas of its penetration, in the profoundness of its impacts and in the number of speakers. Present-day English boasts 375 million speakers who use it as the first language, second to Chinese and Spanish when viewed from the number of native speakers and only next to Chinese when the number of non-native speakers is taken into account. A look-back survey upon the English language around 1,500 years ago gives a completely different picture presenting its evolution from a mixture of British isle vernaculars and northwest Germanic dialects to a modern powerful medium of international communication.

Almost nothing can be found in ancient English literature in relation to the languages used in the British Isles prior to the Anglo-Saxon invasion, and the earliest known reference to the inhabitants of Britain might have come from the records Pytheas, a Greek geographer, kept about his voyage of exploration around the British Isles in the 4th century BC. Recent findings from the Ancient Human Occupation of Britain, known as the AHOB project, have revealed that humans lived in Britain over 800,000 years ago. However, the first occupants the ancient literature now available suggests are probably the Celts, who migrated to the British Isles from the northern part of continental Europe around 500 BC. They spoke the Celtic language, with their initial settlements in Ireland, and they later migrated to Scotland. This is known as the first "intrusion" by the Indo-Europeans.

In 55 BC, the Romans started to invade the British Isles, with their domination lasting for almost five centuries. The collapse of the Roman Empire in the 5th century caused their withdrawal from the Isles. What fell upon the Celts following the withdrawal of the Roman army was relentless plunder and occupation by the Picts in northern Scotland and the Scots in Ireland. As can be inferred from the Ogham inscriptions that came down from the 4th century, the Picts and the Scots spoke the Celtic language. According to *Ecclesiastical History of the English People*, in his fight against the Picts and the Scots, Vortigern, probably a king of the Britons and the "superbus tyrannus", asked his continental relatives Hengist and Horsa for assistance but ended up by taking refuge in North Wales. Around 499, three Germanic tribes – the Jutes, the Angles and the Saxons from northwest Europe – started their conquest in the British Isles and established their kingdom with their own cultural and economic centres. This situation lasted until the early 11th century.

Between the 9th and 11th centuries, Great Britain did not become peaceful as a result of foreign occupation and continued, on the contrary, to suffer from continual plundering assaults by its north European neighbours. Though they came from different parts of north Europe, there were no significant differences between the languages they spoke. After their settlement in the Isles, the Jutes, Angles and Saxons became by and large a

12 The Latin roots in English dictionaries

united nation generally known as Angles. The dialects and vernaculars they used gradually converged into a new language – the Anglo-Saxon language, i.e. Old English (449–1100). Owing to several centuries' intensive Roman and north European contacts, Old English borrowed considerably from Latin and the Scandinavian languages. Part of the borrowings have already become the core vocabulary in modern English, for example, words of Latin origin such as *street, kitchen, kettle, cup, cheese* and *wine* and words of Scandinavian origin such as *anger, cake, call, can, come, die, egg, fellow, folk, get, give, hear, house, leg, man, mine, mother, odd, over, raise, ride, see, skill, sky, summer, take, they, thing, think, ugly, under, wife, will, window* and *winter.*

Old English is by nature a synthetic language rather than an analytic language. Nouns, verbs, adjectives and pronouns were all highly inflected word classes, with the first three classes distinguishing between the strong and weak forms. A large proportion of Old English words originated from the Germanic languages, but only about 15 percent remain as present-day English vocabulary, chiefly formed through compounding, prefixing and suffixing. Word classes were mainly distinguished by grammatical means, and sentence meanings were largely determined by inflections instead of word order in the sentence so that word order was not so rigid as it is in modern English (Fennell, 2005:59).

The Norman Conquest, which took place in the ending period of Old English, exerted unprecedented influences upon the English language and culture in both depth and breadth and marked the transition of Old English into Middle English (1100–1500). Unlike the invasions by the Vikings, what the Norman Conquest brought to the British Isles was, rather than advanced culture, predominating power, tight control and the French gentry. The Norman French dialect they spoke gradually developed into an English-style Norman French. Over a considerably long period of time subsequent to the Norman Conquest, English, Latin and French were in simultaneous circulation. Latin was mainly the Church language, Norman French was the language used by government and English conceded to become the language of the majority of native inhabitants.

From the early 13th century, the British gradually got over the tight Norman French control, and in the 14th century a series of events expedited the heightening of the social status of English and its readoption in political and religious affairs. By the end of the 14th century, poems written in English came out in large numbers, which laid the solid foundation for English to become the literary language. Geoffrey Chaucer (c. 1343–1400), the greatest Middle English poet, composed most of his works in English, though he continued to write in both French and English. Official documents and minute records started to be produced in English, and Henry VI spoke in English when he ascended the throne in 1399. By the early 15th century, English got firmly established as the general language of all walks of life in the British society.

The Latin roots in English dictionaries 13

A textual comparison between Old English and Middle English demonstrates significant transformation in the latter, chiefly reflected in the gradual simplification and even disappearance of inflections, the more stabilized word order and the obvious intensification of language contact and borrowing. All this indicates that Middle English was undergoing a transformation from the synthetic type of language into the analytic type.

1.2 The socio-cultural background of Britain prior to the 16th century

A review of English evolution over the past 1,500 years or so shows that it has never existed independently of itself and has maintained its intimate contact with the languages of continental Europe. As indicated in 1.1, throughout its transformation from Old English into Middle English, English was influenced by all major socio-cultural British events, of which foreign invasions constituted the principal part. Those events brought with them not merely deplorable occupations but led Britain on the way to the glory of today. What follows is a rough scuttle through those major historical events that have exerted direct impacts upon the formation and evolution of the English language and the inception and development of English lexicographical culture so as to trace the interactive links of British English lexicography to the English language, culture and society.

The Roman Invasion Latin, a classic language that was originally a dialect spoken in Latium in the Italian Peninsula, developed through the power of the Roman Republic into the dominating language first within the Italian territories and then beyond the boundaries of the Roman Empire. With the waning power and influence of the Roman Empire around the 5th century, Latin was losing ground as a dominant medium of oral communication in its neighbouring countries but continued to be used only in the central regions of the European continent and evolved into varieties and branches, hence the modern Roman language family. It must be noted that Latin was then still the general language for academic communication in Europe for well over 1,000 years, though it was not spoken in the neighbouring territories.

Latin influence upon English may be traced to 55 BC, when Julius Caesar led his troops and conquered the British Isles. Subsequently, for several hundred years, the Romans annexed two-thirds of southern Britain into their empire. Latin, as the language of the conquerors, was introduced into the British Isles and became spread in the regions where the Roman forces were stationed. In 50 AD, Claudius (10 BC–AD 54), the Roman emperor, led his troops into the Isles. They slaughtered the Celts, drove them to remote regions and made Great Britain part of their empire until the Roman troops retreated in 410. The Roman domination continued for several hundred years but the Celtic language persisted in its use by the Romans, their descendants and a small number of Celts. In addition, the Roman troops came from various regions and spoke languages that differed from each

14 *The Latin roots in English dictionaries*

other in some aspects, which explains why Latin influence upon Old English over that period was limited to only a few Latin borrowings.

The Anglo-Saxon Invasion The withdrawal of the Roman troops from the British Isles left Britain with a great deal of power vacuum, and the internal and external factors of the British Isles, as indicated previously, triggered off the Anglo-Saxon invasion.

Around 449, the Jutes, the Angles and the Saxons landed on the British Isles. They expelled the native inhabitants to remote areas and forced their languages and ways of life upon the conquered people. The Jutes were the first group of invaders among the Germanic tribes, and they settled down in Kent. They were followed by the Saxons, who occupied Wessex and Sussex on the south of the Thames River and the Angles, who occupied the vast land from the north of the Thames River to the Scottish highland. Consequently, there emerged in the history of Britain the seven Anglo-Saxon kingdoms – Northumbria, Mercia, Essex, East Anglia, Wessex, Sussex and Kent.

It can be inferred from the names of the seven kingdoms that Essex, Wessex and Sussex were Saxon settlements, that East Anglia, Northumbria and Mercia were Anglo settlements and that Kent was the settlements of the Jutes. Among them, Kent was originally the major cultural and economic centre, but by the 7th and 8th centuries, Northumbria replaced Kent as the centre because of its academic prosperity. The central role was later shifted to Mercia and eventually to Wessex, which lasted until the early 11th century. The Anglo-Saxon invasion exerted prolonged, profound and extensive influence upon the shaping of British nation and Old English. The Germanic tribal languages merged to form Old English in the end.

The introduction of Christianity into the British Isles The introduction of Christianity into the British Isles is an event of paramount importance in the Anglo-Saxon cultural history. In 596, Pope Gregory I (c. 540–604) sent St Augustine (?–c. 604), together with his missionary delegation, to the British Isles, with the intention of preaching Christianity. Four years later, St Augustine was appointed the first Archbishop of Canterbury, and there ensued Christian churches, Celtic churches, monasteries and numerous followers. By the end of the 7th century, England had become a major force of the Christian family.

However, the transmission of Christianity in England did not go smoothly. Rather, it met with occasional frictions and even conflicts between the St Augustine faction and the Celtic Church faction. With the wider spread of Christianity, the struggle between the two factions for the dominating position became inevitable and fierce. In 664, the church convention was held to determine the Easter and baptizing rituals to be practiced in conformity with the Roman customs, which suggested that the British churches would follow the Roman and European continental practices. The introduction of Christianity into Britain produced immeasurable effects upon the British social life, morals and values and English language and culture.

The Latin roots in English dictionaries 15

The intrusion by the Vikings Peace did not completely come with the Germanic occupation of the British Isles, which were instead plundered from time to time by the Vikings. From 787 to the 11th century, the Vikings, who were treated as heretics, started their continual intrusions upon the churches and monasteries in the British Isles, and two of them left profound impacts upon Old English.

In 865, A Scandinavian named Ragnar Lothbrok sent his two sons, together with their armed forces, to land on East Anglia. In just a few years, the Vikings conquered almost the whole of east England. In the several dozen of years that followed, the invasions by the Vikings increased, including the Danes, the Norwegians and the Swedish. By about 990, East Anglia was still under the British control, but the Danish had made inextirpable imprints upon the British life in both biological and social terms. From the end of the 10th century onwards, new waves of invasions were launched by the Norwegian King Olaf Tryggvason and the Danish King Svein Forkbeard. The Danish domination of England did not end until 1042. The early Vikings invaded England chiefly for the purpose of plundering and looting, but their intention changed in the 10th and early 11th century to assimilation and colonial ruling. The over 200 years of Scandinavian occupation and ruling of the British Isles infused a considerable number of Scandinavian lexical elements into the Old English vocabulary, in particular common everyday words, which is an indication of their willingness to merge with the local people and an outcome of intimate linguistic contacts between the invaders and the invaded.

The Norman Conquest In 1066, King Edward, who ruled England for 24 years, died without heirs to the throne. Harold was chosen as the heir, which directly led to the fight for the throne and the conquest on England by the Norwegian King Harald Hardrada (c. 1015–1066) and Duke William (1028–1087). Shortly after his victory against the Norwegian forces, Harold had no choice but to fight the well–schemed Norman Conquest by the strong French troops. Harold died in battle, and the British troops were defeated. William became the King of England on Christmas of that year, and the French began their rule of England that lasted for over 300 years.

The Norman Conquest is of paramount significance in the British history and has extensive and profound influence upon the British political, social, cultural and religious life. To a very large extent, it brought the French-speaking Normans into the historical scene in the British administration and made them the ruling class in place of the native British, which meant closer ties with the European continent but the waning of the traditional Scandinavian influence. The Norman Conquest also brought about serious consequences to other parts of the British Isles, for, subsequent to the conquest, Wales, Ireland and Scotland became the targets by the Normans and other French-speaking peoples, and the European impacts upon political, social, cultural and linguistic aspects of the British society ensued.

16   *The Latin roots in English dictionaries*

The Norman Conquest radically transformed the British language and culture and brought about subversive effects upon the political status of the English language, its functional mapping, its internal systems and even the whole English linguistic ecology. French became the language of the upper class, and English yielded to become the language of the lower class. Latin was the traditional medium through which to record the major historical events and pass down the British socio-cultural legacies, but, from the mid-13th century, French developed itself into a major supplementary written language and was not replaced by English until the late 14th century. Between the early 11th century and the late 14th century, English completed its transition from Old English to Middle English, which is chiefly reflected in the gradual disappearance of inflections, the gradual stabilization of word order and a huge number of French borrowings as a result of language contacts, which was unprecedented in the history of the English language.

The reestablishment of English as the official language Over a long period of time subsequent to the Norman Conquest, Britain remained a multilingual society. Latin was used for church services, French for government and English by the great majority of ordinary people. Starting from the early 13th century when King John (1166–1216) lost Normandy, the ties between Britain and France became weakened, which was worsened by the outbreak of the Hundred Years' War in 1337, a serious blow to the dominant position of the French in Britain. The awakened common folks used their collective strength to promote the use of English, which restrained to some degree the expansion of French in government.

Some other factors proved more important to the reestablishment of English as the official language. For example, the Bible was translated into English, and great literary masters, such as Richard Rolle (1290–1349), Walter Hilton (1340–1396), William Langland (c. 1332–c. 1400), Thomas Malory (c. 1405–1471) and Geoffrey Chaucer (1343–1400) started to write in English, which immensely enhanced the position and image of English. From 1362 onwards, English became the language used by the court to adjudicate, though the court records were not kept entirely in English until the 18th century. In 1363, the British Parliament officially announced its opening in English, and towards the end of the 14th century, English was already used in official documents and minute records. In 1399, Henry VI's accession to the throne was announced in English. By 1400, when Chaucer died, English was basically re-established as the literary language and as the language for other major fields. (See Algeo and Pyles, 2009:126.)

The application of printing technology in Britain The printing technology is recognized as one of the four major inventions in ancient China and can be traced back to the woodblock printing techniques in the Sui Dynasty (581–618). In the Tang Dynasty (618–907), the great demand for books stimulated its extensive use. The techniques were modified to the more optimized movable type printing by Bi Sheng in the Song Dynasty (960–1279) and were transmitted to Europe via the Mongolians. The widespread

The Latin roots in English dictionaries   17

nature of printing technology substantially facilitated social advancement in Europe, enhanced national literacy education and literary development and created necessary the technological conditions for the Renaissance.

William Caxton, who went to study printing technology in Germany in the 1470s, is the first Englishman to have learned printing techniques and to have established a printing workshop. In 1472, Caxton set up, through joint efforts, a printing and publishing establishment, and, four years later, he applied the printing techniques acquired in Germany and began to print books in large numbers in Britain. He wrote quite a lot in English and translated a considerable number of works from French, Latin and Dutch into English. The number of works he wrote, translated and published amounted to 108 in 87 varieties. His translation of *The Recuyell of the Histories of Troye* (c. 1473–1475) is the first English book printed in Britain. The transmission and wide application of the printing technology in Britain turned out to be of special significance to the standardization of English against the background where spellings were chaotic, dialects were extremely varied, and English was undergoing rapid changes. However, the printing technology did not have immediate obvious effects upon dictionary-making, and the printing of large numbers of dictionaries did not actually happen before the advent of the 16th century, due to economic, technological, cultural and social constraints and the limitations of the printing technology itself.

The Tudor Dynasty After his accession to the throne, Henry Tudor II (157–1509) put an end to the chaos caused by the Wars of the Roses and started to rule the Kingdom of England and its realms from 1485 to 1603. Henry II launched a series of social transformations. He reclaimed land from the churches and confiscated land from the gentry who lost in wars. He recruited key government officials from the grassroots level, concluded trade deals and attempted to set up the British navy so as to reinforce its strong trade and military strength. The Tudors extended their power beyond modern England, achieving the full union of England and the Principality of Wales in 1542 and successfully asserting English authority over the Kingdom of Ireland. All this substantially consolidated Britain's transformation into a strong kingdom, paving the way for Britain to become a world superpower.

The rehearsal of overseas expansion In 1497, John Cabot (1450–1499), who was born in Italy and moved to settle in Britain, helped his family with spice dealings. Inspired by Bartholomeu Dias' (c. 1451–1500) voyage to Southern Africa in 1488 and Christopher Columbus' (c. 1451–1506) adventurous discovery of the New World in 1492, Cabot conjured up the idea of exploring the road to spice trade in India and China. With Henry II's patronage and authorization, he set out on his transoceanic voyage in 1497. After 50 days' voyage, Cabot reached the northern American continent. This discovery later became the testimony for British claim to the North American territories and the prelude to Britain's overseas expansion and the

18 *The Latin roots in English dictionaries*

creation of a sun-never-setting empire, hence a historical opportunity for England to start its journey to globalization.

1.3 The tradition of Latin lexicography and the earliest beginnings of English lexicographical culture

The earliest dictionary compilation, according to historical literature, can be traced back to the Sumerian language spoken by the tribes in south Mesopotamia, which approximates to modern Iraq, between 5000 BC and 2000 BC About 4000 BC, the Sumerians created their civilization, and their representative achievement is undoubtedly the writing system they created and used – cuneiform. Around 3000 BC, the Sumerians started to make a record of their major events via graphics, which developed into the ideographic writing system – cuneiform. Over 2,000 years or so after its formation, the cuneiform writing was the only writing system used in the Mesopotamian region and proved to be significant to the shaping and development of the languages and characters in West Asia.

By 2500 BC, the first libraries in the history of mankind were built in the Mesopotamian region. They collected clay tablets filled with cuneiform characters, which are found to involve the Sumerian glossaries. As a non-Semitic tribe, the Sumerians had as their major opponents the Semitic tribes from their northern neighbour – Akkad. Around 2340 BC, the Akkadians conquered the Sumerians. History demonstrates that successful conquests are most likely accompanied by linguistic and cultural assimilation. The Akkadians accepted and absorbed the most fundamental cultural form of the conquered Sumerians – the cuneiform and compiled glossaries of extensive coverage of lexical items, with a view to further narrowing down their linguistic and cultural distances.

The now-extant Sumerian-Akkadian glossary consists of 24 clay tablets, with 9,700 separately written entries covering a wide range of terms regarding law, administration, wood and wood products, weed and weed products, pottery utensils, leather products, copperware and other metal products, domesticated and wild animals, parts of the human body, botanical plants, birds, fishes, textiles, geography, food, beverage etc. These clay tablets are ascribable as the origins of world lexicography, and the tradition of compiling such glossaries continued in the ancient Mideast until about 1750 B.C., when Sumer and Akkad were annexed into the Babylonian Empire.

There was a period of silence for glossary writing or dictionary-making between 1750 BC and 400 BC, and that silence was broken when the Greek city state system and the Roman Empire came into shape. Around the 5th century BC, Protagoras (c. 490 BC – 420 BC) collected the so-called hard words from Homer's works –*The Iliad* and *The Odyssey* – into a glossary. As remarked by Plato, Homer "educated Greece". It was for the sake of such literacy education that it became necessary for words in Homer's works to be accumulated under one cover, for most of them had become

The Latin roots in English dictionaries 19

unfamiliar to the readers after over 400 years of their publication. It was a common practice for early compilers to collect into glossaries those obscure words that were gathered from classic manuscripts and to mark above each of them with explanatory translations. Around 340 to 284 BC, Philetos wrote a well-known glossary that focused on unusual technical terms, dialect terms and poetry diction. The emergence of such glossaries indicated the sprout of the culture of European lexicography.

From the very outset, ancient Greek lexicography was characterized by diversities and encyclopaedic attributes. In addition to words from Homer's works, early Greek glossaries also collected legal terms, terms of philosophy of language, medical terms from Hippocrates' medical literature, dialect terms and drama terms and words and expressions from great orators in history. Most of the glossaries had been lost, apart from a few fragments out of them, which were occasionally quoted in later works. Lucius Aelius Stilo Praeconinus (152 BC–74 BC), the first scholar in ancient Greece that deserved the title of "philologist", took a keen interest in grammar and etymology owing to the influence of Stoic philosophy, composed a good number of essays and, notably, compiled a glossary.

Marcus Terentius Varro (116 BC–27 BC) was the first important grammarian of Greek, and *De re rustica* is the only one of many of his works that has come down to the present time and is preserved in good condition, and the twenty-five-volume *De lingua Latina* has only six volumes preserved to the present day. Though heavily influenced by Praeconinus and many other Greek thinkers, Varro demonstrated his originality and independent thinking in his works. Varros' contributions to lexicography reside in his *De lingua Latina*, whose academic values were not discovered until the 11th century by Monte Cassino, and, in 1355, Boccaccio Giovanni (1313–1375) had it copied and passed on to his fellow writers. It was eventually incorporated into Ambrosius Calepino's (c. 1440–1510) multilingual *Dictionarium* and subsequent Latin-English dictionaries and English monolingual dictionaries. Ancient Greek and Roman lexicographical culture laid a solid foundation for the birth and development of lexicographical culture of modern Europe and exerted far-reaching influence upon English lexicography. The influence has been so extensive, so profound and so apparent that traces can be easily found from everyday grammar books and dictionaries, and anyone with a smattering of English knowledge can trace back to its earliest ancestry.

It is obvious that English lexicography has been under the influence of the lexicographical culture of ancient Greece and Rome, though the process and its effects might have been slow, long and indirect. In the history of European civilization, ancient Roman and Greek lexicographical culture has left deep and indelible imprints in European dictionary-making, in particular dictionary-making in France, but in the history of English evolution, Latin and French have exerted essential impacts, and British English lexicography can be in no way left out of the scene. Hans Sauer (2009:29) even traces

20 *The Latin roots in English dictionaries*

such influence up to the first Latin glossary by Verrius Flaccus (c. 55 BC–AD 20) in the first century. The general consensus is that the origins of English dictionary-making go back to the Anglo-Saxon period.

There appeared towards the end of the 7th century and the beginning of the 8th century the *glossae collectae* that explained or defined hard Latin words in simple Latin or Old English vernaculars. The extant early hard-word glossaries include *The Leiden Glossary, The Epinal Glossary, The Erfurt Glossary* and *The Corpus Glossary*, which are all named after the libraries that have kept them. However, the practice of annotating words and expressions started in the "prehistoric" Celtic and Germanic times. Those who set the precedent of doing that were usually missionaries, clergymen and then schoolmasters. The books accessible to them were mainly religious gospels and prayers written in Latin, and the annotations between lines or on the margins of pages were either made in the same language as the text or in local languages. They are neither dictionaries nor English, but they turn out to be language data priceless to modern linguists, as they keep records of those words in Old English, Old Irish and Old German that are no longer available elsewhere today. These annotations of hard words between lines and on the margins in early works signify the inception of English lexicographical culture.

1.4 The Latin roots of English glossaries and bilingual dictionaries prior to the 16th century

Prior to the 16th century, accomplishments in English dictionary-making were mainly reflected in glossaries and bilingual dictionaries. For the convenience of preaching and transmitting scriptures, smart monks and schoolmasters collected annotations from between lines and page margins into glossaries, wordbooks and vocabularies. That is the direct source of English lexicography. Early English dictionary compilers also benefited from the classified glossaries that had been made to suit the need for learning and memorizing Latin vocabulary, for example, a glossary for human body parts, a glossary for domesticated animals, a glossary of church furniture etc. The words in these glossaries were all explained or defined in English or in dialects and became "vocabularium" when gathered together. The previously mentioned four glossaries are widely believed to be the earliest ones still extant, but their archetype may be traced back to the late 7th century, which has been touched upon in previous discussions. What follows will concentrate on the making of glossaries and dictionaries between the 10th and 15th centuries.

Almost no such thing as glossary or dictionary-making took place for the whole of the 10th century, apart from *The Cleopatra Glossaries* mentioned in the studies conducted by Sauer (2009:33). This collection of glossaries was made around the mid-10th century and consisted of three Old English glossaries: the first was structured in the alphabetic order from A to P,

The Latin roots in English dictionaries 21

the second was a thematically classified Latin-Old English glossary and the third was also a Latin-Old English glossary, focusing on the explanation of prose and poetry diction gathered from the works of Aldhelm (c. 639–701), a Latin poet and Anglo-Saxon literary scholar. Aelfric (c. 955–1020), the grammarian, is definitely the most noteworthy figure from the perspective of lexicography, "the dominant author around 1000", as Sauer (2009:34) commented. He, in the capacity of clergyman and teacher, "wrote three related works: a Grammar, mainly for the morphology; a Glossary . . . for the vocabulary; a Latin Colloquy, to practise oral skills" (Sauer, 2009:34), which is summarized by Green (1996:59) under the general title of *A Latin Grammar and Dictionary*.

Aelfric's Glossary is "a Latin-OE (OLD English) class glossary", which collects about 3,000 Latin headwords that are divided into 30 sections and "arranged onomasiologically according to word-fields (semantic fields)" (Sauer, 2009:34), covering a wide-range of terms, such as names of parts of human body, names of birds, fish, animals, plants, housing and furniture, colour, garments, weapons, celestial body etc. These terms are generally arranged in a systematic way, following "a hierarchical sequence within the various groups, starting with the higher and proceeding to the lower, thus: God-angel-man; lord-servant-slave". Each headword is explained with one or more Anglo-Saxon synonyms.

In explaining his compiling motives, Aelfric states in the Saxon preface:

> Young men should learn wisdom; it is the business of elders to instruct them; for by learning faith is preserved, and everyone that loves wisdom shall be happy. . . . How should there be a supply of wise teachers for the people of God, unless they have been trained in learning while young? And how should faith be strong, if learning and teachers fail?

Aelfric's Glossary is still extant but in fragments. (See Green, 1996:59.) "Judging from the number of extant manuscripts, it must have been quite popular in the eleventh century, and it was copied until the early thirteenth century" (Sauer, 2009:34).

About one century later, a similar anonymous work came out but collected only 1,300 or so headwords, "making its way through eighteen topics, each of which holds a number of subgroups", including "God, heaven, the angles, sun, moon, earth, and sea; man, woman, and their bodies; blood relations, professional and trades people; diseases; such abstract terms as 'impious' and 'prudent'; fishes; beasts; household equipment; and so on" (Green, 1996:60). At the turn between the 12th and the 13th centuries, Alexander Neckham (1157–1217) became the most outstanding figure. He once taught in Paris. He was "a widely knowledgeable scholar, whose Latin was generally considered as superior to that of many contemporaries" (Green, 1996:62).

22 The Latin roots in English dictionaries

After a successful attempt at making an encyclopaedic dictionary, Neckham compiled several other dictionaries subsequent to his return to England from France. Among them, one treated Biblical terms, one treated terms of tools, instruments and utensils and the other had a more extensive collection and covered a wider range of fields. The work that represented his major achievement in lexicography was *De nominibus* (also known as *De nominibus utensilibus, De utensilibus*, Starnes and Noyes, 1991:199). This is a Latin glossary with Latin, French and occasional English explanations, beginning with descriptions of kitchens, furniture, utensils and cooking methods and extending by association to related terms such as landlord, maidservant, family utensils, architecture, castles, professions, agriculture and agricultural tools etc.

A grammarian almost Neckham's contemporary, John Garland (also Joannes de Garland, c. 1180–1250), is worthy of mention here. He received his education in Oxford and taught in the University of Toulouse. He compiled Latin grammar books and dictionaries, such as *Dictionarius scolasticus, Distigium* and *Synonym. Dictionarius scolasticus* is a collection of annotated Latin words arranged according to topics with the intent of gathering commonly used words for easy consulting and literacy education. According to *OED*, the Latin word *dictionarius* (English equivalent: *dictionary*) was first used in the titles of John Garland's previously mentioned dictionary, and the time was around the year 1225.

Distigium, which was printed in 1481, "is essentially devoted to advising young students". "A rhyming tract with an interlinear gloss in English and Latin, it is 161 lines long". The beginning 41 lines are couplets, proverbs, aphorisms and epigrams that are not related in any way – but coupled with English and Latin explanations. The remaining 120 lines form

> a vocabulary listing vocables associated with these topics: the names of animals; a house and furnishing of a house; the parts of the body; a mill and objects associated with it; a blacksmith's shop; instruments of the household and farm, including distaff, spindle, plow, and wagon; musical instruments; various artificers, such as cobbler, tailor, dyer, tanner, mason, and carpenter; species of trees; dress materials; and various classes of people.
>
> (Starnes, 1954:15)

Synonym is a rhyming dictionary defining its headwords by means of synonyms. It supplies an abundant list of synonyms for writers to choose different diction to express ideas when they write in Latin. Printers, such as Richard Pynson and Wynkyn de Worde, launched several versions of it between 1494 and 1518, which demonstrates that it was popular at that time. No substantial progress was made in dictionary or glossary compilation from John Garland's time to the end of the Middle Ages.

The Latin roots in English dictionaries 23

Boulanger (2003:376) recorded two other multilingual glossaries that appeared between the mid-14th century and the early 15th century. There appeared in about 1350 a Persian-Latin-Kipchak glossary entitled *Codex comanicus*. Kipchak is a Slavic language spoken on the Crimean Peninsula and was very rarely used in early glossaries. In about 1400, Dietrich Engelhus compiled a four-language glossary – *Vocabularius quadriidiomaticus* – with Greek, Hebrew and German equivalents to Latin. This kind of multilingual glossary was rare in early English glossary making.

After the Norman Conquest, the tradition of annotating words continued intermittently, but the practice of annotating in English became scarce, that of annotating in Latin persisted and that of annotating in French began to appear. Throughout the Middle English period, the compilation of Latin-Old English glossaries sustained, which created favourable conditions for the emergence of a new dictionary type – bilingual dictionaries – and laid a solid foundation for the development of Latin-English and English-Latin dictionaries in the 15th century. All that combined to push dictionary compilation in the Middle Ages to its climax.

There is obviously the necessity of introducing the four earliest classic bilingual dictionaries of the 15th century before we go into the 16th century – *Promptorium Parvulorum* (also known as *Promptorium Puerorum, Promptorium Parvulorum sive clericorum*), *Catholicon Anglicum, Medulla Grammaticae* and *Ortus Vocabulorum*. A textual comparison reveals direct or indirect relations between these four works and the works written by Neckham and Garlandes, which has been discussed previously.

As indicated earlier, the headwords in early English glossaries were basically Latin, and the defining language was mainly Latin or/and vernaculars, with occasional explanations made in some other languages. However, glossaries and dictionaries started to appear whose headwords were local languages and vernaculars. As microstructural entries provided very meagre lexicographical information, with most of the headwords explained by means of synonyms or equivalents, the compilation of glossaries with local words as headwords turned out to be no difficult task. What the compilers needed to do was reverse the order of Latin headwords and their explanations or equivalents in the original glossaries. One of the pioneering attempts was the first English-to-Latin bilingual dictionary – *Promptorium Parvulorum* – which was intended for children to learn Latin.

Promptorium Parvulorum was completed in about 1440. It is attributable to Geoffrey the Grammarian, a friar who lived in Lynn, Norfolk, England. It was printed by Richard Pynson in London in 1499, probably the first dictionary printed in England. It consists of around 300 printed book pages with a total of about 12,000 English words arranged alphabetically (I and J and U and V are undistinguished). Under each letter is listed in two groups, one comprising nouns and other word classes, and the other is verbs only. Each headword generally has two Latin equivalents, so that the total

24   *The Latin roots in English dictionaries*

number of words in the work is around 30,000. Besides Latin equivalents, the compiler also provided additional grammatical information regarding the gender and inflections of nouns, the declension of nominative case for adjectives and the conjugation of verbs etc., as well as the citations from authoritative works of the Middle Ages.

Owing to the introduction of printing techniques and the establishment of printing workshops in England, it went through reprints in the early 16th century by the printer Wynkyn de Worde. When the Camden Society republished it in the 19th century, the extended title *Promptorium parvulorum sive clericorum* ("Storehouse for children or clerics") was adopted. For language historians it is a major reference work for the vocabulary of late medieval English. It is a frequently cited reference in today's primary dictionary of late medieval English, the *Middle English Dictionary*. Now this dictionary has five versions in existence, which were made between 1499 and 1528, with two more modern versions that are based on the 15th-centruy manuscripts.

As noted by Ostler (2007:251), *Catholicon Anglicum*, The Universal Remedy or, more literally, the universal purge, as Green (1996:70) put it, is the first dictionary to have been published with a date of publication. It was published in 1460, and currently available are the Lord Monson manuscript and the hand-copied version in the British Museum. The former is dated 1483, and the latter might be much earlier than that, but the formal date of publication is 1881 (Green, 1996:70). It is a small English-Latin dictionary, encompassing a Latin grammar and the dictionary itself. It was completed by Johannes Januensis in 1286 and is intended for clergymen (Ostler, 2007:251). The dictionary collects around 8,000 headwords. The compiler followed Garland's practice of using a good number of Latin synonyms to explain the source-language words and distinguishing them in both meaning and use, which is the most conspicuous feature of the dictionary. He also absorbed extensively the materials from previous works, especially those by William Brito, Joannes Januensis, John Garland and others.

Medulla Grammaticae, according to Starnes (1954:6), has two distinct applications: (1) to 15th-century manuscript versions of a Latin-English dictionary, never printed or, if so, with modifications and change of title; (2) an alternate title to the printed editions of the first English-Latin dictionary, today better known as the *Promptorium parvulorum*. What is discussed here is "the only Latin-English dictionary then available, existing in many manuscripts and having an extensive word list and, above all, many definitions in English" (Starnes, 1954:31). It was printed in the early 15th century, but its manuscript appeared in the late 14th century. There now exist 16 versions of the manuscript with the same title, and the date can be traced to 1440. The authorship is unknown but is ascribable to "a host of obscure persons, unknown teachers: monks, friars, and obscure clerks who expounded the classics and Scriptures in the cloister or in the schools" (Starnes, 1954:26). Judging from the number of extant manuscripts and editions, "it was the

The Latin roots in English dictionaries   25

first and thus the comprehensive bilingual lexicon of the time, of which many copies were in circulation" (Green, 1996:69).

This highly popular and influential dictionary, "arranged in ABC order, contains about twenty thousand words, chiefly Latin, which are defined in Latin or in English. Proper names of persons and places are distributed, alphabetically, throughout" (Starnes, 1954:26). "Running to some 17000–20000 words, depending on the manuscript, the *Medulla* draws on a number of *glossae collectae*, glosses from classical texts and from the Bible. Additional material was apparently gleaned from a number of class glossaries or *vocabularia*" (Green, 1996:69). As it was the only Latin-English dictionary around the year 1500, with numerous versions and English definitions, the Latin-English dictionary makers after that time would use it as the base for their new compilations or abstract material from it, which suggests the strength and extent of its academic penetration.

In 1500, Wynkyn de Worde printed in small folio a Latin-English dictionary of unknown authorship with the title of *Ortus Vocabulorum*, a title that reflects "some of the fascination that words and the study of words had for authors and their public, and were not merely publishers' devices for calling attention to their wares" (Starnes, 1954:28). In explaining his choice of such a title, the author stated,

> Not unworthily called the garden of words, for just as in gardens are found abundance of flowers, of herbs, and of fruits with which our bodies are strengthened and our spirits refreshed, so in this book are diverse words accommodated to beginners desirous of the pleasures of learning. With these words they may furnish the mind, adorn their speech, and finally, if the Fates permit, grow into very learned men.
>
> (Starnes and Noyes, 1991:4)

The motive, as Starnes (1954:31) commented, is that "publication of a Latin-English dictionary as a companion volume to the *Promptorium* would be a most useful, and perchance profitable, undertaking" (Starnes, 1954:30).

Ortus Vocabulorum, which was printed in double columns, draws on *Medulla Grammaticae* as an essential source. It consists of 266 folios and about 27,000 alphabetically arranged entries, "including classical and Biblical proper names of persons and places, with indication of the inflection and gender of nouns and adjectives and the conjugation of verbs" (Starnes, 1954:30). In many of the entries, their Latin or English equivalents take up not more than a single line in the column. Although it "was popular through the first quarter of the sixteenth century" (Starnes and Noyes, 1991:4), "there is little evidence of its influence on subsequent lexicography – a circumstance which might be explained by the desire of the Humanities to start afresh and to avoid the use of medieval sources" (Starnes, 1954:37), to say nothing of inheriting the styles and traditions of the medieval dictionary compilation.

26 *The Latin roots in English dictionaries*

English-Latin and Latin-English dictionaries brought the 15th-century dictionary-making to its peak. However, that is not the only attractive point for the 15th century; the appearance of a new dictionary genre – pictorial dictionary – might be another. That *Pictorial Vocabulary*, "a distinct innovation" in Starnes and Noyes' words (1991:200), was collected by Thomas Wright into *A Volume of Vocabularies* in 1857. Its probable date of appearance is set as 1500, but it was not printed until the middle of the 19th century. "Among its approximately 2500 entries are 70 illustrative sketches, of the most basic quality" (Green, 1996:68).

> As to topics under which words are assembled, this collection is fairly conventional, beginning with names pertaining to the human body, then continuing with words relating to the church, names of domestic animals and wild animals, of fresh water fish and sea fish – distinctions not generally made in the earlier vocabularies.

Though it "includes the conventional elements", this vocabulary is "somewhat more comprehensive and more careful as to classification" (Starnes and Noyes, 1991:200). Its unique feature resides in its crude pictures, or simply the sketches inserted "to fill what would otherwise have been blank portions of the manuscript" and "to focus the reader's mind on his task, a view that seems less than feasible". "Pictorial dictionaries did crop up occasionally before the twentieth century, but on the whole they were rare" (Green, 1996:68). No other vocabulary or dictionary contained illustrations before the 17th century (Starnes and Noyes, 1991:200).

Before the conclusion of the chapter, mention must be made of John Stanbridge (1463–1510) and his two works of high lexicographical value. Stanbridge once worked in schools, hospitals and parishes. He compiled two grammatical works: *Vocabula* (1496) and *Vulgaria* (1508), literally "common things", thus "common words", which were intended for schoolchildren to learn Latin. *Vocabula* is "very typical of the sort of vocabulary or proto dictionary that had been appearing ever since the earliest Anglo-Saxon examples" (Green, 1996:78). This work, which borrowed heavily from his predecessors' work, adopted the usual topical arrangement of the entries, following the human-centred convention of beginning with body parts and radiating from things closest to human life to those least close to human life, including "diseases, the table and things associated with it, a range of occupations that include those of the baker, the carpenter, the smith, the mason, the goldsmith, and the cobbler, the world of agriculture and the countryside, of weapons, and of musical instruments" (Green, 1996:78). Seventeen editions appeared between 1496 and 1631, and six of them between 1510 and 1531, which is a good manifestation of "keeping alive the essentially medieval tradition of the vocabularies and *nominales* into a period of quite different lexicography" (Green, 1996:77–78).

The Latin roots in English dictionaries 27

Vulgaria basically resembles *Vocabula* in structural arrangement and thematic classification. It is somewhat similar to the manual of everyday foreign language conversation for tourists today. It begins with several pages collecting Latin words pertaining to human body parts together with English equivalents, followed by Latin words arranged according to rhymes and their interlinear explanations in English. Its publication became an immediate success as it turned out to be popular not just with children for general use but with students in Oxford as well. Altogether, seven editions came out between 1508 and 1529.

A lot of accomplishments were attained in English dictionary-making during the late 15th century. The printing technology made it possible to enable large numbers of English dictionary users to gain access to or even to possess dictionaries. Merchants, travellers, business agents, book fairs and other channels made dictionaries widely accessible at low prices in Europe and even in the whole world. A new wave of dictionary-making and publication was fermenting and surging, characterized by the emergence of new language dictionaries, scholar publishers' participation, the transformation of glossaries into dictionaries and the synergization of dictionary information. Latin was then still the international academic language, and Latin dictionaries were still being made in small numbers. However, national language dictionaries received unprecedented acclamation among national language users. The role of Latin in dictionaries continued mainly through its combination with major European national languages into bilingual or multilingual dictionaries, particularly with English and French.

1.5 The characteristics and academic value of English glossaries and dictionaries prior to the 16th century

Prior to the 16th century, there was a substantial accumulation of glossaries and vocabularies, whose linguistic data paved the way for later monolingual and bilingual dictionary compilation. Old English glossaries can be classified by nature into monolingual, bilingual and composite types. The glossaries that were purely monolingual or bilingual were rare, but composite glossaries were common, with Latin as the lemma language and Latin and/or Old English vernaculars as the defining language. In terms of contents, some are what are sometimes called *concordances*, collections of annotations of hard words gleaned from classic literature, with headwords arranged in the sequence of their appearance in the text. The greatest problem with such concordances lies in their look-up difficulties, as they are not arranged on the alphabetical basis. Some glossaries are alphabetical, and the others are class glossaries that are arranged on topical or thematic bases.

The previously mentioned classification is far from scientific in the strict sense. Early English glossaries are generally arranged on topical or thematic bases, with only a few being arranged on the mixed basis of thematic

28   *The Latin roots in English dictionaries*

categorization and alphabetization, i.e. first thematic classification of headwords into groups and then alphabetical arrangement of the headwords in A, AB or ABC order in the group. There are also rare cases of a glossary adopting two or more modes of arranging headwords. In the late part of the Middle Ages, some went so far as to list under the root headword all the words derived from the root. That is a major innovation upon the alphabetic arrangement of headwords in previous glossaries. When bilingual dictionaries started to appear in the 15th century, they basically followed the AB or ABC order of headword arrangement, which is a big step forward towards the headword arrangement in modern dictionaries, though, of course, not all glossaries were alphabetical, and random arrangement could be found in quite a few.

The practice of collecting hard words continued to quite modern times, and, in terms of headword selection, Old English glossaries and dictionaries followed the hard-word tradition. The special devotion to Latin hard words is a marking feature of early English glossaries and bilingual dictionaries. Early glossaries may consist of only dozens of pages and collect several hundred headwords, but, by the end of the 15th century, the number of headwords rose to around 27,000, which is remarkable even by today's standard in the eyes of the ordinary users. Early glossaries and bilingual dictionaries have their respective focuses in entry selection. Early glossaries mainly focus on the Latin words that are closely associated with daily life, while the 15th-century bilingual dictionaries have their own norms for headword coverage. Instead of gathering together all the headwords in previous glossaries, they focus more on the words that are related to social life, such as religion, interpretation of classic works, law and so on.

Judging from the ways that headwords are defined, those early glossaries, as well as dictionaries, are still in their infancy. Annotations can only be occasionally found in a few Latin glossaries, though in most are found somewhat more systematic and coherent explanations. When it comes to individual entries, definitions are generally provided in the form of synonyms and/or equivalent explanations, in some cases a combination of a Latin explanation and an Old English synonym, though, in some rare cases, one or several Latin explanations along with an Old English equivalent or explanation. In terms of usage description, they generally provide only a meagre amount of grammatical information concerning the headwords, such as the gender, inflection etc. of nouns and verbs. Word discrimination is also found in *Promptorium Parvulorum* and *Catholicon Anglicum*. For example, in the entry *preyste* of *Catholicon Anglicum*, ten lines are devoted to the discussion of differences in use between *sacerdos*, *presbiter* and *capellanus*. Apart from the information items mentioned earlier, those glossaries and dictionaries are devoid of almost all other information items.

From the very outset, English dictionaries are characterized by their encyclopaedic, pragmatic and subjective nature. From the time of their appearance, ancient glossaries and dictionaries did not confine their attention

The Latin roots in English dictionaries 29

exclusively to collections of linguistic words, and their scope of coverage went far beyond word annotations, taking into account almost every aspect of human life and ranging from word use, poetic language and dialect words to technical words and legal terms as well as specialized jargons. They satisfied to some extent the demands from commercial, legal, religious, administrative and social life of that time. However, it must be pointed out that mistakes and errors became common and unavoidable in them, as their compilers were not equipped with linguistic guides, nor did they know anything about phonetics. Solutions to lexicographical problems were generally worked out according to what they observed and what they pondered upon them. It was not uncommon for compilers to make wild guesses about meanings of words, grammatical usages and even spellings.

A survey of ancient glossaries and dictionaries shows that they were designed for single functions at the outset but have turned out to perform both didactic and scholarly functions when they are in use. In ancient China, Greece and Rome, early glossaries were all intended for literacy education to provide assistance in reading classic works. The chief motive for compilers of early glossaries in Britain was teaching Latin. At that time, Latin was still a living language used in churches, law, religious classics, philosophical reasoning and academic research. It was a language for religion, administration and scholarly activities. Meanwhile, early glossaries became the key carriers for Old English and Middle English words and their variants. They vividly represent the attributes and uses of Old English and Middle English and become realistic reading aids for comprehending Latin texts and for understanding and researching Old English and Middle English.

There were in the 15th century active compilations of Latin-English and English-Latin glossaries, vocabularies and dictionaries. Some compilations remain in the form of manuscripts and some in printed editions. They preserve a great deal of literature dating back to the 11th century. By the end of the 15th century, those glossaries, vocabularies and dictionaries were accumulated into larger printed editions so that they were endowed with supreme authority and naturally became the data sources for later Latin-English and English-Latin compilations and for textual researches in Latin, Old English and Middle English. They have proved to be of significant academic value as the primary literature foundation for textual studies in Old English and Latin.

Early English glossaries also have political and cultural functions to fulfil, reflecting language contacts between and interactive impacts upon Old English and Latin as well as Old English and French, which in turn mirror social activities, political statuses and humanitarian roles of those speech communities. It then becomes possible through the words gathered in the glossaries and dictionaries to trace the line of social, political, religious and cultural development in Britain in the Anglo-Saxon and the Middle Ages periods; reconstruct the scenes of social, political, religious and cultural life

30   *The Latin roots in English dictionaries*

in Britain and provide reliable data for textual researches and diachronic studies in British socio-cultural progress.

It is worth mentioning at the conclusion of this chapter that of the four classic bilingual dictionaries in the 15th century, *Promptorium parvulorum* and *Catholicon Anglicum*, are English-Latin dictionaries, which signifies an obvious tendency towards the localization of English dictionary-making and reflects the increasingly strengthening national awareness and the delicate changes in the status of English in the British society. All this suggests a delicate departure of English lexicography from the traditional Latin track towards nationalization and localization.

2 The early development of English bilingual lexicography and its deviation from Latin traditions

The 16th century witnessed fierce political turmoil, religious conflicts, economic development and social transformations in Britain. It also created a number of literati and thinkers that have shined brightly throughout the history of British literature and the history of world civilization.

In the 16th century, English lexicography continued its concentration on the making of Latin-English and English-Latin dictionaries, with Richard Huloet's *Abcedarium Anglico Latinum* (1552) serving as a line of demarcation. Prior to that line, Latin was basically the source language, and the dictionaries that were made were chiefly Latin-English, while, subsequent to that line, the dictionaries were mainly English-Latin dictionaries, with English as the source language. That line signified an evident transition and inclination of English lexicography from its compiling traditions and previous focuses on Latin towards English, reflecting the delicate changes of roles Latin and English played in Britain's social affairs and cultural communications and heralding the advent of the age of English monolingual dictionary-making.

2.1 The socio-political background for the development of English bilingual lexicography in the 16th century

Between the 14th and the 16th centuries, Europe was dominated by feudalist ideology. The commodity economy began to show its early signs, capitalism germinated and developed to a certain extent and the Renaissance movement was quietly under way. The Tudor Dynasty of the 16th century was a transitional period of great significance in British history. A new gentry class began to emerge in British society, radical changes were taking place in agriculture and, more importantly, industry, particularly the traditional wool industry, developed at an unprecedented rate, which turned Britain from a wool export economy into a wool goods export country.

Industrialization facilitated commercial markets and urbanization. Consequently, the whole of Britain was dotted with large and small towns, which highlighted London as its economic centre. Domestic economic development propelled Britain to expand into overseas markets for colonial plundering

32 *Early development of English lexicography*

and expansion. From the end of the 16th century, Britain started to open up colonial settlements overseas and expedite its capital accumulation through territorial occupation, slavery and even racial extinction. In the struggle between the Roman Catholic forces and the locality separatist forces, Britain's state sovereignty was increasingly strengthened, and national awareness was consolidated. It was the flourishing of Britain's economy and the reinforcement of state and national awareness that prepared social, political and economic conditions for Britain to leap into the modern epoch.

Henry VIII's accession to the throne Henry VIII (1491–1547) was the king of England from April 21, 1509 until his death and was the second Tudor monarch, succeeding his father, Henry VII. During his father's reign, policies of mercantilism were implemented, industry and commerce were protected and the sailing and shipbuilding industry was encouraged, so as to augment trading benefits, increase national strength and expand overseas markets. He also endorsed policies of friendly neighbourhoods and maintained good relations with Scotland, France and Spain through marriage arrangements. Upon his accession to the throne at the age of eight, Henry VIII followed his father's policies and astounded the world with his first marriage to Catherine of Aragon (1485–1536), previously Princess of Wales, as the wife of Henry's elder brother Arthur. Owing to the annulment of his first marriage and its ensuing effects, he initiated the English Reformation, declared the separation of the Church of England from papal authority and appointed himself Supreme Head of the Church of England.

Between 1536 and 1539, Henry VIII closed down over 500 monasteries and confiscated all their property as well as the manors of 90 seminaries and 110 church hospitals. He granted part of what was confiscated to his favourite ministers or sold it to the nobilities, ministers, farm owners and wealthy merchants. Apart from the denial of the authority of the Pope and the partly simplified formalities, no fundamental difference was discernible between the Anglican Church and the Catholic Church, and that is why the Reformation was considered incomplete or not thoroughgoing. Starting from Henry VIII's accession to the throne in 1509, Britain developed itself from a remote and isolated island nation to the northwest of the European continent to a superpower that influenced the world for several hundred years.

Enclosure Movement With the rapid development of the wool textile industry in Britain, the demand for wool was surging, which brought up wool prices. All that combined to make the wool industry a lucrative business. From the 1470s onwards, the British nobilities employed various means to drive the farmers out of their land and enclosed it with fences or ditches to raise sheep in order to benefit from economies of scale in farming huge tracts of land and seek profits.

Movements of land enclosure took place in different countries over different periods. In Britain, it continued until the end of the 18th century. It was not an isolated historical event but associated closely with the social

Early development of English lexicography 33

development, production demand and historical background of that time, hence a cause of the industrial revolution in England. It was a primary means of primitive accumulation that enabled British society to move towards capitalism. It led to improved crop production such as the rotation of crops, turned the British agriculture from small-scale farming economy into agricultural capitalism and changed feudal land ownership into capitalist land ownership in the countryside so that those peasants who had been stripped of their land had to sell their labour as a commodity and made themselves employed workers. All that reserved a huge labour pool for the development of capitalism in Britain, considerably enhanced Britain's industrial development, expedited Britain's urbanization and eventually enabled Britain to become a commercial leader in Europe in the 17th and 18th centuries.

The Acts of Supremacy *The Acts of Supremacy* are the two acts of the Parliament of England that were passed in 1534 and 1559 respectively. They established King Henry VIII of England and subsequent monarchs as the supreme head of the Church of England, thus replacing the Pope of the Roman Catholic Church. The 1534 Act is sometimes cited as marking the beginning of the English Reformation. It was proposed primarily out of Henry's need to obtain an annulment of his marriage to Catherine of Aragon, which was rejected by Pope Clement, as a validly contracted marriage indivisible until death, according to Roman Catholic teachings. So he wanted to take advantage of this act to have his fate and even the fate of his country in his own hands. From the perspective of institutional politics, this act should be considered part of the British institution, whose primary purpose was to reinforce the authorities of the British monarchs, weaken the influence of the Roman Catholic, consolidate his manipulation of the British churches and reclaim the wealth that was in the possession of the Church of England. All that required that he be the supreme head of the Church of England, as had earlier been done in England.

Henry's Act of Supremacy was repealed in 1554 in the reign of Queen Mary I and was reinstated by Queen Elizabeth I when she ascended the throne. Elizabeth declared herself Supreme Governor of the Church of England and instituted an Oath of Supremacy, requiring anyone taking public or church office to swear allegiance to the monarch as head of the Church and state. Anyone refusing to take the oath could be charged with treason. *The Second Act of Supremacy* was passed in 1559, but is dated 1558, because until 1793 legislation was backdated to the beginning of the session of Parliament in which it was passed. It was through that second Act that Elizabeth I officially established the now-reformed Church of England. Supremacy was extinguished under Cromwell but restored in 1660.

Henry VIII's English Reformation Henry VIII reigned as King of England from April 21, 1509 until his death in 1547. He was the second Tudor monarch, succeeding his father, Henry VII. During Henry's reign, dramatic changes took place, and the most far-reaching event was the 16th-century Reformation, a series of events by which the Church of England broke away

34 *Early development of English lexicography*

from the authority of the Pope and the Roman Catholic Church. The English Reformation was conducted from the top level gradually to the lower level. Seemingly, his efforts to have his first marriage to Catherine of Aragon annulled, along with his disagreement with the Pope on the question of such an annulment, led him to initiate the English Reformation. The more profound justification was the intolerance of the increasingly powerful English monarch towards papal supremacy and control over the governance of England purely for political reasons. The crucial issue of it was the political differences between Rome and England, which intensified theological disputes and eventually resulted in the break with Rome. That was consequently affected by the 1534 Act of Supremacy, which declared Henry as the "Supreme Head on earth of the Church of England" and endowed the English monarch with the final authority in doctrinal and legal disputes and, more importantly, with the status of England as a sovereign state and the dignity due to it. Viewed from the perspective of language evolution, this Reformation diminished the absolute authority of Latin in the English society, with the employment and influence of English further heightened, which inclined English lexicography towards a more apparent shift of focus from Latin tradition to the English language itself and led English dictionary-making onto a more English-oriented track of development in the 17th century.

Francis Drake's round-the-world journey Sir Francis Drake (c. 1540–1596) was a sea captain, privateer and political strategist of the Elizabethan era. He began his sailing apprenticeship in his childhood on the Thames River and the English Channel. His first sea voyage did not take place until when he was 23. He started the second circumnavigation of the world in a single expedition close to the end of 1577. He sailed along the west coast of the Americas and returned to Plymouth on September 26, 1580 via the Cape of Good Hope and Sierra Leone. He was the first to complete the voyage as captain throughout the entire circumnavigation. As a vice admiral, he was second in command of the English fleet in the battle against the Spanish Armada in 1588. He was awarded knighthood by Elizabeth I in 1581. His exploits made him a hero to the English, but his privateering led the Spanish to brand him a pirate. He died of dysentery in January 1596.

In the second half of the 16th century, commerce and industries developed at great speed, which demanded urgent expansion of overseas markets through colonization. Spain, the superpower on the sea at that time, constituted a major obstacle to British expansion. The religious conflicts between the two countries directly triggered their intensification and eventually the inevitable military confrontation. The sea battle, which took place in July 1588, dealt a serious blow to the Spanish forces and almost reduced them to nothing. From then on, the British took gradual steps in seeking sea hegemony and colonial expansion into the Americas. Drake's successful circumnavigation undoubtedly accumulated valuable naval battle experience for the British fleet – particularly in their fight again the Spanish

Early development of English lexicography   35

troops – and created necessary conditions for Britain to become the world's number one colonialist. All that consequently laid a solid political foundation for the spread of the English language around the world. The rapid growth of international trade in the 16th century brought about the boom of bilingual and multilingual dictionary compilation with modern European languages as the focus of description.

2.2 The linguistic and cultural background for the development of English bilingual lexicography in the 16th century

The history of language development reveals that all languages undergo gradual changes, and it is hard to specify its segmentation into periods at fixed dates. However, English linguists generally reckon 1500 as the starting year and 1800 as the ending year for early modern English, which may be regarded as a period of transformations both for Britain and for English.

Over the first 100 years in the early modern English period, the Renaissance movement was surging in Britain, the English versions of the Bible and *The Prayer Book* began to be in wide circulation in British churches and among the general masses and Shakespeare's works started to meet their readers in English versions. All this indicated that the 16th century had a special role to play in the transformation of the English language and culture, which caused radical deviations in English lexicography from its traditional reliance upon Latin and a focus on Latin-English and English-Latin bilingual lexicography to a new track of relatively independent development.

Early modern English Upon its entry into the 16th century, early modern English had already borne great structural resemblance to modern English. Word inflections were reduced to the minimum, the word order became basically stabilized and the meaning of a sentence was determined more by word order than inflections. The English system almost completed its transition from the synthetic language to the analytic language. The wide use of printing technology, the gradual implementation of mass education, the increasingly frequent social interactions, the newly emerging communication media and the fast development of natural science gave rise to the wide availability of professional knowledge, the intensification of national awareness and the amelioration of national thoughts. All these novel social elements exerted direct or indirect influence upon and facilitated English evolution.

Like other modern European languages, English confronted similar problems and contradictions in the new age. Relevant to the diachronic study of English lexicography were three major issues. The first was the struggle for the dominant position in the British society between English and Latin. For centuries, Latin enjoyed supremacy in British society, especially in the academic circles, while English remained for long the language for

36   *Early development of English lexicography*

the underclass and was degraded for the barbarous and uncivilized. At the beginning of the 16th century, British writers even had to apologize for using English in the composition of their works. William Tyndale (1494–1536) went so far as to think that English was the language of a ploughboy (Knowles, 1997:77). However, after 50 years, English was used by Queen Elizabeth, and, by the end of the 16th century, British writers took pride in writing in English and felt proud of English. British patriots came to realize that English was equal in importance to the languages of Greece and Rome and that it should enjoy the same social status as Greek or Latin. An overview of the history of the English language demonstrates that the 16th century was the prime time for its development.

The second was the standardization of a consistent writing system. As discussed earlier, numerous dialects coexisted in the Old English period, together with loanwords from Latin, French and northern European languages, which resulted in chaos in spelling. The same words might have been spelt in different ways, thus variations in spelling, and there were no consistent and widely followed spelling rules or systems. Some words underwent gradual changes in their pronunciations, and their spellings had been conventionalized. That brought about obvious discrepancies between spelling and pronunciation. The variability of spelling was an essential part of instability in English, which was especially so compared with languages like Latin. To many, English spelling was random and chaotic (Baugh and Cable, 2001). Although the actual situation was not so complicated, the reality was that spellings varied with individual writers, their educational levels and individual preferences. Therefore, various proposals were put forward for English spelling standardization in the 16th century on the basis of their detailed investigation and researches. In a sense, they produced positive effects upon the establishment of a standardized English writing system.

The third was the wide-ranging enlargement of English vocabulary. English remained to be the language for the British underclass and was used mainly for daily intercourse, while Latin and French were used in government documents, churches, courts and academic writing. Throughout the Middle Age the supremacy of Latin in the academic world downgraded European vernacular languages, such as English, into the predicament of seeking their survival from their meagre existence and thus seriously hindered their development. With the gradual reduction of the roles of Latin and French in British social life and the diminishing supremacy of Latin, English expanded its scope of circulation and assumed its role as a medium of mass communication, but its deficiencies became apparent.

In contrast to classic languages such as Latin, English showed obvious lexical inadequacies in expressing ideas in those languages and an inclination for some degree of retrogression into previous practices. The most effective remedy for overcoming these insufficiencies was naturally borrowing words from those classic languages. Prior to the 16th century, English had already started to borrow expressions from foreign languages, but that

Early development of English lexicography   37

was limited to only words and expressions of everyday use. However, during the 16th century and the early part of the 17th century, English loanwords increased at unprecedented rates. Tens of thousands of words came into use in English from Latin and Greek, and a considerable number were borrowed from French, Italian and Spanish. All that contributed immensely to the expressive power of English.

The Renaissance in Britain As a result of the spiritual confinements of theology, the ancient Greek and Roman cultures were covered up for almost 1,000 years and did not get reviewed until the middle of the 14th century. By the 16th century, they entered into a new era of prosperity, which triggered the ideological movement aimed at the creation of knowledge, the emancipation of human spirit and the exploitation and restoration of the Greek and Roman cultures of the ancient times; pushed European undertakings in the areas of science, culture and arts into a peak period and created the prologue to the history of modern Europe.

The core notion of the Renaissance is humanism, which advocates that mankind is the centre of the universe, affirms humanistic values and dignity, extols the sublime humanity, emphasizes individual development, elevates human dignity, respects human capabilities and wisdom, upholds science, experiments and education and stimulates the desire for knowledge. There appeared between the early phase of the Renaissance to the period of its prosperity a large number of great scientists, artists, men of letters and thinkers, such as Dante (1265–1321), Giovanni Boccaccio (1313–1375), Leonardo da Vinci (1452–1519), Nicolaus Copernicus (1473–1543), Michelangelo Buonarroti (1475–1564), Galileo Galilei (1564–1642), René Descartes (1596–1650) etc.

During the gradual surge of the Renaissance in Europe, Britain was undergoing radical social, political, economic and religious transformations, which explains why the British Renaissance was paces behind Europe. It gained momentum only in the 16th century and did not reach its climax until around the end of the 16th century. Its starting point was the rediscovery of the ancient Greek and Roman cultures. The institutions of higher learning became the major sites and platforms for the teaching and transmission of ancient Greek and the translation of great works produced in ancient Greece and Rome as well as modern Italy and France. The British philosophers, historians, politicians, religious figures and renowned scholars started to publish their works and expressed their humanistic ideas in their desirable ways.

The accomplishments of the Renaissance in Britain were mainly reflected in literary and philosophical undertakings. Under the influence of humanism in Italy, British literature started its prime time in the 14th century, and drama represented its greatest achievements in the Renaissance, giving rise to such great literary figures as Edmund Spenser (1552–1599), Christopher Marlow (1564–1593) and William Shakespeare (1564–1616). Their works gave the best expression of the contradictions and conflicts of the British

38 *Early development of English lexicography*

society then. By the 16th century, humanistic ideas became especially active, giving birth to such great politicians and thinkers as Thomas Moore (1478–1535) and Francis Bacon (1561–1626). The British Renaissance rekindled the public zeal for classic languages, which brought forth several Latin-English and English-Latin dictionaries. English became an equivalent language to Latin.

The first public use of the English Bible the Bible is the classic monument of Christianity. The Old Testament was written in Hebrew, with only a limited proportion written in the Aramaic language. The New Testament was written in Greek. They have been translated into different languages over the past 2000 years. The first attempt to translate the Bible into Old English was made by the Venerable Bede at the end of the 7th century, and John Wycliffe (1320–1385), an English scholastic philosopher, theologian and seminary professor at Oxford, advocated the translation of the Bible into the vernacular. He completed a translation directly from the Vulgate into Middle English in the year 1382, now known as Wycliffe's Bible. It is possible that he translated the entire New Testament, while his associates translated the Old Testament. Wycliffe's Bible appears to have been completed by 1384, additional updated versions being done by Wycliffe's assistant John Purvey and others in 1388 and 1395.

In 1539, Thomas Cranmer (1489–1556), a leader of the English Reformation and Archbishop of Canterbury, published *The Great Bible* with the help of Myles Coverdale (1488–1569), so named because of its size. It was the first English version of the Bible that was authorized for public use in the British history, with seven editions being printed between April 1539 and December 1541. From then on, the Bible was in wide circulation in the British society, exerting prolonged, profound and far-reaching impacts upon various aspects of socio-cultural life in Britain and the world as well.

The Book of Common Prayer The Book of Common Prayer is the general heading for related prayer books used in the Anglican Communion, as well as by the Continuing Anglican, "Anglican realignment" and other Anglican Christian churches. In 1539, the *Six Articles Act* was passed to curry favour with the Catholic France and Spain. However, it was overthrown by the British Parliament in 1547, permitting some degree of freedom of thinking and publication and lifting the ban upon the printing of the Bible. As a product of the English Reformation following the break with Rome, the original book of prayers was published by Thomas Cranmer in 1549 in the reign of Edward VI. The same year, the Parliament issued the *Act of Uniformity*, transmitting orders that Cranmer's book be used for prayers in all churches. The practice of praying in English has continued almost in the same fashion up to the present day.

In 1553, Cranmer completed the *Forty-two Articles of Religion* with the assistance of six other theologians, which was intended to summarize Anglican doctrines. Subsequent to Elizabeth's ascension to the throne, the Reformation was restored. In 1559, the Parliament passed the *Supremacy*

Early development of English lexicography 39

Act, abolishing the authority of the Pope and respecting the Queen as the Supreme Governor. In 1563, the *Forty-two Articles of Religion* was revised into the *Thirty-nine Articles*, stipulating the doctrines of the Church of England and the Bible as the only norm for faith. The supreme authority of the Pope was deprived by the Parliament passage of *The Test Act*, demanding absolute loyalty to the Queen. Queen Elizabeth's reforms met with strong resistance from Rome and Spain. They tried every means, including the use of force, to make Britain succumb, but with no avail. Britain was brought into the golden Elizabethan age, and the Reformation was beginning to take shape.

"Together with the King James Version of the Bible and the works of Shakespeare, the *Book of Common Prayer* has been one of the three fundamental underpinnings of modern English. As it has been in regular use for centuries, many phrases from its services have passed into everyday English, either as deliberate quotations or as unconscious borrowings. They have often been used metaphorically in non-religious contexts, and authors have used phrases from the prayer book as titles for their books" (Wikipedia, "Book of Common Prayer"). With its well-composed language, special rhythmic effects derived from Latin and wide circulation in churches, it is bound to exercise transforming impacts upon the evolution of the English language.

The emergence of Shakespeare's works William Shakespeare (1564–1616) was an English poet, playwright and actor, widely regarded as the greatest writer in the English language and the world's pre-eminent dramatist. In his school days, he learned Latin, the ancient history, philosophy, poetry, logic, rhetoric, etc. Between 1585 and 1592, he embarked upon play writing and quickly rose to stardom, though his concentration was on old play adaptations and collaborative composition. He started to write plays by himself in 1590, and *Venus and Adonis* (1593) became his first independent work published in London. In order to monopolize the performance of Shakespeare's plays, the opera troupes tried every means to control the publication of his works, which accounted for why "pirate versions" dictated by performers were widely circulated. The complete collection of his works did not come out until after his death.

Shakespeare composed 37 plays, covering a wide range of histories, comedies, tragedies and tragicomedies (also known as romances), which have come down to us in numerous editions and versions, such as *Romeo and Juliet* (1595), *A Midsummer Night's Dream* (1596), *The Merchant of Venice* (1597), *Hamlet* (1601), *The Twelfth Night* (1601), *Othello* (1604), *King Lear* (1606), *Macbeth* (1606), and so on. All his works were written in English, which greatly boosted the British public confidence in English and played an enormous role in consolidating the national status of English, heightening the social level of English use, and enriching the expressiveness of the English lexicon. Over the past 100 years or so, his works have been adapted and rediscovered by new movements in scholarship and

40 *Early development of English lexicography*

performance and remained to be most frequently imitated, perused, performed, researched and interpreted from different perspectives and dimensions in all major cultures throughout the world.

2.3 The 16th-century English bilingual dictionary-making and its gradual sublation of Latin traditions

From the very outset, English dictionary-making was deeply rooted in Latin tradition, and Latin played a predominant role in the evolution of English lexicography. However, things began to change without any obvious trace in the 16th century. On the one hand, the status of Latin was once again strengthened in the wake of the Renaissance in the U.K., and dictionaries with Latin as the target language and their vitality in the late 15th century continued to develop with increasing momentum, and on the other hand, English, owing to the intensification of national awareness in England, gained unprecedented elevation of status in all walks of life, especially in areas of literature and religion. Great strides were made in the making of dictionaries with English words as lemmata in the latter part of the 16th century, e.g. English-Latin dictionaries, English-one or more modern European languages dictionaries, and English specialized dictionaries. That signified a preliminary departure of English lexicography from its Latin tradition to a greater concentration upon English itself and created the socio-cultural atmosphere for the first English monolingual dictionary to appear in the 17th century.

Latin-English dictionaries Dictionary-making in the first half of the 16th century was basically limited to the Latin-English type. *Promptorium Parvulorum* and *Ortus Vocabulorum*, which were written in the 15th century, continued in eight and ten new editions respectively to exert their dominating influence until the 1530s, when Thomas Eliot (also spelled Thomas Elyot, c. 1490–1546) published *The Dictionary of Syr Thomas Eliot* in 1538.

However, "there is little evidence of their influence upon subsequent lexicography – a circumstance which might be explained by the desire of the Humanists to start afresh and to avoid the use of medieval sources" (Starnes, 1954:37). Dictionary compilers wanted to put an end to the Middle Ages by avoiding repeated use of the resources left over from the Middle Ages so as to start anew in the innovative fashion. "It was to the Continent that English lexicographers of the sixteenth century turned for models and materials" (Bately, 2009:41).

The Dictionary of Syr Thomas Eliot In England, Thomas Eliot was "the first man to attempt the compilation of a dictionary commensurate with the demand created by changing conditions of life" (Starnes, 1954:47). He once worked as writer and translator. He was quite conversant with ancient Greek and Roman classic works and wrote as well as edited quite a few books. He showed special zeal for English and wrote in English. He

Early development of English lexicography 41

introduced quite a number of loans into English and enriched it by coining many new words. His desire to compile a dictionary was incited by his special feelings towards English, his obsession with English studies, his high expectations of academic activities and his thirst for improving English education through better Latin teaching.

In 1538, Eliot published his Latin-English dictionary – *The Dictionary of Syr Thomas Eliot*. The textual research reveals that his dictionary was the first to have used the word *dictionary* in the title of a dictionary. It is a small folio dictionary and the first English dictionary with pictorial illustrations (McDermott, 2005), bearing basic structural resemblance to a modern dictionary. Apart from the dictionary text, it consisted of the front matter (including the Preface) and the back matter (including indexes and encyclopaedic information about measurements and coins provided in Latin, Greek and Hebrew). The copy of the first edition in the British Museum contains an autograph letter from Eliot to Cromwell, to whom it originally belonged.

According to Starnes (1954:51–65), Eliot did not draw materials from *Promptorium Parvulorum* and *Ortus Vocabulorum*, which were extremely popular in the 1530s. He turned his eyes to the ancient classic works written by the Roman scholars, an obvious indication of the result of the Renaissance surging in Britain. The 1538 edition of the dictionary absorbed materials mainly from the Latin dictionaries compiled by Italian scholar Ambrosius Calepinus.

Calepinus' dictionary became the example Eliot followed in etymological treatment, the arrangement of proper names, the citations from well-known classics and the labelling of verb inflections, as well as those of nouns and adjectives. Eliot arranged headwords in alphabetical order, provided grammatical information of headwords and took illustrations from classic Latin works so as to ascertain word uses and meanings. In addition, Eliot expanded the dictionary text to cover brief introductions to famous people, personal reminiscences, theology, natural history, proverbs etc. All these were accepted as the paradigm for the 16th-centruy Latin-English dictionaries. Such encyclopaedic contents furnished precious materials for subsequent diachronic studies of the Middle Ages.

Eliot made revisions and augmentations of his dictionary in his lifetime in 1542 and 1545, respectively. By comparison with the 1538 edition, the revised and augmented editions showed obvious improvement in terms of contents and organization. After Eliot's death in 1546, the original publisher invited Thomas Cooper, Bishop of Winchester, to carry on with its revision and enlargement, and the result was *Bibliotheca Eliotae* (1548, also called *Eliotis Librarie*), which formed the basis for Cooper's *Thesaurus linguae Romanae & Britannicae* (1565).

Dictionariolum puerorum, tribus linguis, Latina, Anglica, et Gallica conscriptum The Renaissance was flourishing in the 16th century in Britain. In its wake, the British compilers paid more attention to learning and copying from their counterparts on the European continent. Quite a few

42 *Early development of English lexicography*

dictionaries compiled on mainland Europe became the foundation for British compilations. John Veron's (?–1563) *Dictionariolum puerorum, tribus linguis, Latina, Anglica, et Gallica conscriptum* (1552) was just one of them.

Veron was born in France. He travelled to Britain in 1536 and studied in Cambridge University. It is highly likely that Veron started to compile his dictionary after 1542, using as its base the 1542 edition of Robert Stephanus' *Dictionariolum puerorum Latina-Gallicum*, which was reprinted in 1544 and 1547, with the second and third editions coming out in 1550 and 1557 (Starnes, 1954:140–145). Veron's compiling techniques were simple. He inserted the English definitions after those written in Latin and French, turning the original dictionary from a bilingual one to a multilingual one.

Veron's English definitions were chiefly translated from French, but he also transplanted many English definitions from Eliot-Cooper's dictionary series. By 1575, Rudolph Waddington made substantial revisions to and enlargements of Veron's dictionary and deleted its French definitions, making it a Latin-English one. In 1584, Abraham Fleming published its third revised edition, also the final edition. "Although the modest Stephanus-Veron dictionaries contribute nothing new to the technique of dictionary-making in England, they effect a fusion of the Latin-French of the Stephanus and the Latin-English of the Eliot-Cooper" (Starnes, 1954:146). This opened up a new space for the making of English bilingual and even monolingual dictionaries in Britain.

Thesaurus linguae Romanae & Britannicae From the 1540s onward, Eliot-Cooper's dictionary series began to dominate the Latin-English dictionary world in Britain and was taken as the role model for other compilers to follow. Owing to the sustaining impacts from Thomas Cooper's (c. 1517–1594) *Thesaurus linguae Romanae & Britannicae* (1565), its influence extended for almost a century.

Thomas Cooper was born in Oxford. He once taught in school and practiced medicine. He started his literary career in 1548. He spent nearly 20 years turning Eliot's dictionary into *Bibliotheca Eliotae* through considerable enlargement. However, *Thesaurus linguae Romanae & Britannicae* (1565) was his greatest scholarly achievement. This dictionary consisted of 2,000 pages and underwent reprints in 1573, 1578, 1584 and 1587. The historical record has it that Queen Elizabeth highly complimented him on it and gave him promotions several times.

The statistics of Shakespeare's vocabulary in his writing shows that he made use of Cooper's dictionary in composing poetry and drama. Incredibly, Cooper did his compilation under rather miserable conditions. As Winchester (2003) recorded, its making consumed a large fortune of the family, which made his wife so furious that she set fire to the manuscript, and Copper could do nothing but spend another eight years to do it all over again. Starnes' (1954:89–110) contrastive analysis shows that, in his compilation, not only did Cooper make use of materials from *Bibliotheca Eliotae*, but he employed Robert Stephanus' Latin-French dictionary as the basis and

Early development of English lexicography 43

the chief source of materials as well. In his selection of headwords, Cooper excluded those Latin words of the Middle Ages that might be considered "vulgar" but introduced more classic Latin words. He patterned after Robert Stephanus in arranging headwords in the alphabetical order, providing adequate English equivalents or equivalent expressions immediately after Latin headwords, annotating pronunciation for all headwords, illustrating meanings and uses with sufficient grammatical information and copious citations from classic writers and listing derivatives after headwords with meanings and related expressions. The introduction of Stephanus' compiling techniques into the making of English dictionaries is Cooper's major contribution to early English lexicography. Cooper's lexicographical works furnished abundant resources for compilations that were to follow.

Verborum Latinorum cum Graecis Anglicisque *Verborum Latinorum cum Graecis Anglicisque* (1583) was a Latin-English dictionary adapted by Richardus Huttonus from Gulielmus Morelius' (also Guillaume Morel, 1505–1564) Latin-French dictionary.

Morelius was born in Normandy. He was a French classic scholar. He once worked in a firm in Paris as proof-reader and took over Turnebus in 1555 to become the king's printer. The original title of his Latin-French dictionary was *Verborum Latinorum cum Graecis Anglicisque coniunctorum, locupletissimi commentarij*, which could be considered Morelius' most significant work. It took a large number of citations by Greek writers from the unedited and unpublished manuscripts that were kept in the Paris library and was reprinted time and again under the title of *Thesaurus vocum omnium latinarum* in the 16th and 17th centuries. In *Verborum Latinorum cum Graecis Anglicisque*, French definitions were replaced by English ones.

Huttonus' adapted version abstracted numerous materials from Cooper's dictionary but turned out to be innovative in several aspects. He followed the alphabetical arrangement in the original work but supplemented many English definitions on the basis of Cooper's dictionary, provided Greek equivalents to Latin words and gave clear annotations of accentuation, inflection, gender, case, mood, tenses etc. Huttonus' adapted edition did not sell quite well on the British market but served as a bridge between Cooper and Thomas Thomas. His method of arranging headwords became a model for others to follow in the years to come.

Dictionarium Linguae Latinae et Anglicanae Over the last three decades of the 16th century, Thomas Cooper's *Thesaurus linguae Romanae & Britannicae* had always been exemplary for Latin-English compilations. It could be found on the library shelf of every decent grammar school and many upper-class and upper- and middle-class households. Upon the publication of its fifth edition, Cooper's dictionary met with serious challenges from its formidable rival – Thomas Thomas' *Dictionarium Linguae Latinae et Anglicanae* (1587), which became a popular standard work of reference at the turn of the 16th and 17th centuries.

44 *Early development of English lexicography*

Thomas received his education in Eton College and the King's College of Cambridge University. His most remarkable scholarly accomplishment was *Dictionarium Linguae Latinae et Anglicanae*. This dictionary had 1,000 pages, with a collection of nearly 40,000 headwords and quite a few function words with grammatical and usage notes.

Thomas mainly adopted Cooper's and Huttonus' previously mentioned dictionaries as his basis. The former was chiefly employed to expand its number of headwords and enrich its English definitions and the latter to follow its method of alphabetically arranging its headwords and annotating long and short syllables. From its first edition to 1644, Thomas' dictionary had altogether 14 editions, among which 6 editions were produced in the 16th century. The great pity was that Thomas did not experience the glory its success had brought to him, as he passed away less than a year after its publication.

Of the six editions that appeared in the 16th century, three deserve to be mentioned here. The second edition of 1589 was most conspicuously marked by its increase of the number of headwords to 7,500, in addition to a concise supplement of proper names. Three years later, the third edition came out, the number of headwords was further augmented and phrasal and sentential citations were provided for the illustration of meanings and uses. No obvious revision or augmentation was discerned in the fourth edition of 1589, but the last edition of the 16th century in 1596 had a considerable augmentation of headwords and a substantial replenishment of definitions (Starnes, 1954:115–138). Moreover, Thomas provided additional information concerning etymology, grammar etc. Its frequent revisions and reprints manifest that Thomas's dictionary was extensively influential then and won wide recognition as authority.

English-Latin dictionaries From 1552 onwards, there was a shift of focus of dictionary-making in Britain. From Latin to English, resulting in English-Latin dictionary-making with English as the language of headwords. However, a certain degree of inheritance is observable between the dictionaries compiled by Thomas Eliot and Thomas Cooper and those newly compiled English-Latin dictionaries.

Abecedarium Anglico Latinum Richard Huloet was remembered by later generations for his *Abecedarium Anglico-Latinum* (1552). There is no record of Richard Huloet's date of birth, but it can be assumed that he was born in Cambridge. As indicated before, there already appeared in the 15th century two English-Latin dictionaries – *Promptorium Parvulorum and Catholicon Anglicum*. Huloet's dictionary was the third English-Latin dictionary in the history of English lexicography, appearing at the time when *Promptorium Parvulorum* was highly popular. Judging from the fact that it was a product of the Middle Ages and its last edition appeared as early as 1528, it became apparently necessary and even urgent to produce a new English-Latin dictionary to reflect the uses of English in the 16th century and to meet the needs of learning both English and Latin.

Early development of English lexicography   45

In order to keep abreast of the times, Huloet embarked on his dictionary in the 1540s and drew on materials from Robert Stephanus, Thomas Eliot, Thomas Cooper and others. He spent ten years completing his work with a coverage of 26,000 or so headwords. He claimed that he adopted new modes and techniques of compilation. Its highlighting features include defining English headwords in both Latin and English, adopting numerous Latin synonyms for defining headwords and explaining letters by means of paragraphs for the first time in the English dictionary. Like other dictionaries, it provided information concerning Latin grammar but not etymology. Apart from the use of synonyms, its defining techniques appeared oversimplified, and word meanings were generally demonstrated through Latin synonyms and citations. Huloet's employment of English to define English headwords signified a major step towards English monolingual compilation.

According to Gabriele Stein (1991), among the new words or new uses of existing words that first came into English and were collected in *OED*, about 1,000 were first identified for record in Huloet's dictionary, and that is a conservative estimation. Huloet's dictionary was augmented by John Higgins in 1572 and underwent no more editions or reprints, due to fierce competition from John Baret's work.

A Shorte Dictionarie for Yonge Begynners The beginning years of the 1650s witnessed the publication of several Latin-English and English-Latin dictionaries. In 1552, two important such dictionaries came out – *Dictionariolum puerorum, tribus linguis, Latina, Anglica, et Gallica conscriptum* and *Abecedarium Anglico-Latinum*, and the following year John Withals' English-Latin dictionary – *A Shorte Dictionarie for Yonge Begynners* (1553) – followed in the wake.

There is no reliable literature relating to John Withals' biography, but speculation has it that he might be a teacher. His work was based on the users he intended to serve. On the title page, Withals made a clear specification of his dictionary type, user and material sources: *A Shorte Dictionarie for Yonge Begynners*. Gathered of Good Authors, specially of Columell, Grapald and Plini. In fact, the bilingual nature of this dictionary might have led it to take more materials from his predecessors' bilingual dictionaries, such as those by John Stanbridge and Thomas Eliot.

This dictionary is unique in arranging its headwords. Rather than adopting the more conventional arrangement according to the alphabetical order, it groups words together through associations the headwords may invoke. Headword categories gradually unfold from general subjects to specific ones, and each subject has English and Latin subheadings. Under each subheading are listed semantically related lexical items, together with their meanings and uses. For example, you need to consult the "Carpenter" subject in order to find words relating to carpentry. This thematic arrangement of headwords followed the practice of early English glossaries and was of great help to schoolchildren learning Latin.

46 *Early development of English lexicography*

By nature, Withals' dictionary served as a supplementary learning tool to help children to read and write. Sixteen editions were published over a period of over 80 years, and its influence extended well into the 1630s, and its last edition appeared as late as 1634. It is no exaggeration that this learning tool became the most popular over the second half of the 16th century and continued to exert its influence in the early part of the 17th century (Winchester, 2003:21).

Alvearie When Withals' dictionary was still in its heyday, John Baret launched his *Alvearie* in 1573. *Alvearie* means "beehive", and the title drew inspirations from his student assistants at Cambridge University in the course of compilation. They were busy gathering sentences from classic Latin works for the purpose of illustrating meanings and uses, just as bees busy themselves gathering honey. There remain only fragmentary records of Baret's biography. He once studied in Cambridge University, obtained his degree there, and taught in London in his late twilight years. He made his last will and testament in 1578, which academics assume to be his date of death.

In "To The Reader", Baret humbly stated how he came to the idea of compiling the dictionary. In teaching his students Latin, he realized how painstaking it was for them to translate English into Latin. Therefore, he assigned his students several pages of Eliot's dictionary each day, taught them to add English equivalents before Latin and quoted from such great masters as Cicero for illustrations. After a year or two, all the additions came together under one cover and became a huge collection. At the outset, it was mainly intended for personal use but was later published at his friends' suggestion.

It is obvious that this dictionary was a product of collective labour. It was mainly English-Latin, but it also contained a great deal of French and a small amount of Greek. Its headwords were basically arranged alphabetically according to headwords, but that arrangement varied occasionally with spelling variants, headword overlapping and cognate relations. It took the place of John Higgins' augmented edition and was itself revised and enlarged by Abraham Fleming after five years of publication. A new edition appeared in 1580.

Baret failed to achieve his goal of implementing spelling reforms through dictionary-making, but his devotion to etymology became a highlight of his dictionary, and he was the only compiler who devoted attention to etymological treatment during this period (Starnes, 1954:217). His other innovative contribution was his indexing of Latin words and his precedent of providing an index for lexical items in the back matter.

Bibliotheca scholastica One more dictionary that is worth mentioning in the 16th century of English-Latin dictionary-making is John Rider's (1562–1632) *Bibliotheca scholastica* (1589), which was widely used in the 17th century. John Rider received education in Jesus College, Oxford and obtained his bachelor's and master's degrees. He went on to teach and

Early development of English lexicography 47

conduct research there. As "a great, personal favourite" of Elizabeth I of England, he became Dean of St. Patrick's Cathedral, Dublin and was consecrated the Anglican Bishop of Killaloe in 1612, a position he held until his death in 1632, leaving behind him the "character of a learned and religious prelate". He was the first of his family to spell his name Rider/Ryder rather than de Rythre/Ryther, which is a strong manifestation of his innovative spirit.

Bibliotheca scholastica consisted of three parts: a 560-page English-Latin dictionary arranged alphabetically, a 34-page English-Latin dictionary arranged thematically and a 560-page Latin-English dictionary arranged by means of indexation. It is clear from the title page that this dictionary got rid of its convention of targeting chiefly Latin learners, particularly schoolchildren. It expanded its scope of users to include all those who spoke Latin or wrote in Latin, thus endowing itself with the attribute of a bilingual defining dictionary, which, without doubt, furnished theoretical and methodological inspirations for general English monolingual dictionaries to be made in the 17th century.

Apart from the dictionary text, Rider included "To the Reader", "Directions for the Reader", "Index of Latin Words" and a thematically arranged English-Latin glossary of some common headings in his design. To some extent, the index of Latin words endowed the dictionary with the bilingual nature, and the use of numerals to mark the register of Latin words was another mark of Rider's innovation in the dictionary format. That, together with other innovations, is to be dealt with in the following section. Entering into the 17th century, Rider's dictionary underwent revisions and enlargements by Francis Holyoake.

Apart from Latin-English and English-Latin bilingual dictionaries, combinations of English with modern European languages appeared in succession. In 1547, William Salesbury (c. 1520–1584) launched *A Dictionary in Englyshe and Welshe*, the first bilingual dictionary with a modern European language as the source language and English as a "foreign language" (the target language). In 1550, William Thomas appended a concise Italian-English dictionary to his *Principal Rules of the Italian Grammar*. In 1571, Lucas Harrison compiled *A Dictionarie French and English*. Nine years later, Claudius Hollyband published *The treasurie of the French tong*. In 1593, he co-authored with Lucas Harrison a French-English dictionary with a similar title – *A Dictionarie French and English*.

The years 1590 and 1591 respectively witnessed John Thorie's *The Spanish Dictionarie* and Richard Percyvall's *Bibliotheca Hispanica*. Obviously, Percyvall imitated Rider in titling his dictionary. In the final two years of the 16th century John Florio's *A Worlde of wordes, or most copious, and exact dictionarie in Italian and English* (1598) and John Minsheu's revision of Richard Percyvall's dictionary (1599) were published. The former was augmented in 1611 and retitled *Queen Anna's new world of words*, to which Giovanni Torriano added an English-Italian part. Minsheu deleted

48 *Early development of English lexicography*

the Latin part in the original edition and added an English-Spanish index so as to make it possible to perform the functions of a bidirectional dictionary in some way.

One more point to make before the conclusion of this section is the initial shaping of rhyming dictionaries and dictionaries of professional terms. The year 1570 saw the birth of Peter Levins' *Manipulus vocabulorum. A dictionarie of English and Latine wordes*, which is supposed to be the first English bilingual dictionary that was basically arranged according to rhymes, which was useful not only to scholars who needed to use various words but to those who wrote in English rhymes as well. This dictionary was reprinted in 1587. When a new edition was published in 1867, Henry B. Wheatley (1838–1917) wrote the "Preface" and prepared an alphabetical index. Wheatley's "Preface" made a comprehensive exposition of early English and English dictionary-making.

In 1566, Thomas Harman produced the first English glossary of professional jargons, which was appended to *A Caveat or Warening for Commen Cursitors*. Viewed from the angle of textual research, John Awdeley's *The Fraternity of Vagabonds* (1561) lacked the attributes of a glossary or dictionary, though it gathered the terms used by underclass people such as vagrants. Harman collected materials directly from among vagrants and people of similar classes, including their stories, the description of these classes, the introduction about their skills for survival and so on. His glossary of vagrant terms was later reproduced, enlarged or used for enhancing dramatic or publicizing colouring. It inherited the tradition of arranging headwords alphabetically in bilingual dictionaries of the late Middle Ages and initiated the precedent of making dictionaries of professional terms that lasted for several centuries to come. The glossary was in wide circulation at that time, as pirated editions appeared, and two printers were penalized for its copyright infringement in 1567. In the same year of 1568, two editions of the glossary appeared, followed by a revised edition in 1573.

2.4 The design features and academic value of English bilingual dictionaries in the 16th century

The 16th century was a significant transitional period in the history of British English lexicography, in which English dictionaries completed a radical shift of functions from the single function of explaining hard words to diversified functions through providing a great variety of lexicographical information. They incorporated quite a lot of theoretical accomplishments into their compilation, achieved far-reaching breakthroughs in the art and craft of dictionary compilation and demonstrated compiling features never seen before. They proved themselves to be of great social significance and of high scholarly quality.

The 16th-century English bilingual dictionaries are conspicuously characterized as follows. First, owing to the impacts of the Renaissance, the

Early development of English lexicography 49

16th-century English lexicography drew more on the dictionary-making tradition of European continent than on the theoretical enlightenment and materials that could be gleaned from the 15th-century English bilingual dictionaries. The great majority of dictionaries over this period were modelled after or based on Latin dictionaries and Latin-French bilingual dictionaries compiled on the European continent. English elements were inserted into them to make them Latin-English and English-Latin. Latin-English and English-Latin dictionaries constituted the major part of English dictionary-making over the 16th century and dominated the 16th-century dictionary market.

Second, English dictionaries achieved no breakthroughs in creating new types over the 16th century and were confined only to monodirectional bilingual dictionaries. No bidirectional bilingual dictionaries had appeared yet. Latin and English were the major languages involved, and only Baret's dictionary involved a few French and Greek definitions, which signified the advent of a multilingual dictionary type. An index of Latin words was appended to Rider's dictionary, which made it somewhat like a bidirectional dictionary, "A Double Dictionarie" in Rider's own terms, though there was still a great distance from that. Right at that moment on the European continent, the making of bidirectional bilingual dictionaries and multilingual dictionaries was in immense vogue.

Third, a clear line of inheritance is discernible from the development of the 16th-century English bilingual dictionaries. On the one hand, they inherited the compiling styles and formats of Latin dictionaries or a few bilingual dictionaries made on the European continent in the initial stage, capitalizing heavily on their abundant linguistic resources, and, on the other hand, when they were under revision after publication, their compilers would make every effort to explore resources from an identifiable line of sources to enlarge and augment the original dictionaries. With the passage of time, an explicit thread of dictionary pedigree would come into shape, with closely related dictionary groups such as the Eliot-Cooper dictionary family and the Huloet-Higgins dictionary series. All that contributed immeasurably to the steady improvement of dictionary quality and the long-lasting influence they would exert upon users and later compilations.

The 16th-century English lexicography achieved unprecedented transcendence in terms of compiling notions and techniques, displaying high theoretical values, great methodological reference and profound practical significance. First, the dictionary megastructure moved towards greater perfection. Apart from that of the dictionary text, the structure of the front and the back matter appeared to be sounder, and their content became more enriched. Rider's dictionary was especially noteworthy for including "To the Reader" and "Directions for the Reader" in the front matter, which intended to provide users with guidance. That is an indispensable information item found in modern dictionaries but not in the dictionaries of Rider's days. Baret set the precedent of compiling an index as one of the appendixes

50 *Early development of English lexicography*

in his dictionary, and that practice was ameliorated and consolidated in Rider's compilation.

Second, the macrostructural configuration of alphabetically arranging headwords was firmly established. The alphabetical arrangement of headwords was already found in early English glossaries, but in practice with a great deal of chaos, inconsistency and a mixed simultaneous use of several methods in some cases. The 16th-century English bilingual lexicography optimized the previous methods of arranging headwords on the alphabetic basis, established that arrangement on a more orderly and scientific basis and made it a dominating approach to headword arrangement in the 16th-century dictionaries, coupled with the method of arranging headwords on the cognate basis. In Cooper's dictionary, for example, an improved etymological system was adopted by first arranging words according to their cognates – i.e. grouping families of words together – and then cross-referencing them in the alphabetical sequence.

Third, entries had become fuller and more informative, providing information concerning grammar, etymology and so on, in addition to pronunciation, definition and illustrations. In grammar, attention was chiefly given to inflections of verbs, nouns, adjectives etc. "In etymology there was growth in quantity, if not in quality. The principle was not new. . . . In general, etymologies in Cooper, Thomas, and Rider are simple statements of the make-up of compound words". Some progress was made "in the choice, and gradual increase, of classical examples to illustrate usage" (Starnes, 1954:235). These practices of the 16th-centruy English bilingual dictionaries, to a considerable extent, inherited the tradition of Latin dictionaries and drew on elite materials from them. Take illustration for example. That practice came from the European continental lexicographers Calepine and Robert Stephanus, especially Stephanus.

Finally, with regard to compiling techniques, the 16th-century English bilingual dictionaries demonstrated some innovative features by employing some special signs and symbols to indicate lexicographical information. For example, Cooper and Baret adopted the symbols *pen. cor.* and *pen. prod.* to mark accentuation, Thomas, following Calepine, adopted the breve and the macron to indicate short and long vowels, and Rider used the numbers 1, 2 and 3 to indicate the status of Latin words as "proper", "figurative" or "obsolete" (Starnes, 1954:235). In addition, "the exemplification of synonymy and *copia*, the extensive use of proverbs, and the introduction of proper names, together with the historical and legendary matter associated with them" were all noticeable features of English bilingual compilation in the 16th century (Starnes, 1954:236).

The 16th century was of special significance in British history, and, consequently, dictionaries made over that period were endowed with special social responsibilities. Viewed globally, the emergence of Latin-English and English-Latin dictionaries in Britain was an epitome of the intensification of national awareness and the revitalization of national languages. The

Early development of English lexicography 51

awareness of the importance of national languages was well intensified in ancient civilizations other than in European civilization, in which it took place only several hundred years before the printing technology was introduced and without much avail, owing to the fact that Latin, as the medium of academic exchanges, relegated national languages into an inferior and subordinate position. However, things began to change, though gradually, with the intensification of national awareness and the accumulation of literature of national languages. Judging from lexicographical practices, small bilingual glossaries and vocabularies of national languages started to appear in the last few years of the 15th century, with a few of them even completely detached from Latin.

From the socio-cultural perspective, the earliest compilation of glossaries and dictionaries served the purpose of military subjugation and national assimilation, but this function receded to a less important position in their subsequent development, and their didactic function started to play a dominant role, as is evident from the fact that early Latin dictionaries and the ancient hard-word glossaries, to a great degree, were intended for the interpretation of classic works. With the development of trade and commerce and the promotion of religion, dictionary compilation assumed strong religious and commercial colouring from the late part of the Middle Ages. In order to conduct trade and commerce, European merchants were supposed to acquire a basic knowledge of the languages of the countries where such business activities took place. That provided a favourable socio-economic environment for the emergence and development of national language dictionaries.

Prior to the 16th century, bilingual compilations were mostly simple glossaries and vocabularies, with one equivalent provided for every headword in most cases. Owing to a diversity of factors, in particular the highly demanding nature of translation, those simple glossaries were gradually replaced by dictionaries, the more effective and significant form of reference works. The application of printing technology effectively promoted the transmission of knowledge and culture and extensively expanded the circulation of dictionaries. From around 1436, when Gutenberg introduced the printing techniques, to the end of the 15th century, printed products amounted to about 35,000 in all of Europe, most of which were written in Latin, and that number was about 20,000 in Britain only over a span of 140 years after the entry into the 16th century, and they were English works. It is worth noting that the 16th century was a significant period of transition for Latin to be replaced by national languages in the whole of Europe, as a result of the strengthened awareness of national languages as an irreplaceable cohesive force for nations. The 16th-century English bilingual dictionaries were a direct outcome of the increasingly intensified British national awareness and the continuous elevation of the status of the English language, thus laying a solid foundation for the making of English monolingual dictionaries in the 17th century.

3 The bourgeoning of the English monolingual dictionary paradigm and the extension of bilingual dictionary traditions in the 17th century

In the 17th century, English started its journey out of the British Isles, with the establishment of the British East India Company and the first colonial settlement in North America. It developed itself from a language of an island nation into an international language of the modern world. The monolingual dictionary of English started to germinate from an early textbook-like glossary into "a new, distinctive type of reference work, stable in contents, more or less settled in methodology, and such that the modern reader might have felt quite at home in using it" (Osselton, 2009:131). That paved a smooth way and set a shining precedent for the authoritative Oxford dictionary series to be produced with universally recognized scholarship and craftsmanship.

From the first beginnings in Robert Cawdrey's work of 1604, one and a half centuries elapsed before the monolingual dictionary of English was firmly established as a new dictionary genre. The publication of Johnson's dictionary in 1755 made a clear dividing line. Osselton (2009:131) divided that period into three stages according to the dictionary nature: hard-word dictionaries were mainly made in the first half of the 17th century, with a coverage of almost what were considered "scholarly" headwords, and encyclopaedic dictionaries were mainly made in the second half of the 17th century, with all encyclopaedic headwords arranged into the alphabetic macrostructure in the same way as common words, while, in the early 18th century, general dictionaries focused more on their linguistic function and therefore excluded encyclopaedic headwords from the macrostructure, so that as many words for "language" as possible, rather than words for "things", were collected in the macrostructure, even including those simplest and commonest words.

3.1 The socio-political background for the development of English lexicography in the 17th century

With the establishment of the House of Stuart, 17th-century Britain was gradually dragging itself from glory into a mire of domestic turmoil. "Civil war" and "revolution" became the theme words over that period, and the

English monolingual dictionary paradigm 53

British revolution, which lasted for half a century, ended with the Glorious Revolution (1688–1689).

The establishment of the East India Company The East India Company, which is also known as the Honourable East India Company and the British East India Company, was originally chartered as the "Governor and Company of Merchants of London trading into the East Indies" and later became a British joint-stock company. It operated under the Royal Charter granted by Queen Elizabeth I on December 31, 1600 to pursue trade with what is nowadays Maritime Southeast Asia. In 1609, James I (1566–1625) renewed the charter for an indefinite period unless the trade turned unprofitable for three consecutive years.

Around 1670, in a series of five acts, King Charles II granted the East India Company the rights to autonomously acquire territories, mint money, command fortresses and troops, form alliances, make war and peace and exercise both civil and criminal jurisdiction over the acquired regions. All this approximated to the rights of a sovereign state and aimed at turning a commercial power into a military entity and eventually making India a British colony.

Starting from the 1760s, the East India Company went into its decline and was finally dissolved in 1858. However, English began to plant its seeds and grow its roots in this territory when the Company obtained a lease of Madras (now Chennai) with only 600 pounds from the local landlord and set up factories there. With the unbridled expansion of the Company's trade, English spread from the British Isles to South Asia and gradually to the other regions of Asia and became the language connection between what later came to be known as the British Commonwealth nations.

The establishment of settlements in North America Between the 16th and 17th centuries, quite a few European nations vied to open colonies in North America for the purpose of winning a place in the New World, and Britain was no exception. The Jamestown settlement, the first permanent English settlement in the Americas, was set up to gain a permanent foothold in North America by the Virginia Company of London as "James Fort" on May 4, 1607. It was named after King James I and earned huge, quick profits for goldmine investors.

The settlement was located on the east bank of the Powhatan (James) River southwest of the centre of modern Williamsburg out of two considerations – its perfect strategic advantage in building defence works to withstand foreign attacks from waterways and its status of being barren land that had not been inhabited by the aboriginal Indians. Between 1616 and 1699, Jamestown served as the capital of Virginia. However, most of it was coastal mudflat land, isolated from the rest of the world, suffering bitterly from lack of drinking water and farmland, baffled by the bites of breeding mosquitoes, so the capital was moved to Williamsburg, owing to such harsh living conditions. Gradually, Jamestown was deserted, but it must be

54 *English monolingual dictionary paradigm*

admitted that it played the role as a bridgehead for English to be permanently transmitted across North America.

The impacts of the House of Stuart and the Stuart monarchs The House of Stuart, originally Stewart, was a European royal house that originated in Scotland. The royal Stewart line consisted of Kings and Queens of Scots between the late 14th century and its union with England in 1707. Mary, Queen of Scots, was brought up in France, where she adopted the French spelling of the name, *Stuart*. Altogether nine Stewart (or Stuart) monarchs reigned over Scotland alone from 1371 to 1603, in which year Elizabeth I of England (1537–1603) died, and Mary's son, James VI of Scotland (1567–1625) inherited the thrones of England and Ireland, becoming James I of England and Ireland in the Union of the Crowns.

Except for the period of the Commonwealth (1649–1660), the Stuarts were monarchs of the British Isles and its growing empire, until the death of Queen Anne (1665–1714). During the reign of the Stuarts, Scotland developed from a relatively poor and feudal country into a prosperous, modern and centralized state. After the Stuarts reigned over all of Great Britain, the arts and sciences continued to develop; William Shakespeare wrote many of his best-known plays during the Jacobean era, while institutions such as the Royal Society and the Royal Mail were established during the reign of Charles II. All this contributed visibly to the development of the English language, culture and eventually lexicography.

The English Civil Wars Close to the middle of the 17th century, the First English Civil War broke out (1642–1646), the first of a series of armed confrontations and political machinations between Parliamentarians and Royalists between 1642 and 1651, chiefly resulting from the disputes concerning the mode of English governance. The First Civil War ended with King Charles I being handed over to the English Parliament by the Scots and imprisoned in 1646, while the end of the Second Civil War (1648–1649) was marked by a victory the troops of Cromwell won over the Royalists and Scots in 1648 and the execution of Charles I in 1649.

The first two wars were fought between supporters of King Charles I and those of the Long Parliament, while the Third Civil War (1649–1651) took place between supporters of King Charles II and those of the Rump Parliament, ending with the Parliamentarian victory at the Battle of Worcester in September 1651 and Charles II's exile. Apart from the trial and execution of Charles I and the exile of his son, Charles II, the wars brought about the replacement of English monarchy with the Commonwealth of England between 1649 and 1653, the Protectorate under the personal rule of Oliver Cromwell (1599–1658) between 1653 and 1658 and subsequently his son Richard Cromwell (1626–1712) between 1658 and 1659. Another outcome of the wars was the precedent, constitutionally, that an English monarch cannot govern without Parliament's consent, although the conceptualization of Parliament as the ruling power of England was only legalized as part of the Glorious Revolution in 1688, which will be introduced next.

English monolingual dictionary paradigm 55

The founding of the Commonwealth of England Following the execution of Charles I, which marked the end of the Second Civil War, "an Act declaring England to be a Commonwealth" was adopted to signify that England and Wales, later along with Ireland and Scotland, was ruled as a republic, with Oliver Cromwell acting as head of both state and government of the new republic.

In 1653, Cromwell was made Lord Protector of a united "Commonwealth of England, Scotland and Ireland". During the short-lived Commonwealth period (1649–1660), power in the initial stage remained primarily with the Parliament and the Council of State. As a ruler, he enforced aggressive and effective foreign policies. After his death and a brief period of rule under his son, the Protectorate Parliament was dissolved in 1659, and the Royalists returned to power, triggering a process that led to the restoration of the monarchy in 1660.

The Anglo-Dutch wars The Anglo-Dutch wars were fought almost all at sea, mainly over fisheries, trade routes and overseas colonies in the second half of the 17th century, seeking geographical advantages and profits in trade and commerce. After Cromwell united his country into the Commonwealth of England, reorganised the navy and positioned England to mount a global challenge to Dutch trade dominance, the general British mood was growing increasingly belligerent towards the Dutch.

The widening disputes over trade led to a war in the English Channel and the North Sea between the navies of England and the United Provinces of the Netherlands from 1652 to 1654, which resulted in the English Navy gaining control of the seas around England and a monopoly over trade with England and her colonies. That was the first of the Anglo-Dutch wars. The second (1665–1667) and third (1672–1674) wars took place after the English Restoration of the monarchy, and most of the fighting was done in the North Sea. Although England tried to end the Dutch monopoly over world trade, both wars ended in strong victories for the Dutch and confirmed the Dutch Republic's position as the leading maritime power of the 17th century. The Dutch Republic was then at the zenith of its power. The fourth war (1780–1784) was sparked mainly owing to the British disagreements with the Dutch trading with the United States during the American War of Independence. It ended with the Treaty of Paris, an awful defeat for the Dutch. They lost parts of their Dutch Empire.

The eventual victory helped, to some extent, to amplify the British ambition of expansion over the sea and consolidate its determination to realize its dream of building up a great empire where the sun never set. As a result, English went with the expansion of the empire to almost all major parts of the world and became a lingua franca in various parts of the world and a truly international language for communication and transactions.

The Restoration of the Monarchy in 1660 After Cromwell's death in 1658, his son Richard Cromwell succeeded as Lord Protector, and there did not seem to be much chance of Charles' regaining the Crown. However, the

56 English monolingual dictionary paradigm

new Lord Protector had little experience in either military or civil administration, which led to his resignation in the following year.

The Restoration of the English monarchy started in 1660. The Wars of the Three Kingdoms resulted in the Commonwealth of England, Scotland and Ireland, which collapsed in 1659. Out of deep concern of the nation descending into anarchy, politicians such as George Monck (1608–1670) tried to ensure a peaceful transition of government from the "Commonwealth" republic back to monarchy. General Monck led his army into the City of London and forced the recalled Rump Parliament to readmit members of the Long Parliament, which had dissolved itself, and, for the first time in almost 20 years, from 1648, there was a general election. The outgoing Parliament defined the electoral qualifications so as to ensure, as they thought, the return of a Presbyterian majority.

From May 1, 1660, the English, Scottish and Irish monarchies were all restored under King Charles II. The period that followed the Wars of the Three Kingdoms was officially declared an Interregnum. All this contributed to the development of Britain's capitalist society and the primitive accumulation of capital in the growth of British economy.

The Glorious Revolution The Glorious Revolution, also known as the Revolution of 1688, took place in the history of England and Scotland in 1688. On the surface, it was mainly concerned with religion. However, the balance between monarch and Parliament was also its motivation.

The people of England and Scotland did not like the Catholic King James II because he would not let them vote or practice the religion of their choice. On June 30, 1688, a group of English Parliamentarians secretly invited King James II's nephew and Mary's first cousin, the Protestant William III of Orange-Nassau, who was at that time in the Netherlands, to come to England and take over as king. After consolidating political and financial support, William crossed the North Sea and the English Channel with a large Dutch fleet and army in November 1688, landing at Torbay, England.

Following a defeat of his forces at the Battle of Reading, James and his wife Mary fled England for France out of fear. By threatening to withdraw his troops, William convinced a newly chosen Convention Parliament to make him and his wife joint monarchs. On February 13, 1689, Parliament passed the *Declaration of Right*, and William and Mary were crowned together at Westminster Abbey on April 11, 1689. William's successful invasion led to his ascension to the throne as William III of England jointly with his wife, Mary II, James' daughter.

The revolution permanently ended any chance of Catholicism becoming re-established in England. For British Catholics its effects were disastrous both socially and politically: for over a century Catholics were denied the right to vote and sit in the Westminster Parliament; they were also denied commissions in the army, and the monarch was forbidden to be Catholic or to marry a Catholic, this latter prohibition remaining in force until 2015.

English monolingual dictionary paradigm   57

It has been argued that James's overthrow initiated modern English parliamentary democracy, and the *Bill of Rights* (1689) has become one of the most important documents in the political history of Britain, and never since has the monarch held absolute power.

3.2 The linguistic and cultural background for the development of English lexicography in the 17th century

Driven by the continuing socio-cultural momentum of the 16th century, the Renaissance was moving into its prime period in Britain in the 17th century, with unprecedented advancements in cultural, scientific and technological undertakings. The revolution in science and technology was leading the trend of new science and technology in modern times, and the establishment of the Royal Society enabled scientific undertakings to move from the fringes of the society towards the centre of the social stage. That signified the advent of the era that respected science and technology as the first productive force. The boom in science and culture and favourable government policies (such as patent protection) marked the 17th century as an unparalleled period of intellectual ferment in the British history.

Aside from cultural advances and accomplishments in science and technology, substantial changes also took place in the British population. In the early part of the 17th century, it was about 2.5 million, but it soared to 7 million by the middle of the century, and it was nearly 5.3 million in England only. Thanks to the steady promotion of higher and elementary education, the quality of the British population kept improving, which furnished a solid foundation for Britain's social and cultural progress and created a conducive intellectual and cultural environment and market demand for dictionary compilations in Britain.

The printing of *The King James Version* With the conclusion of the Elizabethan reign with the death of Elizabeth in 1603, proposals were put forth for a new English version of the Bible. Upon James' ascension to the throne of England as James I, the primary mission that lay before him was to reconcile various factions of the Church of England. In January 1604, the newly crowned king convened the Hampton Court Conference. That gathering brought forth proposals for a new English version in response to the problems in previous translations as perceived by the Puritan faction of the Church of England, such as in *The Geneva Version* (1557).

Instructions were issued that the translators ensure that "the new version would conform to the ecclesiology of, and reflect the episcopal structure of, the Church of England and its belief in an ordained clergy". Fifty-four scholars were nominated for its translation, but only forty-seven were actually involved in the work, all of whom were members of the Church of England. Like most other translations of the period, the New Testament was

58   *English monolingual dictionary paradigm*

translated from Greek, the Old Testament from Hebrew and Aramaic and the Apocrypha from Greek and Latin.

After six-and-a-half years' efforts, *The King James Version* (also *The King James Bible* or simply *The Authorized Version*), which has come down even to the present day, came into circulation in 1611, 85 years away from the appearance of its first English version. It included the 39 books of The Old Testament, an intertestamental section containing 14 books of *The Apocrypha*, and the 27 books of The New Testament. By the first half of the 18th century, it had become almost unchallenged as used in Anglican and English Protestant churches and supplanted the *Latin Vulgate* as the standard version of scripture for English-speaking scholars. Thanks to the stereotype printing technology in the early 19th century, it became the most widely printed book in history.

The King James Version is well renowned for its "majesty of style", which had enduring impacts upon literary and particularly prose writing in the 300 years or so to come. It has been universally recognized as one of the most significant books in English culture and an undisputable driving force in the shaping of the English-speaking world.

The ups and downs of 17th-century education in Britain The bourgeois revolution in 17th-century Britain opened up new prospects for reform and development in education, but the restoration of the monarchy recklessly diminished the Puritan visions of education reform and deprived non-Anglicans of their rights to be educated so that the number of students enrolled in British institutions of higher learning decreased, college administration decayed, disregard for scientific research became obvious and developments in higher education almost came to a standstill.

The restoration of the monarchy impeded the accelerating progression in British higher education, but signs of university education becoming disentangled from religion and reverting to reality began to materialize in university transformation under the influence of the Renaissance, the Reformation and the blossoming Industrial Revolution. New developments in natural science were introduced into university curriculums, and higher education in Scotland was beginning to assume a new look. After the appearance of the first university in 1412, Scotland surpassed England in the number of institutions of higher learning over a span of 100 years or so and became inclined towards the European continent in educational notions and administrative governance, being less bound by British traditions and less affected by religion. Meanwhile, universities in England were starting to decline. This striking contrast necessitated the transformation of universities in England. Those changes in 17th-century British higher education have left countless imprints in the making of English dictionaries and in dictionaries proper.

The founding of the Royal Society in Britain In the 17th century, the aureole of university education in Scotland started to diminish owing to

English monolingual dictionary paradigm 59

its obstinate adherence to traditional practices, but there surged in the general public a massive force that propelled the pursuit of science and the exploration of truth. In 1648, John Wilkins (1614–1672), who chaired the founding ceremony of the Royal Society, was made Warden of Wadham College, a former royalist stronghold in Oxford, and his presence at Oxford attracted a good number of scientist followers, including even such great masters as William Petty (1623–1697), Robert Boyle (1627–1691), Robert Hooke (1635–1703), Christopher Wren (1632–1723) and Isaac Newton (1642–1727). They gathered to exchange scientific ideas and experimental findings.

By the middle of the 17th century, those gatherings led to the founding of the Royal Society aiming at "promoting excellence in science for the benefit of humanity" (see its webpage), with John Wilkins serving as its first secretary. In 1662, Richard II approved its founding, and so it was named and became highly renowned as the world's oldest independent scientific academy. The Royal Society takes pride in its "determination of Fellows to withstand the domination of authority and to verify all statements by an appeal to facts determined by experiment". *Philosophical Transactions*, which published its first issue in 1665, "established the important concepts of scientific priority and peer review" and "is now the oldest continuously-published science journal in the world". (See its webpage.) The idea of compiling *OED* was conceived in a lecture presented at the Royal Society conference.

The rise of national languages and their standardization Language is one of the significant markers demonstrating the existence of a national society. With the increasingly intensified awareness of the importance of national languages, their standardization was becoming more prominent and pressing, thus one of the social issues that needed to be urgently addressed in most European countries. Dictionary-making was of essential and fundamental importance to their standardization.

Academies of national height were established in some European countries with a view towards effectively promoting the standardization of national languages, consolidating the authoritative position and the scientific nature of dictionaries and addressing the issues of linguistic normative and purity. Typical examples include Accademia della Crusca (Florence, 1582), l'Académie française (Paris, 1635), Academia Española (Madrid, 1713), and Danish Royal Academy of Sciences (Copenhagen, 1743). Although no similar organizations were set up in Britain, controversies and discussions relating to such issues kept arising from the 16th to the 17th century and even became heated from time to time. Those activities, while ensuring linguistic normative and purity, made dictionary compilation a completely official or semi-official government behaviour and facilitated the emergence and flourishing of national language dictionaries.

60 *English monolingual dictionary paradigm*

3.3 The making of the first English monolingual dictionary and its inheritance of European lexicographical traits

As indicated previously, lexicographical culture does not come into shape overnight and needs accumulation and assimilation over centuries. The Middle East region enjoys the longest history of lexicographical culture in the world and has undergone over 40 centuries of dictionary-making, and dictionary-making in China can be traced back to the Western Zhou Dynasty (1046 BC–771 BC) and takes pride in its inheritance of over 3,000 years of lexicographical legacies. Dictionaries, western or eastern, generally follow the line of development, after a period of cultural evolution and accumulation, going from clay tablets or bamboo slips to reading primers, then to glossaries or vocabularies and eventually to character or word dictionaries in the modern form, which demonstrates the general pattern for the development of world lexicographic culture. It can safely be assumed that dictionaries of all languages originate from the most remote reading primers in the history of their languages, and direct or indirect relationships of inheritance are discernible between them. That applies to British English lexicography as well.

Into the 17th century, a considerable number of new words originating from Latin and Greek started to flood into English, which made English dictionary-making a highly demanding task. In 1604, Robert Cawdrey compiled *A Table Alphabeticall*, which is considered the first English monolingual dictionary in the history of English lexicography. However, the tradition of English lexicography dates back to much earlier than 1604, and the practice of providing English marginal notes alongside Latin or French texts started in the Anglo-Saxon period and continued into the Middle Ages. The bilingual glossaries and dictionaries discussed in the previous chapter are all directly or indirectly related to that tradition.

In response to the increasing demand for literacy education, primers were compiled to aid schoolchildren in learning foreign languages and adults in learning English and vernaculars. This tradition of primer compilation extended up to the end of the 15th century and into the early part of the 16th century. Works written by John Stanbridge, William Horman and Robert Whittinton, such as *Vocabula* and *Vulgaria*, all fall into this category. In 1530, John Palgrave, a tutor in the royal household, had his *Lesclarcissement de la langue francoyse* printed in London. Despite its French title, the book was written in English and is said to be the first grammar of the French language. A scuttle through the book reveals that it integrated the functions of a grammar, a French textbook and a French-English glossary into one and set a precedent and paradigm for similar textbooks for the late 16th century.

Starting from the 1570s, English reading and spelling became the focus of literacy education. In order to adapt to the demands of this new situation, textbooks of different kinds were written, and typical bilingual works included Claudius Hollyband's *The Frenche Schoole-maister* (1573), John Florio's *Firste Fruites* (1578) and William Stepney's *The Spanish School-emaster* (1591). All those books were printed with parallel columns on each page in foreign languages and English, including indications about foreign grammars, daily conversation in London, prayers, courtesy expressions and popular expressions, as well as bilingual glossaries that listed all kinds of common words and were arranged at the end of the book. Apart from bilingual textbooks, English monolingual primers started to appear in the 1580s. Influential works include William Bullokar's *Bullokars Booke at large, for the amendment of Orthographie for English speech* (1580), Richard Mulcaster's *Elementarie* (1582), Edmund Coote's *English Schoolemaister* (1596) and Peter Bale's *The Writing Schoolmaister* (1590). They concentrated on English and its grammar instead of foreign languages.

On the title page, Bullokar stated that his intention in compiling the book was to attain "the easie, speedie and perfect reading and writing of English". He went on to list some simple grammatical rules "to no small commoditie of the English Nation, not only to come to easie, speedie and perfect use of our own language, but also to their easie, speedie, and readie entrance into the secretes of other Languages". This perspective represented the original goal of compiling such textbooks. Timothy Bright composed *Characterie. An Arte of shorte, swifte, and secrete writing by character* (1588), an in-depth exploration that was presented to Her Majesty. It should be noted that William Bullokar, Richard Mulcaster and Edmund Coote all appealed for an English monolingual dictionary. Bullokar made a promise that he would compile such a dictionary but left nothing behind except for an English grammar.

Evidence indicates that Mulcaster's work is the first formal English textbook extant, with a collection of 8,300 headwords, which was aimed at standardizing the orthography of English words. He "emphasizes the worth of the English language and advocates a wider use of it" (Starnes and Noyes, 1991:10). He also attached special importance to compiling an English monolingual dictionary in his work. He stated,

> it were a thing verie praiseworthie . . . if som one well learned and as laborious a man, wold gather all the words which we vse in our *English* tung, whether natural or incorporate, out of all professions, as well learned as not, into one dicitionarie.

He did not actually make a dictionary but appended The Generall Table at the end of the book. He listed the so-called hard words without adding equivalent translations or definitions.

Coote's work, which "is nearer to the English dictionary proper" and "the immediate predecessor of the first English dictionary" (Starnes and Noyes, 1991:11–12), contains "the grammar, the catechism, the prayers, and the vocabulary" (Starnes and Noyes, 1991:11). It covered a wide range

62   English monolingual dictionary paradigm

of subjects, e.g. reading, writing, spelling and word classification. It collected about 1,500 difficult English words, designed chiefly for new literacy groups, people with no knowledge of Latin and "gentlemen and gentlewomen engaged in teaching" (Knowles, 1997:87–88). It consisted of three parts. Of the greatest relevance is Part III, a list of 1,357 headwords. This book proved to be extremely popular and was printed in 49 different editions over the 100 years subsequent to its publication. Coote collected not only "difficult words" but added simple definitions in one way or the other. Simplistic though it was, this work should be considered the predecessor of Cawdrey's *A Table Alphabeticall*, which inherited and adopted Coote's compiling techniques.

To put it in a nutshell, English monolingual dictionaries arose out of the following important motivations. First of all, the tradition of compiling bilingual glossaries in the 7th and 8th centuries and bilingual dictionaries in the Middle Ages laid a sound foundation for English monolingual compilations. Bilingual compilations amassed abundant experience for monolingual dictionary-making, and the appearance of English in bilingual dictionaries as source or target language provided a huge amount of data for monolingual dictionary-making. English bilingual and monolingual primers and textbooks stemmed from bilingual dictionaries and started to make their appearance from the Middle Ages up to the early part of the 16th century as a result of structural reorganization so as better to accommodate newly emerging pedagogical demands furnished the most immediate models and lexical data for monolingual compilations.

Coote's book was the first work of English grammar that collected hard words and provided definitions for them, though most of it was taken from Mulcaster's. However, Mulcaster's book did not provide definitions for those hard words (Moon, 2004). Judging by dictionary structure and format, Coote's book has a closer resemblance to a dictionary. It went through 67 reprints, and the final edition came out in 1737. Although its title and part of its contents followed the model of the textbooks of that time, it provided simple definitions for English hard words. That led some to think that Coote should be the father of English lexicography in its real sense. Read (2003) commented that if there had been a creator for English dictionaries, that should be Edmund Coote, absolutely not Cawdrey.

Second, the Renaissance facilitated the awakening of British national sense of language and stimulated fervent desires for explorations in the nature and development of English lexicon and grammar. The change of the social ecology of the English language and the widespread public interest in English studies, particularly in English vocabulary, prompted schoolteachers to compile, in the final three decades of the 16th century, a series of primers and textbooks or supplementary materials that were used to aid language teaching and learning. All this reinforced their consciousness of national language and their sense of pride and set them thinking seriously about the necessity and feasibility of making an English dictionary.

English monolingual dictionary paradigm 63

Mulcaster emphasized in his book,

> But why not all in English, a tung of it self both depe in conceit, & frank in deliuerie? I do not think that anie language, be it whatsoeuer, is better able to vtter all argumēts, either with more pith, or greater planesse, then our English tung is, if the English vtterer be as skilfull in the matter, which he is to vtter: as the foren vtterer is.
>
> (Starnes and Noyes, 1991:11)

He proceeded to propose the techniques of improving and promoting English skills and proficiency, and one of them was to compile "a perfit English dictionarie wished for" (Starnes and Noyes, 1991:11). Thanks to the experience accumulated in previous bilingual compilations, the intensification of awareness of English as a national language, the substantial promotion of the status of English and the increasing interest in English vocabulary study, there was just one more step away from making a real monolingual English dictionary.

Third, from the most remote time of Roman invasion of the British Isles in 55 BC, English had remained in the state of close contact and even assimilation with European continental languages, though degrees varied significantly from period to period. Over several hundred years of the formation of Old English and another several hundred years subsequent to the Norman Conquest, English underwent great changes that were rarely seen in the history of world languages. Not only did it absorb an enormous number of words from contact languages, in particular "pompous" and "inkhorn" words from Latin and French, but it experienced modifications and evolution in its formation, structure and grammar as well. Prior to the 17th century, two radically different attitudes were taken towards the borrowing of "inkhorn words", which stirred up the "inkhorn controversy" between linguistic purists and non-purists. A certain degree of compromise was reached between them in the 17th century. Consequently, all loanwords that were considered acceptable and useful found their way, almost unnoticeably, into English, and those that were doomed to be redundant disappeared quietly from English. Those "inkhorn words", which were newly borrowed from Latin, Greek and even Arabic and Hebrew, were no longer despised. They enjoyed the same status as Old English hard words and were reasonably classified into the category of "hard words".

The term "hard word", a translation of "mots difficiles" in French, was first used in John Day's glossary *A gatheryng of certayne harde wordes in the newe Testament, with their exposicion* (1551). Among the academics who borrowed such words, they would not create barriers to reading and comprehension, but outside the academic circle, they were undoubtedly words from a sealed book. However, they have become an integrated part of standard English and now prove to be in wide and even everyday circulation. They were favourites for those merchants, artists and newly emerging

64 *English monolingual dictionary paradigm*

noblemen who aspired to higher social status and extraordinary styles of conversation. An English monolingual dictionary, which intended to cater to this sort of linguistic demand, was well on its way to explaining difficult inkhorn words.

3.4 Robert Cawdrey and the first English monolingual dictionary

It is certainly necessary, before a detailed account of the first English monolingual dictionary, to know something about its compiler Robert Cawdrey. It is hard to determine the date of his birth. One story says that he was born sometime in 1537, but another says it was 1538, and he died in 1604 or sometime after that. He did not have the chance to receive higher education. In 1563, he became a schoolteacher in Oakham, Rutland. He was ordained deacon in 1565 and priest in 1570 and, one year afterward, rector of South Luffenham in Rutland. He got into trouble with the Church authorities time and again for being sympathetic to Puritan teachings, not reading the approved texts in his sermons, performing a marriage without authorization and violating other Church rules. In spite of powerful friends who tried to defend him, he was deprived of his rectory in 1588 and had to return to his teaching post to support himself. In the same year, Cawdrey composed an article "A Short and Fruitefull Treatise of the Profit of Catechising". Later he revised it and had its second edition printed in 1604. In 1600, he also published a booklet called *A Treasurie or Store-House of Similes*, which was reprinted in 1609.

Throughout the 16th century, English borrowed numerous words from foreign sources. Cawdrey was concerned about the flooding of those new words into English, which were totally unintelligible to the general British public. He was even extremely upset about the increasing adoption of such words by the rich and powerful people in daily social intercourse. He commented, "They forget altogether their mothers' language, so that if some of their mothers were alive, they were not able to tell or understand what they say" (Preface). He provided a vivid description of how those noblemen who travelled overseas far and wide learned those new words and what pride they took in their ability to use foreign languages. He saw the need of writing an instructional book. With the assistance of his son Thomas Cawdrey (1575–1604), who taught in a London school, Cawdrey compiled what was supposed to be the first English monolingual dictionary *A Table Alphabeticall* and published it in 1604. Obviously, what Cawdrey had on his mind was a strong need for national awakening and an urgent awareness of unexpected development in English. Cawdrey's dictionary opened a prelude to the era of hard-word dictionary compilation, which started in the early 17th century and went through the whole of it.

The full title of Cawdrey's dictionary was *A table alphabeticall conteyning and teaching the true writing, and understanding of hard vsuall English*

English monolingual dictionary paradigm 65

wordes, borrowed from the Hebrew, Greeke, Latine, or French, &c. With the interpretation thereof by plaine English words, gathered for the benefit & helpe of ladies, gentlewomen, or any other unskilfull persons. Whereby they may the more easilie and better vnderstand many hard English wordes, vvhich they shall heare or read in scriptures, sermons, or elswhere, and also be made able to vse the same aptly themselues. Speaking of its compilation, Cawdrey said that it had been written a long time before, that most of it was composed by himself and that it was revised, augmented and eventually completed by his son.

Starnes and Noyes' textual researches proved Cawdrey's words. Cawdrey's book was mainly based on Coote's, from which he "borrowed about 90 per cent" "of words and definitions" and Thomas Thomas' *Dictionarium Linguae Latinae et Anglicanae*, from which "more than 40 per cent" of "words together with the definitions come directly". "50 per cent of the definitions which Cawdrey borrows from Coote he supplements generously by matter from Thomas" and "17 to 18 per cent of his word list and definitions from sources other than Coote and Thomas" (Starnes and Noyes, 1991:15–18). It is worth noting that Cawdrey also drew on marginal annotations from works on religion, law, science and technology and literary texts, such as Arthur Golding's *An exposition of certein words* (1569), John Rastell's *Exposition of Certaine Difficult and Obscure Wordes and Termes of the Lawes of this Realme* (1598), Gregory Martin's *Explication of Certaine Wordes* (1600), Thomas Speght's *The old and obscure words of Chaucer, explained* (1600) etc. (Starnes and Noyes, 1991:14; Knowles, 1997:87–88).

A Table Alphabeticall is a little octavo volume of only 120 pages, which collects 2,652 headwords, a result of word-by-word calculation by the author, rather than following other sources with inaccurate numbers, such as 2,511; 2,543; 2,500; 2,560 and so on. As the title page indicates, all the words are "hard vsuall English wordes, borrowed from the Hebrew, Greeke, Latine, or French. &c" rather than "inkhorn terms" (Moon, 2004). In some entries, labels are given to indicate their sources, such as the use of *[fr]* to show their French origin and (*g*) or (*gr*) to show their Greek origin. For headwords of Latin and Anglo-Saxon origin, no labels are given. In addition to its initial issue, there are three other editions of 1609, 1613 and 1617. There is a successive increase of headwords from the second edition, ranging from 3,009; 3,089 and 4,886, respectively, which shows no great augmentation from the second edition over the third but substantial improvement and enlargement from the third over the fourth. By the early 17th century, William Shakespeare had completed two-thirds of his dramatic writing, and his tragedies, which brought him greater fame and prestige, were under composition. An estimation of Shakespeare's vocabulary demonstrates his possession of about 15,000 words, a surprisingly huge distance Cawdrey's collection keeps from Shakespeare's word power.

66 *English monolingual dictionary paradigm*

Somewhat contrary to what the title says, *A Table Alphabeticall* does not have all the words arranged strictly in the alphabetical order, although the author gives special prominence to this macrostructural arrangement, as it forms a sharp contrast to the thematic arrangement in previous works. Cawdrey's entries provide no phonetic transcription or other information about word usage, except for French and Greek origin and synonym definitions. Headwords are defined by (a) synonyms (e.g. *altitude*, height; *rubicunde*, red, or ruddie), (b) synonyms plus explanations (e.g. *tripartite*, threefold, or deuided into three parts; *succeede*, followe, or come in another place), and (c) explanatory notes (e.g. *records*, writings layde vp for remembrance; *[fr] rallie*, gather together men dispersed, and out of order). The great majority of headwords are defined in the first and second methods, and the third method is used only in a small proportion of entries. No examples are given to illustrate usages.

"Cawdrey was not . . . a man of one book" (Starnes and Noyes, 1991:15) and epitomized all previous works available to him. He made no breakthroughs in compiling techniques but adopted mainly Coote's practices. Coote used labels like (g), (gr) and [fr] to indicate words of Greek and French origin and signs like "*" to identify those words whose forms changed from original spellings, as he believed that more attention should be given to their forms instead of meanings and that users would more likely misspell them. All those practices continued into Cawdrey's works.

Certainly, Cawdrey's work is not without flaws, which will be discussed in 3.7.

3.5 The development of English monolingual lexicography and the fading of English hard-word traditions

The 17th-century English dictionary compilation started with *A Table Alphabeticall*, but its appearance did not bring with it the immediate flourishing of English monolingual dictionary-making. Not until 1616 did the second come out, followed by another five. Though quite limited in number, they intensified the hard-word tradition of British English lexicography. No other English monolingual dictionary was published between 1604 and 1616, but glossaries of different types that concentrated on one single discipline or one aspect of social life appeared as appendixes to specialized works. They were extensions of lexicographical tradition in the 15th and 16th centuries. For instance, early in 1480, John Trevisa (1326–1412) compiled a glossary of legal terms – *De legibus legumque vocabulis*. It is likely that compilers of the early 17th century extracted useful materials from those glossaries.

The first "hard-word" dictionary after Cawdrey's was *The English Expositour: Teaching the Interpretation of the hardest words used in our Language, with sundry Explications, Descriptions and Discourses* (1616), which was written by John Bullokar (c. 1580–1641) at the invitation of

English monolingual dictionary paradigm   67

the wealthy gentlemen. Its headwords amounted to about 5,000, almost twice the number of *A Table Alphabeticall*, with a focused coverage of difficult and outmoded words, typically words from Latin and Greek. It offered more detailed and accurate definitions, coupled with a small number of pictorial illustrations and citations from encyclopedic works. Labels such as "obsolete" and usage notes were given, together with indications of disciplines that those terms fell into in their definitions.

Bullokar was the first to have indicated subject categories of specialized terms or classification of their industry. His dictionary went through three editions in his lifetime, and each new edition contained extractions and augmentations from other dictionaries (Béjoint, 2010:57). That explained why each was well received by its users, especially the revised and augmented edition of 1663, which absorbed selectively from Henry Cockeram's work. Its final revision was completed by R. Browne in 1707, and another four reprints appeared over the 24 years up to 1731.

A forceful rival work was published after Bullokar's dictionary. That was Henry Cockeram's *The English Dictionarie or, an Interpreter of Hard English Words* (1623), "the first monolingual to use the word *dictionary* in its title, almost a century after the bilingual *Dictionary* of Elyot" (Béjoint, 2010:57). Cockeram's dictionary was based on Cawdrey's and Bullokar's. It collected about 5,000 headwords, with a special focus on hard words that were taken from the 16th-century Latin-English dictionaries. It consisted of three parts. Part I collected words and terms in general use, Part II was "was original in that it included 'vulgar' words, glossed by more refined equivalents, clearly intended as a help for those users who wanted to express themselves elegantly" (Béjoint, 2010:58) and Part III collected words and encyclopedic terms relating mainly to well-known figures, god, giants and demons, monsters and serpents, beasts and birds and so on. A dozen pictorial illustrations were provided for clearer clarification of those words and terms.

Obviously, the third part followed the pattern of Cockeram's contemporary Latin-English dictionaries, but he set the precedent of providing such words and terms in an English dictionary. His inclusion of encyclopaedic terms intended to endow his dictionary with encyclopaedic attributes and thus promote its practicality. In spite of his lack of linguistic knowledge, he attempted to classify his headwords on the stylistic basis and divided them into such categories as "general", "vulgar", "elegant". That is his major contribution to linguistics and lexicography. On the whole, Cockeram's dictionary proved to be a success. It went through 11 editions between 1623 and 1658. Up to 1656, Bullokar's work remained to be his only rival, and his final edition was published in 1670 (Béjoint, 2010:58).

The tradition of compiling "hard-word" dictionaries reached its peak with the publication of Thomas Blount's (1618–1679) *Glossographia* (1656) and Edward Philips' (1630–1696) *New World of English Words: or a General English Dictionary*. Blount was a zealous Roman Catholic but practiced law

68   *English monolingual dictionary paradigm*

for some time. His religion interfered with the practice of that profession at a time when Catholics were excluded from almost all areas of public life in England. He abandoned law for literary pursuit and returned to his world of law only when he needed to explore the mysteries of legal terms so as to satiate his spare-time tastes. In 1670, he published a legal dictionary intended to explain difficult terms in ancient and contemporary legal literature.

As indicated in the title, *Glossographia* aimed at

> Interpreting all such Hard Words, Whether Hebrew, Greek, Latin, Italian, Spanish, French, Teutonick, Belgick, British or Saxon; as are now used in our refined English Tongue. Also the terms of Divinity, Law, Physick, Mathematicks, Heraldry, Anatomy, War, Musick, Architecture; and of several other Arts and Sciences Explicated. With Etymologies, Definitions, and Historical Observations. . . . Very useful for all such as desire to understand what they read.
>
> (See its title page)

It collected about 10,700 hard words and words that were not in wide use, including those that had not been collected in previous dictionaries and not even in subsequent dictionaries. His purpose was not to provide a complete list of the English lexicon but to explain hard words that might be encountered in literary reading or in performing professional duties so as to offer assistance to the expanding middle class, who were not well educated.

Glossographia was the largest English monolingual dictionary at the time of its publication and also the last largest and most authoritative one during that stage. Blount was quite keen on new words and refused to accept their exclusion by the conservative force. He believed that "our best modern Authors . . . have both infinitely inriched and enobled our Language by admitting and naturalizing thousands of foreign words" (See "To the Reader"). This view went quite against the trend for linguistic purity. The treatment of etymology in Latin-English dictionaries before Blount's was a novelty, and examples could already be found in dictionaries by Cooper, Thomas, Holyoake and a few others. However, Blount "is the first lexicographer of a purely English dictionary to attempt etymology of words" (Starnes and Noyes, 1991:46). What's more, *Glossographia* was also the first to have had pictorial illustrations and to have indicated the sources of the defined words. "To Blount belongs the credit for being the first English lexicographer to cite the authorities he had consulted" (Starnes and Noyes, 1991:47). Despite fierce competition from a few other dictionaries, it proved itself to be highly popular and went through revision and augmentation in 1661, 1670, 1674 and 1681 and new editions with numerous reprints. Its latest edition came out in 1969 and is still the treasure that stimulates the British taste and interest in reading.

Two years after Blount's *Glossographia*, Edward Philips, the nephew of the poet John Milton, brought forth his *New World of English Words*,

English monolingual dictionary paradigm   69

which was encyclopaedic in nature. It was the first folio English dictionary. Its tediously long title demonstrates that, apart from the words of the
language it covered, collections were also made from Arabic, Syriac, Dutch
and other languages. It selected terms from an extensive range of subjects,
almost all conceivable subjects. Philips collected common words, as well
as hard words, foreign words, proper nouns and other specialized terms,
a tradition he followed in the making of his dictionary. That highlighted a
striking difference between his dictionary and his predecessors' and marked
an end to the tradition of hard-word dictionary-making. In addition, he
used dagger signs to indicate words that he believed to be unrefined. He
was the first to have appended to a dictionary a history of the English language in the long course of lexicographic development and making (Béjoint,
2010:59).

The first edition of *New World of English Words* covered around 11,000
headwords, including proper nouns, and made subjective judgments upon
them (Béjoint, 2010:59). The number of headwords increased to 13,000
when the third edition appeared in 1671, to 17,000 when the fifth edition
appeared in 1696 and to 38,000 when the revised and augmented edition
by John Kersey appeared in 1706 (Starnes and Noyes, 1946:84). Besides
doubling the number of headwords, Kersey also discarded old and useless
materials but introduced important and fresh materials so that he became
the first British lexicographer to collect the terms relating to strange plants
on American plantations (Read, 2003:223). As a result, he changed "general" in the original title to "universal" and renamed his work as *New
World of English Words: or Universal English Dictionary*. That new title
agreed more with the range of his headword selection and the contents of
the text. He revised and augmented Philips' dictionary so much that it was
widely recognized as a new compilation and a forerunner for Johnson's
great work.

Philips' work became a formidable competitor to *Glossographia*, but it
relied so heavily on his predecessors' works, especially Blount's dictionary,
that he plunged himself into a prolonged copyright dispute with Blount,
which lasted until their death. Philips' major contribution was his special
emphasis on the compiling techniques that were previously adopted but
without consistency, such as providing information concerning personal
names and places, consulting people with expertise, classifying and indicating subject categories of specialized terms and so on. Amid heated disputes of copyright issues between Blount and Philips, Elisha Coles (c. 1640/
another story says 1643–1680) published *An English Dictionary* (1676).
Coles' dictionary marked a departure from the tradition of compiling Latin
and Greek hard-word dictionaries, and it was the first to have collected
slang, colloquialism and the like in an English dictionary.

Coles was born of a well-educated family. His father worked as teacher,
and he received education in Oxford, though without obtaining a degree.
From 1663 onwards, he taught foreigners English and Latin in London and

70 English monolingual dictionary paradigm

remained in the teaching profession until his death. Coles carried in his work the style of exaggerating his selection and coverage of headwords on the title page in previous compilations, claiming on its title page that his work explained

> the difficult Terms that are used in Divinity, Husbandry, Physick, Phylosophy, Law, Navigation, Mathematicks, and other Arts and Sciences. Containing Many thousands of Hard Words (and proper names of Places). . . . Together with the Etymological Derivation of Them from their proper Foundations. . . . In a Method more Comprehensive, than any that is extant.

Coles' work is encyclopaedic by nature, with a coverage of about 25,000 headwords and an increase of over 8,000 compared with Philips' fourth revised edition. Coles' materials were mainly taken from Philips' dictionary, with dialect words from John Ray's *Collection of English Words* (1674) and colloquial words from Richard Head's *The Canting Academy* (1673).

What was special about his dictionary was that it "corrected many of Phillips' errors" and "included slang and dialect words, a first in general lexicography, and proper names with encyclopedic developments" (Béjoint, 2010:59). "Coles is the first consciously to introduce them (i.e. canting terms) into an English dictionary proper", though "as early as the sixteenth century separate collections of such terms had been made" (Starnes and Noyes, 1991:63). He gave greater attention to how to make definitions more compact. Many of his definitions were considerably condensed, and though succinct owing to space condensation, his definitions were generally refined and well composed. Coles proved his originality and special features in the making of his dictionary. In "To the Reader", he expressed his strong dislike for tasteless repetitions and therefore attempted to explain words in an independent and yet interrelated way so that definitions would be made such that they were interconnected into a meaningful chain. For example,

> *Lupa*, a She-wolf that nourished *Romulus* in the
> *Lupercal*, a place near *Rome*, where they celebrated the
> *Lupercalia*, feasts in honour of *Pan*, performed by the
> *Luperci*, Priests of Pan.

Though it was never revised or augmented, Coles' dictionary went through 11 reprints, and the final reprint was made in 1732. It kept its record of sales for over 50 years on the highly competitive dictionary market in Britain, which is a good testimony to its practicality and popularity. Starnes and Noyes (1991:62–63) summed up Coles' contributions to English lexicography in six major aspects. The most significant innovation is definitely his grouping of related words and his rejection of his predecessors' practice of

English monolingual dictionary paradigm 71

randomly choosing the adjective, the noun or the verb form to represent the group, as shown in the previous example. This way of grouping words may give a better demonstration of lexical relations in both form and meaning and make it easier to establish lexical associations and to learn, acquire and consult.

The last English monolingual dictionary that appeared in the 17th century was called *Gazophylacium Anglicanum* (1689). Its authorship is unknown, but scholars ascribed it to Stephen Skinner (1623–1667), as it was mainly based on Skinner's Latin-written dictionary *Etymologicon Linguae Anglicanae* (1671). Its second edition came out in 1691 and was renamed *A New English Dictionary Showing the Etymological Derivation of the English Tongue*. It traced and indicated all general English words and arranged all proper names into a separate second part. Despite numerous defects, errors and mistakes in it, its publication paved the way for the development of philology and lexicography. The treatment of etymology, from that time on, became a paradigm for English dictionary-making. With the closing of English monolingual dictionary-making in the 17th century, the hard-word era of English lexicography gradually came to its end.

Before the conclusion of this section, mention must be made of the beginnings of English dialect lexicography. The diversified distribution of geography and the inconvenience of transportation and communication within the British Isles, from the outset, gave rise to a great variety of vernaculars and endowed Old English with rich linguistic varieties. However, records of findings from observations concerning English regional differences did not appear until around 1125. Edmund Coote's (1597) strong dislike for dialects and his views about the harms that were thought to have been brought about by dialects dominated the minds of the public from the 16th to the 18th centuries. The British public showed a strong inclination for "best English", and the abidance by the standards of "educated language" was expected to become their voluntary and conscious action (Penhallurick, 2009:292–295). Fortunately, that did not impede the interest in and attention to Old English vernaculars and dialects on the part of amateur groups, represented by Laurence Nowell (c. 1515–1570).

Nowell was the first to have intended to compile an Old English dictionary, and his *Vocabularium Saxonicum* was only completed in 1565. Two years later, he passed it on to his son William Lambarde (1536–1601) for revision and augmentation. The augmented revision was not published until 1952 as part of a series of ancient rare texts. The process from compilation to publication spanned over 400 years, and the dictionary should be reckoned as spanning over the longest period of time from its making to appearance in the history of world lexicography. Its manuscripts became the main source of linguistic materials for William Somner's (1598–1669) *Dictionarium Saxonixo-Latino-Anglicum* (1659). Nowell collected about

72 *English monolingual dictionary paradigm*

190 dialectal words, which became valuable materials for studies in Old English dialects and their history. What is interesting is that Coote, Cooper and Alexander Gil (1565–1635), who compiled *Logonomia Anglica* (1619), all labelled them as "barbarous" in their dictionaries. That attitude towards dialects and dialectal words was not put right until Skinner (1671) and Coles (1676) acknowledged dialectal words as regional language elements (Penhallurick, 2009:294).

John Ray (1627–1705), a member of the Royal Society, was the first to make a systematic collection of dialectal words on a national scale and amass them into a dictionary. In 1670, he published *A Compleat Collection of English Proverbs* and *A Collection of English Words Not Generally Used* four years later. Its revised reprint was made in 1691. The revised version consisted of two main parts: North Country Words (1–86) and South and East Country Words (87–121). Ray invited a large number of volunteers to assist in collecting dialectal words, among them Skinner, Ralph Thoresby (1858–1724) and others. His purpose was

> not in this book to be a general English Glossary; (of which sort there are many already extant,) but only, as the Title imports, a Catalogue of such as are proper to some Countries [i.e. counties], and not universally known or used.
>
> (See Postcript 169)

Ray distinguished between "general words" and "regional words", which laid a theoretical demarcation and foundation for the making of dialect dictionaries in the real sense in the 18th century.

Our final mention is made of B. E.'s *The New Dictionary of the Terms Ancient and Modern of the Canting Crew* (c. 1698). Its full title is *A new dictionary of the terms ancient and modern of the canting crew, in its several tribes, of gypsies, beggers, thieves, cheats, &c. with an addition of some proverbs, phrases, figurative speeches, &c.* While borrowing heavily from previous glossaries and vocabularies of similar nature, it collected jargons, cants, slangs, colloquialisms and popular new expressions in London commercial areas. They altogether amounted to over 4,000. Keen observations were made of different aspects of the collected words, and discriminations were made of senses with fine subtlety. All that contributed to its status as the largest and the most widely used nonstandard English dictionary of that time. No dictionary could replace it until Francis Grose's (1730, and another story has it as 1731–1791) *A Classic Dictionary of the Vulgar Tongue* (1785). Such collections were, as a rule, added as appendixes in previous works of the same kind, and that dictionary was the first to have been published as an independent work and also the first to have provided citations in a slang dictionary. The materials it provided, particularly jargons and cant words, became priceless sources later compilers could draw from.

English monolingual dictionary paradigm 73

3.6 The continuation of English bilingual lexicographical traditions and innovations in bilingual dictionary compiling techniques

The development of British English bilingual lexicography gained such forceful momentum in the 16th century that, in the first half of the 17th century, the dominating role was played by the revised or enlarged versions of the Latin-English and English-Latin bilingual dictionaries that were made in that century, represented by the Rider-Holyoake dictionary series. New bilingual compilations did not appear until 1662, and they were mostly bidirectional. Owing to the substantial amelioration of the national status and social function of English, those bilingual, bidirectional dictionaries firmly established English as a source language and a major target language, marking an obvious departure from the Latin-dominating tradition in the 16th century and a leap forward towards more combinations of English with other European continental languages.

In the history of English lexicography, relations of inheritance and even plagiarism are traceable to the middle and late part of the 15th century. Such relations were discernible not only between monolingual dictionaries but, more apparently, substantial between bilingual dictionaries. Into the 17th century, such relations were realized mainly through revision and augmentation, which pushed the 16th-century bilingual dictionaries to a higher level of glory in the 17th century. What became the first choice for revision and augmentation was naturally the latest edition of John Rider's *Bibliotheca scholastica*, which was published at the end of the 16th century and was later given the honorary title of *Riders Dictionarie* as the trademark for the publisher. As great a success as his work turned out to be, he did not involve himself directly in its subsequent revision.

The revision of *Bibliotheca scholastica* was first completed by Francis Holyoake (1567–1653) in 1604, and the first revised edition came out in 1606. The effort Holyoake put into the revision of Rider's dictionary extended its influence into most of the 17th century. By 1659, nine of the revised and enlarged editions were directly authored by Francis Holyoake. In 1664, Francis Gouldman (c. 1607–c. 1688) published *A Copious Dictionary in Three Parts* on the basis of Holyoake's work. In 1677, Thomas Holyoake published *A Large Dictionary in Three Parts* on the basis of the works written by his father and Gouldman. More will be discussed about these two works later. Here an end can be put to the discussions concerning revision and augmentation of Rider-Holyoake dictionary series and related compilations.

Rider-Holyoake's dictionary series outshone almost all other compilations in the first half of the 17th century, until Christopher Wase (1627–1690), an English scholar, writer, translator and educationalist, published *Dictionarium minus* in 1662. This dictionary consisted of two parts – English-Latin and Latin-English. The Latin-English part was completed in 1661, and the

74 *English monolingual dictionary paradigm*

English-Latin part the following year. Wase made a strict selection of headwords in the Latin-English part. He selected only classic words, arranged them according to the etymological sequence with their derivatives following their roots and provided necessary grammatical information.

Wase might be the first in the 17th century to have listed metaphorical meanings before basic or natural meanings (Starnes, 1954:273). From Thomas Cooper's time, Latin-English bilingual dictionaries had the tradition of appending a special list of proper nouns to the dictionary text, but Calepine broke away from the tradition and set the precedent of inserting them into the dictionary text and arranging them alphabetically in its macrostructure. However, Wase believed that information about proper nouns could easily be found in specialized works and that their selection in the dictionary would be of no great value to the teaching and learning of Latin. This idea started to exert dominating influence upon decisions about whether to select or drop out proper nouns. Compilers continued to follow that practice till the end of the 20th century.

Another contribution Wase made was the application of explanatory notes to English dictionary-making so as to identify different senses of words. In 1675, Wase published the enlarged and abridged edition. Apart from some additions and deletions, not many substantial revisions were made in it, and so there was no great change in its size. One more thing to be noted is its bidirectional configuration, which became a popular pattern for later bilingual compilations to follow (See Green, 1996:177–178).

Two years after the appearance of Wase's dictionary, Gouldman published *A Copious Dictionary in Three Parts*. As indicated in its title, this dictionary consisted of three parts: I. The English before the Latin, Enriched with about Ten Thousand Words more than any former Dictionary contains; II. The Latin before the English, With correct and plentiful etymological Derivatives, Philological Observations, and Phraseological Explications. III. The Proper Names of Persons, Places, And other things necessary to the understanding of Historians and Poets. Obviously, Gouldman restored the tradition Wase attempted to overthrow. According to Starnes (1954), Gouldman basically adopted Rider-Holyoake's wordlist in his selection of headwords, which was supplemented by Wase's list, but his claim of an increase of around 10,000 headwords in his dictionary is highly doubtful. In defining words, Gouldman chiefly used the materials from Thomas and Holyoake's works. He followed the pattern that was established in Thomas' and Rider-Holyoake dictionaries and incorporated pure and vulgar words altogether into the macrostructure of his dictionary, as he suggested in the preface that it was generally hard to distinguish between "pure" and "vulgar" words and that the Latin-English part was intended for reading rather than writing, an intended division between encoding and decoding functions in dictionary-making.

In addition, he brought back in his dictionary Baret's practice of providing the background introduction to each letter in the alphabet, which was

English monolingual dictionary paradigm   75

passed down from one generation of compilers to the other. In the front matter, Gouldman wrote an introductory article about the evolution of English lexicography that traced its history from the most remote Roman beginnings down to Wase, his direct inheritor. Viewed from the lexicographical perspective, Gouldman adequately demonstrated the advantages of his dictionary in his preface but proposed many ideas that were thought-provoking and had rich theoretical implications and references (Green, 1996:178–179).

Francis Holyoake was the first to have undertaken the task of revising Rider's dictionary. It was not after over half a century that his son Thomas Holyoake took over his work. Around the 1660s, Thomas copied his father's mode of compilation and started to work on *A Large Dictionary in Three Parts* on the basis of Gouldman's dictionary and with supplementation from Wase's work and a few other sources. That voluminous folio dictionary was published in 1677 and consisted of three parts – "The English before the Latin", "The Latin before the English" and "The Proper Names of Persons, Places, and other things". Like other previous compilers, Thomas spared no effort boasting about his dictionary and stated on the title page, "Together with very considerable and ample Addition, carried on by a diligent search into and perusal of very many Authors both Ancient and Modern. Whereby this Work is rendered the most Compleat and Useful of any that was ever yet extant in this kind". A comparison of what is said on the two title pages shows that it is an apparent reproduction of the title page in Gouldman's work with modifications only in wording and the number of headwords selected. Owing to its heavy reliance upon the works by his father, Wase and Gouldman, Thomas' work manifested no obvious advancement in compiling techniques and structural organization. No reprints were made as a result of strong competition from previous works and the dictionary by Elisha Coles. However, "containing the essential matter" of his predecessors and printed in folio, in larger and more legible type, as Starnes (1954:299) says, this dictionary "is for consultation preferable to any one of these".

The second year after the publication of his English monolingual dictionary, i.e. the same year as the publication of Thomas' dictionary, Coles' *A Dictionary, English-Latin, and Latin-English* (1677) came off the press. This bidirectional dictionary contained "All the things Necessary for the Translating of either Language into the other. To which end Many things that were Erroneous are rectified, many superfluities retrenched, and very many Defects supplied. And All suited to the meanest Capacities" (See its title page). Coles followed a rigid alphabetical arrangement of headwords with common nouns and proper nouns treated in exactly the same way. Those terms that denoted birds, beasts and other creatures and were listed only in appendixes in the Rider-Holyoake dictionary series were without exception inserted into its macrostructure in the alphabetical sequence.

In the three-page appendix specially appended to the English-Latin part, Coles collected an extraordinary list of homophones, "with their Several Significations explained by English for the Benefit of our own Nation, and

76 *English monolingual dictionary paradigm*

the Latin for the Good of Strangers". That design appeared for the first time in the history of English dictionary-making. Coles' bilingual dictionary had an extensive coverage of headwords, fairly succinct expression and much simplified format and layout. It was no wonder that 15 editions came out over a span of 73 years between 1677 and 1749. The publisher indicated in the thirteenth edition that there was an annual sale of 2,000 copies since its first publication. It followed that its total sales amounted to no fewer than 1,400,000 copies. By even today's standards, it was a huge success. It is not hard to see what extensive and enduring impacts Coles' dictionary had exerted upon his contemporaries and later compilers (Starnes, 1954:306–308; Cormier, 2009:66–67).

In the late part of the 17th century, what could be mentioned in the same breath as Coles' dictionary was Adam Littleton's (1627–1694) *Linguae Latinae Liber Dictionarius Quadripartitus* (Latine Dictionary, in Four Parts). That large quarto dictionary consisted of four parts – English-Latin, Latin-English, Latin proper nouns and Latin vulgar words. The Latin-English part was the largest of all parts and took up two-thirds of its proportion. In its foreword, the compiler explained that the English-Latin part focused chiefly on those English words of actual use, which was coupled with proper Latin equivalents and supplemented with several thousand words absent from previous compilations. The Latin-English part provided the origin, meaning and use of the headwords, together with such grammatical information as word classes. It employed special signs and marks to indicate the style of use of the equivalent words, e.g. capital letters standing for word roots, asterisks for words of Greek origin, equation marks for synonyms, and so on.

The part of proper nouns followed the tradition of providing historical, legendary and geographical information about the proper nouns, and the part of Latin vulgar words distinguished between orthodox standard words and vulgar words so that young users could identify one from the other and the classic attributes of the dictionary could be maintained. Littleton claimed that his greatest intention in compiling the dictionary was to "carry the purity of the Latine Tongue throughout" (Cormier, 2009:67–68), which is where the idea of English purity originated in the 18th century. (See Green, 1996:179–182.)

Littleton's treatment of information outside the dictionary text is also noteworthy. He inserted two maps, i.e. the map of ancient Italy and the map of Rome, immediately after the Latin-English part, and, at the end of the dictionary, he inherited Thomas and Rider's model and appended a list of legal terms, a Roman calendar, anecdotes and events of famous figures, Roman measurements, a table of currency etc. In terms of macrostructure, such a configuration is almost complete and assumes all the structural attributes modern dictionaries should possess. Littleton's dictionary underwent six editions, and the last edition appeared in 1735. Its influence lasted for over half a century until the 1730s, when Robert Ainsworth's (1660–1743) new dictionary gradually took its place.

English monolingual dictionary paradigm 77

English dictionary-making in the 17th century was dominated by Latin-English and English-Latin dictionaries, but there also appeared a few new combinations of English, bilingual or multilingual, with French and with Dutch. English combinations with French included Randle Cotgrave's (?–c. 1634) *Dictionarie of the French and English Tongues* (1611), Guy Miège's (1644–c. 1718) *A New Dictionary* (1677) and Abel Boyer's (c. 1667–1729) *The Royal Dictionary* (1699). English combinations with Dutch included Willem Sewel's (1653–1720) *A Large Dictionary of English-Dutch* (1691). Those dictionaries were limited in variety, but they incorporated a lot of innovation into their making and exercised far-reaching influence. Sewel's dictionary experienced at least five editions for over 60 years after its publication, and an augmented edition was published by Egbert Buys in 1766, which adequately demonstrated its academic value and popularity. (See Cormier, 2009:70–85.) Multilingual dictionaries in the 17th century mainly included John Minsheu's (also known as John Minshew, 1560–1627) *Ductor in Linguas: Guide into the Tongues* (1617), William Somner's *Dictionarium Saxonixo-Latino-Anglicum* (1659) and James Howell's (c. 1594–1666) *Lexicon Tetraglotton* (1660). (See Cormier, 2009:64.) Minsheu's dictionary is actually "a blend of a polyglot etymological dictionary and an incomplete etymological synonym finder in ten languages other than English" (Liberman, 2009:271).

3.7 The academic and social values of English dictionaries in the 17th century

The 17th-century English dictionaries, monolingual and bilingual, have preserved priceless treasures for studies in British social transformation, cultural progression and language change. They have become inexhaustible resources for English dictionary-making over the three centuries to follow. They are a mirror that reflects the evolutional projection of Britain's social, cultural and linguistic changes. It goes without any exaggeration that without the accumulation of the 17th-century English lexicography there would never be Johnson's lexicographical accomplishments nor the glory of the Oxford dictionaries in the 19th and 20th centuries, It follows that the 17th century is both a sedimentary and foundation-laying period for the development of English lexicography.

Owing to their development over the 16th and 17th centuries, English dictionaries developed into various types, covering bilingual, monolingual and bidirectional as well as specialized dictionaries, which constituted major dictionary genres of modern times. Meanwhile, their megastructural configuration was maturing, including such main components as front matter, body part (dictionary text) and back matter. It was becoming clear that the appearance of a modern dictionary was taking shape. During the Renaissance period, no specialized dictionary came into existence, but that did not mean that proper names and technical terms were completely overlooked.

78 *English monolingual dictionary paradigm*

For example, personal names and place names were scattered in the macro-structure of Eliot-Cooper dictionaries, and, for the first time in the history of English lexicography, Cooper selected proper names and treated them as a separate part in his *Thesaurus*. This way of treating proper names in a separate part after the dictionary text became a common practice and an outstanding feature in most of the Latin dictionaries in the 16th and 17th centuries.

From the time that Francis Holyoake brought forth the 1606 revision of *Bibliotheca scholastica* and added the Latin-English part and a separate section for proper names, the design of a bidirectional dictionary incorporating an English-Latin part, a Latin-English part and a section of proper names began to take shape and became a reality. That "three-in-one" combination was well recognized and accepted by the majority of large bilingual dictionary compilers. It became a mainstream model for bidirectional dictionaries and continued to be in use for over half a century. The "four-in-one" combination also appeared, as few dictionaries devoted a separate section to vulgar and colloquial words to cater to the special need to distinguish between register and styles. The "three-in-one", "four-in-one" and bidirectional combinations demonstrated a major structural attribute that marked differences between the 17th-century English bilingual dictionaries and those previous to them.

Three macrostructural arrangements were common in the 16th century – alphabetical, thematic and etymological. In terms of thematic arrangement, Withals set a precedent. He followed the tradition of arranging words in bilingual glossaries in the Middle Ages and came under heavy influence of Latin dictionary compilers. However, the thematic arrangement was obviously not suitable for large dictionaries. As a result, it became especially popular in primers and textbooks for children and continued into the 18th century. Eliot inherited the etymological arrangement that was adopted in Calepine's dictionary, but the difficulty in entry retrieval deemed that this way of arranging headwords would not be in wide use in large dictionaries. Consequently, in its augmented and revised edition, macrostructural arrangement was reverted to the rigid alphabetical order.

Comparatively speaking, the alphabetical arrangement is easy to follow and convenient for headword retrieval, but for inflectional language, the scattered distribution of conjugate and homonymic words in macrostructure indisputably has its defects. Probably owing to this, up to the 17th century, not a single dictionary stuck to any one of the three arrangements consistently and throughout. However, the alphabetical arrangement could after all be accepted as the dominating mode, as it had been tested in use for centuries and became gradually established in large and important dictionaries.

"The ultimate test of a dictionary is in the accuracy and completeness of definition" (Starnes, 1954:345). In the 16th-century English lexicography, definitions were neither standardized and consistent nor informative. Some

English monolingual dictionary paradigm 79

were merely literal translations of Latin words; others were extensions of English synonyms. Some were detailed and meticulous and succinct and to the point, but others were ambiguous and vague and lacking in precision. Thanks to the arduous efforts on the part of generations of Latin dictionary compilers, bilingual dictionaries became increasingly refined in definition and in art and craft. There is no doubt that Cawdrey's defining methods were obviously derived from the practices of previous compilers. In dictionaries compiled by Wase, Coles, Littleton and others, more attention was paid to their definitions, and that laid a good foundation for the improvement in defining quality and methodology in later compilations.

From their inception, Latin-English and English-Latin dictionaries provided information concerning word grammar to varying degrees and in varying amounts. That practice was taking shape in Cooper's 1548 revision of *Bibliotheca Eliotae* and was well developed when *Thesaurus linguae Romanae & Britannicae* came out in 1565. It went on to cover word classes, pronunciation, the gender of nouns and adjectives and their conjugation, verb inflections, derivatives from roots etc. There had also been a tradition of Latin dictionaries providing information about word origins, but they confined their attention to only Latin words of Greek origin, combinations of Latin elements and cognate Latin words, with the exception of John Baret's and Francis Holyoake's dictionaries.

Baret devoted some attention to the origin of English words but only to a limited extent. Holyoake's dictionary made a more extensive use of etymological information taken from other Latin dictionaries to enrich its contents, though a great many were merely guesses. Their practice was extended into works by compilers such as Gouldman, Thomas Holyoake, and Littleton. It was amply reflected and given due attention in English monolingual dictionaries as well, especially in Blount's *Glossographia* (Starnes, 1954:344–345).

For dictionaries of the 15th and 16th centuries, it was quite a fashion to quote classic authors to illustrate the meaning and use of words, as that could heighten the prestige and reputation of their dictionaries. Consequently, compilers took pride in acknowledging the authors they quoted. Thomas Eliot, for example, missed no opportunity to keep up with the latest trends by transplanting a large number of citations from Latin-French dictionaries for the purpose of raising the quality of citations and ultimately heightening the quality and prestige of his dictionary.

However, from the time that Eliot's dictionary appeared, the compilers of the Middle Ages were no longer treated as authorities that were followed and imitated for new compilations. The compilers shifted their eyes onto those authors and compilers whose works were more of a classic nature. As a rule, no acknowledgement was made, and the names of those authors who were quoted were drowned in the tedious list. Throughout the 16th century, the issue of etymological treatment became extraordinarily complicated, as compilers took resources from the same sources and very often quoted from

80   *English monolingual dictionary paradigm*

each other's works (Starnes, 1954:347). In some cases, the tracing of authorship could be an extremely difficult riddle. Over the 17th century, disputes over whether it was lexicographical inheritance or plagiarism kept popping up, and the root cause lay here. As the illustration and supplementation of definition, the quotation from classic works by well-known authors later constituted a major theoretical underpinning for the ideology of linguistic purism.

Regarding the provision of lexicographical information, progress was obvious in the 17th-centruy English dictionaries, particularly in the design and application of notational marks and signs. Littleton's work was a concentrated reflection of such aspects of dictionary-making in English bilingual lexicography. For example, he employed "capital letter" to indicate "roots", "asterisk" to indicate "Greek origin", "obelisk" to indicate "obsolete" or "specialized", "equation" to indicate "synonym" and so on. As far as monolingual compilation is concerned, Cawdrey is without doubt a pioneer. He applied Coote's specially designed signs and typefaces for the identification of word origins to his dictionary-making, e.g. the use of italics such as "*(g)*" or "*(gr)*" to show Greek origin, "*[fr]*" to show French origin, and "***" to show words of foreign origin that had undergone changes in form. He also used "(k)" [a kind of] to indicate "vague" or "ambiguous", such as artichok, (k) herbe; citron, (k) fruit; crocodile, (k) beast, and so on.

Substantial advancement was made in the development of new types and functions and in the art and craft of 17th-century dictionary-making, most noticeably with unprecedented breakthroughs being achieved in monolingual compilation, but, in contrast to bilingual compilation of the same period, there existed serious drawbacks. Definition in Cawdrey's dictionary is a case in point. A scuttle through Cawdrey's dictionary will show that his definition was coarse and crude, e.g. "*vertigiousnes*, lightnes, or a swimming of the heade", his senses were not discriminated, e.g. "*collation*, recitall, a short banquet", the word classes of headwords and defining words were mismatched, e.g. "*vegetable*, springing, or growing, as herbes" and even in definitions the classes of defining words were inconsistent, e.g. "*conference*, communication, talking together".

One of the motivations for Cawdrey to compile his dictionary was to make a record of correct spellings. What was interesting was that spelling inconsistencies were not uncommon in his dictionary, e.g. "wold-wolde; to be-to bee". In addition, inconsistency was also found in his defining format. The defining of verbs, for example, employed root verbs in some cases and the to-infinitive form in other cases. The use of punctuations at the end of entries was random, e.g. "." and "," in some cases, ":" and no punctuation at all in other cases.

A review of the educational background of English dictionary compilers in the 16th and 17th centuries demonstrates that they generally had education in Oxford or Cambridge and served in ecclesiastical posts. Some even held Oxford or Cambridge high degrees, and the majority of them had teaching experience in schools. Those qualifications, together with their experiences, contributed considerably to the quality of the works they completed and the steady and sustainable development of British English lexicography in the 17th century.

4 The termination of hard-word traditions in English lexicography and its pursuit of prescriptivism

English lexicography arose out of the need of explaining the "hard words", and English monolingual dictionaries, which began to appear in the early 17th century, strengthened the tradition of explaining difficult words, as well as representing the standard use of language, especially the standardization of English orthography, directly in the course of dictionary-making. Driven by the language standardization movement that was surging in Europe featured by purity, normalization, prescription and ethnicity, dictionary compilers naturally considered linguistic standardization and codification their priority and produced dictionaries in response to the intensifying needs for linguistic normalization, which was typified by Johnson's dictionary of 1755.

> The eighteenth century was a period of rapid evolution for monolingual dictionaries, at a time when many other things were also changing in European societies. Because of the general fascination for knowledge and its dissemination, because of the development of science and technology, because there were more people writing, to a wider public, because periodicals appeared in many countries at that time, there was a need for reference works of all kinds, and particularly a need for authority on what words meant.
>
> (Nunberg, 1994)

It was for this reason that a succession of authoritative dictionaries began to come out in the 18th century, typically Johnson's dictionary, as well as a few "first" dictionaries, such as the first dictionary to have covered American usage – Kersey's augmented edition of New World of English Words and the first English dictionary to have included woodcut illustrations – *Glossographia Anglicana Nova* (1707). These dictionaries suggested transformations in compiling notions, the rising market demands for diversified dictionaries in response to economic, social and cultural development and a radical transition of orientation in dictionary-making from compiler-centred, hard-word-focused and "inkhorn" tastes to user-first and more

The termination of hard-word traditions   83

general tastes for diversified demands. That explains why hard-word traditions could no longer be sustained in later compilations.

4.1 The socio-cultural background for the shaping of British English lexicography in the 18th century

Over 300 hundred years' influence of the Renaissance gradually pushed Europe into the Age of Enlightenment, an intellectual movement, which started in the late 17th century and sustained its domination of the world of ideas in Europe for the 18th century. It advocated reason as the primary source of authority and legitimacy, ideals like liberty, fraternity, government through constitution and church-state separation, scientific methodology and the spirit of "*Sapere aude* (daring to know)", such that it came to be known as the second ideological emancipation movement in the history of mankind. Thanks to the widespread nature of the Enlightenment ideals, philosophy, literature and science in Europe received unprecedented attention and achieved unparalleled advancement.

Following the Industrial Revolution of the 1750s, the victory over France in North America in the 1760s, and the occupation of the vast territories in India, Britain became the world's superpower in every sense of the word. The Industrial Revolution in Britain radically changed the social, political, economic and cultural life of humanity, and, by 1700, the total population of England and Scotland amounted to 7.5 million. All this furnished fertile socio-cultural soil for the amelioration of English dictionary-making in the 18th century.

The appearance of the world's first English daily On March 11, 1702, Elizabeth Mallet started to publish the first British daily newspaper – *The Daily Courant* in London, with her publisher Edward Mallet, but it was soon sold to Samuel Buckley, who moved it to premises in the area of Little Britain in London. The title was taken from *The Courant*, a newspaper that was initially published in London in 1621. In its early days, it consisted of only one page with two columns and with advertisements printed on the reverse side. It covered news in Dutch and French without titles or headlines. Her intention was to publish swiftly, correctly and objectively foreign news without her own comments, as she believed that readers would have "sense enough to make reflections for themselves".

The edition of April 7, 1712 dragged the newspaper into serious controversy and even trouble with the Parliament, and that was worsened by excessive burden of subsidies. It had to stop publication in 1735 and was merged with *The Daily Gazetteer*. Although *The Daily Courant* is not Britain's first paper, it is the first English paper published on a daily basis. It played an important role in transmitting information and formulating and leading public opinion. Under its extensive influence, several other newspapers came out in Britain. The transmission of newspapers was of extraordinary

84 *The termination of hard-word traditions*

help in promoting the standardization of English orthography and furnished abundant sources in terms of references and citations for the making of English dictionaries.

The establishment of the United Kingdom of Great Britain England and Scotland were historically independent states. In the late 13th and early 14th centuries, England attempted to annex Scotland by force but to no avail. In the 1560s, Mary, queen of Scots, pledged, in order to gain the throne of Scotland, to annex the two states by peaceful means. From 1603 onwards, the two states had the same monarch, but the royal families continued without change. The Parliamentary acts of 1606, 1667 and 1689 made serious efforts to annex the two. However, the consensus was not reached until 1707, at which time the Parliaments of both sides granted consent to the annexation agreement that was reached on July 22, 1706.

Obviously, the two sides had different political intentions for the annexation. From England's point of view, the annexation could ensure that Scotland would neither appoint its own monarch nor unite with neighbouring states against England, while Scotland expected to pull itself out of the fiscal mire with England's assistance. The act for annexation took effect as of May 1, 1707, and England and Scotland combined into the United Kingdom of Great Britain. On the same day, the parliaments on both sides became unified, and the Parliament of Great Britain came into effect in London. As commented by some historians, that unification turned out to be one of the most astounding social transformations in the history of Europe. In addition to the expansion of geographical territories, the annexation laid a solid foundation for further strengthening Britain's political, economic and social power needed for its overseas operations and for English to go global.

The birth of the first modern English novel Daniel Defoe (c. 1660–1731), an English pamphleteer, journalist and writer as well as one of the earliest proponents of the form of the novel and one of the founders of the English novel, is best-known for *Robinson Crusoe* (1719), which is reckoned as the first modern English novel. Defoe was born in London and received only limited boarding school education, but he travelled far and wide. He showed keen interest in politics and was later jailed for his ruthless satirization of both the High church Tories and those hypocritical Dissenters. In 1719, when he was nearly in his sixties, he published *Robinson Crusoe*. That novel presents an autobiographic portrait of a castaway spending 28 years on a remote tropical desert island near Trinidad fighting with wisdom and courage against cannibals, captives and mutineers before ultimately being rescued and taken back to his homeland. Since its publication, it has been well received by both the literary world and the enthusiastic readership. It is often credited as marking the beginning of realistic fiction as a literary genre and is generally recognized as the first novel that is written in modern English.

The Great Awakening in American colonies With the increasing exchanges between Europe and the American colonies, new immigrants from Europe,

The termination of hard-word traditions 85

especially those from England, Holland and Germany, flocked to North America in order to elude religious persecution, cherishing their visions, faiths and wishes. Those newcomers introduced great advances in the social, cultural and commercial life of North America. Meanwhile, the new ideology, science and technology and the strong appeal of philosophical thinking brought by newcomers to the new land radically transformed the churches and the ways religion affected local social life. The public enthusiasm for religion was fading away day by day. Their zeal and attention became focused on how to make the colonies develop and prosper. Religion, which played such an enormous role in the early stage of the colonies, met with serious crises of belief.

Faced with such predicaments, pious clergymen could not hold back any longer. They set out preaching to the local communities and trying to call back the public zeal for and faith in religion. From the 1720s, an evangelical and revitalization movement, initiated by Theodore Jacobus Frelinghuysen (1691–1747), Jonathan Edwards (1703–1758), George Whitefield (1714–1770) and others, surged through British America, particularly the American colonies. It reached its climax in 1740 and lasted for about half a century, ultimately leaving profound and far-reaching impacts on American Protestantism and making it a social event of special importance to New England. The Great Awakening converted numerous believers back to Christianity and brought the religion to every corner of the American colonies, making Christianity an indispensable part of the spiritual life of not merely the colonial people but even the blacks and the indigenous Indians and turning the disintegrating colonies into a common home for them all. It exerted profound impacts upon the shaping of the spiritual life in North America and even in Britain and the European continent as well.

Captain James Cook's adventurous voyage to Australia James Cook (1728–1779), an 18th-century British explorer, navigator, cartographer and captain in the Royal Navy, made detailed maps of Newfoundland prior to making three voyages to the Pacific Ocean. His first voyage started on August 26, 1768 from Plymouth, England to Cape Horn, South America and then to New Zealand and the east coast of Australia. He continued to sail westward to South Africa and reached England on July 13, 1771. His second voyage started on July 13, 1772 again from Plymouth to Cape Town, South Africa and then to Bouvet Island close to the mainland of the Antarctic. He sailed from Cape Horn to the Cape of Good Hope and returned to England on July 29, 1775, completing his successful but highly dangerous circumnavigation of Antarctica.

He began his third voyage on July 12, 1776 by sailing along the west coast of Africa and then eastward into the Indian Ocean to New Zealand via Cape Town. He continued his voyage to the Sandwich Islands (now Hawaii) and further north to Alaska for the purpose of discovering a northwest passage to Europe but with no avail. He got killed in a fight with the

86 *The termination of hard-word traditions*

indigenous people in the Sandwich Islands on February 14, 1779. Cook's adventurous expedition dramatically deepened the European perception of the world, and as navigator and projectionist, he filled up quite a few blanks in the world atlas. His contributions to 18th-centruy science further stimulated explorations of the unknown world and opened up pathways and space for the English to spread towards Oceania. In 1788, the first group of Englishmen came to settle down in what is now known as Sydney, Australia and became the first English-speaking group on the Australian island.

The 1775–1783 American War of Independence As mentioned earlier, Britain started to set up their colonial settlements along the east coast of North America at the beginning of the 17th century, and, after over a century, the number amounted to 13. Those settlements were all governed by representatives from the British Isles, with the majority of inhabitants migrating from Britain, in addition to indigenous Indians, migrants from other parts of Europe and African black slaves. Apart from their work in the textile, iron and mineral industries, they also worked on plantations. The economic growth of American settlements lured the British government to levy heavy taxes on the settlers, which, together with philosophical and political differences, triggered widespread protests, escalating boycotts and conflicts between Great Britain and its American colonies, especially in the province of Massachusetts Bay.

The British attempts to seize the munitions of Massachusetts colonists initiated the first open combat between the Crown forces and the Massachusetts militia – the Battles of Lexington and Concord on April 19, 1775. The colonies formed the Continental Congress to coordinate their resistance, and George Washington was appointed to take command of the militia, later as commander-in-chief of the newly formed Continental Army. On July 2, 1776, the Continental Congress formally voted for independence, issuing its Declaration on July 4. The signing of the Treaty of Paris on September 3, 1783 ended the American War of Independence and signified the independence of the United States of America. The American victory over the British colonial ruling caused a huge crack in the colonial system of the British Empire, setting a good example for the national liberation movement in Latin America and to some extent pushing forward the revolution in Europe.

During the American War of Independence, the United States contributed priceless legacies to human civilization, such as the Declaration of Independence, the 1787 Constitution and the new-type political institution that was derived from it. The war gave enormous momentum to the birth of the first independent English-speaking country within the colonial system of the British Empire. The war forced a large number of colonial settlers to flee from America to settle in Canada. They brought the English language to remote parts of North America. From a linguistic perspective, the American War of Independence radically changed the international distribution and boundaries of the English language, exerted profound impacts upon

The termination of hard-word traditions   87

its developmental trend and laid a solid foundation for it to become an international language. The awakening national linguistic awareness and its enhancement directly or indirectly facilitated changes in English and the emergence of English dictionaries in America.

4.2 The codification of the English language and the establishment of prescriptive traditions

As indicated previously, tremendous political, economic, social and techno-logical transformations took place in Britain between the 15th century and the end of the 18th century. They changed world geographical territories, international political climate, development paths and modes of evolution. They also brought changes to the regional distribution of English, the cultural inclination for evolution and the width and depth of its influence upon the international communities.

Early in the middle of the 15th century, modern languages on the European continent started their replacement of classic Greek and Latin as the academic medium and the channel for knowledge transmission, while in the early 16th-century Britain there were frequent cases of writers making their apologies for writing in English, as English was then still the language of the British underclass and was considered vulgar, decayed and barbarian. William Tyndale (c. 1495–1536) went even so far as to describe it as the language of a ploughboy (Knowles, 1997:78). However, less than just one century elapsed and brought about tremendous changes in the status of English as a medium of communication, which made it possible to replace Latin and French and establish its legitimacy in Britain's political, legal, and scholarly life as well as in government administration. It gained its position as the official language for religion, law, academics and government. British writers showed keen interest and increasing confidence in English and took great pride in writing in English.

Viewed from a structural perspective, early Modern English bore much resemblance to contemporary English but, compared with classic Greek and Latin, there existed in it unwelcome variations in spelling and pronunciation, absence of words for proper expression of ideas, capricious uses and meanings, and numerous linguistic uncertainties, which mirrored foreign invasions, impacts of European continental languages, Britain's socio-cultural transformations and fluctuations in the historical and social status of English and their consequences. Chaotic spellings are inevitably the direct outcome of phonetic changes. The conceptualization of spelling in the Middle Ages was based on the principle of phonetic spelling, which meant strict correspondence between spelling and pronunciation. However, language is in constant change as long as it enjoys users, and the same can be said of its pronunciation. The reality is that changes in spellings always take place after pronunciations and that spellings tend to represent pronunciations generations and even centuries later.

88 *The termination of hard-word traditions*

The Great Vowel Shift, which started early in the 15th century and went on for almost 300 years, exerted not merely long-lasting influence upon English spelling and literacy education but affected to a considerable extent the ways that English words and words of Latin origin were pronounced, leading to great discrepancies in pronunciation between Latin words in English and those spoken by European continental neighbours. The disjoints between spellings and pronunciations that were caused by those systematic phonetic changes had become evident in the 16th century, and it was those changes that made the 16th-century English spelling rather outmoded. Some became stabilized and fossilized in the late part of the Middle Ages as a result of the application of printing techniques, and their traces can be discovered even in present-day English. As the English language of that time could not accommodate and satisfy the expressive demands of academics, science and technology, law and the like, it became gradually expanded and enriched in the late part of the early Middle English period, especially in the borrowing and enlargement of vocabulary, which made the already highly varied spellings, pronunciations and uses even more chaotic. Reforms in pronunciation and reforms in spelling that ensued became inevitable.

In 1528, Desiderius Erasmus (1469–1536) published his *De recta Latini Graecique sermonis pronuntiatione* and proposed reforms in pronunciations so as to make them conform with their corresponding spellings. That aroused strong interest among the French in language reforms, while in Cambridge University the issue of English spelling reform drew serious attention from John Cheke (1514–1557), professor of Greek. He attempted to launch small-scale reforms to make English spellings correspond to pronunciations and advocated the omission of silent letters. In 1551, John Hart completed his *The Opening of the Unresonable Writing of Our Inglish Toung* and after 18 years published *Orthographie*, which made a comprehensive exposition of his ideas of reforms in English spellings and his great expectations of a perfect language.

The first work on English spelling that proved to be of the greatest importance in Britain – *De recta and emendata linguae anglicae scriptione, dialogues* – was written in 1568 by Cheke's friend Thomas Smith. That work was based on two basic suppositions: spelling should be the mirroring of pronunciation, and each letter should correspond to a natural sound. He believed that in written texts there should be one-to-one correspondence between letters and sounds. However, English did not possess enough letters to correspond to all sounds. He was opposed to one letter corresponding to different sounds and thought it an abuse of letters, so he created a couple of letters. Obviously, Smith adopted a different approach, which made spelling and pronunciation match through reforms in spelling.

The ideas Smith and Hart proposed echoed in the works by Baret, Bullockar, Mulcaster and others. Baret strongly supported the idea of setting up a national organization to put language under control. Bullockar proposed

The termination of hard-word traditions   89

the application of dictionaries towards maintaining reformed spellings and grammar towards stabilizing language so that English would become perfectly orderly. Mulcaster raised sharp objections to the view of spellings being based on pronunciations and insisted that reasoning and conventions should have a role to play. He thought it necessary to compile a dictionary that would contain all the words in English used by people of every profession, whether natural or mixed, decent or vulgar (Knowles, 1997:85–86). It was becoming apparent that English standardization was a serious issue to consider.

Language standardization is the outcome of the standard language developing norms for its varieties such as regional dialects and social variations, which involve orthography, spelling, pronunciation, grammar, word formation etc. Language norms are generally considered to be associated more intimately with the written form and apply to the written text. However, under most circumstances, language norms may exert influence upon speech and ways of expression. They constitute the source of standards for spoken language. Most western languages have some kind of standards or norms. They are incorporated into grammar books and dictionaries and taught in classrooms. They are usually formulated by government through joint efforts with language research institutions, educational administrations and institutions of higher education. They are reviewed and evaluated on a regular basis so as to adapt to the changes that are already taking place in language. For example, modifications need to be made in word spellings so as to accommodate their phonetic changes.

The idea of linguistic standardization sowed its seeds in the 1560s, but the proposal for establishing the Royal Academy with the intent to standardize language was not put forward until 1617. It was drafted up by Edmund Bolton (c. 1575–c. 1634) but came to nothing, though he was the first individual who devoted attention to that issue. The organization that first paid attention to the issue of linguistic standardization and purity was The Society of Antiquaries, which was established around 1580 on the initiative of Archbishop Parker (Mathew Parker, 1504–1575).

William Camden (1551–1623) and Richard Verstegan (c. 1550–1640) should be counted as the most influential scholars in this regard. Camden was an English antiquarian, historian, topographer and herald. He was better known as the author of *Britannia* – the first chorographical survey of the islands of Great Britain and Ireland – and of the Annales, the first detailed historical account of the reign of Elizabeth I of England. Verstegan was an Anglo-Dutch antiquary, publisher, humourist and translator. They frequented the residence of Sir Robert Bruce Cotton (1570–1631), a member of Parliament and an antiquarian who founded the Cotton library, discussing issues concerning antiques and history as well as reforms in language. However, the radical political atmosphere of the British society then overshadowed their interest in research into Old English, and their attempts to standardize and purify English were bound to bear no fruit.

90 *The termination of hard-word traditions*

In New Atlantis, which was begun by Lord Verulam – also known as Francis Bacon – and was summarized and continued in 1660 by R. H. Esquire, a mysterious figure of dubious background, was unfolded a portrait of an ideal Utopia as well as the idea of setting up a national academy as one of its major attributes. This idea found immediate support among celebrities such as John Dryden (1631–1700), an English poet, literary critic, translator and playwright who was made England's first Poet Laureate in 1668 and John Evelyn (1670–1706), an English writer, gardener and diarist.

Several months later, the Royal Society of London for Improving Natural Knowledge, commonly known as the Royal Society, which was established in 1662 with its major interest in promoting science and its benefits and recognizing excellence in science, passed a resolution in December 1664 concerning the setup of the English Reformation Committee and the fulfilment of functions performed by national academies in European continental countries. The Committee consisted of 22 members, including such celebrities as Dryden and Evelyn. They met once or twice a month in Peter Wyche's (c. 1593–c. 1643) residence and submitted the proceedings of their meetings to the Royal Society. Members absent from the meetings were supposed to submit written reports. Evelyn, for instance, submitted several written reports and proposals regarding grammar writing, spelling reform, dictionary compilation and elegant writing styles, due to his absence from the meetings.

An ideal dictionary in Evelyn's mind was one that collects purely English words, without any sort of innovation or at least without any biases until there is a need to compile a new one. Evelyn's ideal was not put into operation. The English Reformation Committee gathered only three or four times altogether. Against Britain's socio-political background then, the committee could be nothing more of a political tool than a scholarly organization. Considering the fact that the Royal Society did not have keen interest in language issues and that most of the members on the committee had basically no knowledge of language science, it is not difficult to understand why nothing eventually came out of it. However, the committee's proposals did bring forth several English dictionaries in the late 17th century. It must be noted that they were all made single handedly and were hardly affected and controlled by government in terms of language normalization and purification.

Dryden's ideas continued to exert impressive influence upon later generations as he was committed to pushing the committee to fulfil the functions of national academies in European continental countries and had come up with more constructive suggestions. In 1697, Daniel Defoe reiterated the notion of establishing a national academy so as to create an equal to L'Institut de France. That proposal was repeated 15 years later in Jonathan Swift's *Proposal for Correcting, Improving, and Ascertaining the English*

Tongue. Swift believes that "our Language is less Refined than those of *Italy, Spain,* or *France*" and

> is extremely imperfect; that its daily Improvements are by no means in proportion to its daily Corruptions; and the Pretenders to polish and refine it, have chiefly multiplied Abuses and Absurdities; and, that in many Instances, it offends against every Part of Grammar.

He strongly opposed any action that might "corrupt" English, such as abbreviating polysyllabic words, contracting verb conjugations, coining fashionable words etc. He also came up with theories of language origins and decay in the hope of preventing linguistic corruption. It is obvious that Swift's conservative ideas of language came down in one continuous line with his conservatism in politics and religion.

Starting from the 14th century, Britain adopted step by step the nationally unified writing system, as a result of the combined impacts of social forces and printing techniques. Between King Charles II's (1660–1685) Restoration in 1660 and the early part of the 18th century, the awareness of the new writing norms became increasingly strengthened with the changes in social and political situations, and English standardization came into a transition of primary importance. Prior to 1660, there were both endorsements for and objections to linguistic purity, but after that the public came to a gradual consensus, and the differences became narrowed down to a considerable extent, thanks to the notions that were proposed by Swift, Dryden and some others in terms of linguistic purity, standardization and correctness and their impacts upon the general public. Although changes in views of language would not exert instant influence upon language itself, the notions put forward by Swift, Dryden and others permeated people's thinking and led them to consciously adjust language use, abide by rules of "correctness" and retain linguistic purity.

The period between 1700 and 1760 (some say 1789) is known as the Augustan Age in the history of British literature, also its golden age. A typical feature of the British society over that period was the pursuit of stability and perpetuality. It was generally felt that English still had the defects of being uncertain, irregular and nonstandardized in its use despite varying degrees of improvement made prior to that time. Consequently, the orientation for normalization, purity and codification was becoming more and more apparent, and English standardization and codification became a direct manifestation of the attributes of British society in linguistic context, in such ways as to "reduce the language to rule and set up a standard of correct usage", "refine it – that is, to remove supposed defects and introduce certain improvements" and "fix it permanently in the desired form" (Baugh and Cable, 1993:252).

92 *The termination of hard-word traditions*

Early in the first half of the 17th century, scholars in Britain had voiced the view that language change is inevitable. However, it became the best wish of the 18th-century language scholars in Britain to fossilize English in some ideal form. By the end of the 18th century, written standard English had evolved to a certain extent into the form of modern English (Knowles, 1997:118). Viewed from the sociolinguistic perspective, language normalization takes place owing to both language-inherent motivations and pragmatic social motivations. In the first place, the notion of standard language was first put forward by European scholars in the Renaissance and was intimately associated with the invention and application of printing techniques. The printing technology made it possible for books to be circulated far and wide, which required that the written language be recognized by the great majority of users. Consequently, language norms widely accepted would create greater demand for book markets. The more standardized language norms are, the larger number of people who would accept and use the language, the wider circulation and consumption of books and eventually the greater profits for publishers.

Second, the heightening of educational expansion, industrialization and public literacy stimulated the birth of norms of language used in classroom texts, scientific literature, government papers and other official documentation, which was especially noteworthy in the 19th century and the early part of the 20th century.

Third, the increasingly flourishing mass media started to play an indispensable and irreplaceable role in establishing and promoting language norms. The emergence and rapid development of the British press and publishing industry became the catalyst and the major means of English standardization, which can be made even more transparent through observations of the interactive impacts between the internet and the internet language in the 20th century.

Finally, the standard variety of a language is generally for the use of the ruling elites of a society, and, as a result, language norms are associated with power, status and influence and are regarded as symbols of correctness, identity and superiority. Those who have the authority for language norms are generally considered superior, better educated and more capable of arbitrating linguistic issues. A command of language norms and standards is a means of achieving power, privilege and economic benefits, which makes them different from regional and more popular forms of the standard variety. Regional forms of the language tend to be considered inferior and vulgar, and it naturally follows that people who use such forms are treated as being uncivilized, intellectually underdeveloped and less influential. Consequently, the standard form of a language mirrors, strengthens and consolidates the power and privilege of the ruling elites, which provides an important explanation of the social and political motivations for English standardization in dictionaries.

4.3 Samuel Johnson and his monumental *Dictionary of the English Language*

While the seeds of linguistic standardization were sprouting and stirring up controversy in Britain, the continental countries in Europe were already setting up special bodies with the intent to materialize their great ambition of standardizing languages. Early in 1582, Accademia della Crusca was founded in Italy for the purpose of purifying the Italian language. Its best-known accomplishment in this regard was *Vocabolario degli Accademici della Crusca* (1612). The huge controversy that dictionary caused eventually turned into the most effective advertisement for its promotion and publicity. After several revisions and reprints, the fourth edition that came out between 1729 and 1738 amounted to six volumes and was recognized as a role model in language reform. That inspired a widespread interest in language standardization and purification in other European countries, which followed suit by setting up national academies to serve the purpose.

In 1635, L'Académie Française, which originated from an informal literary group deriving from the salons held at the Hôtel de Rambouillet during the late 1620s and early 1630s, was formally established with the support of Cardinal Richelieu (1585–1642), a French clergyman, nobleman and statesman best known as King Louis XIII's "Chief Minister" or "First Minister". The Académie was "to labor with all the care and diligence possible, to give exact rules to our language, to render it capable of treating the arts and sciences". It published Antoine Arnauld and Claude Lancelot's pioneering work in the philosophy of language – *Grammaire de Port-Royal* (originally *Grammaire générale et raisonnée contenant les fondemens de l'art de parler, expliqués d'une manière claire et naturelle*, "General and Rational Grammar, containing the fundamentals of the art of speaking, explained in a clear and natural manner") in 1660, as well as a dictionary of the French language in 1964, known as the *Dictionnaire de l'Académie française*, which is widely recognized as an official reference work in France. Throughout the 17th century, several language associations were set up in Germany. In 1713, Real Academia Española was established in Spain, and similar institutions were founded in Denmark 1743 and in Portugal in 1779.

With the passing of the 18th century, an increasingly strong desire to create national language standards was surging in the British academic circles, particularly among dictionary makers and publishers. The appeal was growing like a raging fire for a language that should be ameliorated, standardized and codified and that could be compared with any language in the world and could match European continental languages, especially French. To achieve this end, various approaches and proposals were put forward, but, in the case of lexicographers, the ideal choice was undoubtedly the making of a new-type dictionary that could cover all the lexicon in the English language and keep a complete and thorough record of the language. While the British were deploring the absence of such a dictionary, the

94   *The termination of hard-word traditions*

Italians and the French had already set an example for them. The institution that was supposed to be solely responsible for such an undertaking did not come into existence, but Johnson's dictionary of 1755 met, to a considerable extent, the expectations of British society.

Johnson, who was born into a poor bookseller's family in Lichfield, Staffordshire, is described by Pat Rogers (2006) in the *Oxford Dictionary of National Biography* as "arguably the most distinguished man of letters in English history", a man who made lasting contributions to English literature as a poet, essayist, moralist, literary critic, biographer, lexicographer and editor. As a child, he demonstrated signs of great intelligence, though he was weak and often got sick. He attended Pembroke College, Oxford, for 13 months, and a shortage of funds forced him to drop out without a degree.

In December 1731, his father passed away, leaving behind him 20 pounds and a pile of books. At the age of 25, he was introduced to a young lady but fell in love with her mother, a widow who was 21 years older than himself. After his marriage with the widow, he moved to London, where he began to write for *The Gentleman's Magazine*. His early works include a collection of poems titled *London* (1738), a biography titled *Life of Mr Richard Savage* (1744), the poem *The Vanity of Human Wishes* (1749) and the play *Irene* (1749). In spite of all that, he continued to live a miserable life. In 1747, he started to embark upon his famous dictionary, which came out in 1755. Upon its publication, he was awarded the degree of Master of Arts by Oxford University, an honorary doctorate in 1765 by Trinity College Dublin and in 1775 by Oxford University again.

During the nine years of his dictionary-making, Johnson also composed numerous essays, sermons and poems pertaining to morals and religion. In 1750, he decided to produce a series of essays under the title *The Rambler* that were to be published every Tuesday and Saturday and were to sell for twopence each. Those essays were not well received at that time but were highly commended upon their publication as a collection, which underwent nine reprints during his lifetime. In July 1762, an annual pension of £300 was granted by the 24-year-old King George III in appreciation for his dictionary.

On May 3, 1777, Johnson wrote to Boswell that he was busy preparing a "little Lives" and "little Prefaces, to a little edition of the English Poets". He had been asked by Tom Davies (1712–1785), the bookseller in London; William Strahan (1715–1785), the printer, publisher and MP and Thomas Cadell (1742–1802), a well-renowned bookseller, to create this final major work – *Lives of the English Poets*, which "allotted to every Poet an Advertisement . . . containing a few dates and a general character", as he justified in the advertisement for the work.

Johnson died on December 13, 1784, shortly after he fell into a coma, and he was buried on December 20, 1784 at Westminster Abbey with an inscription that reads: "Samuel Johnson, LL.D. *Obiit XIII die Decembris, Anno Domini* M.DCC.LXXXIV. *Ætatis suæ* LXXV". James Boswell

The termination of hard-word traditions   95

(1740–1795), a Scottish biographer and diarist, wrote *The Life of Samuel Johnson* (1791), which made Johnson not only a household name in Britain but an internationally renowned figure of letters as well.

In 1746, several publishers approached Johnson with the intention of discussing with him the possibility of creating an authoritative dictionary of the English language. A contract with William Strahan and associates, worth 1,500 guineas (equivalent to about £220,000 in 2017), was signed on the morning of June 18, 1746. Johnson claimed that he could complete the project in three years, while sneering at the Académie Française taking 40 scholars 40 years to complete their dictionary, saying "This is the proportion. Let me see; forty times forty is sixteen hundred. As three to sixteen hundred, so is the proportion of an Englishman to a Frenchman".

The second year after the contract was signed, Johnson published the first piece of writing in the history of British English lexicography that made a systematic exposition of the making of English dictionaries – the plan of a dictionary of the English language. That plan, which consisted of 7,277 words (according to the author's calculation) and had a strong flavour of prescriptivism, became the programmatic document that dominated the writing of his dictionary, covering a wide range of topics involving its structural design, principles and methodology and their application to the making of the dictionary, hence a theoretically foundation-laying work for the dictionary. Of the total number of words, Johnson spent 652 to express his sorrowful feelings about the work that

> is generally considered as drudgery for the blind, as the proper toil of artless industry; a task that requires neither the light of learning, nor the activity of genius, but may be successfully performed without any higher quality than that of bearing burdens with dull patience, and beating the track of the alphabet with sluggish resolution.

He went on to "determine by what rule of distinction the words of this dictionary were to be chosen" and discuss the difficulty, "which extended itself to the whole work". He deemed that "the chief intent of it is to preserve the purity, and ascertain the meaning of our English idiom", so it was required that "the words and phrases used in the general intercourse of life, or found in the works of those whom we commonly style polite writers, be selected, without including the terms of particular professions". Johnson held that "this is, perhaps, the exact and pure idea of a grammatical dictionary" and that "the value of a work must be estimated by its use; it is not enough that a dictionary delights the critick, unless, at the same time, it instructs the learner". He considered it

> necessary to the completion of a dictionary, designed not merely for criticks, but for popular use, that it should comprise, in some degree, the peculiar words of every profession; that the terms of war and navigation

96 *The termination of hard-word traditions*

should be inserted, so far as they can be required by readers of travels, and of history; and those of law, merchandise, and mechanical trades, so far as they can be supposed useful in the occurrences of common life.

The second major issue Johnson discussed in his plan was "the orthography, which was long, vague and uncertain". Pronunciation changes with the passage of time, and the changes in pronunciation give rise to discrepancies between pronunciation and spelling, which result in the gaming between English etymology and pronunciation, hence the long-standing chaos in spellings. Johnson proposed that "the present usage of spelling, where the present usage can be distinguished, will, therefore . . . be generally followed" and thought it "sometimes proper to trace back the orthography of different ages, and show by what gradations the word departed from its original". He concluded that "closely connected with orthography is pronunciation, the stability of which is of great importance to the duration of a language, because the first change will naturally begin by corruptions in the living speech", and consequently it was considered to be of primary significance to codify pronunciation in the dictionary.

The next issue to be discussed in his plan was etymology, derivation and inflections, as well as the discrimination of words on the basis of their classes, which, in Johnson's view, "will much facilitate the attainment of our language", as "now stands in our dictionaries a confused heap of words without dependence, and without relation".

By tracing in this manner every word to its original, and not admitting, but with great caution, any of which no original can be found, we shall secure our language from being overrun with *cant*, from being crowded with low terms, the spawn of folly or affectation, which arise from no just principles of speech, and of which, therefore, no legitimate derivation can be shown.

Johnson's plan also included discussions concerning word classification, definition, sense relations and so on. He finally generalized from his discussions that

this . . . is my idea of an English dictionary; a dictionary by which the pronunciation of our language may be fixed, and its attainment facilitated; by which its purity may be preserved, its use ascertained, and its duration lengthened.

According to the conventional belief, Johnson laboured on the dictionary tirelessly for nine years with the assistance of six copyists before its completion. However, after serious research, McDermott (2005) discovered that it was not entirely true. Johnson was once in such a predicament that he was on the verge of giving up its compilation, thrusting aside the publisher's

The "Preface" "has almost unanimously been praised as one of the best
expressions of the problems of lexicography" (Béjoint, 2010:66). It sets out
two clear objectives, i.e. explaining "the words and phrases used in the general intercourse of life, or found in the works of those whom we commonly
style polite writers" and preserving "the purity, and ascertain the meaning
of our English idiom". In the course of his compilation, he drew on and
made frequent references to earlier works, such as those by Philips, Bailey,
Ainsworth, Martin and others and was inspired by them in both methodology and techniques (Béjoint, 2010:68).

Johnson's dictionary was published in two volumes but was later changed
to four volumes for consideration of costs. It weighed 9.5 kg. Its pages were
18 in (46 cm) tall and nearly 20 in (51 cm) wide when opened. The paper
was of the finest quality available, the cost of which ran to a height almost
impossible for anyone. No bookseller could possibly hope to print this book
without help, and, apart from a few special editions of the Bible, no book
of this heft and size had even been set to type. It sold at what is equivalent
to £650 today. Owing to its extremely high price, only about 6,000 copies
were sold over the 30 years after its first edition, with an average of 200 copies per year, though it went through five editions. One copy was sent to the
Académie Française in return for a promise to "repay with a new edition of
its own masterpiece as soon as the new edition should appear" (Sledd and
Kolb, 1955:146), which was fulfilled in 1761. That act of Johnson's can be
interpreted as an obvious intention of a contest with his French counterpart
and a show-off gesture of his confidence.

On the title page, Johnson wrote, "A **DICTIONARY** of the **ENGLISH
LANGUAGE**: in which The WORDS are deduced from their ORIGINALS,
and ILLUSTRATED in their DIFFERENT SIGNIFICATIONS by EXAM-
PLES from the beft WRITERS. To which are prefixed, A **HISTORY** of the
LANGUAGE, and AN **ENGLISH GRAMMAR**". The first edition of the
dictionary contained a list consisting of 42,773 headwords, from which
were excluded proper names, many compound words collected in previous works, action nouns ending in -ing, participle forms of verbs, obsolete
or outmoded words and those so-called ghost words, to which only a few
more were added in subsequent editions. All headwords were arranged in
alphabetical order.

One of Johnson's important innovations was to illustrate the meanings
of his words by literary quotation, of which there are around 11,4000. The
authors most frequently cited by Johnson include William Shakespeare,
John Milton and John Dryden. As a rule, Johnson included definitions

98 *The termination of hard-word traditions*

and citations in his entries. His definitions are objective, succinct, readily understandable and full of wit, with occasional exceptions (Hanks, 2005). He surpassed his predecessors in the length of definitions and their scope, polysemous arrangement and indications of citation sources. His dedication to and treatment of polysemous headwords were unusually adorable. His 114,000 quotations from well-known literary works adequately illustrated the meanings, uses and stylish elegance of the headwords. The care he took of some of the headwords was so meticulous that it has remained commendable even by today's standards.

For instance, the entry "take" has 134 definitions, which runs as long as 8,000 words and takes up five pages, and the entry "put" runs to the length of 5,000 words and takes up over three pages, the great proportion of which is devoted to illustrative citations. The entry "turn", for example, has 16 definitions, coupled with 15 citations, and the entry "time" has 20 definitions, coupled with 14 citations. A look at the entry "opulence" may reveal more:

> Opulence: wealth; riches; affluence
> "There in full *opulence* a banker dwelt,
> Who all the joys and pangs of riches felt;
> His sideboard glitter'd with imagin'd plate,
> And his proud fancy held a vast estate". – Jonathan Swift

Some entries contain Johnson's comments and annotations about word usage, from which dictionary users can feel Johnson's sense of humour, his sentimental inclinations and even biases, as is shown in the following entries:

> **EXCISE:** a hateful tax levied upon commodities and adjudged not by the common judges of property but wretches hired by those to whom excise is paid
> **LEXICOGRAPHER:** a writer of dictionaries; a harmless drudge that busies himself in tracing the original and detailing the signification of words
> **MONSIEUR:** a term of reproach for a Frenchman
> **OATS:** a grain which in England is generally given to horses, but in Scotland supports the people

Citations, which appear in the great majority of entries, make Johnson's dictionary conspicuous and distinct from others. They are mostly taken from the works of major writers from the late 15th century to the time of his compilation. According to Hitchings (2005), Johnson quoted around 250,000 paragraphs from his favourite writers, selected from them about half the number, arranged them chronologically as the database for illustration and eventually decided on about 110,000 sentences of various length from about 500 writers to be used as examples. Johnson "cited only the authors he liked, refused to quote from" (Béjoint, 2010:69) "any wicked

The termination of hard-word traditions   99

writer's authority for a word, lest it should send people to look in a book that might injure them forever" (Preface). Citations, according to Reddick (1990), are to prove the existence of words, show their meaning in context, ascertain their use by best writers, demonstrate how they are used by them and before contamination and share their didactic and moral values.

Johnson offered critical comments and stylistic labels in many of his entries. Some are positive and appreciative, such as "a good word", "elegant and useful", and "elegant and expressive", some are sentimental and reproachful, such as "neither elegant nor necessary", "ought not to be admitted into the language", and "unworthy of use". The systematicity and elaboration that went into his stylistic labelling proves to be far beyond that of previous works. Cassidy (1997) made a statistic investigation of the "sentimental and reproachful" labels, which shows that "low" appeared 217 times, "improper" 96 times, "corrupt" 94 times, "cant" 94 times, "barbarous" 38 times, "ludicrous" 32 times and "erroneous" 27 times. In addition, Johnson also used other forms, such as adjectival labelling (e.g. affected, bad, burlesque, colloquial, inelegant, provincial, uncircumstantial, vile, wanton), nominal labelling (e.g. impropriety, colloquial barbarism, scarce English), prepositional labelling (e.g. without authority), adverbial labelling (e.g. ignorantly) and so on.

Johnson's dictionary was a great success but was not without defects. He included in his list such headwords (e.g. abactor, absonous, adcorporate) as had never come into use, but missed some common words, e.g. ambush, athlete, bank-note, blond, euphemism, inaugural, malaria, virus, zebra, zero (Hitchings, 2005). He provided etymologies, which were very much simplified and erroneous in many cases, and his definitions were sometimes obscure. (Congleton and Congleton, 1984) Some definitions were merely a sequence of synonyms, as in the entry "*plagu*: to trouble; to teaze; to vex; to harass; to torment; to afflict; to distress; to torture; to embarrass; to excruciate; to make uneasy; to disturb".

On the whole, etymological labelling represented Johnson's major drawbacks in his compilation, which may be ascribable to his assessment of the difficulty of overtaking his predecessors and thus his reluctance to spare more of his precious time and energy. His treatment of pronunciation was rough and sketchy, as in *cough*: "a convulsion of the lungs, vellicated by some sharp serosity. It is pronounced coff". His indications of citation sources were at times random, which provided no other information than the names of the writers, and at other times only abbreviations, which might drag users into an awkward situation. Some spellings in the dictionary text turned out to be inconsistent, as in "nought" and "naught".

Johnson did not attach extravagant hopes for its perfection. He stated in the Preface, "To interpret a language by itself is very difficult; many words cannot be explained by synonimes . . . nor by paraphrase", "Some words there are which I cannot explain, because I do not understand them", "thus to persue perfection, was, like the first inhabitants of Arcadia, to chace the

100 *The termination of hard-word traditions*

sun". In spite of its errors, mistakes and defects, its prescriptive keynote in compilation, its conservative attitude towards language issues and its advocacy of traditional ways of word spelling (e.g. *olde*), his dictionary was universally recognized as the most excellent of his times and firmly remained a milestone in the history of British English lexicography. Undoubtedly, all present-day dictionaries have benefited from his dictionary to varying extent.

Since its publication in 1755, Johnson's dictionary has gone through at least 52 editions, 12 revisions, over 120 compact editions, 309 pocket editions, 4 abridged editions and several electronic editions. "Johnson came to be known as Dictionary Johnson, and his Dictionary soon became the dictionary in the English-speaking world" (Béjoint, 2010:75). This landmark work was "produced by a single man rather than by committee" (Hitchings, 2005:182) and "superseded only by the Philological Society's historical dictionary and by the 'utility dictionary' of the Merriam Company" (Sledd and Kolb, 1955:205). It was acclaimed as the "dictionary Bible" and was the most popular and most extensively emulated and copied dictionary in the two centuries subsequent to its publication, with far-reaching influence upon modern lexicography. "After 1755, English dictionaries were never again exactly the same" (McDermott and Moon, 2005:153).

Numerous researches have been conducted concerning Johnson's dictionary and the compiler himself. Some scholars focus on Johnson's biography and its relation to the dictionary, some on his linguistic views and compiling philosophy, some on his views on lexicography, some on his compilation of the dictionary and some others on bibliographic issues pertaining to his lexicographical writings and citation sources. According to incomplete statistics, relevant research monographs have reached at least 350, in addition to a large number of academic papers and other writings, over a span of more than 250 years. The most representative of such researches are Reddick (1990, 1996, 2005), Horgan (1994), Crystal (2005), Kolb and DeMaria (2005), Lynch and McDermott (2005), etc.

All these have furnished valuable first-hand literature for explorations in the dictionary as well as its compiler. (Lynch and McDermott, 2005) They indicate not only the enduring humanistic charm and strong vitality of Johnson's dictionary but its profound influence upon modern English studies, especially the studies in British English lexicography. That has created an unparalleled landscape in the history of English lexicography, which is beyond comparison even in the case of OED.

> The century down to 1850 saw great changes in the notion of what a dictionary should be: it came to be seen as a scholarly record of the whole language; in method, it became inductive . . . the emphasis came to lie far more than hitherto on the literary rather than the technical

The termination of hard-word traditions   101

language; and the dictionary now assumed an authoritarian or normative function.

(Osselton, 1983:17)

Fierce criticism was vented upon Johnson's dictionary and even Johnson
himself, describing him as "a wretched etymologist", but his dictionary
"easily ranks as one of the greatest single achievements of scholarship,
and probably the greatest ever performed by one individual who laboured
under anything like the disadvantages in a comparable length of time"
(Bately, 2009). Until the completion of the *Oxford English Dictionary*
173 years later, Johnson's dictionary was viewed as the preeminent English
dictionary.

4.4 Other major English monolingual dictionaries in the 18th century and their adherence to prescriptivism

English lexicography had been trudging along the tradition of hard words
from earliest glossaries to Latin-English and English-Latin dictionaries, and
then to English monolingual dictionaries. Early in the 17th century, Cawdrey gave special attention to usual hard words, though unusual hard words
also made their appearance in his collection. Bullokar and Cockeram developed an extraordinary preference for difficult words and succeeded in their
competition with their rivals by including the most difficult, the most weird
and the most specialized headwords in their revised or updated versions.

By the middle of the 17th century, the publication of Thomas Blount
and Edward Philips' dictionaries signified the acme of English hard-word
dictionary compilation and at the same time the fading-away of the hard-
word tradition of British English lexicography, which was moving towards
a more rational, comprehensive, systematic and scholarly track of recording words. Coles was a forerunner of this transformation and was "open-
minded enough to include archaic words, dialect, and even cant but still
neglected everyday words". "The importance of this work, then, lies
in its introduction into the English dictionary of the bulk of the English
language – that is, of the essential words of daily speech, writing, and reading"
(Starnes and Noyes, 1991:71).

The 17th-century English dictionaries recorded only a limited number of
common words, but there had been a long tradition of collecting daily used
words in reading primers and English grammars. The disconnection was not
made up until John Kersey and Nathan Bailey published their dictionaries
in the 18th century. Their practices reinforced the transition from a sheer
collection of hard words to a more comprehensive record of all sorts of
English words. Johnson's dictionary pushed this transition to its climax and
brought English monolingual dictionary compilation into its peak period.
From then onwards, Johnson's dictionary outshone all his predecessors, as

102 *The termination of hard-word traditions*

well as exerting its dominating impacts upon English lexicography for one century and a half. What follows is a scuttle through other major English monolingual dictionaries in the 18th century, together with an analysis of their compiling features.

The second year of the 18th century witnessed J. K.'s *A New English Dictionary, or a Compleat Collection of the Most Popular and Significant Words, Commonly Used in the Language; with a Short and Clear Exposition of Difficult Words and Terms of Art* (1702), which is small in terms of size. The identity of its compiler J. K. remains a mystery even up to the present day. However, it is generally ascribable to the outstanding compiler John Kersey, who published the revised version of Edward Philips' *The New World of Words* (1706). Two years later, he published his own work – *Dictionarium Anglo-Britannicum*.

J. K.'s *A New English Dictionary* purposefully collected "the Most Proper and Significant Words, Commonly used in the Language; With a Short and Clear Exposition of Difficult Words and Terms of Art", amounting to about 28,000, most of which made their first appearance in an English dictionary and were collected from the 17th-century popular reading primers, such as Nathaniel Strong's *England's Perfect School-Master* (1676) and Edward (?) Cocker's *Accomplish'd School-Master* (1696), "chiefly designed for the benefit of Young Scholars, Tradesmen, Artificers, and the Female Sex, who would learn to spell truly; being so fitted to every Capacity, that it may be a continual help to all that want an Instructor" (See its title page).

For a dictionary that made its first attempt to collect common vocabulary, definition posed a formidable challenge to its compiler. The commoner the vocabulary, the richer social, linguistic and cultural implications it carries, and the more profound its connotations. Obviously, it is no easy task to make a full representation of its implications and connotations in definitions. Amazingly, the compilers neither borrowed definition resources or defining methods from those popular primers nor made enough efforts in cracking the hard nuts, still presenting a headache even to modern lexicographers. In explaining hard words, the compliers quoted some definitions mostly from Elisha Coles' dictionary but with identifiable modifications, and the proportion of such borrowings was low. They provided almost no definitions in cases where derivatives, head-word-related words and common words were explained. In some cases, only their meanings or their contexts of use were explained. For example,

> **ABROAD:** To sit abroad upon eggs, as a bird does
> **AKE [MODERN ENGLISH: ACHE]:** Ake, as, my head akes
> **ARM:** An Arm of a man's body, of a tree, or of the sea
> **MAY:** May, the most pleasant Month of the Year

A revised edition was published in 1713, with its entry number being reduced to about 21,000, but its practical value was immensely enhanced. It

The termination of hard-word traditions   103

provided definition for every entry, and the defining techniques were significantly improved. Its influence extended well into the second half of the 18th century. In *The Art of Reading and Writing English* (1720), Isaac Watts (1674–1748) recommended it as "the best dictionary that I know" for the educational purpose. Watts insisted, despite Bailey's and other fine dictionaries then available, J. K.'s is

> very entertaining and useful to persons of a polite education, yet for the bulk of mankind . . . much more convenient . . . and . . . in the hands of all young persons, to acquaint them better with their mother-tongue.
> (Starnes and Noyes, 1991:75)

Compared with *A New English Dictionary*, *Cocker's English Dictionary* (1704) appeared inferior in terms of compiling techniques and popularity, and there remained a great deal of controversy as to whether its authorship should go to Edward Cocker (1631–1676), as there was a great gap between his date of birth and the date of publication. *Cocker's English Dictionary* consists of four parts. The first part is the main body "Interpreting The most refined and difficult words in Divinity, Philosophy, Law, Physick, Mathematicks, Husbandry, Mechanicks, &c. With an Exposition of those hard words, which are derived from other Languages". The other three parts are appended to the principal part, with "An Historical-Political Dictionary, containing the Proper Names of Men, Women, Rivers, Countries, Cities, Castles, Towns, Mountains, &c. in England, Scotland and Ireland, &c. And the feigned Stories of Heathen Gods, with other Poetical Inventions", "The Interpretation of the most usual Terms in Military Discipline" and "The Terms which Merchants and others make use of in Trade and Commerce; Ad the Coins of most Countries in Europe, and several Parts of the World" (See its title page). This dictionary selects about 22,000 words, with the bulk of the first and second part taken from Elisha Coles' work, some entries only slightly modified and polished, and the third and fourth part mainly taken from the publications of 1670 and 1697 (Starnes and Noyes, 1991:79).

A revised edition was published in 1715, with a considerable addition of local historical and cultural materials of the UK after the letter H and a listing of those lexical items that should belong somewhere after the letter H under a general heading, such as "King and Queen". "The ghostly reviser of a ghostly author and a ghostly editor" deemed it "very Necessary for all Persons, who desire to understand the Affairs of the World, as well as the Language and Transactions of their own Country" (Starnes and Noyes, 1991:83), which was an evident expression of the UK's inflated national sentiments towards colonial expansion and ambitious annexation in dictionary-making. The compilers' visions went far beyond the British Isles. Nine years later, a third edition came out. That was the final edition, and no more revision was made after that.

104 *The termination of hard-word traditions*

In 1707, a work of unknown authorship – *Glossographia Anglicana Nova* – was published, altogether 576 pages with a coverage of 14,500 headwords. Considering the normal size of a dictionary at that time, this dictionary was rather small, written for the purpose of "instructing the Ignorant . . . for the use of such as are not able to read a good Historian, or any Polite English Writer without an Interpreter". Its title page says "A Dictionary, Interpreting Such Hard Words of whatever Language, as are present used in the English Tongue, with their Etymologies, Definitions, &c." "Also, The Terms of Divinity, Law, Physick, Mathematicks, History, Agriculture, Logick, Metapgysicks, Grammar, Poetry, Musick, Heraldry, Architecture, Painting, War, and all other Arts and Sciences are herein explain'd". Its materials are mainly taken from the best "Modern Authors", such as Evelyn, Dryden and Isaac Newton, and its technical terms were mainly selected from John Harris' (c. 1666–1719) *Lexicon Technicum: Or, A Universal English Dictionary of Arts and Sciences* (1704). This dictionary was revised in 1719, but, apart from the addition of 1,000 or so headwords, there was no substantial augmentation. (Starnes and Noyes, 1946:94)

According to Starnes and Noyes (1991:92–94), the special point about this dictionary was its more serious efforts in promoting science and scientific knowledge to the general public in a less costly but more convenient way, though John Kersey was accredited with ushering in the practice of introducing scientific terms into general English dictionaries. It is worth mentioning that it was the first English dictionary to have adopted a certain number of woodcut illustrations for terms of armorial bearings. The method of pictorially illustrating headwords first appeared in Blount's *Glossographia* but only twice. No other dictionaries surpassed this one in the number of pictorial illustrations until after Nathan Bailey's Volume II of *An Universal Etymological English Dictionary* (1727), in which the method was applied to not only armorial bearings but scientific terms as well, hence a more extensive lexical coverage.

John Kersey was an outstanding lexicographer in the 18th century in the UK, playing a key role for the beginning ten years. He integrated the tradition of writing reading primers and elementary school books that focused on grammar and spelling and that of making hard-word dictionaries that focused on difficult words of Latin, thus creating the precedent of collecting commonly used words in English dictionaries. He discarded outmoded materials and made serious efforts in lexicographical innovation. His dictionary attempted to cater to the needs of all walks of life in the British society of his days. In addition to the dubious authorship of J. K.'s *A New English Dictionary*, he was highly recognized for his revision and augmentation of Edward Philips' *New World of English Words*.

In 1708, another work of Kersey's – *Dictionarium Anglo-Britannicum, or a General English Dictionary* – was "designed as a reference work for advanced students of literature, science, and the arts" (Starnes and Noyes, 1991:69–70). It was claimed on the title page, "a General English

The termination of hard-word traditions   105

Dictionary, comprehending a brief, but emphatical and clear explication of all sorts of difficult words . . . and also of all terms relating to Arts and Sciences both liberal and mechanical". This dictionary monopolized the English dictionary market for 13 years after its publication, in which period no new dictionary came out. After a contrastive analysis, Starnes and Noyes (1991:96–97) discovered that it was in fact an abridged version of the revised and augmented edition of Edward Philips' *New World of English Words* (1706). It made abridgements and reductions of definitions and deleted rare cross-referencing information but added a small number of obsolete words and word variants.

It must be noted that it was the first abridged dictionary in the history of British English lexicography (Starnes and Noyes, 1991:70). Its successful practice provides workable solutions to and sets up a basic model for the making of abridged dictionaries. It is "the first ever abridged English dictionary, and thus launches a tradition that persists today in the Shorter, Concise, and other Oxford dictionaries, the many 'college dictionaries' of America, and all their varied peers" (Green, 1996:229). It was revised in 1715 and 1721 but to only a limited extent and with no obvious addition of headwords. John Kersey tried a series of innovations when he revised and augmented Edward Philips' *New World of English Words* (1706) but failed to give due attention to etymological treatment. He left about half of the headwords unattended and indicated the other half simply by means of letter annotation. This way of treating word histories obviously has its pragmatic considerations but departs from the traditional practice of English dictionaries tracing word origins by hard and thorough search.

That defect was remedied in a consistent and systematic manner in Nathan Bailey's "first work" (Green, 1996:229) – *An Universal Etymological English Dictionary* (1721), which was "most popular of all dictionaries antedating Johnson" (Starnes and Noyes, 1991:98) and "spanning eighty years . . . may logically be considered the most popular and representative dictionary of the eighteenth century" (Starnes and Noyes, 1991:107) "on the basis of sales" (Green, 1996:230). Bailey "has never been accorded the degree of reverence allotted his successor and rival, Samuel Johnson" (Green, 1996:230), but his dictionary series undoubtedly laid a solid foundation for Johnson to make his dictionary.

An Universal Etymological English Dictionary (1721) is "compil'd and Methodologically digested, as well for the Entertainment of the Curious, as the Information of the Ignorant, and for the Benefit of young Students, Artificers, Tradesmen and Foreigners", as the title page indicates. It collected 40,000 or so headwords, with a coverage of the commonest words; words from classic works by such great figures as Chaucer, Spenser and Shakespeare; dialect words; slang; proverbs; outmoded words and so on. It drew upon a great many materials from previous compilers, "particularly Kersey's *Dictionarium Anglo-Britanncum* (1708)" (Béjoint, 2010:64), which signifies a change in the way of thinking about what is described

106 *The termination of hard-word traditions*

about words and how they should be treated in the dictionary. The dictionary text contains numerous citations, more than 500 woodcut illustrations, and simple definitions for common words, for example, for "goat" "a beast", for "cat" and "dog" "a creature well known", adding additional information "a Mongrel or Mastive" to "dog". This way of defining words is not desirable in any way.

"Bailey is the first lexicographer really to lay out the language as it is, taboo words, slang, and all. He also offers usage guidance, notes on word stress, pronunciation, and so on" and is "one also of the first dictionary makers to aim for comprehensiveness" (Green, 1996:230). Bailey continued the use of the sign of "dagger" to indicate four-letter words, dialect words, obsolete words and those so-called vulgar words and the use of asterisks to indicate commendatory words. Landau (1989:72) concluded that it is "the first English dictionary to treat etymology with consistent purpose and seriousness" and "is credited with having established etymology as 'one of the requisites of any reputable dictionary'" (Landau, 1989:99). The treatment of etymologies is a conspicuous feature as well as a selling point for its promotion. Moreover, its ways of handling dialect words deserves special attention, too. That will be discussed later.

Quite a few compilers made attempts to treat word histories in their dictionaries from the appearance of the first English monolingual dictionary to the publication of Kersey's dictionary, but there existed serious defects and deficiencies in terms of systematicity, consistency, comprehensiveness, profundity and precision in such treatment. Bailey, however, achieved breakthroughs in his ways of providing information concerning word histories and roots as well as close and distant sources and exploring the evolutional traces. It designated etymology as the essential information every authoritative dictionary should contain, which established a model for later compilations.

An Universal Etymological English Dictionary experienced 30 editions over a period of 81 years after its publication. The number of headwords it collected kept increasing to around 50,000 by the time the 25th edition came out in 1783. That number remained almost unchanged till the final edition was published in 1802. In 1727, Bailey published an "erratic" (Starnes and Noyes, 1991:117) "Volume II", which bore the same title as *The Universal Etymological English Dictionary*. In fact, it might be well considered a supplement to the original dictionary, with a significant addition of common words, specialized terms and encyclopedic terms, of definitions and etymological information, of woodcut illustrations and with annotations of accentuation. For nearly half a century after its publication, it underwent several revisions and additions and had altogether seven editions.

In 1730, another work of Bailey's – *Dictionarium Britannicum* – came out, with a subtitle of "or a more compleat universal etymological English

The termination of hard-word traditions   107

dictionary than any extant". It amounted to nearly 900 pages, with a comprehensive range of lexical items, including hard words and technical terms. The collection totalled about 48,000, including those taboo words that were excluded by Johnson in his selection, such as *shite* and *fuck*. That number soared to 60,000 when a new edition was published in 1736. Proverbs that appeared in previous editions were dropped out in the new edition, but etymology was provided and was for the first time signalled by means of square brackets.

"Far more comprehensive and more competently executed than any predecessor", this dictionary "is justly famous in its own right as well as for the important role it later played as working base for Johnson's dictionary", "thus the second milestone on the road that leads to Johnson and on to scholarly modern lexicography" (Starnes and Noyes, 1991:117). Though it was made on the basis of two previous editions, a great deal of innovation was introduced, as is evidenced in the listing of cognate word families and proper nouns in separate indexes, the number of definitions surpassing that in Johnson's dictionary (Green, 1996:230) and the meticulous refinement and consideration of the defining language and lexicographical information. Not surprisingly, Johnson used it as a major basis for his dictionary.

In 1735, *A New General English Dictionary* was completed for publication by William Pardon after Thomas Dyche (?–c. 1733) passed away. Dyche once worked as a schoolteacher and wrote several books on English. His novel work – *A Guide to the English Tongue* was first published in 1709 and again in 1716 in India. The Indian edition was considered the first English book ever published in Asia. By the time the final edition appeared in 1830, it went through nearly 50 editions over a span of over 120 years. Its distinctive feature was its special attention to pronunciation and the classification of words according to syllabication. His remarkable contribution to English phonetic studies was the priceless legacy he left behind him and paved a smooth way for the compilation of his dictionary.

A New General English Dictionary had so far been one of the few products of collaborative work in the history of British English lexicography. It contained an English grammar, which probably made it the first English dictionary to have included a grammar. (Béjoint, 2010:65) Starting from the 1720s, Bailey's dictionary series held a dominating position on the British dictionary market. Against this backdrop, its publication posed a great challenge to both compilers and publishers. However, its extraordinary popularity and influence is detectable from its prolonged attraction to the dictionary users for over half a century and its 18 editions and several reprints between 1735 and 1798.

A New General English Dictionary was intended for schoolchildren and ill-educated adults. The number of headwords amounted to about 20,000 in the initial edition and rose to about 30,000 when the 17th edition came

108   *The termination of hard-word traditions*

out in 1794. Its principle for the selection of headwords appeared special, as it basically focused on hard words that were rarely used or not readily intelligible, geared to those whose intellectual demands were limited, so that

> Derivations and Etymologies are entirely left out: First, because of their Uncertainty . . . secondly, upon account of their Uselessness to those Persons that these Sort of Books are most helpful to, which are commonly such, whose Education, Reading, and Leisure, are bounded within a narrow Compass.
>
> (See its title page)

A general review of the dictionary shows that its definitions were written through mature deliberation and in such meticulously chosen language, though they seemed verbose in a few cases. They were mostly straightaway and easily comprehensible, coupled with many practical, concise and helpful citations. That defining style was determined by its intended users. "In many ways this can be seen as a 'hard-word' dictionary for the mass market" (Green, 1996:238). The compilers went against the tradition of serving elite users by limiting its use for those who are "unacquainted with the Learned Languages" (see its title page) and reverting to "earlier lexicographical tradition by focusing on a lower level", "particularly recommended to those Boarding-Schools, where English only is taught; it addresses the less educated and, specifically, those who have no knowledge of foreign languages and no desire to repair that deficiency" (See its title page).

The most noticeable feature of the dictionary was its treatment of phonetic, spelling and grammatical information, which turned it into a guide to pronunciation, spelling and grammar. The compilers followed Bailey's method of annotating pronunciation – in particular accentuation – and made it an indispensable part of the English dictionary. In terms of spelling, the compilers proposed a set of reforms, such as abbreviating -*ck* into -*c* (e.g. *logick-logic*, *physick-physic*), -*our* into -*or* (e.g. *authour-author*), -*ll* into -*l* (e.g. *alphabeticall-alphabetical*), etc. Such spelling reforms predated American dictionary compilers by almost a century, and many have become the spelling norms for modern English.

As regards grammatical treatment, the compilers provided a nine-page treatise discussing basic grammatical issues such as word classes and inflections, emphasizing the importance of a dictionary in including grammar, and indicating word classes only by the use of letters. All these practices provided high reference values for the treatment of similar issues and created the precedent for the making of learner's dictionaries that were to come only 200 years later.

Upon the advent of the second half of the 18th century, Benjamin Martin (1704–1782) published *Lingua Britannica Reformata* (1749), six years earlier than Johnson's dictionary. Martin was born into a poor family and began his life as plough boy, but he later became well known as a teacher

The termination of hard-word traditions   109

and a spectacle manufacturer. He lectured on natural philosophy and published *Biblioteca Technologia* – a survey of natural philosophy – in 1737, as well as *Martin's magazine,* the periodical formally known as the *General Magazine of Arts and Sciences* between 1755 and 1764. Good things never last long. His business collapsed as a result of poor management, and he went bankrupt in 1781. His failure to commit suicide left him an incurable wound, and he died the following year.

Lingua Britannica Reformata made a careful selection of about 24,500 headwords, including common words and hard words. Compared with previous dictionaries, it reduced its collection of technical terms. He showed special talent for advertisement and highlighted on the title page the features of the dictionary with eight capitalized words: I. UNIVERSAL; II. ETYMOLOGICAL; III. ORTHOGRAPHICAL; IV. ORTHOEPICAL; V. DIACRITICAL; VI. PHILOLOGICAL; VII. MATHEMATICAL; VIII. PHILOSOPHICAL. Those eight features represent his inheritance of previous accomplishments in the making of dictionaries and his theoretical reflections, generalizations and innovations upon lexicographical practices.

First, he abandoned the idea of codifying English through dictionary-making. He believed that it would be mere fantasy to formulate norms for linguistic purity and perfection, as no language would be permanently fixed and would be in constant change, and polite and elegant usages in one age could become vulgar and even barbarian in another. This dynamic view of language evolution became recognized by the community of lexicographers and was adopted as one of the core notions that guided later dictionary compilation.

Second, he offered a full exposition of the ideas and the plan for making his dictionary in the front matter and developed it into a serious work that was based on meticulous planning and systematic thinking. He made a detailed list of objectives to achieve in his compilation on the title page and set up an example for subsequent compilers, including Johnson. He remedied the defects of randomly selecting headwords in previous dictionaries and demonstrated how headwords could be determined in a careful, strict and consistent manner.

Third, his dictionary was the first English dictionary that adopted the method of numbered definitions and arranged definitions according to the logical sequence. He strove hard for the precision of definitions, the logical division of senses and their arrangements by numbers. He listed the cognate or the original senses first, followed by metaphorical or extended senses. This mode of definition arrangement better accorded with the evolutional characteristics and rules of word senses, better reflected the inherent evolutional relationships between word senses and better accommodated the cognitive demands of dictionary users.

Finally, he carried on with Dyche's spelling reforms, such as the deletion of silent word endings for the simplification of spellings (e.g. *logick-logic*) and made it possible for spelling reforms to last and spread. In spite of his

110 *The termination of hard-word traditions*

inconsistency and preference for Latin origins in etymological treatment, his creation of a more convenient spelling system and a more practical guide to pronunciation embodied an obvious improvement upon previous dictionaries.

Lingua Britannica Reformata appeared in its second edition in 1754, with modifications. The grammar part in the first edition was deleted, 2,500 or so headwords were added, with an additional supplementation of encyclopaedic information regarding European kingdoms, capital cities, townships of Great Britain and Ireland and counties of England and Wales. Where the new letter in the alphabet started in the dictionary text, some space was devoted to discussions concerning its composition, pronunciation and special use in numerals and abbreviations. The second edition was also the last one. The reason was quite obvious, and Johnson's monumental work was launched the following year after the second edition came out.

There also appeared anonymous dictionaries in the 18th century. Some were of high quality and in vogue for some time, some others were reprints and even private versions. The reason for their being anonymous was either that the compiler did not care about the authorship despite his long and arduous labour, that it was improper for reproductions to mark authorship or that it was inconvenient for collective compilations to mark authorship.

The next anonymous dictionary was *A Pocket Dictionary* (1753). Judging from its style and methodology, it was apparently a well-conceived work that could not be ignored. It contained a selection of 18,500 or so headwords, each of which was provided parts of speech, pronunciation and accentuation, as well as precise definitions that were arranged in the proper way and followed by word histories. Its title page said,

> to render this Book complete, many modern Words are introduc'd, which are not to be found in other Dictionaries; and to make it more concise and protable, such Words are omitted, as being neither properly English, nor ever used by good Authors, would only serve to mislead and embarrass the Learner.
>
> (See its title page)

Another feature that made it distinct from others was its clear-cut segmentation of users, "A Work entirely new, and design'd for the Youth of both Sexes, the Ladies and Persons in Business" (see its title page). Its selection of headwords and definitions all centred around this user segment, such that it went so far as to provide the distance from London, fairs and their dates in entries of major cities and towns, which was really amazing from the angle of a pocket dictionary. Its second edition was published in 1758 with numerous revisions and additions, with its total number of headwords amounting to 25,000. Two more reprints were produced between 1765 and 1779 but without revision and augmentation.

The termination of hard-word traditions 111

The same year as *A Pocket Dictionary* was published, *The Complete English Dictionary* came out without indicating its authorship on the title page, only claiming "By a Lover of Good English and Common Sense" (see its title page). However, its authorship can be safely ascribable to John Wesley (1703–1791) (Starnes and Noyes, 1991:172). This unique dictionary consisted of only 144 pages. In addition to terms of astronomy, medicine and music, the author intentionally avoided classic words, technical terms and professional jargons that were common in the 17th-century dictionaries but collected "most of those hard words which are found in the English writers" (Preface), i.e. "words that were used in literature but which would confuse the simple reader" (Preface), which ran to about 4,600 words, "the shortest since Cawdrey" (Green, 1996:242). Its definitions were succinct, fairly simple, and generally less than one line. It

> is not published to get money, but to assist persons of common sense and no learning to understand the best English authors: and that, with as little experience of either time or money, as the nature of the thing would allow.
>
> (Preface)

It took up some proportion of the market owing to its clear segmentation of users and its catering to practical user needs. Its second edition came out in 1764 and was reprinted in 1777 and 1790, with its influence extending over a period of more than 40 years.

The year of 1755 was a milestone in the history of British English lexicography, which marked the appearance of not only Johnson's monumental *Dictionary of the English Language* but also Joseph Nicol Scott's *A New Universal Etymological English Dictionary*, which pushed Bailey's etymological dictionary-making to its peak and became the most sizable of his dictionary series with the best quality, the most optimized functional design, the most meticulous internal organization and the most sophisticated compiling techniques.

Rather than a new compilation, which the title claimed, it would be more accurate to regard *A New Universal Etymological English Dictionary* as a revised version of Bailey's dictionary, as suggested on the title page, "Originally compiled by N. Bailey". This version retained the vocabulary of the original edition, with a supplementation of newly added words from Johnson's dictionary and words that were missing from the original edition and Johnson's dictionary. Its total collection amounted to about 65,000.

In microstructural treatment, Scott basically followed the original edition. No obvious innovation was attempted except for his absorption of new elements from Johnson's dictionary. He discriminated between senses, annotated pronunciation, provided the close and distant sources of words, illustrated uses with citations from the best authors and explained common terms of humanities, natural science, manufacturing and commerce and

112 *The termination of hard-word traditions*

trade. The adoption of copperplate illustrations was its big selling point. This dictionary was reprinted in 1764 and 1772. As successful a work as it was, it was not born at the right time and was very much overshadowed by its formidable rival – Johnson's dictionary.

In addition to the monolingual dictionaries mentioned earlier, four other dictionaries appeared between 1735 and 1741, namely B. N. Defoe's *A Compleat English Dictionary* (1735), an anonymous work *A New English Dictionary* (1737), J. Sparrow's *A New English Dictionary* (1739) and James Manlove's *A New Dictionary of All Such Words* (1741).

After serious comparative studies, Starnes and Noyes (1991:139–145) demonstrate that they all had a coverage of about 16,000 headwords, including common words, the biblical figures, and place names in Britain. They were of different authorship, but they were basically similar in contents and were, to a great extent, abridgements of previous dictionaries, especially those of Bailey's. The entries contained only definitions, devoid of information concerning etymology, grammar, pronunciation and usage. No discernible differences were discovered in compiling techniques. It can be safely assumed that they were the reprints of the same work by different publishers, and the authorships were merely fictitious. Those reprints did not receive much attention, as popular dictionaries, such as Bailey's, Dyche's and Pardon's, had already been well recognized by their users.

1775 saw the publication of *The New and Complete Dictionary of the English Language*, which was compiled by John Ash (1724–1779). This dictionary was extraordinary in selecting slangs and even four-letter words, such as *foutra* (i.e. *fuck*), which were strictly forbidden in such previous authoritative works. From that practice arose a great deal of controversy and rebuke.

> Dictionaries containing common words became dominant in the course of the eighteenth century, while the dictionary of hard words all but disappeared, undoubtedly the sign of a change in the role of the dictionary. It is probably not a coincidence that the word *lexicography* appeared during the seventeenth century.
>
> (Béjoint, 2010:61)

All that indicated that English lexicography would undergo profound transformations in notions and compiling techniques.

4.5 The extension and emergence of other types of English dictionaries in the 18th century

The flourishing of English monolingual dictionaries in the 18th century outshone all other types of English dictionaries. The glory and glamour of bilingual dictionaries, which made their appearance in the 15th century, began

The termination of hard-word traditions 113

to fade away, other existing types were quickening their steps of transformation, and new types were beginning to emerge in succession.

English-Latin dictionaries started to withdraw from the historical scene of British English lexicography after Robert Ainsworth published his *Thesaurus Linguae Latinae compendiarius* (1736). After school education, Ainsworth took up a teaching post. He founded a school on the outskirts of London and taught there until several years before his retirement. In addition to his fondness for ancient coins and other antiques, he published several treatises, including "A Short Treatise on Grammar".

After about 20 years' hard labour, Ainsworth completed his dictionary and dedicated it to Richard Mead (1673–1754). His intention of compiling it was explained in the "Preface to the Reader" on the basis of a survey of the history of English and Latin bilingual dictionaries. "The defects of all Latin dictionaries" "have made additions rather than reformed errors or rejected barbarous Latin words", wishing "to preserve Latin pure for the British youth" (Starnes, 1954:328). The contribution of his dictionary to English monolingual lexicography resided in his discrimination of senses, his numbered sequencing of them on the logic basis and according to the principle of intelligibility and his indication of the authors and text sources from which his classic citations were taken. His methods of sense discrimination and numbered ordering were directly inherited by Benjamin Martin. Not only did Johnson model after Martin but Ainsworth as well (Starnes, 1954:349). Ainsworth's dictionary was later revised and enlarged by Samuel Patrick, John Ward, William Young, Thomas Morell, John Carey and others. It came out in different editions and sizes. There was an abridged edition by Young and Morell, as well.

Subsequent to Ainsworth, other bilingual dictionaries included:

(1) English-Italian dictionaries, such as Ferdinando Altieri's bidirectional dictionary *Dizionario Italiano ed Inglese* (1726–1727) and Giuseppi Baretti's (1719–1789) *A Dictionary of the English and Italian Languages* (1760);

(2) English-Spanish dictionaries, such as Captain John Stevens' (c. 1662–1726) *A New Spanish and English Dictionary* (1705–1706), Peter Pineda's *Nuevo Dicionario, Español e Inglés e Inglés y Español* (1740), Joseph Giral Delpino's *A Dictionary Spanish and English, and English and Spanish* (1763), and Thomas Connelly and Thomas Higgins' *A New Dictionary of the Spanish and English Languages* (1797–1798);

(3) English-German dictionaries, such as Christian Ludwig's (1635–1706) *A Dictionary English, German and French* (1706), Theodore Arnold's adapted version of Bailey's dictionary of 1736 – *Neues Deutsch-Englisches Wörterbuch* (1739), Johann Christoph Adelung's (1732–1806) *Neues grammatisch-kritisches Wörterbuch der englischen Sprache für die Deutschen* (1783–1796);

114 *The termination of hard-word traditions*

(4) English-Dutch dictionaries, such as John Holtrop's *New English and Dutch Dictionary* (1789) and Samuel Hull Wilcocke's (c. 1766–1833) *A New and Complete Dictionary of the English and Dutch Languages* (1798).

Among those bilingual dictionaries, almost none were independent compilations. They were basically adapted or even translated directly from previous English monolingual dictionaries, such as Bailey's and Johnson's. Some were simply augmentations and supplementations of previous works (Cormier, 2009:65–85).

As a newly emerging genre, English pronouncing dictionaries were especially noteworthy. The precise phonetic annotation of words was a significant attribute and signifier for the maturing standardization of English dictionaries in the 18th century, and the making of English pronouncing dictionaries pushed that attribute and signifier to a new level of amelioration and perfection. Bailey's *An Universal Etymological English Dictionary* (1721) was a pioneer of English monolingual dictionaries that set the precedent of annotating pronunciation, in particular accentuation.

Two years later, that practice was carried over into Thomas Dyche's *A Dictionary of All the Words Commonly Used in the English Tongue* (1723) and into Johnson's dictionary as well, notably in accentuation, but Bailey, Dyche and Johnson did not make further explorations and attempts. James Buchanan became the first to have made such attempts in *Linguae Britannicae Vera Pronuntiatio* (1757) subsequent to Johnson's dictionary, thus making his dictionary the first "to use macrons and breves to indicate quantity", "to use semi-phonetic respelling" and "to indicate 'silent' letters systematically" and himself "the first to produce a dictionary specifically designed to regulate pronunciation" and eventually being credited with "the first English pronouncing dictionary" (Hüllen, 2009:153). William Johnston's *The Pronouncing and Spelling Dictionary* (1764) was published with the view of "providing a guide to the pronunciation of every word", "certainly the first to give a complete account of the pronunciation of English, and had a moderate degree of commercial success and influence" (Hüllen, 2009:154).

"A cluster of dictionaries appearing from 1773 onwards attempted to provide clearer and more consistent [phonetic] notation" (Hüllen, 2009:156). William Kenrick (c. 1725–1779) was a representative compiler of such dictionaries. He was an English novelist, playwright, translator and satirist, who compiled *A New Dictionary of the English Language* (1773). What was unique about this dictionary was that it was the first to have employed diacritic marks for phonetic transcription and to have divided headwords according to their syllables. These methods were not carried over by William Perry into his *Royal Standard English Dictionary* (1775). Instead, Perry heaped serious criticisms upon his rival and proposed "a way of indicating pronunciation without disturbing traditional orthography"

The termination of hard-word traditions   115

(Hüllen, 2009:163) and "rendering it intelligible to the weakest capacity" (See its title page).

However, Kenrick's techniques were copied by John Burn (?–1793) in his *A Pronouncing Dictionary of the English Language* (1777). His intention in compiling the dictionary was mainly to help people read or transmit written language elegantly so that no offence would be meant for any acute British ear. Obviously, it was an extremely important and helpful aid for the Scottish to mingle into the decent English society heavily influenced by London then. There was a reprint of it in 1786, which suggested that it was, to some extent, a popular work of reference then.

Thomas Sheridan (1719–1788), an Irish stage actor and educator, inherited and developed Kenrick's techniques of transcribing pronunciation in *A General Dictionary of the English Language* (1780) so as to establish a simple and permanent standard pronunciation system. However, John Walker (1732–1807), philologist and lexicographer, was the first to have provided a truly systematic description of the pronunciation of English words. He followed his predecessors' steps and made continuous improvements in *A Rhyming Dictionary* (1775) and *A Critical Pronouncing Dictionary* (1791). The former turned out to be quite a success and was reprinted several times, and the latter became a role model for English pronouncing dictionaries in the 19th century. It had over 40 editions and over 100 reprints. Its last edition came out in 1904. It dominated the English pronouncing dictionary market for over 120 years and eventually became an authoritative work on English pronunciation stretching over the 18th and 19th centuries. Its influence did not recede until its replacement by Daniel Jones' (1881–1967) *English Pronouncing Dictionary* (1917).

There also appeared in the 18th century dictionaries of quotations. This dictionary genre originated from the 17th-century collection of pearls of wisdom such as famous aphorisms and maxims in poems and other literary writings. The earliest extant dictionary that may be associated with this dictionary genre is Edward Bysshe's *The Art of English Poetry* (1702). It consists of three parts: (1) rules of poem composition; (2) *A Dictionary of Rhymes*; (3) "A Collection of the most Natural, Agreeable, and Sublime THOUGHTS, viz. Allusions, Similes, Descriptions and Characters, of persons and Things; that are to be found in the best ENGLISH POETS". The third part, the longest of the three parts, is by nature a collection of quotations carefully designed to serve as a writing aid and model on the basis of the first and second parts. It was not until the end of the 18th century that D. E. Macdonnel's *A Dictionary of Quotations* (1797), the first dictionary of quotations, in the strict sense of it, came out. Its third edition appeared in 1799, followed by another two editions by 1811, which is a strong indication of its popularity at that time.

Thanks to the sound foundations laid by Skinner, Coles and Ray, dialect dictionaries continued to develop steadily. Samuel Pegge's (1704–1796) *An Alphabet of Kenticisms* (1735–1736) collected about 600 words and

116 *The termination of hard-word traditions*

expressions specific to Kent. Some proverbs and aphorisms were supplemented when the augmented edition was published in 1873. Bailey collected a good number of dialectal words in his *Universal Etymological English Dictionary* so that William Edward Armytage Axon (1846–1913), who worked for The English Dialect Society, extracted them out of it and compiled a separate collection – *English Dialect Words of the Eighteenth Century as shown in the "Universal Etymological Dictionary" of Nathaniel Bailey* (1883). As well as collecting dialectal words, Bailey also provided many annotations of where those words were used. Identification and supplementation were also done in Axon's compilation. Both were valuable resources for the 18th-century British dialect studies and served as important references for The English Dialect Society to develop British dialect dictionary projects.

For the 18th century, mention should be made of the last collection of dialect words – Francis Grose's (1731–1791) *A Provincial Glossary, with a Collection of Local Proverbs, and Popular Superstitions* (1787), which was augmented and renamed as *A Glossary of Provincial and Local Words used in England* (1839). Grose, an antiquary and lexicographer, received good education with a great fondness of drawing and art. He served twice in the army as well as playing an active part in several academic and social organizations and publishing several works.

Grose made a more careful sub-classification of Ray's criteria for dialect word collection with focus on three major types: (1) obsolete words that were out of use for long or were replaced by more fashionable ones and yet were still in use only in remote areas; (2) foreign words whose origins were difficult to identify but were passed on mouth by mouth among common folks; (3) words with strong local flavour. It excluded generally used words with differences only in pronunciation. (See Preface.) The enlarged edition of 1839 consisted of 188 pages, with headwords arranged alphabetically and annotations added at the end of the entry. Indications, such as *S, N* and *W*, were provided in some entries to show the regions of their uses (i.e. South, North and West). *E* was omitted for lack of adequate words used in the "East" region, and *C* was used for words that were used in various regions, sometimes marked as *Var. Dial.* In some entries, word origins were given, even along with references to famous writers and earlier dictionaries. Obviously, Grose's work was a considerable improvement upon previous ones.

Finally, let's turn back to English etymological dictionaries mentioned earlier in this section. "The earliest etymological dictionary of a new West-European language was of Dutch (Kiliaen, 1599)" (Liberman, 2009:271). C. Kiliaen's *Etymologicum teutonicae linguae* (1599) can be reckoned as the first of its kind, and English etymological dictionaries had their roots in Latin-English and English-Latin dictionaries, and their direct origin can be traced to English linguist and lexicographer John Minsheu's *Ductor in Linguas* (*Guide into the Tongues*, 1617). Relevant work was carried on by

The termination of hard-word traditions   117

Skinner, Franciscus Junius (1591–1677) and a few others. Unfortunately, neither of them saw the publication of their own etymological dictionaries before their death. Junius' *Etymologium anglicanum* was completed and published in 1743 by Edward Lye (1694–1767) on the basis of his lifetime work.

4.6 The humanistic and academic values of English dictionaries in the 18th century

The 18th century was indisputably a significant period in the history of British English lexicography. The middle part of it signified the advent of a new era of English dictionary-making, which brought English monolingual compilation into its first real climax, endowed British social and lexicographical culture with more profound, embellished humanistic and scholarly implications and left over to the British and world lexicographical culture priceless legacies that are hard to come by.

Lexicographical culture is concomitant with the times in which it originates and develops and with the advancement in social civilization. It is interwoven with and interactively promoted by literacy education, language evolution, writing system reform and scientific and technological development. Under specific circumstances, civilizations are all characterized by their own mainstream humanistic demands, distinctive values and spiritual accomplishments, which certainly lead the direction of lexicographical culture in these specific times and make it possible for dictionaries to encapsulate and reflect the extent of civilization and spiritual values of these times. Dictionaries thus become the representative cultural achievements that symbolize their times. The making of dictionaries in prosperous times is a conspicuous attribute in the history of Chinese culture, which is typified by the peak periods in the Han (206 BC–AD 220), Tang (618–907), Song (960–1279), Ming (1368–1644) and Qing (1616–1911) dynasties. Those peak periods are all marked by landmark lexicographical works, which embody admirable accomplishments of previous times, epitomize Chinese cultural and lexicographical legacies and give full expression to cultural advancement and spiritual values in ancient China.

British English dictionaries represent a major part of world lexicographical culture and constitute a typical form of Britain's socio-cultural life and carrier. They are bound to reflect Britain's accomplishments in social undertakings and advancement in civilization. In the 18th century, Britain underwent significant events that exerted extensive, profound and long-lasting impacts upon British political and socio-cultural life, as well as the progression of civilization in the history of mankind, such as the Enlightenment, the Industrialization, the establishment of the United Kingdom of Great Britain, the British-French war fought overseas and the annexation of Indian territories. Captain Cook's voyage to Australia and the victory of the American Independence War radically transformed the distribution of English-speaking

118 *The termination of hard-word traditions*

areas in the world territories and turned English into a language spoken in all the major parts of the world. The favourable circumstances inside and outside Britain conduced to leading English into the status of an international language in its real sense. The rich humanistic implications English embodied were duly and fully reflected in the 18th-century English dictionaries, with Johnson's dictionary as its typical representative.

Johnson's dictionary is a philological dictionary. However, over the past two or three decades, quite a few British scholars began to adopt an entirely different perspective by treating it as an attempt to construct a system of encyclopaedic knowledge, which is an integrated manifestation of humanistic values, social concepts and language wisdom. "Imperialism, profit, and philology had, by the mid-nineteenth century, become important ingredients of British lexicography – often prioritized in that order" (Bailey, 2006:207). Much more than that, the dictionary inevitably contains numerous historical sketches and miniatures, as Hitchings, (2005:182) commented, and Johnson's dictionary is a typical exemplar. Compared with any other English dictionaries before his time, it has a greater wealth of historical legends, mysterious information, family anecdotes, interesting trifles and mythological stories. To put it in a nutshell, it is simply a treasure house.

After a systematic analysis of a huge multitude of citations in Johnson's dictionary, DeMaria (1986) came to the conclusion that it is not merely a reference work of language, as it carries in its citations judgments regarding moral values and represents a complete system of cultural knowledge independent of the language system. Its essence resides not only in explaining the signification and use of language but in promoting cultural attainments and moral values of dictionary users and building up a huge system of cultural knowledge as well. DeMaria is a representative of this school of thought, and further researches are needed to determine whether those views are well-grounded. Johnson's dictionary is only a representative of this type, and, like many others, they all carry humanistic values and abundant social knowledge.

In Johnson's dictionary, some definitions are frequently taken as proofs to illustrate his one-sided or even biased opinions, but those biased definitions, more or less, reveal even profound humanistic implications and precious information of social significance, and they afford food for even more in-depth thought. What follows are two classic examples, which demonstrate various discrepancies from their counterparts in modern English dictionaries.

> Excise: a hateful tax levied on commodities and adjudged not by the common judges of property, but wretches hired by those to whom excise is paid (Samuel Johnson, *A Dictionary of the English Language*, 1755)
> Excise: a tax levied on certain goods and commodities produced or sold within a country and on licences granted for certain activities (*The New Oxford English-Chinese Dictionary*, 2007)

The termination of hard-word traditions 119

"Excise" is a variety of taxes levied in Britain, and its definitions in the previous two dictionaries show radical differences in their compilers' attitudes towards it. *The New Oxford English-Chinese Dictionary* holds an objective and moderate stance and is free from affectations, while Johnson's dictionary displays an obvious disapproval and even grievances towards it, as well as depicting public sentiments and images evoked by "excise", particularly the images of the collectors in the public eye. This definition presents an ugly portrait of tax imposition in the British society of that time.

> Oats: a grain, which in England is generally given to horses, but in Scotland supports people (Samuel Johnson, *A Dictionary of the English Language*, 1755)
>
> Oat: an Old World cereal which is cultivated chiefly in cool climates and is widely used for animal feed (*The New Oxford English-Chinese Dictionary*, 2007)

As indicated in the second definition, oats chiefly grow in cool climates and are mainly used for animals nowadays. However, in Johnson's times, things were quite different. In Scotland, oats were generally used for horse feed, while in England, they were used to maintain human survival. Some critics blame Johnson for not being objective in the definition, believing that Johnson was biased against the Scots. The conclusion may not be the case if the definition is interpreted under the historical context of Johnson's times. It is widely known that England was developed earlier than other areas in Britain and therefore went ahead of others in terms of economic strength and social advancement. Comparatively, Scotland was some distance away from England in terms of social and economic progress, though it made considerable headway in the 17th and 18th centuries. It was no surprise at all that the impoverished Scots ate oats for subsistence. That definition provides a vivid picture of the society the Scots lived in and the miserable life they had at that time.

The 18th-century English dictionaries not only contain abundant information concerning Britain's socio-cultural life with rich humanistic values but also manifest innovation and breakthroughs in lexicographical theorization and practices. As a result of the impacts from prescriptive traditions of dictionary-making in Europe and English standardization in Britain, prescriptive ideas were deeply rooted in Johnson's mind and were beginning to sprout and blossom. *The Plan of an English Dictionary*, which was based on the principles of prescriptivism, came to be known as Johnson's manifesto of prescriptivism. His dictionary became a test field for his manifesto and a solid scholarly foundation for his status as the representative lexicographer of prescriptivism.

The 18th-century English dictionaries not only contain abundant socio-cultural information that has high values for humanistic development but also embody innovation and breakthroughs in lexicographical theorization

120 *The termination of hard-word traditions*

and practices. As a result of the impacts of prescriptive traditions of dictionary-making in Europe and English standardization in Britain, prescriptivism sowed seeds deep in Johnson's mind that started to sprout and blossom. His "Plan of an English Dictionary" (1747), which was based on the prescriptive principles, can be viewed as the manifesto of Johnson's prescriptivism, while his dictionary, which laid a solid scholarly foundation for his status as the representative of prescriptive lexicographers, can be reckoned as the test field for the practice of his manifesto.

Some critics hold that descriptivism is discernible in his plan and in the making of his dictionary, but it is undeniable that prescriptivism went through the whole dictionary-making and dominated the whole process. Johnson's dictionary made the prescriptive principles well established in English dictionary compilation and turned them into one of the fundamental paradigms for modern dictionary-making. For the first time, his plan gave a systematic account of how the prescriptive principles could be applied to dictionary-making and enabled English dictionary-making, also for the first time, to proceed under systematic theoretical guidance. That is the most significant theoretical contribution made in the 18th century to British English lexicography.

Early in the 16th century, English dictionary-making was affected to varying degrees by pedagogical traditions, and the direct outcome was the primers and textbooks designed for the delivery of English literacy education to school children. Those early predecessors focused on simple common words with phonetic annotations and were aimed to standardize spellings and provide assistance in comprehending texts. However, viewed from the perspective of the language functions of dictionaries, those pedagogical traditions could only meet insignificant consultation needs. They overlooked the functions that dictionaries should perform as reference tools in removing doubts, suspicions and problems that could arise out of text comprehension. Hard or difficult words formed an indispensable part of the dictionary macrostructure. The hard-word tradition in British English lexicography was gradually intensified in the 17th century, reached its peak in the mid-18th century and began to decline from then on.

Running parallel to the hard-word tradition was the potential need of the general public to comprehend the strange and pompous words they frequently encountered in reading historical and legendary literature, and that need materialized the reference function of English dictionaries in the real sense and pushed dictionaries to play their due role and expand their core function. In the 18th century, dictionary functions became further specified and more clearly oriented, and that paved a smooth way for the development of British English lexicography in the 200 years to come.

Dictionaries prior to the mid-18th century were structurally incomplete by modern standards, for there was no comprehensive plan for the making of dictionaries before their compilation started. Consequently, the front matter did not cover such relevant materials as notes of compilation, explanation

The termination of hard-word traditions 121

of styles and formats, guides to use etc. What appeared in it was, more often than not, some poorly conceived ideas or some views regarding some controversial issues. In the front matter of the 17th-century dictionaries, Philips provided a brief history of the English language, Bailey gave explanations of the methods and forms of etymological treatment and Dyche and Pardon offered the knowledge about English grammar.

Those front matter items actually contained rather limited information, which was far from what should appear in a complete plan for the making of a dictionary. However, they embodied previous thoughts and reflections about English and English dictionary compilation and constituted sound foundations for Martin and Johnson to formulate the plans for making their dictionaries. Martin's was most probably the first English dictionary made according to a well-conceived plan and set a good example for Johnson to follow. Johnson's admirable success in his dictionary was directly ascribable to the plan he formulated for its making. From then on, it became a normal practice to formulate a plan before the making of a dictionary so that the dictionary was made according to the plan. The detailed plan for compiling *OED* is a typical case in point, which took a dozen years or so to formulate, after meticulous thinking, numerous discussions, heated debating and repeated adjustments and revisions between 1844 – the year when the interest in making a new dictionary was expressed – and 1857, the year when work began on the dictionary.

At the outset of the 17th century, English dictionary compilers began to pay attention to etymological treatment. Cawdrey might be considered the forerunner in treating etymology in English dictionaries by adopting special signs to indicate word origins, though in a considerably random way. The treatment of word histories in Bullokar and Cockeram's dictionary seemed somewhat redundant due to their collection of classic words, so their dictionary devoted almost no attention to this aspect of word treatment. Blount was the first lexicographer who gave great prominence to etymological treatment in his dictionary by providing word roots so as to indicate their origins. Sometimes, he went so far as to annotate the semantic composition of word roots as well as indicating their origins. In different versions of his dictionary, Philips took scarce notice of etymologies and provided speculative annotations to just a few words. Coles differed from his predecessors in this regard. He employed simply one letter to indicate word origins, and his indication was precise and scrupulous. No previous dictionaries surpassed his work in terms of consistency and comprehensiveness. Two other dictionaries – *Glossographia Anglicana Nova* and *Dictionarium Anglo-Britannicum* – noted etymologies by using the names of the source languages, but the proportion of the noted words was rather low.

Bailey's treatment of etymology was superior to others' in several aspects. He indicated not only the source languages and the roots of words but the close and cognate sources as well. What is more noteworthy was that a great proportion of his Preface was devoted to how etymologies were treated in

122 *The termination of hard-word traditions*

his dictionary as special attributes and contributions to British English lexicography. Numerous errors and mistakes were found in his treatment, and some were even inherited from Skinner's *Etymologicon Linguae Anglicanae* (1671), but he lived up to the self-appointed title of the first person to have attempted at treating word origins in English dictionaries. (See Preface.)

Bailey made etymological treatment one of the dispensable attributes all reputable dictionaries should possess and set up replicable examples for others to follow. Regrettably, throughout the 18th century, the treatment of etymologies stopped at lexicographical practices, without in-depth systematic theoretical generalization. Consequently, no scientific solutions were worked out until the 19th century, when new theoretical breakthroughs were achieved in the preparation of *OED*.

Etymological treatment was one of the features that made the 18th-century dictionaries better than previous ones, and there was another aspect that was not obviously neglectable, i.e. new attempts at defining words. "Definitions have at last been accorded their proper place as the prime concern of the dictionary" (Starnes and Noyes, 1991:195). Definitions were far from satisfactory in the early 18th century. Let us have a look at how words were defined in J. K.'s *A New English Dictionary* (1702). This dictionary provided basically no definitions for derivatives, words relating to headwords or commonly used words. For some words, it provided only meanings or contexts of usage and notes, as in "Accent, to accent Words", "Any, anyone, anywhere", "Apron, An Apron, for a Woman", and for others it used one word to explain another, as in the case of using "beast" to explain "elephant" and "goat". Obviously, those so-called definitions were unintelligible and were likely to cause serious misunderstanding.

However, definitions, as well as the art and craft of defining words, were continuously improving, as can be shown through comparing the two versions of J. K.'s *A New English Dictionary*:

1702	1713
A Gad of steel	A Gad, a measure of 9 or 10 feet, a small bar of steel
A Gag	A Gag, a stopple to hinder one form crying out
To Gaggle like a goose	To Gaggle, to cry like a goose
A Gallop	A Gallop, the swiftest pace of a horse

English dictionaries in the mid- and late 18th century made great strides in definitions, which can be summarized as follows:

(1) By avoiding ambiguous and broad-brush definitions that were common in previous dictionaries, they used more precise and appropriate language to define words;

(2) They made fine discriminations of word senses by identifying original, basic and extended senses and matched usages and citations with the

The termination of hard-word traditions   123

contexts in which the senses developed and were applied. The number of senses identified in some entries amounted to more than 100;

(3) They conducted some preliminary surveys concerning the methods of arranging senses so as to better suit the cognitive needs of users and started to arrange them in the sequence of basic senses first and then extended senses, basically following the mode of going from original senses to metaphorical senses;

(4) They devised various systems for arranging senses by use of numerals, signs and other devices and made it possible to arrange senses in a traceable and orderly fashion. It is obvious that Martin and his dictionaries played a role of agglomeration and transition in the methodological amelioration of arranging senses, while Johnson brought the techniques of defining words into their empyrean.

From the time of the publication of the first English dictionary, compliers aspired to make their dictionaries capable of all roles and functions they could conceive and intended them to meet all the imaginable user needs. Consequently, their range of users was all-inclusive, which might be the ideal the compilers wanted to realize, though there might also be elements of advertising their dictionaries. However, the hard fact was that no dictionaries in the world could really achieve such desirable effects, for it was inevitable for dictionaries to make clear segmentation of user groups on the basis of market analyses of potential users, their language needs and reference demands.

Over the past three decades or so, user studies, especially studies in user cognition, started to draw serious attention from lexicographers, linguists and educationalists, though they came later and developed more slowly than they should, without much avail. Early in 1735, Dyche and Pardon conducted investigations of market prospects and user needs and tried to narrow down or even completely exclude the range of users the dictionaries such as Bailey's had already covered by targeting those user segments other compilers chose to ignore. Bailey's dictionary claimed to be chiefly intended for those well-educated, intelligent and elite users with strong sensitivity to language, while others turned to the general user market. That awareness of user needs and market diversities intensified and echoed to varying degrees in later compilations, as in Wesley's *The Complete English Dictionary*, whose attention to young school pupils sowed seeds for the making of learner's dictionaries in the 20th century.

5 The European philological traditions and the creation of the diachronic dictionary paradigm in the 19th century

Political and social turmoil were commonplace in British society in the early 19th century. However, viewed from the perspective of the entirety of the century, Britain enjoyed the most stabilized and the best developed century ever since remote times. Industrialization was expedited and deepened, science and technology, especially the steam engine technology, was promoted and employed and the population clustering resulting from the "world factory", the speedy development of railway transportation and the gradual flourishing of overseas trade turned Britain into the world's first industrialized and urbanized society. The enthronement of Queen Elizabeth opened up a new era of prosperity and dazzling glory, followed by an obvious transition from a wealthy and powerful nation into a gradually declining power.

Starting from the 19th century, English underwent no radical change within its internal system, but the external environment experienced sharp continuous transformations. Owing to British colonial expansion, the increasing territories of the British Empire and the rise of America on the New Continent, English had spread to all the major parts of the world, resulting in a substantial increase of its speakers. With the strengthened flourishing of trade and commerce, science and technology and international intercourse, English became an international medium of communication that boasted unprecedented influence and scope of transmission by the end of the 19th century. The 19th century gave birth to such great literary figures as Jane Austen (1775–1817), Charles Dickens (1812–1870), Robert Louis Stevenson (1850–1894) and Thomas Hardy (1840–1928). Their immortal works written in Modern English considerably enriched the cultural implications of English and literary charm and held English in high esteem.

The year 1842 witnessed an event of far-reaching sociolinguistic significance – the establishment of the Philological Society (also London Philological Society), the oldest learned society in Britain designed to "investigate and promote the study and knowledge of the structure, the affinities, and the history of languages". Its activities catalysed the erection of the gigantic monument in the history of world lexicography – *OED*. Its compilation

The European philological traditions   125

and publication pushed English dictionary-making into full blossom and into its peak period. What follows is an exploration of the environment, evolutional track and features of English dictionary-making in Britain in the 19th century.

5.1 The socio-cultural background for the development of British English lexicography in the 19th century

In the 19th century, British society was undergoing profound social transformation, remarkable economic development and high-speed advancement in science and technology. Starting from the 1830s, Britain continued to expand its overseas colonies, resorting to its huge economic strength and its monopolistic status in the international trade, and its territories extended so far and wide as to surpass the ancient Roman Empire. The reform bills passed through Parliament in 1832 strengthened the political status and social privilege of the bourgeois class with economic power.

In the 1850s and 1860s, Britain had occupied the absolute leading position in the world economy. Its population accounted for only 2 percent of the world population and 10 percent of the European population, but it manufactured more than half of the world's industrial products and became the "world factory" in every sense. From the 1870s onwards, it was beginning to lose its dominant position in the world economy, with its total economic output diminishing from 40 percent of the world's total in the 1850s to 32 percent in the 1870s. By the beginning of the 20th century, America replaced Britain and became the world's first, with its total output accounting for 31 percent of the world's total, and Germany overtook it as well.

Britain underwent a period of population expansion in the 19th century. Take London for example. Its population was about 500,000 in 1700, rose to over 3,000,000 in the early 1860s and reached nearly 5,000,000 by the early 20th century (Fennell, 2005:185). In 1801, Britain's entire population was around 9,000,000, the majority of whom were engaged in farming and its related industry, with a great part of products made manually. About 20 percent of its population lived in towns with low living standards and poor living environment.

By 1851, half of its population lived in towns, and, after 30 years, about two-thirds became urban residents. Its total population soared to 41,000,000 by the early 20th century. When factories became widespread, a large proportion of products were made by machinery, and at least 80 percent of its population became the working class. However, the disparity between the rich and the poor was widening in British society throughout the 19th century. By the end of the 19th century, over 25 percent could only earn a meagre living, and about 10 percent lived in extreme poverty. In addition, around 15,000,000 people fled from Britain to America and Australia between 1815 and 1914 to avoid starvation and religious prosecution. That caused a substantial increase of population in the New World of America

126 *The European philological traditions*

and Australia and laid a solid foundation for the expansion of English to other parts of the world territories.

In the history of human civilization, the 19th century can be reckoned as a century of science, and the scientific spirit is the main feature of those times, which is especially conspicuous in the British society where the industrial revolution first took place and was still taking the lead. In the 19th century, accomplishments in science and technology were made at an unprecedented pace in terms of their amelioration and promotion. In its early part, they were chiefly reflected in the areas of physics and life science. Charles Darwin (1809–1882) published *The Origin of Species* in 1859, which triggered heated debates concerning evolution, the nature of mankind and society, human beings and nature and religion and morals and brought about radical transformations in British ideology, culture and religious faith.

In technological innovation and promotion, the steam engine George Trevithick invented in 1801 directly propelled the extensive application of the steam engine technology in fields other than the textile industry, which even covered the printing industry. The printing innovations meant lower costs in the publication of books and newspapers, the radical improvement of publishing speed and greater affordability for the general public. The new technology of telephones and wireless telegrams narrowed down the social distance between people in communication and made social life immensely easier and more convenient. The advancement in ideology and science and technology infused a huge number of new words and expressions, hence considerable dynamics, into English.

British education made great strides in the 19th century. In 1870, the General Education Act made child education compulsory, bringing overall British education to a new level. More and more British citizens could read and write, and their socio-cultural quality was visibly enhanced. All this furnished abundant socio-cultural soil and strong momentum for British English lexicography to move into another peak period. What follows is a scuttle through those events that are of major significance for causing that to happen in the 19th-century British English lexicography.

The founding of the United Kingdom of Great Britain and Northern Ireland About 8,600 years ago, human beings began to inhabit the island of Ireland. During the 4th and 5th centuries, the Irish inhabitants were converted to Christianity. With the Normans' occupation of Ireland in the mid-12th century, England gradually penetrated into and dominated the Irish politics and culture, until its full occupation of Ireland in 1609. Although various kingdoms existed in the British history, the Kingdom of England had performed a dominating role. Prior to its creation, the United Kingdom had conquered and annexed Wales. Thus, the United Kingdom created by the 1707 Acts of Union between England and Scotland encompassed all of Great Britain. The Acts of Union in 1800 united the Kingdom of Great Britain and the Kingdom of Ireland in 1801, forming the United Kingdom of Great Britain and Ireland. Following the partition of Ireland and

The European philological traditions 127

the independence of the Irish Free State in 1922 as a result of the Anglo-Irish Treaty, five-sixths of Ireland seceded from the United Kingdom, but the state had the status of dominion until 1937, when a new constitution was enforced, which effectively turned it into a republic, though it was not officially declared until 1949, following the Republic of Ireland Act 1948. Consequently, the name "United Kingdom of Great Britain and Northern Ireland" was adopted, which was highly conducive to the elevation of English as an international language.

The Battle of Trafalgar Subsequent to the Norman Conquest in 1066, Britain took away some French dominions, which gradually fostered hostilities and even intensified confrontations. In order for France to succumb, Britain tried every means to form the First and Second Coalition against France, which the newly born Napoleonic Empire broke through with resort to military strength and political struggles.

However, the French were well aware that peace would not come by itself without defeating or signing peace treaties with Britain. The Treaty of Amiens was signed on March 25, 1802 but was short-lived. Direct confrontation broke out between the two countries again in 1803, followed by the anti-French Third Coalition forged by Britain between August and December 1805. A naval engagement was fought on October 21, 1805 by the British Royal Navy against the combined fleets of the French and Spanish Navies on the Atlantic Ocean off the southwest coast of Spain, just west of Cape Trafalgar.

The British navy won a decisive victory by dealing a destructive blow to the combined fleets. The battle considerably reduced the French threat on the seas and enabled Britain to continue its maritime supremacy. It added enormously to the glory of the British Empire and substantiated the global influence of not only the British Empire but the English language as well. Meanwhile, it diminished, to a considerable extent, the potential impacts of France and the French culture upon Britain's social, cultural and linguistic life.

Alexandrina Victoria's ascension to the throne Alexandrina Victoria (1819–1901) inherited the British throne on June 20, 1837, at the age of 18, initiating the glorious Victorian era. She remained Queen of the United Kingdom of Great Britain and Ireland until her death, reigning over the empire for 63 years and 216 days. Upon her ascension to the throne, the United Kingdom was already an established constitutional monarchy, in which the Queen could only exert private influence upon government policy-making and ministerial appointments, but, publicly, she was a national icon with strict standards of personal morality. The overseas colonial plundering, the domestic industrial development, the booming railway transportation, scientific inventions and culture and art combined to create the strong and prosperous Victorian era.

The world exposition (also known as World Expo), which had its roots in the French tradition of national exhibitions, has become a large global

128 *The European philological traditions*

exhibition designed to showcase dazzling achievements of nations, which has been characterized by industrialization, cultural exchanges and national branding. In 1851, London held the first World Expo in The Crystal Palace in Hyde Park under the title "Great Exhibition of the Works of Industry of All Nations", which demonstrated to the world the remarkable innovative accomplishments of the century and promoted the image of Britain as the world centre of commerce, trade and science and technology in the Victorian era. The upholding of morality and strict etiquette observation (especially table manners) made Britain a land of gentry.

The Victorian era was the prime period of economic growth, sociocultural progression and scientific and technological advancement of the British Empire, culminating in radical transformations and rapid advancement in almost every field. However, those transformations and developments started with confidence, optimism and economic booming but ended in swelling anxieties about the future and the gradual declination of the empire. Contradictions were sharpening inside and outside the empire, the polarization between the rich and the poor was widening, and the newly emerging industrial nations, such as America and Germany, were catching up with and overtaking Britain. All this eventually led to the collapse of the Crystal Palace, together with the huge empire and the Victorian era.

The Philological Society of London Traditionally, philology studies language in its written and oral sources from the diachronic perspective, which attempts to focus more on literary texts, establish their authenticity, trace their origins and discern their meanings and evolution. The Philological Society of London is the oldest learned society in Great Britain, established in 1842 to "investigate and promote the study and knowledge of the structure, the affinities, and the history of languages". Its predecessor was the Society for Philological Inquiries founded by Thomas Hewitt Key (1799–1875) and George Long (1800–1879) in 1830 for the heightened interest in comparative philology and in pursuit of the "Philological Illustration of the Classical Writers of Greece and Rome".

While pursuing the tradition of European continental philology, a group of British scholars were beginning to create their own path of philological research. Among them was Edwin Guest (1800–1880), a self-taught Anglo-Saxon scholar and an English antiquary, who first came up with a plan to found a society for the advancement of philological inquiry in his initial composition of *Origines Celticae* (1883). On May 9, 1842, he formally announced an open invitation for interested parties to attend a meeting on May 18 for the "purpose of forming a Philological Society". The preliminary meeting was held as planned and chaired by Connop Thirlwall (1797–1875), its first and longest-serving president (1842–1868). As a scholarly organization dedicated to language inquiries, its most remarkable accomplishment was definitely the *New English Dictionary on Historical Principles*, based partly if not exclusively on the notions of a comprehensive

The European philological traditions   129

historical dictionary of English proposed by Trench in his paper "On some Deficiencies in our English Dictionaries" (1857).

The Philological Society of London has had extensive and ever-lasting influence in different walks of British life, and its aims and fundamental principles remain unchanged even to the present day. It continues to play an active and leading role in the research of frontier issues of historical and comparative linguistics by publishing on modern English varieties, structure and changes. Its devotion to both traditional and modern issues of language, problems concerning modern languages, and theories of language is well worth commending. In the wake of its influence were established such organizations of similar nature as The Cambridge Philological Society and The Philological Society, New York. Under these umbrellas, language experts and specialists from relevant fields come together to study language in a more comprehensive and systematic manner, to improve English dictionary-making from different perspectives and to make dictionary compilation a more glorious socio-cultural undertaking.

The First and Second Industrial Revolution Just as the Industrial Revolution (1760–1840) transformed Britain into an "empire on which the sun never sets", so the Second Industrial Revolution (1871–1914) became an evident indication of the decline of the British Empire.

The First Industrial Revolution, which started in Britain and gradually spread to the European continent, North America and Japan, was a significant turning point in the history of mankind and brought about radical transformations in and exerted far-reaching and ever-lasting influences upon every field and walk of the socio-economic life of the world, especially textile, manufacturing, mining and transportation as well as scientific and educational undertakings. Thanks to the strong momentum generated from the First Industrial Revolution, Britain developed itself into the world's number one power in the Victorian era.

However, when the manufacturing of frontier industrial goods, such as iron and steel products, chemical products, electrical products and petroleum products, signified the advent of the Second Industrial Revolution, the British were still indulging in their accomplishments generated from steam engine technology. The newly emerging industrial nations, such as Germany, America and even Japan, were already catching up and even aspiring to overtake. Upon entry into the 20th century, the fact that America and Germany were already surpassing the then number one power of the world, thanks chiefly to the widespread application of electrical technology, reshaped the world's political and economic landscape, redirected the development trend of English in the world territory and revised the distribution pattern of core regions in which English was spoken as the first and the second language on major continents. The domination of British English over the English-speaking world was about to become history.

Just as Baugh and Cable (1993:290) said, "The events of the nineteenth and twentieth centuries affecting the English-speaking countries have been

130 *The European philological traditions*

of great political and social importance, but in their effect on the language they have not been of revolutionary". In the 19th century, no substantial changes took place in the pronunciation, grammar or structure of English, except for the continuing expansion of its lexicon. English had become basically stabilized in terms of pronunciation and grammar in the modern English period.

5.2 The English and linguistic background for the evolution of British English lexicography in the 19th century

As a result of the expansion of the British Empire, English gradually spread to almost every corner of the globe in the 19th century through three major channels: migrating with English native speakers to non-English speaking regions, coexisting with native languages and being introduced as official language or being assimilated with native and vernacular languages so that Pidgin English and Creole were formed.

The first case is amply demonstrated by the English development in America, Australia, Canada, New Zealand and a few other regions. The newcomers to those primitive lands paid almost no attention to the already existing aboriginal languages, to say nothing of learning those languages. What somewhat interested them was understandably the languages of those previous conquerors, such as French and Spanish. The second case was especially apparent in countries and regions such as India, South Africa and the Philippines. Just as French became the language of the British upper class after the French occupation of Britain, so English became the official language of the occupied territories, and their native languages were reduced to the "inferior" languages spoken by the ordinary people. The third case was typified by the colonies established mainly by Britain, France, Spain and Portugal. Pidgin languages and creoles were particularly commonplace in East Africa, West Africa, the Caribbean and those regions along the rim of the Pacific Ocean. They still exist in many parts of the world today, and a few of them have become officialized.

Thanks to the widespread use of printing techniques, the gradual popularization of education, the increasing convenience of transportation and social intercourse and the ever-strengthening national and social awareness, the 19th-century English language became more steady and stable, with no obvious changes taking place within the language system, its grammatical structure being somewhat perpetuated, its inflections basically fading away and grammatical irregularities (such as "you was") being eliminated. However, English spelling reforms, phonetic normalization and the movement for linguistic purity did not come to a complete halt. English regional varieties gradually materialized in different parts of the world. All these became the outstanding evolutionary features of English in the 19th century.

The European philological traditions 131

Ever since early modern English, problems of English spelling had been perplexing British academia.

> For nearly 400 years the English have struggled with their spelling. It was one of the chief problems that seemed to confront the language in the time of Shakespeare, and it continued to be an issue throughout the seventeenth and to some extent in eighteenth century.
>
> (Baugh and Cable, 1993:328)

From the late part of the 19th century, they became a focal point again in language studies. Researchers from both Britain and America came up with various proposals, set up spelling reform committees and publicized their spelling reform schemes on a periodical basis, but little had come out of such efforts owing to the obstinate adherence to linguistic conventions, the etymological values and cultural implications residing in traditional spellings. It became evident that spelling reforms had to be undertaken gradually and fractionally, without causing systematic damages to the existing language system. English dictionaries played their due role in such reforms, and it is particularly true of American English dictionaries.

The establishment and final adoption of Received Pronunciation (abbreviated as RP, also known as Queen's English, King's English, Oxford English), is a major accomplishment of English phonetic normalization in the 19th century. The term was coined by the French American philosopher and linguist Peter Stephen Du Ponceau (1760–1844) in 1818 and was later adopted by Alexander Ellis (1814–1890) in his *Early English Pronunciation* (1869). The word "received" conveys its original meaning of "accepted" or "approved", as in "received wisdom". It is often believed that RP is based on the dialect and the accents of southern England, though it has a great deal in common with the Early Modern English dialects of the East Midlands, which was the most populated and most prosperous area of England during the 14th and 15th centuries. Standard English was established in the City of London by the end of the 15th century, though RP did not get widespread and universally recognized until Daniel Jones (1881–1967) published *An English Pronouncing Dictionary* (1917). RP provides a reliable aid and guide for English phonetic transcription in dictionaries. The majority of English dictionaries published in Britain (including *OED*) now give phonetically transcribed RP pronunciations for all words. British pronunciation dictionaries are all based on RP, though not necessarily using that name.

English is extraordinary in terms of its ever-lasting contact with other languages and the degree of the impacts of such contacts. Due to such extensive contacts and even all-round in-depth penetration by other languages (such as French), some began to pay close attention to the problem of English purity and the trend of its development. To varying degrees,

132   *The European philological traditions*

linguistic purity became a highly controversial issue and triggered heated debates from the middle of the Old English period. Consequently, the Society for Pure English was called into forth to perform the duty of maintaining linguistic purity.

The debates concerning English purity gradually went into their climax in the early and mid-18th century, during which period the idea of upholding linguistic purity prevailed and the views became popular and well recognized that linguistic changes should be considered decay and corrosion from outside English should be resisted. Those principles dominated the design, innovation and development of British English dictionary-making at that time. Johnson gave full play and full expression to those principles in the compilation of his dictionary and made it a classic work representative of English dictionaries compiled according to the doctrines of linguistic purity and codification.

Despite the prevailing notions of prescriptivism, descriptivism was still discernible in the making of the 18th-century English dictionaries and even in Johnson's dictionary and his plan for making the dictionary, though it was claimed that prescriptivism was strictly followed in its entire compilation. This descriptive practice can be traced back to Blount's treatment of word origins in *Glossographia*, where a precedent was set for conducting in-depth etymological research. It was inherited and somewhat fully implemented in Bailey's *Universal Etymological English Dictionary*.

So far no systematic investigation has been made regarding whether comparative philology and diachronic linguistics in the 19th century exerted direct impacts upon the treatment of word origins in Latin-English bilingual dictionaries and English monolingual dictionaries, but affinity does exist between language origin research and studies in word origin. The former is a macro-level investigation into the beginning and evolution of the whole language system while the latter is a micro-level investigation into the beginning and evolution of words within the system. They share some common methodology and research goals, which turn out to be complimentary in many aspects.

As suggested earlier, comparative linguistics (also comparative grammar, comparative philology) originated from the studies in the origins of Indo-European languages with focus on the explorations into whether two or more languages share cognate relations and diachronic correspondence. In 1786, William Jones (1746–1794) claimed that there existed some kind of relatedness between Sanskrit and Latin, Greek and German, which greatly stimulated scholarly interest in the comparative studies of phonology, morphology, syntax and lexicon from the diachronic perspective. Thanks to the long-term optimization and development, the comparative approach, which aimed to reconstruct language affinities to establish language families, especially the existence of a relationship between European and Indian languages, came into shape in the 19th century and was successfully applied to such researches. Diachronic (or historical) linguistics, a new linguistic

The European philological traditions   133

branch, ensued from the comparative approach to language, with broader visions, more scientific methodology, more general objects and more specific goals to achieve.

From the 19th century to the 20th century, comparative and historical linguistics provided huge methodological enlightenments and referential values for explorations in language origins and evolution, pursuit of humanistic truth and spirit and discovery of beginnings of civilizations. The influence of comparative and diachronic approaches and their accomplishments extended far beyond language systems, and a case in point is their application to the hypothetical reconstruction of human gregariousness and migration in prehistoric times.

The proposals for compiling historical dictionaries and their successful implementation were the direct outcome of applying diachronic concepts and the comparative approach in the study of language origin and families to English dictionary-making. Research findings in diachronic linguistics infused fresh insights and momentum into historical dictionary-making, broadened the theoretical visions and scholarly foundation for English dictionary-making and led English dictionary compilation for the first time, wholly and systematically, out of the confines of prescriptivism onto the track of diachronic description.

5.3 The tradition of European philology and the theoretical conceptualization of *New English Dictionary on Historical Principles*

OED has become a legend and miracle in the history of world lexicography and has erected a glorious monument in world scholarship. However, this legendary milestone stemmed from some ideas and concepts that were neither systematic nor complete at the very outset, though they had their roots in European philology and the remote lexicographical tradition.

William Jones (1746–1794), an Anglo-Welsh philologist and a scholar of ancient India, was especially well-known for his observation and proposition of the genetic relationship between European and Indian languages. In his third annual discourse to the Asiatic Society of Bengal on the history and culture of the Hindus, which was delivered on February 2, 1786 and published in 1788, Jones stated,

> The Sanscrit language, whatever be its antiquity, is of a wonderful structure; more perfect than the Greek, more copious than the Latin, and more exquisitely refined than either, yet bearing to both of them a stronger affinity, both in the roots of verbs and the forms of grammar, than could possibly have been produced by accident; so strong indeed, that no philologer could examine them all three, without believing them to have sprung from some common source, which, perhaps, no longer exists.

134 *The European philological traditions*

Jones' speech shattered the traditional philosophical foundation that underpinned 18th-century language studies, brought into practice the mainstream approaches that eventually led historical and comparative linguistic studies in the second half of the 19th century and the early part of the 20th century in Europe and paved a smooth way for the birth and development of "new philology" and for what later came to be known as "comparative philology". They provided theoretical guidance for the shaping of the historical paradigm for German dictionary-making and the sparks that ignited the compilation of *Deutsches Wörterbuchvon Jakob und Wilhelm Grimm*.

The idea of compiling an English dictionary similar to *Deutsches Wörterbuchvon Jakob und Wilhelm Grimm* and making it a real monument erected in the history of English lexicography started to germinate in the 1850s. The original plan was to compile an English lexicon, which would start from early modern English and would be more systematic, inclusive and complete than any of previous dictionaries. Thanks to the strenuous efforts and promotion by The Philological Society of London, the plan was put into operation. At the beginning of the 19th century, a great fervour for comparative philology was surging on the European continent under the advocacy of the Danish scholar Rasmus Kristian Rask (1787–1832) and the German scholars Franz Bopp (1791–1867) and Jakob Grimm. Bopp published a book about comparative studies in verbs in 1816, Rask wrote an article that explored the origin of the Norwegian language in 1818 and Grimm wrote a German grammar between 1819 and 1837. "They were laying the foundations of what later came to be known as comparative linguistics" (Béjoint, 2010:97). Out of keen interest in comparative philology, the Cambridge classicist scholars Thomas Hewitt Key (1799–1875), George Long (1800–1879) and others founded the Society for Philological Inquiries in 1830 and hosted a series of informal seminars. Meanwhile, many scholars began to ponder upon the development of philology in Britain and were determined to forge their own path. Edwin Guest, the founder of the Philological Society, was a representative among such scholars.

In the early stage of writing *Origines Celticae* (1883), Guest proposed the idea of setting up a society aiming for philological studies. On May 9, 1842, he delivered formal invitations to those who had expressed their wishes to become a member of the society so that they would come together to discuss its establishment. Among those were included Thomas Hewitt Key, Henry Malden (1800–1876), John Mitchell Kemble (1807–1857), Benjamin Thorpe (1782–1870) and Hensleigh Wedgwood (1803–1891). The first meeting was held on May 18 of the same year. Connop Thirlwall (1797–1875) presided over the meeting and formally declared the founding of the society. The Philological Society carried on with the mission of the Society for Philological Inquiries, striving to continue the existing tradition of tracing citations from Greek and Roman classic authors and "investigate and promote the study and knowledge of the structure, the affinities, and the history of languages".

The European philological traditions 135

Naturally, the report on the research findings and latest developments of the structure, the affinities and the history of languages in the European continental countries became part of the new society's agenda. The accomplishments by the continental scholars such as Rask, Bopp and Grimm were reported at the society's regular meetings. It is obvious that, from the very outset, the Philological Society regarded the comparative studies in language as one of their research focuses. However, it was not merely a reproduction of the philological studies on the European continent but attached greater prominence to word origins, classic philology, the structure and history of language, and even the dialects of Papuan tribes and the lingo of Australian emigrants.

The Philological Society absorbed figures of the greatest prominence in the British academic and social circles of that time; among them were included the best-known phoneticians in 19th-century Britain – Alexander Ellis (1814–1890) and Henry Sweet (1845–1912). Ellis laid a solid foundation for phonetic studies in Britain, and Sweet made major contributions to the advancement of the new discipline of phonetics. They participated regularly at the society's meetings and delivered annual reports and keynote speeches. They also made contributions to the Society's journal – *Transactions*. Sweet acted twice as its interim president (1875–1876; 1877–1878). Ellis' and Sweet's participation in and contribution to the society's activities ensured its continuing heightened success and strengthened its influence in the 1860s and 1870s. Certainly, its most significant single achievement to date remains the key role it played in formulating the compiling notions of *OED* and the sophisticated plan for making its compilation and publication possible.

Early in 1844, the British statesman and man of letters Cornewall Lewis (1806–1863) came up with the proposal of compiling a historical dictionary concentrating on English obsolete words and regional terms. That view gained favourable responses from the philological circle, associating for the first time and in a coherent way the diachronic approach to language with the compilation of dictionaries. On June 18, 1857, the Philological Society formally announced the establishment of The Unregistered Words Committee, whose duty was to collect all the words previously unlisted or poorly defined in any dictionary of English. The committee comprised a Literary and Historical section and an Etymological section. The former consisted of Richard Chevenix Trench (1807–1886), Herbert Coleridge (1830–1861), Frederick James Furnivall (1825–1910) and the latter Wedgwood and Malden.

In July 1857, the committee issued its first circular, which was revised in August 1857. In November, Trench, then Dean of Westminster and subsequently Archbishop of Dublin, delivered to the Society a "little Essay" — "On some Deficiencies in our English Dictionaries", which "is the substance of two papers that were read before the Society". His speech dealt with "some, and not with all their deficiencies" but "leaves wholly aside the

136 *The European philological traditions*

etymological aspect" and treats only of the imperfect registration in them of the words of our language, and the imperfect use of our literature in the illustration of the words". That can be explained by the fact that by Trench's time etymological treatment in English dictionaries was already rather advanced.

The "principal shortcomings" Trench listed go as follows:

(1) Obsolete words are incompletely registered; some inserted, some not; with no reasonable rule adduced for the omission of these, the insertion of those other;

(2) Families or groups of words are often imperfect, some members of a family inserted, while others are omitted;

(3) Much earlier examples of the employment of words oftentimes exist than any which are cited; indicating that they were introduced at an earlier date into the language than these examples would imply. So, too, on the other hand, in the case of words now obsolete, much later examples might frequently be produced, marking their currency at a period after, and sometimes long after, that when we are left to suppose that they passed out of use;

(4) Important meanings and uses of words are passed over; sometimes the later alone given, while the earlier, without which the history of words will be often maimed and incomplete, or even unintelligible, are unnoticed;

(5) Comparatively little attention is paid to the distinguishing of synonymous words;

(6) Many passages in our literature are passed by, which might be usefully adduced in illustration of the first introduction, etymology, and meaning of words;

(7) And lastly, our Dictionaries err in redundancy as well as in defect, in the too much as well as the too little; all of them inserting some things, and some of them many things, which have properly no claim to find room in their pages.

Trench especially pointed out that, for the history of words and families of words and for the changes of form and sense which words had historically passed through, the existing English dictionaries gave hardly any help whatsoever. No one could find out from all the dictionaries extant how long any particular word had been in the language, which of the many senses in which many words were used was the original or how or when these many senses had been developed; nor, in the case of words described as obsolete, were we told when they became obsolete or by whom they were last used. He added that the obsolete and the rarer words of the language had never been completely collected, that thousands of words current in the literature of the past three centuries had escaped the diligence of Johnson and all his supplementers. He called upon the Philological Society, therefore, as the

The European philological traditions   137

only body in England then interesting itself in the language, to undertake the collection of materials to complete the work already done by Bailey, Johnson, Todd, Webster, Richardson and others and to give quotations illustrating the first and last appearance and every notable point in the life-history of every word.

Trench's list of major deficiencies in the existing English dictionaries and his exposition of the compiling notions and techniques provided illuminating insights into the making of a new dictionary and eventually came to form the basis for the proposal to be put forward to the society. He played a key role in the project's first months, but his ecclesiastical career meant that he could not afford the time the dictionary project demanded. After his withdrawal, Herbert Coleridge became the first editor.

In December 1857, Coleridge, who was taking charge of the dictionary project, reported to the Unregistered Words Committee regarding the production of a comprehensive historical dictionary "worthy of the great English nation" (*The Times* 1869). On January 7, 1858, *Proposal for the Publication of A New English Dictionary by the Philological Society* was submitted to the society's first meeting of the year and met the public in August. In the same year, Coleridge came up with his *Glossarial Index to the Printed English Literature of the Thirteenth Century* and *Canones Lexicographici; or Rules to be observed in editing the New English Dictionary.* Interestingly, George Perkins Marsh (1801–1882), a diplomatist, philologist, America's first environmentalist and a precursor to the concept of sustainability, offered to organize American volunteers to collect materials for the making of the dictionary.

Simultaneously, far beyond the Atlantic Ocean, a war of dictionaries was beginning to surge in America, which was poised to surpass its British counterparts, which is to be dealt with under a separate cover. The British kept making strong appeals to compile a large comprehensive dictionary that could match Noah Webster's (1758–1843) *An American Dictionary of the English Language* (1828). By then, the dictionary project emerged as a matter of national attention and significance. In 1859, the Society's *Proposal* was published, and on January 16, 1860, the council passed a resolution to produce a dictionary of four volumes, covering the entire English language from past to present. That was followed by the publication of Coleridge's dictionary plan on May 12, 1860 and his research immediately afterwards. On May 30, Coleridge stated with confidence that the society could publish the first fascicle of *A New English Dictionary on Historical Principles; Founded Mainly on the Materials Collected by The Philological Society* (hereinafter abbreviated as *NED*) within two years.

Coleridge's house was the first editorial office. He arrayed 100,000 quotation slips in a 54-pigeon-hole grid. In April 1861, the first sample pages were sent out for comments. However, its compilation did not go as smoothly as expected, and a series of setbacks hindered its progress. The worst thing was Coleridge's premature death on April 23, 1861, caused by the tuberculosis

138 *The European philological traditions*

he contracted as he was sitting through a meeting of the society with only damp clothing on. That happened two weeks after he presented to the society the first set of words he had collected for the letters *A–D*. When told he would not recover, Coleridge extracted a deathbed promise from Furnivall to oversee the project through to completion.

Furnivall joined the Philological Society in 1847 and remained its secretary from 1853 almost to his death. He worked as the second editor of *NED* between 1861 and 1870. Despite his scholarship and enthusiasm, his stint as its editor nearly brought the project to an end owing to his lack of patience, discipline and accuracy. His serious defects in personality, typically irascibility and caprice, caused the resignation of subeditors responsible for letters *A, I, J, N, O, P* and *W*. His final resignation as editor, however, did not prevent him from contributing to the project by providing citations for the dictionary until his death in 1910 at the age of 85.

> He has been by far the most voluminous of our 'readers', and the slips in his handwriting and the clippings by him from printed books, and from newspapers and magazines, form a very large fraction of the millions in the Scriptorium,

said James Murray of Furnivall. Furnivall did not see the completion of the project and died before the appearance of the last fascicle of the dictionary. In 1876, he persuaded James Augustus Henry Murray (1837–1915) to work part time for the project, which not only ensured the continuation of the project but turned to be a significant decision, making for its eventual success.

During the 1870s, the Philological Society was somewhat concerned with the publication of its dictionary. Although sample pages of the dictionary were printed by publishers, no publication agreement was reached. In 1876, Macmillan approached Murray and discussed the likelihood of compiling a standard English dictionary with the aid of the materials the Philological Society collected, but the negotiations came to a halt. Furnivall started his contact with the Oxford University Press and discussed issues relating to the publication of the dictionary of the Philological Society. In 1877, in his capacity as president of the Philological Society, Sweet sent a formal letter to the Oxford University Press and gave a clear articulation of the compilation of the dictionary. At the same time, the Cambridge University Press was also approached. In 1879, after two years of contact, a publishing agreement was reached between the Philological Society and the Clarendon Press. The dictionary was to be published as interval fascicles over a period of ten years, with the final form in four 6400-page volumes. On February 1, 1884, the unbound fascicles began to be published under the title of *NED*. That date was over 20 years later than Coleridge's prediction of only two years before its debut. By that time, several well-renowned contributors, such as

The European philological traditions 139

Coleridge, Guest, Malden and Key, had all passed away. They did not see the dictionary come out, and neither did Murray.

With the publication of the last fascicle on April 19, 1928, the compilation of *NED* came to an end. Regretfully, Murray died in 1915, 13 years prior to the publication of its last fascicle, when its compilation proceeded to letter *T*. Murray kept sending manuscripts to the publisher for 33 consecutive years in his 78-year lifetime and edited 7207 pages, almost half of the entire dictionary (Ramson, 2002:2). Facts proved that it was wise and farsighted for Furnivall to invite Murray to join in the compiling team and recommend him as his successor. Otherwise, the fate, history and scholarship of *NED* would have to be rewritten, most probably presenting a completely different picture. In 1933, when *NED* was reprinted in its 12-volume edition and with the new title of *OED*, its connections with the Philological Society came to an end. The plan for *NED* signified the birth of the historical paradigm for British English lexicography, and the publication of *OED* became a forceful testimony of its successful implementation in English dictionary-making.

5.4 *The Oxford English Dictionary* – an epic of inheritance, innovation and perseverance

Among the members of the Unregistered Words Committee, Trench was certainly the founder of *NED*. However, he was not directly involved in its compilation, as his Church of England appointment as Dean of Westminster would not allow him to devote as much time as the project required. Therefore, he decided to withdraw, and Coleridge, the secretary of the Committee, took the responsibility of pushing the project forward. In 1859, Coleridge was formally appointed to become technically the first editor of *NED*. Coleridge received his education in Eton and Oxford, and his zeal for philology led him into the Philological Society and made him a member on the Unregistered Words Committee. Unfortunately, he died in 1861 at the age of 31. His deathbed was covered with books and slips of quotations.

The dictionary Coleridge planned was "a tripartite work that was far broader than that actually produced and which in some ways recalled an older tradition". It would consist of "a section devoted to mainstream language, which would include provincialisms, dialect, slang, Americanisms, and colonialisms" and a second part that "concentrated on technical and scientific terms, as well as the proper names of people and places", while the third offered an "Etymological Appendix". He "also called for the inclusion of 'every word in the language, for which sufficient authority, whether printed or oral, can be adduced" (Green, 1996:367). Numerous volunteers were mobilized and participated in word hunting and slip quotation, and numerous citation cards were sent to the Unregistered Words Committee.

140   *The European philological traditions*

Coleridge initially designed 54 pigeon-hole spaces for 100,000 cards, but that number rose to 2,500 by 1911; citation cards amounted to 5 to 6 million and about one-fourth of them were directly used in the compilation. Coleridge proposed some new ideas. The most noteworthy was the innovative adoption of spoken materials in the making, which went straight against the traditional way of thinking that laid almost exclusive focus on written literature. However, some modern scholars hold that his ideas of compilation did not get out of the conventional shackles, meaning that *OED* would never be what it is today if it had been compiled in the way Coleridge mapped out. Upon his death, Coleridge had his last words that Furnivall would take over the work and oversee its completion. That year, Furnivall was only 36.

Furnivall had good education and studied in several private schools, London University College and Trinity Hall, Cambridge. During his stay in London University College, he became conversant in European philology and its developments. He was particularly keen on the study of early English literature and was the founder of the Early English Text Society, the Chaucer Society, the New Shakespeare Society etc. With some of the successful and yet controversial societies, he made remarkable contributions to English literature. He joined the Philological Society in 1847 and acted as secretary from 1853 till his death. In 1857, he worked together with Trench and Coleridge to form the Unregistered Words Committee. He became a member of the British Academy in 1902 and vice president of The Spelling Reform Society in 1907. His manuscripts and writings covered a wide range of areas and left behind him rich scholarly treasures.

On May 23, 1861, Furnivall delivered his first speech in the capacity as editor of *NED* to the Philological Society. After his takeover of the project, he implemented a series of measures to intensify progress and organization. He recruited more volunteers, expanded the range of data collection, increased the sources of citation selection and employed those interested in compilation as assistants.

On February 22, 1910, Furnivall recalled in the *Morning Post*, London,

> In November 1858, Trench wrote us a paper on the duty of making a supplement to the dictionaries of Johnson and Richardson . . . then I said, "People who want a word will first look at Johnson and then at Richardson, and then at ours. Why not amalgamate it and have one dictionary?" I communicated my idea to Trench. He said, "It is a very fine idea if you can carry it out, but I do not think you can." So we went on collecting words.

At the Philological Society meeting on January 7, 1858, a resolution was made that a new dictionary of the English language, instead of a supplement, be compiled under its supreme authority so as to match the status English had built up. Thanks to the extensive influence and appeal of the

The European philological traditions 141

Philological Society, more and more volunteers joined in word hunting and collection and provided an endless flow of word resources so that the smooth progression of the project was ensured.

In November 1858, the Philological Society signed a publishing agreement with Messrs Trübner & Co., which was followed by the publication and promotion of Proposal for the Publication of the *New English Dictionary* by the Philological Society in 1859. The proposal specified the rules and guidelines for data collection and provided a book list for that purpose, emphasizing that dictionaries must include every individual word in English literature and adhere to the principle of diachronism. Apparently, an idea of Furnivall's changed the initial intention of the Philological Society and the original cause of the project and entailed the formulation and implementation of the proposal for compiling *NED* on the historical principle.

It can be assumed, without exaggeration, that *NED* might have run aground if Coleridge had not chosen Furnivall and that *NED* might not have achieved today's glamour and glory if Furnivall had stuck to the old cause set by Coleridge. After Coleridge's death, Furnivall worked as the second editor overseeing the compilation of *NED* for nearly ten years. He once claimed that the project would be accomplished within five years. In March 1862, he proposed the initial compilation of a concise dictionary, which he believed would conduce to the completion of the whole project, and he made a promise to the publisher that it would take merely three years to complete. However, as a rule, a concise edition of a dictionary is very often derived from an unabridged edition. After a few setbacks, the plan for compiling a concise dictionary had to be abandoned, and *The Concise Oxford English Dictionary* did not come out until 1911.

Despite the huge amount of energy, confidence and self-dedication Furnivall put into the project, the compilation of *NED* almost came to a halt in the early 1870s. Volunteers began to diminish in number, and the Philological Society no longer paid as much supportive attention as previously to the project so that no progress report was published as it was annually. Furnivall admitted that almost no progress was made and that there was no need to publish new reports. At a 1868 meeting of the Philological Society, the then president Ellis hinted that the society would only prove equal to word and citation collection rather than dictionary-making. Ellis also thought, in the eye of the Philological Society, Henry Sweet, rather than Furnivall, would make an ideal editor for *NED*. "Furnivall lacked the patience and the perfectionism to make the ideal editor of what he termed 'the Society's Big Dictionary,' but no one could have rivaled his perseverance" (Green, 1996:381). Enthusiasm, confidence, dedication and perseverance were all the fine qualities and spiritual values Furnivall left to the Philological Society and his successors and are what are needed professionally and spiritually in modern lexicographers to guarantee the success of dictionary-making projects.

142   *The European philological traditions*

From the early 1870s, Furnivall started to look for ideal editors for *NED*. He recommended three candidates, and the Philological Society settled on Henry Sweet, who turned down the offer. Henry Nicol (1845–1880), the second candidate, French philologist and Henry Sweet's nephew, accepted the offer but could not afford the time and energy the project demanded due to his poor health and other engagements. Persuaded by his ten-year assistant editor George Wheelwright (c. d1813/1814–1875), Furnivall came to realize the seriousness of the issue and determined to invite James Murray, who was already a member of the Philological Society and was teaching as his profession. From 1875 onwards, Furnivall kept lobbying the Philological Society to appoint Murray as editor and tried to negotiate with the publishers.

The fact that the dictionary would be a huge project made the Philological Society somewhat concerned about its publication. Sample pages were already made by several publishers, but no publishing agreements were reached. Negotiations continued for two years on the part of Sweet, Furnivall and Murray. While the Oxford University Press was still uncertain about whether to accept its publication, Furnivall went up to meet them, promising that the then president of the Philological Society Murray would be its next editor, that nearly 400 volunteers were doing word hunting and collection and that the dictionary would bring huge profits for the publisher. In 1878, Murray was formally appointed as editor, and on February 7, 1879, the Oxford University Press agreed to sign the publishing contract and to give Murray a rewarding payment of 175 pounds.

It was agreed that the dictionary would be published in the form of fascicles, but the final dictionary would appear in four volumes consisting of altogether 6,400 pages. It would take ten years to complete. When all was set, Furnivall resigned from his titular editorship. He did not even edit a single entry, but

> there were few who doubted that his importance to the work was enormous . . . he contributed some 30 000 quotations to the finished work, making him one of the leading collectors. Nor did he stop. Only months before his death, he was still scanning the press for new words, cutting and annotating and forwarding his discoveries to Murray.
>
> (Green, 1996:382)

William Alexander Craigie (1867–1957) and Charles Talbut Onions (1873–1965) said in the preface to the 1933 single-volume *Supplement*, "Through his early organization of the collecting and sub-editing, and his lifelong contributions, the work of Furnivall pervades every page of the Dictionary, and has helped in a great degree to make it what it is".

Murray was born of a draper's family and was "a precocious child with a voracious appetite for learning". He took a teaching post at seventeen in Hawick Grammar School. He was keen on languages and etymology and

The European philological traditions   143

was claimed to be conversant in major modern European languages. His publication of *The Dialect of the Southern Counties of Scotland* (1873) contributed considerably to his reputation in philological circles. By 1869, he was on the council of the Philological Society and by 1873 had quit his administrative job at the Chartered Bank of India. He became a teacher again at Mill Hill School.

On April 26, 1878, an invitation from Oxford brought Murray before the delegates of Oxford University Press, and, almost a year later, a formal agreement was reached between the two parties so that Murray was to become the editor of *NED*. The first thing Murray did after his takeover of the work was collect the slips that the Unregistered Words Committee gathered, especially those that scattered in various parts of the UK and even the world when Furnivall took charge of the work, and it was saddening to discover that some slip pigeonholes became the comfortable homes for rats. The slips that were collected and sorted out were stored in 1,029 pigeonholes, and, at the same time, over 2,000 volunteers from different parts of the world kept sending slips of citations to Murray and his team. Some volunteers worked for 15 successive years, and one volunteer sent over 165,000 slips (Krache, 1975:22).

During the early stage of the compilation, Murray had to work in his extremely crowded house, where more than three million slips weighing over two tons were piling up. A corrugated-iron shed, which was called "the Scriptorium" and nicknamed "Scrippy" by his family, was set up in the backyard of his house on the premises of Mill Hill School to accommodate the compiling team, his two daughters and four assistants and the numerous slips that were flooding over to him as a result of his appeal. In his dictionary, "Scriptorium" was defined as "a writing-room; spec. the room in a religious house set apart for the copying of manuscripts". In the summer of 1884, Murray, along with his family, moved to north Oxford, where another "Scriptorium" was built in its back garden, with more storage space for the slips that kept flowing in to "Mr Murray, Oxford". A blue plaque was installed in 2002 in honour of him on the pillar box at 78 Banbury Road, Oxford, where Murray resided. He remained the primary editor from 1878 to his death.

In collecting and classifying the slips gathered under Furnivall's charge, Murray discovered that the majority of them concentrated on rare and interesting words rather than common words. New appeals were sent out through bookshops, libraries and newspapers for volunteer readers to provide citations of common, rare, obsolete, outdated and eccentric words, and to continue with the collection of new resources and the hunting for new words. He invited Professor Francis March (1825–1911) – American philologist, lexicographer and chairman of English language and comparative philology at Lafayette College in Pennsylvania from 1857 to 1907 – and put him in charge of such work in North America. Thanks to his enormous efforts, data collection and word hunting were again on the right track, with

144   *The European philological traditions*

about 1,000 slips being delivered to the team. By 1882, the slips totaled 3,500,000.

Murray, together with his team, worked day and night, chained themselves to the compilation for 16 hours a day. However, after five years, their compilation went just as far as *Ant* in letter *A*, and almost 27 years had elapsed before the first fascicle covering *A* to *Ant* finally came out on February 1, 1884, with the full title proposed by Murray – *A New English Dictionary on Historical Principles; Founded Mainly on the Materials Collected by The Philological Society*. The first fascicle ran to 352 pages, and around 4,000 copies were sold at a price approximating to 250 pounds today. In order to ensure the smooth progression of the project, he gave up his teaching post in 1885 and became fully engaged in the compilation of *NED*.

In 1886, Henry Bradley (1845–1923) was employed as an assistant in editing letter *B* so as to prepare him for full editorship. Bradley was born of a humble farmer's family, but, in his adolescence, he had already familiarized himself with several languages of Classical learning, and he was said to have learned Russian in only 14 days. He spent quite a long time working for a cutlery firm in Sheffield. In addition to *The Making of English*, his erudition as a columnist in a weekly literary magazine *Academy* was demonstrated in his review of the first fascicle in February 1884, particularly his challenge of Murray's etymological treatment. His comments were objective, quite to the point and, above all, well-tempered. Murray recognized a worthy peer in him and decided to hire him as assistant editor and as joint senior editor.

Bradley "had little formal education but was a remarkable philologist" (Béjoint, 2010:99). After his succession of Murray as senior editor in 1888, he led his team working on the dictionary in the British Museum. His work earned him the recognition and the titles he deserved, such as honorary degrees from Oxford and Heidelberg, fellowship of Magdalen College and the British Academy, presidency of the Philological Society and one of the founders of the Society for Pure English. By 1894, 11 fascicles were published, almost one fascicle a year, with letters *A* and *B* taking up four, letter *C* five and letter *D* two. In 1895, Charles Talbut Onions (1873–1965), an English grammarian and lexicographer, joined the compiling staff of *NED* at Murray's kind request and began his independent editorial work as its fourth editor with the help of his own assistants in 1914.

Onions was born of a metal designer and embosser's family. He received good education and obtained his degrees at Mason College, the present-day University of Birmingham. He once served as a fellow and librarian of Magdalen College, Oxford and acted as president of the Philological Society from 1929 to 1933. In 1934, he was appointed Commander of the Most Excellent Order of the British Empire and was elected a Fellow of the British Academy in 1938. His dedication and most remarkable contributions to *NED* earned him a series of honorary degrees from the University

The European philological traditions   145

of Birmingham, the University of Oxford and the University of Leeds. His other accomplishments in relation to the Oxford dictionaries include the *Supplement* to *OED* (co-edited with William Craigie, 1933), *The Shorter Oxford Dictionary* (co-edited with William Little) and *The Oxford Dictionary of English Etymology* (1966). Onions died just before the dictionary of 1966 went to press.

Onions came to familiarize himself with lexicography under the influence of A. J. Smith, the headmaster of the King Edward VI Camp Hill School. In 1895, the same year Onions joined the compiling team, the title *OED* was first used unofficially on the cover of the fascicle of *DECEIT* to *DEJECT*, and it then appeared only on the outer covers of the subsequent fascicles. The original title was still the official one and was used everywhere else. In 1911, he published *Shakespeare Glossary*, and, three years later, he assumed independent editorship after Craigie, with the help of his own assistants, compiling the remaining ranges of *Su – Sz*, *Wh – Wo*, and *X – Z*.

In 1897, William Alexander Craigie (1867–1957), a graduate of the University of St. Andrews and a Scottish philologist and lexicographer, joined the compiling team, worked on letter *G* under Bradley's guidance and became the second joint editor and the third editor between 1901 and 1933. Craigie developed a keen interest in Icelandic during his study in Copenhagen, then the centre of Norse philology. He worked as Rawlinson and Bosworth Professor of Anglo-Saxon in the University of Oxford from 1916 and 1925. He lectured on lexicography at the University of Chicago while working as chief editor of the four-volume *Historical Dictionary of American English* (1926) and the twelve-volume *Dictionary of the Older Scottish Tongue* (1931–2002), a project he pioneered but whose completion he did not live to see. He also co-edited with Onions the *Supplement* of 1933. He took pride in quite a few 20th-century American lexicographers, such as Clarence Barnhart, who had attended his lectures.

Murray once predicted that the whole project could be completed by 1896. Unfortunately, it did not go on so smoothly as expected. A series of events happened after 1910 and affected the progress of the project to a considerable extent. Also in 1910, Furnivall died, and, four years later, the First World War broke out, which caused a great reduction in the compiling staff – especially those young members – and a great delay in the work. The compilation proceeded to only letter *T* by the time of Murray's death on July 26, 1915. The unfavourable impacts of those events did not end until the war was over. On May 23, 1923, Bradley died, and, two years later, Craigie accepted an invitation from the University of Chicago to undertake teaching, though he was still involved in the compilation of the project.

Seventy-one years had elapsed before the seed of Trench's original aspirations were sowed in the minds of Furnivall, Murray, Bradley, Craigie, Onions and many others, who endeavoured to turn his aspirations into an ambitious plan and develop it into a dictionary of unparalleled scholarship and world admiration in the history of British lexicography, the last and the

146 *The European philological traditions*

125th fascicle of which went from the entry *Wise* to the end of *W* and came out on April 19, 1928, "44 years after publication of the first fascicle, about 70 years after compilation had started, and exactly 100 years after Webster's main dictionary and almost 200 after Johnson's" (Béjoint, 2010:100).

In 1928, the complete dictionary was republished in ten bound volumes and with three columns on each page, under the full title of *A New English Dictionary on Historical Principles, Founded Mainly on Materials Collected by the Philological Society*. It consisted of 15,487 pages and 252,000 entries, with the defined headwords and sub-headwords amounting to 414,000 and citations running up to 1,827,306. The dictionary was presented as a gift to King George V (George Frederick Ernest Albert 1865–1936) and the then American president Calvin Coolidge (1872–1933). Craigie was conferred the title of knighthood for his outstanding contributions to the dictionary. In 1933, the title *OED* fully replaced the former name in all occurrences in its reprinting as twelve volumes with a one-volume supplement.

Among the major editors, neither Murray nor Bradley lived to see the accomplishment of this great undertaking, but they, along with their assistants and countless volunteers, lived up to the high expectations of the general public and forged with hard labour and sweat the glorious status of the dictionary as an ultimate English authority, which Murray, Bradley and many others were striving to achieve. Its making proves it to be a truly historical dictionary of language, with profound linguistic and philosophical inspirations, immense socio-cultural implications and enormous potential values for future lexicographical undertakings, which has been well summed up by Béjoint (2010:101–110). It reproduces a magnificent historical epic that was written with inheritance, innovation and perseverance and turns over a splendid chapter in the history of world civilization.

5.5 The traditional inheritance and theoretical innovation of other major British English dictionaries in the 19th century

From the mid-18th century, Johnson's dictionary overshadowed his contemporary works, and Johnson became a synonymous substitute for almost all English dictionaries. Likewise, by the mid-19th century, for almost one century to come, the planning and making of *NED* and the appearance and serialization of *OED* drowned their contemporary works and made the publication of even some excellent English language dictionaries almost unknown, but a good number of them are well worthy of our serious attention and study. Apart from such English monolingual dictionaries, for the whole of the 19th century, there were other dictionary types that deserve our explorations.

English encyclopaedic language dictionaries certainly come first. They were a rare species prior to the mid-19th century, but two large such dictionaries appeared right in the middle and late part of the 19th century, i.e.

The Imperial Dictionary of the English Language: A Complete Encyclopedic Lexicon, Literary, Scientific, and Technological (1847–1850) by John Ogilvie (1797–1867) and *The Encyclopædic Dictionary – A New, Practical and Exhaustive Work of Reference to all the Words in the English Language, with a Full Account of their Origin, Meaning, Pronunciation, History and Use* (1879–1888) by Robert Hunter (1823–1897). Second, among bilingual dictionaries, fewer English-Latin dictionaries were compiled, while bilingual dictionaries of English and modern European languages mushroomed, such as combinations of French, Spanish, German, Italian, Russian and so on. Obviously, the countries that had those languages were strong powers in Europe. Third, a great deal of serious attention was paid to dialectal studies and dialect dictionaries, and quite a few high-quality dialect dictionaries appeared, covering all the major dialects spoken in important regions of Europe, and became an attractive highlight in the 19th-century English lexicography. Fourth, a succession of slang dictionaries, quotation dictionaries and etymological dictionaries were published, with slang dictionaries being the most influential upon later generations of compilers. Finally, there occurred for the first time in the history of British English lexicography a dictionary of synonyms, which nevertheless turned out to be well developed in both structure and contents, leaving behind it valuable experiences in the making of this type of dictionaries and setting up a role model for later compilations.

Let us discuss Charles Richardson's (1775–1865) English monolingual dictionary first. For nearly a century after the publication of Johnson's dictionary, no strong rivals appeared until Richardson's *A New Dictionary of the English Language* was published by William Pickering in parts between 1835 and 1837. Richardson, a philologist and lexicographer, started a legal career in his early life but abandoned it for scholarly and literary pursuits and then took up an English teaching post. His *Illustrations to English Philology* (1815) contained a critical examination of Johnson's dictionary demonstrating his extensive, profound and yet hostile insights about his dictionary as well as dictionary-making. It was reissued in 1826.

In the preface to his dictionary, Richardson stated in a more-or-less complacent way that no one could compile a genuinely English dictionary unless he chose a course different from the steps Johnson had set. Three years later, the opening portions of his lexicon appeared in the alphabetical order in volumes 14 to 25 of *Encyclopædia Metropolitana* (1818–1845). In 1834, he issued the prospectus of a new English dictionary, and the result was a revised, augmented and heavily etymologically oriented republication of his lexicon, entitled *A New English Dictionary* (1836–1837), with copious quotations from the best English writings, which reduced definitions to a less important position. These ideas originated from his mentor, politician and philologist John Horne Tooke (1736–1812), who believed that word histories reveal the most primitive meaning, including all the significations and those of its derivatives. (See also Zgusta, 1971:599.) "Richardson also

148   *The European philological traditions*

believed that the etymologist's or lexicographer's task is to locate similar words, usually in the same language, from which the full meaning of the word could be derived", and "etymology offered an organic theory of language" (Reddick, 2009:174).

With those compiling principles in mind, Richardson provided basically no definitions but quoted extensively from the works of the best authors from 1,300 up to his lifetime, thus preserving a huge amount of literature and language data for later researchers and compilers. All quotations were examples of word meanings and usages over different periods of time. His countless quotations surpassed all previous works of a similar nature. However, he was severely criticized by Noah Webster for his principle of treating etymology, especially for his ignorance of oriental languages. Despite the fact that it contained obvious technical defects, particularly problems with compiling styles and treatment of definitions that hardly accommodated user needs and the fact that the compiling prospectus doomed it impossible for it to become a well-received work, the dictionary was commended by such popular magazines as the *Quarterly Magazine* and the *Gentlemen's Magazine* and was the only one Trench endorsed as the most excellent in his lifetime. An abridged single volume edition, which was devoid of quotations, came out in 1839, with a new preface but uncorrected.

In 1867 James Donald compiled *Chambers Etymological Dictionary*, which received considerable recognition after its publication and was reprinted several times. In 1872, W. & R. Chambers published *The Chambers English Dictionary*, in fact an augmented version of his previous etymological dictionary. Its second edition was published in 1898, followed by its compact edition of *Chambers Twentieth Century Dictionary* in 1901.

The 19th century becomes noteworthy also owing to the publication of two English encyclopaedic dictionaries – *The Imperial Dictionary of the English Language* and *The Encyclopædic Dictionary. The Imperial Dictionary of the English Language* was an augmentation of the second edition of Noah Webster's *American Dictionary* (1841) and was edited by Rev. John Ogilvie (1797–1867) and published by W. G. Blackie and Co. of Scotland in two large volumes between 1847 and 1850, followed by a supplement volume in 1855, thus a substantial increase in word coverage from Webster's 70,000 to over 100,000, which included words from science, technology and the arts; much British usage omitted in Webster's dictionary; an unusual number of provincial and Scottish words; well-selected quotations and encyclopaedic information for many words and over 2,000 exquisite woodcut illustrations. It was the first significantly illustrated dictionary after Bailey, setting the trend that continues today.

In the last days of his life, Ogilvie was still revising his dictionary, but he did not complete his revision before he died, and the work was taken over by Charles Annandale (1843–1915), who published a revised and expanded

The European philological traditions 149

four-volume edition between 1882 and 1883, with over 3,000 pages, about 130,000 entries and 1,000 more illustrations than the first edition. The number of words covered in this edition was not very impressive by today's standards, but it was the largest English dictionary existent then. This edition went through numerous printings in various forms well into the 20th century. The most conspicuous of all revised and enlarged versions was published in 1897.

In 1883, The Century Company acquired rights to Annandale's 1882–1883 dictionary and adopted it as the basis for a much larger American work — *The Century Dictionary and Cyclopedia* (1889–1891). A good number of derivatives stemmed from *The Imperial Dictionary of the English Language* even in the 19th century, such as *The Comprehensive English Dictionary, Explanatory, Pronouncing, and Etymological* (1863); *The Students' English Dictionary, Etymological, Pronouncing, and Explanatory* (1865) and *The English Dictionary, Etymological, Pronouncing, and Explanatory, for the use of Schools* (1867). Only four years into the 20th century, in 1904, an adapted work of the original edition by George W. Ogilvie (1860–1917), called *Webster's Imperial Dictionary*, came out, whose versions and revisions have been issued under various titles, including *Webster's Universal Dictionary* and *Webster's Twentieth Century Dictionary*.

The Encyclopædic Dictionary was the principal English-language encyclopedic dictionary of the 19th century, which was published by Cassell between 1879 and 1888. It consists of seven volumes, surpassing *The Imperial Dictionary of the English Language* in size and considered the largest English encyclopaedic dictionary in Britain then. A great many reprints were issued after its publication and even well up to 1910, under different titles when reissued in America. In making the dictionary, Hunter was assisted by zoology author Henry Scherren and a small team of domestic assistants at his house in Loughton. Its page design and other styles left discernible imprints upon James Murray's *The New English Dictionary*, whose headword arrangements, numbered divisions of definition, senses written in the form of paragraphs and many other aspects of its making can all be traced back to *The Encyclopædic Dictionary*.

Starting from the early part of the 19th century, Latin basically lost its function as a literary and academic medium. In the first half of the century, there were still science reports written in Latin, though mainly limited to the fields of natural science and medicine. The rise of European national languages gradually took the place of the role Latin played. By the end of the 19th century, English had been firmly established as an international language, and its role in international trade and academic exchanges became unparalleled to other major European languages, while French persisted in international cultural exchanges and diplomatic communication. Consequently, compared with other European languages, Latin and French held a conspicuously extraordinary position in the 19th-century English bilingual dictionary-making.

150   *The European philological traditions*

Latin-English dictionaries of this period mainly include Ethan Allen Andrews' (1887–1858) *A Latin-English Dictionary* (1850, another story 1852, see Marello, 2009:87) and Charlton T. Lewis' (1834–1904) and Charles L. Short's (1821–1886) *A Latin Dictionary* (1879). Andrews' dictionary was adapted from German philologist Wilhelm Freund's (1806–1894) *Wörterbuch der lateinischen Sprache* and underwent several revisions. Its final edition was *Harper's Latin Dictionary* (1907). *A Latin Dictionary* was based on Andrews' dictionary through revision, augmentation and adaptation. From it was derived a Latin learner's dictionary – *An Elementary Latin Dictionary* (1891).

Other major European languages involved include French, Spanish, Italian, German and Russian. Representatives of English-French combinations include John Bellows' (1831–1902) *The Pocket Dictionary French-English and English-French* (1891) and Henry Neumann's *A New Dictionary of the Spanish and English Languages* (1802). Neumann's dictionary was published again and again with revisions and enlargements by Baretti, Mateo Seoane y Sobral, Mariano Velázquez de la Cadena and others. The 19th-century English-Italian dictionaries inherited the chief attributes of Baretti's *A Dictionary of the English and Italian Languages* of 1760, which continued its influence for over half a century through revisions and reprints. The new edition of Baretti's dictionary came out in 1854 through considerable revision and augmentation by J. Davenport and G. Comelati, followed by John Millhouse's *A Dictionary of the English and Italian Languages for General Use* (1849, 1853), etc.

Representative of the 19th-century English-German combinations are J. G. Flügel's *A Complete Dictionary of the English and German Languages* (1830) and Felix Flügel's (1820–1904) *A Universal German-English and English-German Dictionary* (1891) translated and adapted from John Francis Davis' (1795–1890) German dictionary (fourth edition). The first English-Russian dictionary that appeared in Britain is Adam Kroll's *A Commercial Dictionary, in the English and Russian Languages with a Full Explanation of the Russia Trade* (1800) – in fact a 60-page English-Russian glossary with Russian equivalents. In the beginning part of the 19th century appeared Michel Parenogo's multi-volume English-Russian dictionary with the title of *A New Dictionary of English and Russian* (1808–1817), the first of its kind, which was based on M. Robinet's *The Great Dictionary English and French* and composed of 1,400 pages and a selection of about 45,000 headwords. In 1838 and 1849, respectively, James Banks published a two-volume *Angliisko-russkii slovar* and *Russko-angliiskii slovar*, which was followed, almost 40 years later, by A. Aleksandrov's two-part collaborative work – *Polnyi anglo-russkii slovar* (1879) as well as *Polnyi russko-angliiskii slovar* (1883/1885). Both hold a significant position in the history of English-Russian bilingual lexicography (Farina and Durman, 2009:108).

Glossaries of English dialectal words began to appear in close succession in the early 19th century for multifold purposes. First, the British have been

The European philological traditions   151

described as having a national complex of nostalgia and have developed a special fondness for rare books and antiques. The lingering memories of those gradually extinct British dialects and regional vernaculars caused by such a complex of nostalgia stimulated the collection of language data by language fans and amateurs, who eventually compiled them into glossaries. Second, various kingdoms existed in ancient Britain, which was not vast in territories but abundant in dialectal resources. As is well known, dialects are usually closed associated with the status, position and pride of the people who speak them. It thus becomes inevitable and necessary that glossaries be made to preserve the precious dialect resources and the cultural memories of different speech communities. As indicated previously, 19th-century Britain was undergoing rapid industrialization and urbanization, which provided favourable conditions for more in-depth research in dialects and paved a smooth way for the making of English dialect glossaries, which would certainly facilitate intercommunity communication. Finally, thanks to the language research findings in the 17th and 18th centuries, the public cognition of dialects and their attitude towards dialects underwent a radical transition from "barbarous language" and "vulgar language" to "social language" and "regional intercourse". The academia and even the religious circles made their efforts to promote dialect research so as to enhance the public interest and understanding of dialects and regional vernaculars. A more important fact was the adoption of dialects in literary writing. William Barnes (1801–1886) went so far as to compose poems in dialects.

Though glossaries of dialectal words mushroomed, many failed to survive through the time and come down to the present day. Only a few may be mentioned here, such as James Orchard Halliwell's (1820–1889) *A Dictionary of Archaic and Provincial Words, Obsolete Phrases, Proverbs, and Ancient Customs, from the Fourteenth Century* (1847), Thomas Wright's *A Dictionary of Obsolete and Provincial English* (1857), Frederick Thomas Elworthy's (1830–1907) *The West Somerset Word-book-A Glossary of Dialectal and Archaic Words and Phrases Used in the West of Somerset and East Devon* (1886) as well as William Barnes' *A Glossary of the Dorset Dialect* (1886).

Halliwell, an English Shakespearean scholar, antiquarian and collector of English nursery rhymes and fairy tales, received his education in Cambridge and published over 60 works. His dictionary of 1847 came out in two volumes, consisting of 954 pages with a coverage of more than 51,000 headwords. Headwords can be easily identified through capitalization, and what ensue are definitions, coupled with indications of regional labels of usage in some entries, usually one or two citations from early writers and concise treatment of etymology. The dissertation "The English Provincial Dialects", which served as a preface, elucidated the origins, boundaries and development of British dialects. Even today, this dictionary remains a precious gem for studies in ancient British dialects. Wright's dictionary of 1857 consisted of 1,039 pages and collected words that were in use prior to the

152   *The European philological traditions*

19th century and were out of use at the time of its compilation, words that had acquired new meanings and uses and words that were only found in regional dialects and vernaculars. The microstructure of Wright's dictionary bears striking resemblance to that of Halliwell's, except that Wright gave indications of grammatical classes after headwords.

More than two centuries had passed before the recognition and acceptance of dialectal words in social intercourse and dictionaries, counting from Skinner's serious research. In "On Some Deficiencies in our English Dictionaries" (1857), Trench insisted, "provincial or local words . . . have no right to a place in a Dictionary of the English tongue", but he regretted the absence of

> many such, which belonging once to the written and spoken language of all England, and having free course through the land, have now fallen from their former state and dignity, have retreated to remoter districts, and there maintain an obscure existence still.

By so doing, Trench factually excluded dialectal words from possible inclusion in dictionaries. In 1873, under the advocacy of Walter W. Skeat (1835–1912) and a few others, the English Dialect Society was established in Cambridge for the purpose of collecting materials for the publication of *The English Dialect Dictionary*, and Skeat became the chief founder and the only president of the society from 1873 to 1896. The society was dissolved in 1897, but the new notions, methodology and principles it proposed for dialectal research were deeply rooted and exerted their far-reaching influence.

By the end of the 19th century, a solid foundation had already been laid for the compilation of English dialectal glossaries and dictionaries, particularly dictionaries of dialectal words in major regions in England, such as southern, western and central England. With the increasing maturity of comparative philology in Europe, the deepening explorations in British dialects, the gradual perfection of compiling techniques and the smooth development of *NED*, appeal had been surging with the passage of time for the production of a large-scale comprehensive dictionary that would distinguish between different types of vocabulary, i.e. core, general, standard and dialectal words. The establishment of the English Dialect Society provided strong organizational support for such a project.

The English Dialect Society published and reissued a great number of bibliographies, glossaries and miscellaneous collections from its founding to its disbandment in 1896, among them valuable dialect materials. In 1884, when Skeat delivered a speech at the annual meeting of the English Dialect Society, he put forward the proposal of compiling a dialect dictionary. Two years later, a fund was launched for the *English Dialect Dictionary*. Abram Smythe Palmer (1844–1917) was appointed interim editor, and simultaneously tens of thousands of volunteers were recruited for the collection of

The European philological traditions 153

materials. Joseph Wright (1855–1930) drew special attention from Skeat for his remarkable accomplishments in dialect grammar and comparative philology. Skeat sent an invitation letter to Wright on June 13, 1887 to formally ask him to act as editor for the dictionary, to which a positive reply was received. The Oxford University Press offered office space for editing and an agreement for publication, but Wright had to take care of all the expenses pertaining to its editing and publishing.

After 20 years or so, Wright's *English Dialect Dictionary* (1898–1905) met its readership. It consists of six volumes (Volume I A-C; Volume II D-G; Volume III H-L; Volume IV M-S; Volume V T-Z; Volume VI a bibliography of dialect works arranged in the order of counties), with a text of 4,700 pages and 70,000 entries, as well as supplementation, bibliography and grammar. Its subtitle is "Being the Complete Vocabulary of All Dialect Words Still in Use, or Known to Have Been in Use During the Last Two Hundred Years". It is the most commendable milestone dialect work that appeared at the turn of the 19th and 20th centuries and has kept its record of being the largest English dialect dictionary so far.

From the late 18th century to the end of the 19th century, several slang dictionaries were published, represented by Francis Grose's *A Classic Dictionary of the Vulgar Tongue* (1785) and John Camden Hotten's (1832–1873) *A Slang Dictionary* (1859). Grose published several books, and the dictionary, which went through three editions until 1796, is the most influential and gives a vivid presentation of words of daily life that were not gleaned in the standard dictionaries of that time and about 9,000 terms that would go unnoticed in academic works. Dictionaries of slang and vulgar expressions in the first half of the 19th century are basically the augmentation, revision or reissuance of Grose's dictionary but, from 1859, that segment of market was almost occupied by Hotten's.

Close to the end of the 19th century, comparative philology and historical linguistics exerted impacts upon slang lexicography and gave birth to historical and comparative slang dictionaries. Several important works were published, such as Heinrich Baumann's *Londonismen* (1887), an English-German comparative slang dictionary, Albert Marie Victor Barrère's French-English comparative *Argot and Slang: A New French and English Dictionary of the Cant Words, Quaint Expressions, Slang Terms and Flash Phrases Used in the High and Low Life of Old and New Paris* (1887); Albert Marie Victor Barrère and Charles Godfrey Leland's (1824–1903) *A Dictionary of Slang, Jargon & Cant* (1889–1890), which integrates slang of British, American, pidgin English, gypsy and other origins under one cover; and John Stephen Farmer's (c. 1845–c. 1915) and William Ernest Henley's (1849–1903) *Slang and Its Analogues* (1890–1904), which is a seven-volume dictionary, "A dictionary, historical and comparative, of the heterodox speech of all classes of society for more than three hundred years. With synonyms in English, French, German, Italian, etc." (see its title page), printed in London for subscribers only with its first edition limited to 750 signed

154 *The European philological traditions*

and numbered copies and an abridgement appearing in 1905, representing many improvements in English slang lexicography.

By the 19th century, Macdonnel's *A Dictionary of Quotations* was exerting its continuing influence. After its fifth edition in 1811, several other revised and augmented editions were issued. It was replaced 20 years later, when Huge Moore's *A Dictionary of Quotations from various Authors in ancient and modern languages* (1831) was published. There followed in succession L. C. Gent's *Familiar Quotations* (1852), John Murray's *A Handbook of Familiar Quotations from English Authors* (1853), *An Index to Familiar Quotations* (1854), the British essayist and novelist James Hain Friswell's (1825–1878) *Familiar Words, A Collection of Quotations* (1865), Henry George Bohn's (1796–1884) *A Dictionary of Quotations* (1867) etc.

In the 19th century, the British lexicographers' interest in etymology was kindled and got increasingly intensified as a result of the impacts of Indo-European and Germanic philology and the historical and comparative linguistic approach. Consequently, several important etymological dictionaries were published, such as John Thomson's Etymons of English Words (1826), the etymologist and philologist Hensleigh Wedgwood's (1803–1891) A Dictionary of English Etymology (1859, second edition 1872), Eduard Müller's (also spelled Mueller) Etymologisches Wörterbuch der englischen Sprache (1865), Skeat's four-volume The Etymological English Dictionary (1879–1882) and The Concise Dictionary of English Etymology (1884). Thomson's work contained a lot of things that were unscientific, imprecise and even erroneous. Wedgwood's was a great improvement upon previous compilations and a recognized authoritative reference work over the decade after its publication, until Skeat's replaced its position.

Before the conclusion of this section, something must be said about Peter Mark Roget's (1779–1869) *Thesaurus of English Words and Phrases Classified and Arranged so as to Facilitate the Expression of Ideas and Assist in Literary Composition* (1852), which has exerted profound and everlasting influence upon the making of thesauruses and synonym dictionaries even up to the present day. Roget was born to a Swiss clergyman in England. He received education at the Edinburgh University and graduated in medicine. He became a successful physician, philologist and inventor. During his fellowship in the Royal Society, he served as secretary for over 20 years. He wrote papers on a wide range of topics, such as natural theology and phenology and contributed to several encyclopaedias of the time.

After retirement from medicine in 1805, he spent the rest of his life compiling his *Thesaurus*, partly as an effective therapy for his depressive disorder caused by his sadness over the loss of his father and wife. Worked got started in 1805 and completed in 1852. It groups words thematically rather than alphabetically, which is more in line with its function and ease of consultation. What can be seen from its preface is that it was designed as

The European philological traditions   155

a small-scale classified collection of related words, which is then expanded into six categories in the first edition, and those categories consist of subcategories, which are further divided into semantic groups, in which synonyms, near synonyms and semantically related lexical items are collected together. The whole dictionary covers about 15,000 words, thus offering the user a much more creative and subtle means of finding new ways to express their thoughts and enhance their command, creative use and enjoyment of English in composing whatever kind of texts.

Roget's *Thesaurus* was reprinted 28 times in his lifetime. Time and again, it was revised and augmented after his death by his son John Lewis Roget (1828–1908) and his grandson Samuel Romilly Roget (1875–?). Roget's semantic categorization and classificatory spectrum is based on German philosopher Gottfried Wilhelm Leibniz's (1646–1716) philosophical studies and has come down from generation to generation to the present day. His *Thesaurus* ranks as one of the greatest English language reference works. It is the world's most famous and trusted word-finder and the indispensable desk companion for generations of speakers and writers of English. Its sales have now exceeded 32 million copies and, indeed, it has never been out of print since its first publication

5.6 The humanistic and academic values of British English dictionaries in the 19th century

Unlike the 18th century, no substantial monolingual dictionaries were made for the whole of the 19th century, owing to the continuing influence of Johnson's dictionary in the 19th century, the appearance of Richardson's competitive dictionary in the mid-1830s and the plan looming up for making *NED*, which attracted unprecedented attention from the British public, though the actual compilation met with serious setbacks. British scholars, social elites and the general public harboured high expectations for *NED*. They displayed extraordinary enthusiasm and actively participated as volunteers in the collection and assortment of language data, which made the making of *NED* a huge social project unparalleled in the British history.

It can be safely assumed that many things would be entirely different without this monumental work and the notions and approaches it generated. Studies in English would not be going so much ahead of other major modern languages and would not take such a predominant position in the arena of world languages without it or the ideology, philosophy and research methodology of language that were derived from it. That predominance would belong to *Deutsches Wörterbuchvon Jakob und Wilhelm Grimm*, or Paul Imbs' *Trésor de la Langue Française: Dictionnaire de la Langue du 19e et du 20e siècle* (1971–1994) or even Salvatore Battaglia (1904–1974) and Giorgio Bàrberi Squarotti's *Grande dizionario della lingua italiana* (1961–1990; *Supplements*, 2002). *NED* has remained an immortal milestone in the journey of international scholarship, which has contributed immeasurably

156 *The European philological traditions*

to the development of world lexicography, modern linguistics and philology and to some extent human civilization.

The 19th century can be reckoned as a transitional period from prescriptivism to descriptivism in the history of English lexicography. Despite the obstinate tradition of Latin grammar and the extensively influential 18th-century English dictionaries, especially the profound impacts of the leading principle of prescriptivism in Johnson's dictionary, the 19th-centruy lexicographers had come to realize the defects and negative impacts of prescriptivism in dictionary-making and had become keen on European philology, in particular the fresh theories generated from the booming comparative philology and the research methodology stemming from historical descriptivism. Sparks of historical descriptivism kept bursting out, and serious expressions of it were found quite frequently in academic discussions and works and even discovered in newspapers and magazines that targeted the general public.

Literature of European philology demonstrates that Franz Passow (1786–1833) was the first to advocate the principles of historical descriptivism in dictionary compilation. As early as 1812, he published his ideas, strongly upholding the provision of citations in the diachronic sequence so as to illustrate the history of the uses of every word (Singleton, 2000:198). In 1819, he went to such an extent as to propose that dictionary makers should be historians and believe that dictionaries should be able to explain the origins and development of the uses of every word. Dictionaries should show the complete evolutional trajectory of all words and track their changes in pronunciation, uses and significations. That gave a clear indication that European philologists had broken out of the shackles of Latin prescriptivism and come to understand that language would not be fixed in a certain state and would be in a constant state of change.

That point of view was actually discernible from time to time in Johnson's proposal for the making of his dictionary. "We have seen the ways in which Johnson especially, and Richardson to a lesser extent, moved lexicography towards a more empirical and descriptive orientation" (Reddick, 2009:180–181). However, Johnson's dictionary was by nature prescriptive. "One of the ways in which the early *Oxford English Dictionary* lexicographers sought to be pioneering was in breaking free from the prescriptivism of Johnson and the other lexicographers who had followed him" (Brewer, 2006:41).

Trench defined an ideal dictionary as a treasure house of word description and lexical exposition. He stated, "It is no task of the maker of it to select the *good* words of a language. If he fancies that it is so, and begins to pick and choose, to leave this or to take that, he will at once go astray. . . . He is a historian of it, not a critic". He insisted that historical descriptivism would be a guiding principle for making *NED*. The establishment of such a compiling principle certainly landed *NED* on a new historical starting point and elevated it to a new theoretical height, laying a solid theoretical

The European philological traditions 157

foundation for NED to become an immortal monument for the studies and development of world languages – especially English – and modern linguistics.

There are generally three ways of arranging senses in dictionaries, i.e. in their historical sequence, according to their frequencies of use and in their logical order. Historical ordering did not originate with *NED*. It was adopted in Passow's *Handwörterbuch der griechischen Sprache* (1819–1924), which was a revised version of John Gottlob Schneider's (1750–1822) dictionary and exerted dominant influence upon Henry George Liddell's (1811–1898) and Robert Scott's (1811–1887) *Greek-English Lexicon Based on the Work of Franz Passow* (1845), "the product of nine years' work" and "generally seen as an exemplary piece of lexicography" (Green, 1996:364). Even in Britain, historical ordering could be occasionally found in Bailey's work, but it was used more extensively in Richardson's.

> Richardson's dictionary was noteworthy for the clarity with which it displayed related words and word families, and was influential on modern lexicography through its attempts to ascertain etymologies. The diachronic listing of quotations marked a major step towards the study of historical semantics.
>
> (Reddick, 2009:181)

Liddell and Scott stated the notion in the preface to their dictionary, "Our plan has been that marked out and begun by Passow, viz. to make each article a History of the usage of the word referred to". That notion was implemented systematically and scientifically in *NED*, which carried out historical ordering to such an extent as to be impeccable. That ordering objectively reflected the evolutional trace of senses, faithfully depicted the pedigree map of sense development and brought theoretical generalization and methodological construction to a perfect height.

In ancient China, there were two major schools of thought regarding the issue of how "name" and "content" are related, one being represented by Xun Zi (313 BC–238 BC), who proposed the theory of conventionalization, and the other being represented by Liu Xi (c. 160–?), who believed in their natural relatedness. It was Liu Xi's thought that there exist intrinsic connections between "name" and "content" and that this connection between "name" and "content" is realized through the pronunciation of words. Coincidentally, the defining theories in the 18th-century English lexicography were basically based on the classification of the cognition of categories, irrespective of a philosophical perspective or a semantic point of view, trying to seek exemplification from language, base word histories upon speculations concerning language origins and conclude that the primitive meanings of words stemmed from their origins. In the eyes of the 18th- and 19th-century lexicographers, word senses are intertwined with their origins and inseparable from each other.

158 *The European philological traditions*

Bailey attempted to demonstrate the "real" meaning of words through his analysis of their etymology. Johnson inherited Bailey's basic ideas, treated etymology as a workable approach to mapping out basic meanings and identifying real meanings from referential meanings and defined etymologists as "one skilled in searching out the true Interpretation of Words". "Horne Tooke claimed that the etymology revealed the 'primordial meaning . . . compris[ing] all the senses of the word and those of all its derivations', and "his lexicographic disciple Richardson further insisted, 'when the intrinsic meaning is fixed, every lexicographical object is firmly secured'".

Although word origins and senses remained interdependent in *NED*, its compilers endeavoured to explicate senses and their changes through meticulous collection of language data and precise analysis of their transformation in forms and uses. In this sense, *NED* made conscious attempts to separate senses from etymological analysis and turn semantics into a relatively independent field of study with focus on rigid empirical investigation. To some degree, *NED* furnished fertile theoretical soil and abundant empirical preconditions for the birth and development of semantics – especially historical semantics – and historical linguistics. *NED* also provided unparalleled practical experience and methodological reference for later compilations. Prior to *NED*, the great majority of English dictionaries were made single handedly. *NED*, however, was blessed with a strong enterprising team, assisted by thousands of volunteers from almost all parts of the English-speaking world in citations. Volunteers combed through a great variety of literature, including newspapers, magazines, technical books, song lists, cookbooks, opera scripts, government documents and even family wills. They looked into word usage, collected numerous citations and discovered new uses and meanings. In order for volunteers to do citation collection more effectively, the Philological Society, especially Murray himself, revised reading lists several times so as to guarantee detailed, comprehensive and accurate collection of citations.

The most representative picture of *NED* compilation is probably the classic image of Murray standing before a shelf of citations and reading them with absorbed concentration, but behind Murray stood countless volunteers with admirable enthusiasm, perseverance and determination. They made unknown sacrifices to forge *NED*'s glory and constructed networks and modes useful for later data collection and compilations. In December 2010, *NED* launched its new online version, accessible to users by previously unimaginable means. It opens an incredible window for them to enjoy the full-range landscape of more than 1,500 years' history of English and its evolution through internet searches, online reading and interrelations of over 600,000 entries and 3,000,000 citations. It might have been far beyond the imagination of Edwin Guest and his collaborators that their fragmentary ideas eventually created an everlasting scholarly icon of the Philological Society and *NED*.

The European philological traditions 159

Since 1842, the charter of the Philological Society has remained the guiding rules for its operation, and the foundations on which its academic research and transactions have been built have remained its basic principles for conducting its academic activities. Even today, it still regards such traditional fields as historical linguistics and comparative linguistics as its major areas of research and continues to publish in relation to modern English structure, its present-day development and regional varieties, in addition to hot and difficult issues in modern linguistic theorization. This strategy of incorporating new elements and developments of English studies in modern times while preserving its research traditions makes it possible for the Philological Society to become the most prolonged, endurable and influential academic body in Britain, which dedicates itself almost exclusively to philological studies and linguistic inquiries.

A careful contrastive analysis of the innovative developments of *NED* and later *OED* and the scholarly activities and theoretical explorations of the Philological Society reveals the fact that, since the very outset up to the present day, the society has remained a valuable and inexhaustible source of ideas, wisdom and theoretical innovation for *NED* and *OED*, just like a research and development centre of a firm, which provides underpinning, motivation and influence, direct or indirect, upon its development and transformation. On the European continent, the glory the German dictionary enjoyed gradually faded away, and the French and Italian dictionaries failed academically and in many other ways to reach the height of *OED*. The absence of such a dynamic, purposefully active and highly scholastic body as the Philological Society might help to explain the reason.

The work on *OED* started over 160 years ago. Since its birth, it has been universally recognized as an authoritative work, a crowning achievement, a culmination of hard work, time and wisdom and a priceless guide to the history, pronunciation, meaning and use of English words that is hardly insurmountable in the foreseeable time to come. Its academic significance and socio-cultural implications have far surpassed its values as a sole cultural product. It has been fossilized as an icon of scholarship, a totem of culture, a signifier of British civilization and a symbol of national identity. Despite criticisms of its failing to collect American words and usages, taboo words and other dissatisfaction, Roy Harris, Britain's lexicographical critic, commented that it was hard to make criticism of *OED*, as what would be discussed was not merely a dictionary but "a national institution".

6 The transformation of lexicographical traditions and the prosperity of British English lexicography

The 20th century underwent radical transformations and, compared with other periods in the history of human civilization, only in that century, they were so complicated and wide-ranging that they involved social, cultural, economic, political, technological, military and many other areas, so pervasive and overwhelming that they shook the foundation of almost every aspect and walk of life and so complicated and profound that their impacts are strongly felt even today. It is surprising that all those fundamental changes took place within such a relatively short duration of time. As some statistics indicate, the world's gross value of production amounted to less than 2 trillion dollars in 1900, and its population only 1.6 billion. However, that soared to 30 trillion by 2000, and the world's population increased to 6 billion. There were only over 40 independent sovereign states in the 19th century, but the member countries of the United Nations had reached 189 by 2000.

The two world wars reshaped the world with a new political structure, the economic depression in the 1920s and 1930s dealt devastating blows to the international communities, the cold-war mentality that dominated international geopolitics for nearly half a century eventually dragged the world into two extremes, the application of computer and internet technologies brought mankind into the age of information and the unprecedented advancements in political, economic, social, cultural and technological fields caused fundamental changes in life, production and ways of thinking and raised living standards and life quality. The ever-changing scientific explorations, convenient and efficient interpersonal communication and all-pervading telecommunication technology enabled people to view the world from a more scientific, comprehensive and objective perspective, to have a better command of sophisticated means to gain knowledge, capabilities and visions that were needed to transform the world and to make better plans for self-development and the progress of the world under the context of globalization.

Early in the 20th century, the British power was declining, but it remained among the most powerful countries in the world, and the rapid rise of the United States created the situation of two English-speaking powers

Lexicographical traditions 161

coexisting in the English world. That determined the evolutional trend of English and its position as an international language in the 20th century. The importance of a language is determined not by its internal structure and attributes but by the extensive and ever-lasting influence of the people who speak it in world politics, economy, culture, science and technology, military strength and so on. Whether a language really has an international position and influence is chiefly decided by whether it can play the special role recognized by major countries and regions in the world.

With the continuing strengthening of British and American economy in the 20th century and their continuous rise of both hard and soft powers in international politics, culture and military force, it was natural for English to be universally accepted as a general international medium of communication for international organizations, international conferences and regional and global collaboration. It also became spread as a second language or foreign language in major countries and regions outside the English-speaking world. English dictionaries, as a significant carrier of the English language, eventually became an extraordinarily outstanding family in the 20th-century world lexicography owing to its solid foundation in the 19th century and its subsequent development. Representative of such foundation and development were the Oxford and the Webster English dictionary series, which were leading the theoretical innovations in dictionary-making and transformations in compiling techniques in the 20th century and even beyond. The emergence and gradual maturity of brand-new areas, such as modern linguistics, cognitive science, information science and computer and internet technologies provided unprecedented theoretical and technological underpinning for dictionary research and making and brought forth new dictionary media and types, such as learner's dictionaries, electronic dictionaries and internet dictionaries, thus achieving revolutionary breakthroughs in lexicographical theories and practice and in technological platforms.

6.1 The social and technological background for the prosperity of British English lexicography in the 20th century

Language is a carrier of culture, and, in a sense, the dictionary is a carrier of language. The dictionary is a cultural product, an outcome of human communication, language development and civilization advancement, which evolves towards perfection with the deepening understanding of language and the progress of human society. Lexicographical culture will not evolve in a vacuum and independently of social civilization and national culture. The progression of social culture is the external motivation for dictionaries to appear and develop, and the social and cultural demand is the direct orientation for dictionary-making and use. Lexicographical culture is an essential component of national culture, and lexicographical development can mirror the historical trajectory of civilization advancement and the ups

162 *Lexicographical traditions*

and downs of a nation. What follows is a survey of social, political and technological factors behind the flourishing of British English lexicography in the 20th century and the historical and actual background for English to develop into an international lingua franca so as to reveal the impacts of social culture upon lexicographical culture and the interactive association between them.

Attempts were made to create an international lingua franca in the first half of the 20th century, and the most representative was Esperanto, which failed to achieve much success. However, the awareness of a common work language for international communication was becoming intensified owing to the establishment of the United Nations and the increasing demand upon international affairs and intercourse. Experience shows that it is unlikely for a language to be accepted by the international community as lingua franca simply because of its structural attributes or convenience of use. The reason why English has become such a medium of communication is not the intrinsic features it possesses but the unrivalled influence of the people who speak it in world affairs.

If English is compared to the Earth, then it can be described structurally in terms of "crust", "mantle" and "centrosphere". Its distribution around the world can be demonstrated by analogy, and so can their interrelated integration. The "centrosphere" is naturally the core, where the "base camp" is situated and English is used as the native and official language. It is represented by Britain, Ireland, America, Canada, Australia, New Zealand, Jamaica, Bahamas, Barbados and Guyana. The "mantle" is an outward extension of "centrosphere", where English is a non-native language that plays a major communicative role or a second language under the multilingual context. Examples of such countries and regions include Sweden, Norway, Holland, Denmark, Kenya, South Africa, Zimbabwe, Malaysia, Singapore, India and Hong Kong, China. It is, to a great extent, the consequence of colonization. The "crust" is the outermost periphery of the English-speaking world, including mainly countries and regions where part of their territories was colonized with English not being used in administration, courts or related areas but as a foreign language taught in schools and as a common language for international communication and exchanges, for example, Japan, South Korea, China and so on. The three layers display the distribution, roles and interrelations of English among major countries in the world and, to some extent, demonstrates the political background and historical track for their formation and development.

From the 16th century onwards, with Britain's overseas colonial expansion and the establishment of the "empire where the sun never sets", colonialism brought English to almost every corner of the world and made it a sun-never-setting language. In the 17th century, industrial revolutions took place in Britain and in America and pushed steam and electrical technologies into wide application, which brought about a great leap forward in economic growth in both countries and gave English an advantage of being

Lexicographical traditions 163

used as a language of international technologies. In the 18th century, the English-speaking territory and population expanded drastically as a result of the inhabitation of the Australian continent, Britain's ruling of Canada, the independence of America from Britain and the pervasive adoption of English in South Africa, western Africa, eastern Africa, southern Asia, southeast Asia and other regions.

Between the end of the 19th century and the beginning of the 20th century, America's economic superiority and political power, along with the establishment of the United Nations in New York after the Second World War, shifted the centre of the world from Britain to America, where the English-speaking people accounted for 70 percent of its population, and that once again speeded up English globalization. Towards the latter half of the 20th century, America's strong position in world politics, economics, science and technology, education, culture and military force further consolidated the foundation of English as an international language. The revolution of computer science in the 1980s and 1990s sent English to another commanding height as an international language of technology, a language of computer technology and of internet communication.

As a language of sophisticated technology, English is a stepping stone to the acquisition of relevant technology and knowledge, and, as a language of international intercourse, it is a travel pass for telecommunication, commerce, tourism and academic activities. In the early stage in Britain, English was the language for developing telegraphy, and operators of international telegrams must speak English. English became the sole choice for international telegrams, which prepared it to be a medium of international wireless communication and telecommunication. In the early stage of transportation industry, telegram cables went hand in hand with railway construction, and railway lines became a roadmap for English expansion. In the field of airline industry, America dominated aircraft technology, manufacturing and services in the initial stage of development. It followed that almost all materials pertaining to that industry were written and circulated in English, and English was bound to be the language for international airline services. With the launching of more and more international airlines, English is now the first-choice language for airline travels across the world. So it is, undoubtedly, in present-day navigation, commerce and academic exchanges.

Currently, English is adopted in over 90 countries as their official and semi-official language and is used as the official or working language of international organizations in non-English-speaking regions, such as the Association of Southeast Asian Nations and the European Central Bank (ECB). Surprisingly, no member states use English as their native language in ECB. According to a survey, 43 percent of the population on the European continent claims to speak English along with their mother tongues. That proportion reaches 89 percent in Sweden, and in the southern region of Europe, such as Spain and Portugal, it gets to 36 percent. According to the statistics by Crystal (2008:424), the native population of English reaches

164 *Lexicographical traditions*

about 400 million. Another 400 million use it as a second language, and about 600 to 700 million learn it as a foreign language.

It is obvious that the status of English as an international lingua franca is ascribable to education and culture. Lack of educational and cultural underpinning will make it impossible to sustain. Since the 1960s, English has become a language of higher education in many countries and regions, including those where English is not an official language. University courses are normally conducted in English in Holland, for example, and it is the same with most of the African universities, where courses are not generally conducted in native languages. Over the past three decades or so, the "crust" has been expanding at an unprecedented speed, and English educationalists and experts have been sent in large numbers from major English-speaking countries, such as Britain, America, Australia and Canada, to the "crust" countries and regions to promote English teaching and learning. As a medium of international communication in education, culture, commerce, tourism and science and technology, English has become a must-learn foreign language in primary and secondary schools in many parts of the world. It is not uncommon for it to be part of preschool education in some countries, such as China, where classes are conducted in English or bilingually in some kindergartens.

English, as a channel of cultural communication, not only plays an instrumental role in education but provides a forceful and yet invisible impetus to the promotion and transmission of British and American culture. Public media, such as newspapers, movies, broadcasts, publications, sports, advertisements, music and even cuisine and delicacies, have all exerted subtle influences upon the transmission of English and intensified its acceptability where it has reached. As a language of journalism, English has got a history of over 400 years. At the turn between the 19th and 20th centuries, nearly 2000 newspapers were published in America, and today the great majority of newspapers are published in English in countries where English is a native language or a major official language (Crystal, 2008:424).

In the 1920s, sound motion pictures appeared in America, and what viewers heard was English. By and by, English became the language for films, television and broadcasts and a fashionable language with the increasing popularity of Hollywood movies. It is still the most frequently used in public media around the world. English publications in the fields of humanities and social and natural sciences take an increasingly large proportion. According to an incomplete statistic, the proportion of English publications of humanities and social sciences increased from 66.6 percent in 1974 to 82.5 percent in 1995 and that of natural sciences from 74.6 percent in 1980 to 90.7 percent in 1996 (Mair, 2006:10), though the latest statistics show a slight decline owing to huge numbers of publications in Chinese, Spanish, French and German over the past few decades. All that points to the fact that English has established itself indisputably as a language for international academic communication and exchanges after Latin and French faded

Lexicographical traditions 165

out of the scene. American tycoons, such as KFC and McDonalds in the fast food industry, Coca-Cola and Pepsi in the beverage industry, BBC and VOA in the global mass media and America's sport brand NBA, have all served as strong propellers for the promotion of the image of English-speaking nations and the identity of English as an international lingua franca.

Aside from the social and cultural superiority Britain and America enjoy, the 20th-century British English lexicography also benefited from advancements in science and technology, in particular technological breakthroughs in computer development, information processing and internet and their application to the creation of databases and corpuses and dictionary compilation. Towards the end of the 19th century, Edward Sapir (1884–1939) and other structural linguists laid great emphasis on the natural abstraction of linguistic data and their objective analysis. Importance was also attached to research methodology with corpuses as bases, thus bringing corpus-based approaches into linguistic inquiries. In the 1920s, Edward Lee Thorndike (1874–1949) created a language databank consisting of 4.5 million words for the purpose of compiling a hierarchical list of English vocabulary to assist in English pedagogy.

The appearance of the first computer in America in 1946 brought digitalized linguistic databases into existence, typified by Randolph Quirk's Survey of English Usage (SEU) in the 1950s, the Brown Corpus (BC) in America in the 1960s and the Lancaster-Oslo/Bergen Corpus (LOB) in Britain in the early 1970s. There was a gradual expansion of scale and intensification of functions with manual keyboarding being upgraded to optical character recognition (OCR). The application of Longman/Lancaster corpus in the 1980s and Cobuild corpus to the making of *LDCE* and *Collins Cobuild Dictionary of the English Language* (1987) was a pioneering attempt and a role model for corpus employment in dictionary-making. Thanks to the popularization of word processing software and desktop printing systems, the mushrooming super corpuses that are represented by British National Corpus have developed into powerful platforms for language research, natural language processing and dictionary-making in the 21st century. The integration of information processing, corpus and internet technologies has given rise to multimedia dictionaries, such as electronic dictionaries and internet dictionaries.

The application of information processing technology and corpuses has caused revolutionary transformation in the art and craft of dictionary-making, which has exerted radical impacts upon data collection, assortment and retrieval as well as information processing, storage and transmission. In fact, it has affected every aspect of dictionary-making and made manual cards, scripts and look-ups history in lexicography. It has substantially shortened the cycle of dictionary-making and revision and improved the efficiency of dictionary-making and information consultation as well as the precision of lexical information, citation selection, frequency counting and usage check. The inclusiveness of present-day corpuses and technological

166 *Lexicographical traditions*

means of corpus development are helping to deepen human cognition of language, intensifying their capabilities of language understanding and processing and in one way or another exerting influence upon the ways they think and behave.

6.2 The linguistic and academic background for the prosperity of British English lexicography in the 20th century

Behind the prosperity of dictionary-making in any language always are hidden deeply rooted social, cultural and academic factors. In the previous section, discussions are conducted in relation to the socio-cultural causes for the prosperity of British English lexicography in the 20th century, and this section will make explorations in linguistic and academic rationales with a view towards further revealing the interactive links of socio-cultural transformation to changes in English and the flourishing of British English dictionaries.

Over the period of modern English, especially after the entry into the 21st century, English structure and grammar have basically become stabilized. English has developed into an analytic language in its true sense. However, due to international political turmoil, economic ups and downs, socio-cultural changes and technological innovation and upgrading, English continues to undergo changes in vocabulary power and lexical usage. Changes are even more obvious in its scope of use, fields of intercourse, population size and levels of employment. As a result, its international impacts have also been on the rise. Vocabulary is the most active component of language that demonstrates in the most straightforward manner its changes with the passage of time. In 1755, Johnson's dictionary appeared in only two volumes and with a coverage of only 42,773 headwords, but there were 10 volumes and over 400,000 headwords when the first edition of *OED* came out in 1928 and 20 volumes and over 500,000 headwords when the second edition was printed in 1989. It is estimated that the third edition will appear in the electronic and online versions rather than in its print form due to its massive size. Its lexical coverage will exceed 600,000, which is a good testimony of English lexical enlargement since the 1990s.

Motivations for changes in language can be found not only in its internal mechanism of self-regulation but also in external forces that may trigger them. Both internal and external causes may interact with each other and work interdependently. No substantial changes have been observed in the internal mechanisms of English lexical evolution in the 20th century, and conventional ways of word building, such as compounding, derivation, backformation, conversion and borrowing, continue to play a predominant role. However, inducing factors are extremely varied and difficult to predict, and they are the major external forces that incite lexical changes and dramatically expand English vocabulary. Throughout

Lexicographical traditions 167

the 20th century, international politics experienced turmoil and constant changes. Significant events took place in succession, which may still exert extensive and profound influence upon the material and spiritual life of mankind. New notions, new thinking, new technology and new things added numerous lexical items to the English lexicon. The two world wars, along with subsequent local wars, arms races and military technological advances that ensued, tremendously transformed world political, economic and social situations, giving rise to war-related words and terms, such as *air raid, dugout, gas mask, periscope, tank, appease, blitz, jeep, parachutist, shelter, task force, barrage, camouflage, hand grenade, jungle war, sector* and so on.

The innovation and progress in science and technology in the 20th century is unparalleled in the history of mankind. New fields were created and expanded, and new technologies and inventions mushroomed. Consequently, numerous technical terms appeared, such as *ecology, bionics, cybernetics, pragmatics, transistor* and so on. Some are now in everyday use, for example, *rocket, computer, spacewalk, internet, clone, ecommerce* etc. Some have acquired new uses and meanings. "Memory", for example, has extended to mean "the part of a computer where information is stored", and "mouse" "a small device that is moved by hand across a surface to control the movement of the cursor on a computer screen". Technological innovation and progress have been the main motivations for the rapid enlargement of English vocabulary, particularly the emergence of new words in the 20th century.

Another major cause is transformations in international politics, economics and cultural life. The 20th-century international politics, for instance, left behind quite a few political terms, such as *gestapo, lebensraum, Bolshevik* and *Kremlinology*, as well as terms that were derived from world-renowned political figures, e.g. Tony Blair (1953–) and Bill Clinton (1946–), and went into popular use, such as *Clintonian, Clintonism, Clintonomics, Clintonite, Clintonise, Blairism, Blairite, Blairification* etc. In addition, cultural exchanges, trade and commerce and environmental activities also created new words or developed new meanings for existing words, such as *rock and roll, Mickey Mouse, motel, hippies, ecofriendly, subhealth, client* etc. In order to strengthen expressive power, it was not uncommon for identical or similar things and ideas to be expressed in different words. For instance, nearly 50 words and expressions were developed over the first half of the 20th century to denote "drunken", e.g. *ginned* (1900), *ossified* (1901), *pot-eyed* (1901), *shellacked* (1905), *piped* (1912), *illuminated* (1926), *shit-faced* (1940s), *sloshed* (1950s) etc. Most of the existing words acquired new meanings via metaphorical extension, some by means of affixation, and others by changing their stylistic colouring. The need to express is a determining factor that catalyses the birth of new vocabulary and expressions and of course through such ways of word formation as abbreviation (e.g. *TV*), blending (e.g. *smog*), compounding (e.g. *crop circle*), derivation

168 *Lexicographical traditions*

(e.g. *worker*) and borrowing (e.g. *limousine, kungfu*). All these new words and new meanings must be codified and reflected through dictionaries.

Just as the rapid expansion of English vocabulary in the 20th century created preconditions for the making and updating of English dictionaries, so the development of linguistics in the 20th century provided greater theoretical space and more solid foundation for lexicographical practice. The 20th century was an era for new linguistic theories, with existing theories being questioned and challenged and new ones being put forward one after another. There was an obvious turning from the diachronic and comparative description of language to its structural description and from structuralism characterized by the analysis of inherent components of language system to cognitivism marked by the explanation of the transformational generative mechanisms of language use for the purpose of disclosing the attributes of human mind. In addition to improving themselves, modern linguistic theories have pushed forward the development of related disciplines and their branches as well as other disciplines so that they become better covered and identified in types, better developed and structured in form and better substantiated and ameliorated in connotation. As a special branch of linguistics, lexicography undoubtedly draws what is needed for self-development from linguistics and more conventional subjects, such as phonetics, grammar, lexicology, philology etc. It is especially worth noting that branches of modern linguistics, such as semantics, pragmatics, stylistics, structural linguistics, descriptive linguistics and cognitive linguistics, furnished strong theoretical support and methodological guidance for lexicographical generalization and practice in the 20th century.

Explorations were conducted in the introduction for the purpose of tracing linguistic contributions to the evolution of English dictionary paradigms, with focus on major influences of traditional linguistics, historical linguistics and descriptive linguistics upon English dictionary-making. Further explorations are to be made here to demonstrate the direct and extensive impacts of English grammar, semantics, pragmatics and stylistics upon English dictionary-making and research in the 20th century. It is the theoretical contributions of those branches of modern linguistics that made the 20th-century English dictionaries, especially learner's dictionaries, unique and distinctive from previous periods in methodology, compiling techniques, structural organization, defining modes, information option and other aspects.

Let us first explore how English grammar affected the making of English dictionaries. Out of practical needs of orthography and English standardization, compilers of the 18th and 19th centuries tended to pay more attention to the forms and basic meanings of words. However, the 20th century presented a completely different picture of grammatical description in English dictionaries. For the first time, Hornby's *The Oxford Advanced Learner's Dictionary of Current English* introduced English grammar in a systematic way into an English dictionary. The reason for this was that English grammarians in the early 20th century, such as George Oliver Curme

Lexicographical traditions 169

(1860–1948), Otto Jespersen (1860–1943) and Harold Edward Palmer (1877–1949), paved a smooth way for his endeavour and that he himself conducted a great deal of relevant research and experiments overseas. In the latter part of the 20th century, the treatment of grammatical information was considerably improved and heightened owing to the monumental work *A Comprehensive Grammar of the English Language* (1985) by Randolph Quirk, Sydney Greenbaum, Geoffrey Leech and Jan Svartvik.

In the front matter of *LDCE* (1978), there was a separate section, "Grammar in the Dictionary", which was exclusively devoted to the treatment of grammar and an unambiguous expression of the compilers' attitude towards how grammar should be treated in the dictionary. It was their view then that grammar is nothing more than an additional or appended part in the dictionary. That was also the way most of the previous compilers looked at grammar in the dictionary. However, a radical change of attitude was adopted towards grammar in the 1987 edition of the dictionary, which is obvious even from the section title "Grammar and the Dictionary" and its coordinate rather than subordinate structure. The structure of the title implies a change of the subordinate position of grammar in the dictionary, puts it in a parallel position with the neighbouring disciplines of lexicography and recognizes its status as an indispensable component of the dictionary. Judging from scientific, systematic and practical points of view, the new edition of 1987 is extraordinarily outstanding in its grammatical treatment and annotation, which is marked by the continuation of previous practices, their improvement as well as innovations according to user needs, such as the substitution of tedious notes by codes, the marking of word collocation and the provision of idiomatic usages, discrimination of uses, usage notes and so on.

Word defining lies at the core of dictionary-making and has direct relevance to dictionary quality. Traditionally, a great deal of attention was devoted to "conceptual meaning" in philological dictionaries, as it is a highly generalized reflection of the world, a basis for human beings to communicate and the essential part of dictionary definition. The challenge that compilers face is how to take due notice of connotative meaning, social meaning, affective meaning, reflective meaning, collective meaning and thematic meaning (Geoffrey Leech, 1981) while retaining their prominence to conceptual meaning. Viewed from the user's perspective, conceptual meaning is the focus of vocabulary acquisition but not the difficult part. Their difficulty lies in the other six types rather than the conceptual type. More often than not, they may cause perplexity, deviations and even obstacles in comprehension. The semantic classification makes it likely for dictionaries to present word meanings in a more comprehensive and orderly manner and for users to be readily guided in the acquisition, employment and configuration of lexical semantics.

Another major contribution of semantics to definition is componential analysis. The theory of "componential analysis" holds that there exist in

170 *Lexicographical traditions*

human cognitive structure linguistic universals and that words, as the basic meaningful unit of language, are where linguistic universals reside. As a result, every lexical item contains a certain number of "features", which are derivable from its semantic decomposition and are used as the basis for analysing similar lexical items. The theory of "componential analysis" enables compilers to define words in a more precise, standard and scientific manner. Owing to the fact that compilers may come from different social, educational and academic backgrounds, discrepancies in lexical interpretation may sometimes occur. There is a lack of due attention to how words should be defined in that way, and the theory creates a set of basic rules to serve as a yardstick for compliers with different linguistic and socio-cultural backgrounds and with different preferences, tastes and styles to follow.

Although doubts have been raised by scholars at home and abroad regarding the feasible application of this theory to lexical definition, and no dictionary has been entirely made on the basis of this theory, the truth is that it has been, consciously or unconsciously, applied to word defining in dictionary-making. It has demonstrated unparalleled advantages in analysing the conceptual meaning of specific items (including some abstract words), explaining six other categories of meaning, discriminating between synonyms and making diachronic semantic explorations. It has opened enormous prospects for the deepening of lexicographical research and the continuous development of computation linguistics.

In 1852, by compiling *Roget's Thesaurus of English Words and Phrases*, Peter Mark Roget created a brand-new dictionary type – thesaurus. His dictionary was not reprinted until 1911, and no new edition came out in the first half of the 20th century. Surprisingly, after the third edition of 1962, revised and augmented editions were published in close succession. By 2000 there were altogether 16 editions, with a total sale of 32 million copies. From the 1970s onward, it induced the publication of quite a few works of similar nature, such as Jerome Irving Rodale's (1898–1971) *The Word Finder* (1947), Laurence Urdang's (1927–2008) *The Synonym Finder* (1961), Tom McArthur's *Longman Lexicon of Contemporary English* (1981) and Stephen Glazier's *The Word Menu* (1997). This dictionary strain was naturally a derivation from accomplishments in semantics, particularly the semantic field theory, which was proposed in 1931 by German scholar J. Trier to describe sense relations and semantic configuration of lexical items. The theory provided a more coherent and scientifically based theoretical framework for the making of thesauruses and synonym dictionaries and added the function of finding synonyms to the traditional philological dictionaries. It thus created a new type of "two-in-one" dictionary with a new compiling mode and a new entry structure that incorporates definitions and synonym lists.

The tradition of prescriptivism sowed seeds of linguistic norms and correctness deep in the minds of language users and led them to think that the correct use of language was a necessary skill in language acquisition and

Lexicographical traditions   171

even that it was all language learning was about. The truth is that correctness in language use does not equate with language learning and that grammatically correct sentences do not necessarily express ideas appropriately. In some cases they may become meaningless. A well-known example is American linguist Noam Chomsky's "Green ideas sleep furiously". In addition, there might be disconnections between sentence meaning and speaker meaning, which shows that it does not suffice to grasp linguistic knowledge and understand how to apply grammatical rules correctly in learning a language. Language users must also be equipped with pragmatic knowledge and competence, i.e. the skills of using a language in an appropriate way and interpreting "speaker meaning", hence the birth of pragmatics.

Pragmatics raises new issues and poses new challenges to dictionary-making, i.e. as a language-learning tool, how the dictionary should take into account pragmatic knowledge in describing language knowledge. The 1978 edition of *LDCE* made no allusion at all to pragmatic issues. Nine years later, the 1987 edition condensed its previous description of grammar, changed its section title to "Grammar and the Dictionary" and added a two-page section about "Pragmatics and the Dictionary". That appeared to be a slight modification but implied a major change of orientation towards pragmatic aspects of lexical use, i.e. the relevance of pragmatics to dictionary compilation and its status in the dictionary, suggesting the compilers' recognition of the special role of pragmatics in English dictionaries.

Pragmatics was then a newly emerging branch of linguistics and was still in its infancy. It was not so full and well developed as grammar, and no systematic attempt had been made to formulate a set of pragmatic rules for compilers to absorb and adopt in their dictionary-making. What was encouraging was that compilers had made empirical researches into English learners' needs and taken wise steps to deal with pragmatic issues through "usage notes", "language notes" and explanations in definitions or before citations. Many issues awaited exploration. If pragmatic knowledge was only scattered and dotted in the 1987 edition of *LDCE* and appeared to be incomprehensive and unsystematic, an entirely different and inspiring landscape unfolded in *Collins Cobuild Dictionary of the English Language*, which was published in the same year. It can safely be assumed that its compilers made the best and fullest use of pragmatic principles to such an extent that every entry and each of its definitions could serve as the best pragmatic note of the headword and each of its lexical uses. They demonstrated, to the greatest possible extent, the penetration of pragmatic principles into dictionary-making and its pervasive and revolutionary impacts.

From the user's perspective, *Collins Cobuild Dictionary of the English Language* has three features that make it distinctive from other dictionaries of similar nature, i.e. information type, information quality and modes of information transmission, which combine to embody the pragmatic spirit in dictionary compilation. Traditionally, almost exclusive attention is paid to the conceptual meaning that is refined and abstracted from the context of

172 *Lexicographical traditions*

actual uses in English philological dictionaries as well as in contemporary English dictionaries similar in nature to *Collins Cobuild Dictionary of the English Language*. The information users glean from their consultation is naturally the decontextualized abstract meaning. In order to get a correct understanding of the individual meaning of a specific lexical item under specific contexts, users have to restore "conceptual meaning" to its original context so as to comprehend what it truly meant.

Collins Cobuild Dictionary of the English Language defines in a way that avoids the previously mentioned detour users have to take in understanding lexical meaning. Instead of highly condensed and abstracted definitions that are numbered in previous compilations, it defines words in paragraphs. That method creates a context that builds up a connection between context and meaning and a continuum for them to permeate into each other, as conceptual meaning is put back into its context. In this way, what users get is not merely conceptual meaning but a complete picture of lexical senses that integrates both conceptual meaning and other meanings. What each entry and each definition describe is a complete and coherent context, thus providing high quality information that is intuitive, stereoscopic, objective and readily understandable. It helps to narrow down and even eliminate the distance between sentence meaning and speaker meaning and avoids possible linguistic and cultural barriers in communication, particularly in cross-cultural communication.

Linguistic variations may arise as contexts, objects and ways of language use differ, and they are the best evidence of language being used in an appropriate way. Stylistics classifies linguistic variations on regional, contextual, functional and other bases. Regional factors classify English into British English, American English, Australian English and other varieties. Contextual factors classify English into oral and spoken English, formal and informal English and other genres. Functional considerations divide English into literary English, journalist English, legal English, commercial English, technological English and so on. Stylistic labelling started to appear in Cawdrey's dictionary, but English lexicographers did not realize the importance of stylistic information until the 1970s, when they tried to cover it as much as possible in their dictionaries, with particular attention paid to regional varieties (e.g. British and American English) and contextual varieties (e.g. formal and informal English, oral and spoken English). Other branches of modern linguistics, such as sociolinguistics, corpus linguistics, cognitive linguistics and so on, have exerted positive and lasting impacts upon compiling modes, notions and methodology, new-type dictionary-making, lexicographical information selection, internal structural organization and presentation, accessible interfaces and media, consultation modes and tools, retrieval paths and contexts and so on. No more discussion will be made here due to already-existing research findings.

Now into the 21st century, there is every reason to assume that English will play a more powerful role on the world stage. A good proof is that,

Lexicographical traditions 173

through heated debate, the French National Assembly passed the bill that proposed English teaching in French institutions of higher learning so as to legalize courses being conducted in English in French universities, though it covered only courses for European or international programs. It marks a significant development in the 21st century for English to be used in previously untrodden areas, and it is certain that future linguistic breakthroughs will provide stronger impetuses for heightened theoretical generalization of lexicography and innovation in dictionary compilation.

6.3 The continuing development and prosperity of British philological dictionaries in the 20th century

As discussed previously, the sound development of European philology in the 19th century laid a solid theoretical foundation for the making and success of *OED* and made the *OED* series the major theme and mainstream of Britain's dictionary-making in the 20th century. The notions, principles and methodology imbedded in conventional European philology exerted tremendous impacts upon the making of diachronic dictionaries in Britain, but 20th-century English lexicography obviously benefited more from modern linguistics, in addition to innovations in theorization and research methodology and increasingly sophisticated science and technology.

Among the 20th-century philological dictionary families, *OED* is undoubtedly a landmark in world lexicography and is the most remarkable, unparalleled and unique accomplishment in English lexicography. It stands like a huge tree, with its trunk well developed in the 19th century. By the 20th century, the tree became robust with luxuriant foliage, thanks to the exceptional advantages Britain's social, cultural, academic and technological environment created for its making and development. According to the *Guinness Book of World Records*, *OED* is the most inclusive monolingual print dictionary in the world. Although publishers claim to have earned no profit, the undeniable fact is that the dictionary has become the most highly reputed brand and an irreplaceable icon of British lexicographical culture.

The continuation of *OED* in the 20th century assumed the characteristics of being serialized, electronized and network-based, with "trunk" (mainstream) and "branch" (derived) dictionaries being developed along parallel lines and even synchronously. When the first edition of the ten-volume dictionary came out in 1928, it retained the title of the first fascicle, but it was formally renamed *OED* in 1933, when it was reprinted in twelve volumes. In the same year, a 866-page single-volume *Supplement*, a joint work by Onions and Craigie, was published "seeking in particular to record the burgeoning volume of technical language relating to both arts and sciences" and also "the varied development of colloquial idiom and slang, to which the United States of America have made a large contribution, but in which the British dominions and dependencies have also a conspicuous share" (preface). It includes words that appeared too late for inclusion in

174 *Lexicographical traditions*

the 12-volume edition, new uses of existing words, a list of spurious words, and a bibliography. The 13-volume edition of 1933 altogether amounted to 16,500 pages. Out of consideration of time and cost, there was no revision and augmentation for nearly 40 years following Onions and Craigie's publication of *Supplement*.

"After what was recognized, with some relief, as a *tour de force*, the publisher hoped to close the Oxford English Dictionary enterprise down" (Brewer, 2009:263). That explains the absence of serious lexicographical activities relating to *OED* for about 20 years. It was not until 1957, coincidentally the 100th anniversary of Trench's delivery of his innovative speech, that Robert Burchfield was appointed editor for a new supplement, which would replace the 1933 single-volume edition and reflect English changes that took place after its publication in Britain and other parts of the world, including "much new information on the language (especially on twentieth century vocabulary) obtained in the intervening years" as well as "considerably more words from North America, Australia, New Zealand, South Africa, South Asia, and the Caribbean", as indicated in "History of the *OED*" on public.oed.com. Burchfield planned to complete the project within 7 years, but the compilation took 29 years. That new *Supplement* came out in four volumes, with the first volume (A to G) published in 1972, the second (H to N) in 1976, the third (O to Scz) in 1982 and the fourth (Se to Z) in 1986.

Burchfield's *Supplement* is substantially longer than the original 1933 edition and consists of 5,730 pages and a collection of 69,300 headwords. In the introduction (under Editorial Policy), he stated that "our aim had been first and foremost to ensure that all common words and senses in British written English of the period 1884 to the present day (of those not already treated in the Dictionary) were included". In addition to words from the previously mentioned regional varieties of English, four areas of vocabulary were specified for inclusion, i.e. literary language, World English, scientific and technical English and colloquial and coarse expressions referring to sexual and excretory functions along with racist terms, slang, colloquialisms and contentious usages. Burchfield's *Supplement* "represents a substantial and significant achievement". His "definitions are precise and lucid, and he treats an extraordinarily wide range of words with admirable thoroughness". However, it contains "inconsistencies and imperfections", such as the failure to put right a good number of mistakes and errors in the first edition, the inclusion of excessive citations and the inclusion of too many obvious lexical collocations (Brewer, 2004, 2007, 2009). It increased the number of volumes of the dictionary to an incredible height of 17.

Work on *OED* and its supplementation, from data collection to compilation, revision and augmentation, was basically done manually, and major data sources were citation cards volunteers sent to the editing team from different parts of the world. In 1982, upon Burchfield's completion of his *Supplement*, the Oxford University Press hosted a debate seminar on how to

Lexicographical traditions   175

bring the Oxford dictionaries into the new era. Participants reached quick consensuses that traditional compiling techniques should be upgraded and that Oxford dictionaries should undergo a transition of medium from paper to electronic means. Led by Timothy J. Benbow in 1984, over 120 text operators, systems engineers and lexicographers, along with 55 proof-readers, worked together on both sides of the Atlantic Ocean to launch "the most adventurous computerization project seen in the publishing industry at that time" to turn "a multi-volume, century-old, print-based reference work" into "a machine-readable resource", "publish an integrated print edition in 1989" and "provide a full, electronic text to form the basis of future revision and extension of the Dictionary". Over five years, 13.5 million dollars were spent to build bespoke computer systems for both pre-processing the text, editing it in electronic form and marking it up in the (then) novel SGML encoding scheme ("History of the *OED*" on public.oed.com). By 1988, the text of *OED* and its supplements was completely digitalized and converted into the CD-ROM version. Compared with the print dictionary, the electronic version had the advantage of being handy, highly compact and cost effective.

In the course of computerization, the New Oxford English Dictionary Project was launched in Oxford by John Simpson and Edmund Weiner, together with a core group of lexicographers for the revision, correction, addition and editing of this new electronic dictionary. "The culmination of this mammoth task was the setting in type and subsequent printing of the *Oxford English Dictionary*, Second Edition". In 1989, the Second Edition, an integrated work of the first edition, the four-volume *Supplement* and over 5,000 newly collected words and senses, was published as scheduled. It comprises 21,728 pages that are bound in 20 substantial volumes, with a total of 59 million words, 291,500 entries, 615,164 defined words and over 2.43 million citations. (See preface.) It was presented to Queen Elizabeth II and was received with wide acclamation by the general public. Its publication was reported by the *Los Angeles Times* as the greatest publishing event of the century and by the *Guardian* as one of the wonders in the world.

In 1992, through joint efforts of both British and Canadian scholars and technicians, *OED* again made history by creating and publishing a CD-ROM edition. "Suddenly a massive, twenty-volume work that takes up four feet of shelf space and weighs 150 pounds is reduced to a slim, shiny disk that takes up virtually no space and weighs just a few ounces" ("History of the *OED*" on public.oed.com). The CD-ROM edition turned out to be a great success and was reputed to be the most advanced and exemplificative of CD-ROM dictionaries. "The electronic format has revolutionized the way people use the Dictionary to search and retrieve information", and "its audience now embraces all kinds of interested readers beyond the confines of the scholarly community" ("History of the *OED*" on public.oed.com). In 1993, *The Oxford English Dictionary Additions Series* was published in two small volumes, followed by a third volume in 1997. That was the last

176 *Lexicographical traditions*

supplement or addition to the dictionary, which heightened the number of volumes to an unprecedented level of 23, with each collecting 3,000 or so new words and new uses.

It was once an issue of common interest and concern whether there would be a third edition of the work. Reports had it that the third edition was under way, with revision and augmentation being done by 80 lexicographers, and that, by March 24, 2011, work had reached Ryvita, with an annual increase of 4,000 to 6,000 new words. According to a news report by the *Telegraph* on January 7, 2011, the Oxford University Press was recruiting volunteers to assist its editors in collecting hot words of high frequency from newspapers, journals, manuals, books and other publications with intent to facilitate the third large-scale revision and enlargement. Its selected sources even included movie and television scripts, recipes, song words and emails, but only new words of over ten-year circulation were eligible for inclusion. John Simpson, chief editor, predicted that the third edition would meet its audience around 2035.

Work on the third edition does seem to be endless, as new words and new uses of existing words continuously pop up every year, and even every day on some special occasions. Authoritative sources even go so far as to speculate that there is no likelihood of the third edition appearing in print owing to its massive size and the increasingly shrinking market for paper dictionaries. Close to the end of August 2010, Nigel Portwood, CEO of Oxford University Press, indicated that the third edition would not come out in print, considering its challenges arising from various electronic devices and the generally presumed lifespan of paper dictionaries, probably only 30 years. No evidence shows, however, that that is finalized. On August 1, 2012, at the invitation of Simpson, 50 world renowned lexicographers, etymologists, lexicologists and software engineers, as well as linguists, including applied linguists and corpus linguists, came together in Oxford to discuss the ongoing revision and the future trend of the dictionary.

"Today, once again, the *Oxford English Dictionary* is under alteration". Its content is "being comprehensively revised", and "the entire work is being updated". "The result of this ambitious undertaking will be a completely revitalized *Oxford English Dictionary*". "The remedial work of revising original 19th and early 20th century editorial material is in progress, and the results of the revision programme and additions of new words will be published online every three months". "The *Oxford English Dictionary* is a living document that has been growing and changing for 140 years". It is "an irreplaceable part of English culture", which "not only provides an important record of the evolution of our language, but also documents the continuing development of our society" ("History of the *OED*" on public. oed.com.)

The seeds of serializing *OED* were sowed and sprouted in the initial stage of its compilation, where its series came out in succession, such as Henry Watson Fowler (1858–1933) and Francis George Fowler's (1871–1918) *The*

Concise Oxford Dictionary of Current English (1911) through adaptation, followed by Francis George Fowler and Henry Watson Fowler's *The Pocket Oxford Dictionary* (1928); George Ostler's *The Little Oxford Dictionary* (1929); William Little, H. W. Fowler, E. A. Coulson et al.'s *The Shorter Oxford English Dictionary on Historical Principles* (1933); J. Coulson, C. T. Carr, Lucy Hutchinson and Dorothy Eagle's *The Oxford Illustrated Dictionary* (1965), a 2-volume compact edition (1971) from the original 13 volumes; Albert Sydney Hornby and Christina Ruse's *The Oxford Student's Dictionary* (1978) and Della Thompson's single-volume *The Oxford Compact English Dictionary* (1996). In terms of sales, Thompson's fell far behind the two-volume edition.

Special mention should be made here of a few of Oxford derivative dictionaries. *The Concise Oxford Dictionary of Current English* must be discussed first. It was published 17 years earlier than the original first edition, at which time its compilation only reached letter *R* (Allen, 1986). A comparison between them shows their discrepancies in compiling methods and principles owing to space condensation, such as the avoidance of too many encyclopaedic terms, the provision of examples only where definitions need further clarification, the provision of phrasal illustrations where necessary, the succinctness in expression etc. (See preface.) Obsolete and out-of-date words, vernacular words, non-British English words and usages and most of technical terms are excluded in order to condense more space and cater better to user needs. Instead of arranging senses in the historical sequence, as was done in the original first edition, this dictionary arranges its senses in the logical order, which fits in better with user habits of information retrieval. Moreover, its etymological treatment is considerably simplified. Its second edition was published in 1929, and the third, fourth and fifth editions in 1934, 1951 and 1964, respectively. By 1999, there were ten editions all together. Four revisions were made in 2001, 2006, 2008 and 2009. Its eleventh and twelfth editions came out in 2004 and 2011.

The Shorter Oxford English Dictionary on Historical Principles is a two-volume dictionary condensed from the original first edition and is therefore its closest follower among Oxford derivative dictionaries in observing its compiling principles. Plans for making such a dictionary started at the time when Oxford University Press took over the *New English Dictionary* project in 1879, but compilation did not begin until 1902, when William Little was formally appointed editor. Unfortunately, upon his death, Little finished only letter *A* to *T* and letter *V*. His editorship was resumed by Onions, but specific work was done by H. W. Fowler and E. A. Coulson. Fowler completed letters *U*, *X*, *Y* and *Z*, and Coulson completed letter *W*.

Its first edition was published in 1933 and reprinted three times in the same and following years. Its second edition met its audience in 1936 with over 3,000 revisions and additions. It was reprinted three years later. Its third edition came out in 1944, with such appendixes as supplements and corrigendum. It was reprinted with revisions and additions in 1947, 1950,

178 *Lexicographical traditions*

1952 and 1955, and the 1955 reprint had an additional addendum of new words. After extensive correction, revision and augmentation, the third edition was published in America under the title of *The Oxford Universal Dictionary on Historical Principles*, with a total of 2,515 pages. It was re-typeset and reprinted under the same title in America in 1973, after G. W. S. Friedrichsen rewrote "Addendum", which was expanded to over 70 pages and included considerable revision of etymologies.

In 1993, Lesley Brown's *The New Shorter Oxford English Dictionary* was published. It is actually the fourth edition based on the completely revised text of the third edition and covers all the English words in use after 1700, including those used by William Shakespeare, John Milton, Edmund Spenser and other famous writers and those used in the 1611 edition of the Bible. It employed many resources that had not been used in the previous editions. When the fifth edition was published in 2002, it used the title of the original British edition, simply to show its strengthened relatedness to it. It was edited by William R. Trumble and Angus Stevenson. It consists of 3,792 pages, and its collection includes not only technical terms and words from English varieties in different parts of the world but over 3,500 new words and new uses of existing words. Its total definitions exceed one million, coupled by ample citations and wide-ranging sources. More than 83,500 citations were quoted from over 7,000 authors. In 2007, Stevenson's sixth edition was published, conspicuously marked by its omission of hyphens in over 16,000 words (e.g. *ice-cream/ice cream*) and citations from contemporary journals, online sources and even blogs.

Oxford dictionary series have been basically derived from its first edition and the previous three early compilations. For example, from the base dictionaries, *The Pocket Oxford Dictionary* was compiled, and it in turn brought about numerous reprints and revised and augmented editions, which were again used as the base for English-variety dictionaries, such as *The Australian Pocket Oxford Dictionary*, *The New Zealand Pocket Oxford Dictionary*, and *The Pocket Oxford American Dictionary*, as well as compilations of foreign languages and online versions, such as *The Pocket Oxford Spanish Dictionary*, *The Pocket Oxford Italian Dictionary*, *The Pocket Oxford Greek Dictionary* and *The Pocket Oxford Latin Dictionary*. *The Pocket Oxford Dictionary* is only a small-scale member of minor importance in the whole of the Oxford dictionary family, and its derivations amply demonstrate the reproductive and generative capacity of the Oxford dictionaries and their dynamic life force that sustains their continuous development.

In the late 20th century, the sustainable continuation of Oxford dictionaries is ascribable to the significant contributions made by Judy Pearsall, who edited *The Concise Oxford Dictionary*, *The Concise Oxford English Dictionary: Plain Edition*, *The Oxford English Reference Dictionary*, *The New Oxford English Dictionary* and others. *The Oxford English Reference Dictionary*, which Judy Pearsall and Bill Trumbleell published in 1996,

Lexicographical traditions 179

consists of 1,781 pages. It covers a good number of new words, with succinct definitions, illustrations and usage notes only where necessary and
concise etymological information for each headword. Its "reference" value
lies in its inclusion of a huge number of encyclopaedic terms (e.g. proper
names, events) and information regarding countries, prime ministers, presidents, national events and so on. Indeed, it is entirely different from conventional British English dictionaries and is highly notable for its innovations
in compiling principles and its tentative practices. Its second edition came
out in 2002.

In 1998, Judy Pearsall co-edited with Patrick Hanks *The New Oxford
English Dictionary*. This dictionary amounts to 2,152 pages and collects
350,000 headwords, among which one-fourth are technical and encyclopaedic terms. It is the most significant dictionary of the greatest international
reach that was launched by Oxford University Press at the end of the 20th
century. Its popularity is evidenced by the appearance of a new edition only
two years later. In 2001, Erin McKean published its American edition –
The New Oxford American Dictionary. It shares compiling styles and lay-
outs with most American dictionaries. Its second edition met its audience
in 2005.

There is no doubt that Oxford dictionaries constituted the mainstream
of British philological dictionaries in the 20th century. They accounted for
a lion's share of the British dictionary market and did not allow for much
space for the survival of other brands. Understandably, few new philological dictionaries were launched. Rare examples are *Chambers Twentieth
Century Dictionary* (1901, which was modelled after *Chambers Etymological Dictionary*), Henry C. Wyld's (1870–1945) *The Universal Dictionary of
the English Language* (1932) and Patrick Hanks' and Lawrence Urdang's
Collins English Dictionary (1979). *Collins English Dictionary* is reckoned
as a milestone in dictionary-making in Britain, as it is the first dictionary
that was based on English corpus and typeset by computer. Its headword
selection amounts to over 160,000. It incorporates some striking features in
American English dictionaries, provides usage notes and covers encyclopaedic and technical terms. New editions came out every three to four years,
and the tenth edition, which marked the thirtieth anniversary of its publication, appeared in 2010, and a new edition was published in 2011. Though
remarkable in quality, they were to some extent overshadowed by Oxford
dictionaries.

It is natural that British and American English lexicographers learn from
each other's experience, as English is the linkage between the two countries and Americans share their ancestry with the British. The dictionaries Americans used in the early stage were imported from Britain, and,
consequently, early American dictionaries were chiefly modelled after the
imported dictionaries. However, after Webster's dictionaries, the layout and
style of American dictionaries attracted serious attention from British compilers, who took advantage of them and started to absorb useful elements.

180 *Lexicographical traditions*

Part of Webster's inspirations came from Johnson. Webster's dictionaries were known to British compilers and users and were used and even copied by them. *OED* "used Webster's 1864 edition as a benchmark" (Béjoint, 2010:155). Some special features in American English dictionaries, such as usage notes and synonym discrimination, were gradually accepted by British compilers and reflected in British dictionaries. "The efforts of British publishers to sell dictionaries in the USA have not always been successful", but they "never stopped trying" (Béjoint, 2010:155).

6.4 The emergence and thriving development of British learner's dictionaries

No systematic discussion will be made here regarding the interactive influence of English learner's dictionaries and philological dictionaries in the 20th century, but there is clear evidence that early learner's dictionaries certainly exerted some influence upon headword selection, phonetic notation, definition and usage explanation in subsequent philological dictionaries, and, in the latter part of the 20th century, some features in English philological dictionaries were modelled after in learner's dictionaries, such as usage notes and synonym discrimination. In Britain, the development of learner's dictionaries was not coherent or steady. No obvious progress was discernible after their initial emergence, and that was followed by a dormant period and a period of slow progression. Development was accelerated from 1978 into a booming time in the late 1980s. Through nearly three decades' development, especially after 1995, learner's dictionaries assumed a completely new look and became a pacesetter for English learner's dictionaries worldwide.

As suggested previously, learner's dictionaries in Britain underwent three generations of evolution. West's *The New Method English Dictionary*, together with Palmer's *A Grammar of English Words* and Hornby's *The Idiomatic and Syntactic English Dictionary*, formed the basis for the first generation. It culminated in *The Advanced Learner's Dictionary of Current English* (1948), which was marked by a transition from notional integration to framework configuration. The second generation mainly had the second (1963) and third (1974) editions of *The Advanced Learner's Dictionary of Current English* as the foundation, represented by the first edition of *LDCE* (1978), which signified the beginning of competitive development for English learners dictionaries. The third generation mainly had *The Oxford Advanced Learner's Dictionary of Current English* (1989) and the second edition of *LDCE* (1987) as the foundation and the first edition of *Collins Cobuild Dictionary of the English Language* as its representative work. Their appearance indicated the entry of learner's dictionaries into a period of accelerated development and full-scale competition.

Numerous reprints and editions have appeared since the publication of *The Advanced Learner's Dictionary of Current English* in 1948. The first edition underwent 12 reprints, the second 19 reprints after its publication in

Lexicographical traditions 181

1963, the third 28 reprints after its publication with a new Oxford-prefixed title in 1974, the fourth 50 reprints after its publication in 1989, the fifth 65 reprints after its publication in 1995 and the sixth 117 reprints after its publication in 2000. The seventh and eighth editions came out in 2005 and 2010. Its successive new editions, strong market demand and highly frequent reprints stimulated British publishers, attracted heavy investments from other dictionary brands and lured them into that lucrative competition through functional innovation and the incorporation of strikingly unique features.

1995 was an extraordinary time for the development of learner's dictionaries in Britain. It witnessed the publication of *Cambridge International English Dictionary*, almost simultaneous with the fifth edition of *The Advanced Learner's Dictionary of Current English*, the third edition of *LDCE* and the revised second edition of *Collins Cobuild Dictionary of the English Language*, which are collectively reputed as "The Big Four" of English learners dictionaries. In 2002, Macmillan Publishers Ltd. published *Macmillan English Dictionary for Advanced Learners*. Its second edition came out in 2007 with a huge wealth of new materials, while building on distinctively innovative features, such as the most frequently used 7,500 English words printed in red, graded with stars and explained with greater detail concerning how to use them properly. All that combined to win it immediate public recognition, as well as The Duke of Edinburgh English Language Book Awards and The British Council Innovation Award. By then, Britain's major dictionary publishers had all published learner's dictionaries of their own brands.

It is a strategy of paramount significance for British publishers to develop English dictionaries that are geared towards the specific needs of foreign users, another noteworthy path of development for learner's dictionaries in Britain. In addition to the previously mentioned learner's dictionaries for international users, they also developed new-type dictionaries that catered to the special needs of American English learners, most notably the American edition of *The Pocket Oxford Dictionary* (1927) and Virginia French Allen, David E. Eskey and Don L. F. Nilsen's *Longman Dictionary of American English* (1983, fourth edition in 2008 and with e-Tutor CD-ROM that offers a wide range of practice material and help in understanding and using English correctly).

Learner's dictionaries in Britain catalysed the approach of the user-friendly era. As a result, bilingualized dictionaries came into existence, a new dictionary genre that is based on learner's dictionaries but prove to be more user-friendly owing to the insertion of definitions written in the target language(s). The first bilingualized edition of *The Advanced Learner's Dictionary of Current English* came out in 1970 with inserted Chinese definitions immediately after their original English ones, and that first edition was followed by other editions with embedded definitions in Japanese, Hindi, Greece, Italian, Spanish, Portuguese, Norwegian and a few other languages. Its bilingualization pushed forward similar endeavours by

182 *Lexicographical traditions*

Longman, Macmillan, Collins and other publishers, with English-Chinese versions dominating the scene. That formed an overwhelming trend of new-type development for learner's dictionaries, which played an increasingly conspicuous and significant role in English learning and teaching.

6.5 The digitalization of printed dictionaries and the booming growth of British electronic and online dictionaries

The breakthrough in compiling technologies in the 20th century is chiefly characterized by the integration of computer science, technologies of electronic information processing and internet technologies, which propelled the revolutionary transition in dictionary-making, use and research. Since the University of Birmingham was granted funds in 1969 by Office for Scientific and Technical Information of the UK and took the lead in launching the OSTI project, English corpuses, typically The Bank of English and British National Corpus, mushroomed to provide indispensable foundations for English studies, dictionary compilation and textbook composition, particularly for the creation of electronic and online dictionaries.

Electronization and networking are the inevitable path for 21st-century dictionaries to maintain their academic vitality, serve user needs for information about lexical items and their latest changes in use, satisfy their requirements for fastest and most straightforward retrieval and keep compiling techniques continuously upgraded and improved. They have proved to be the effective weapon for Oxford English dictionaries to triumph on the world dictionary market. Only three years after the publication of the second edition of *OED*, its milestone CD-ROM edition was brought into existence with huge success. Though its 1999 supplemented and 2002 enlarged editions failed to meet expectations, confidence was regained in the new CD-ROM editions of 2007 and 2009.

In 1997, The Oxford English Dictionary Online project was formally launched and got online for the first time on March 14, 2000, marking a major breakthrough in the electronic networking of Oxford dictionaries. It became possible to revise, supplement and update them online every three months. According to the news report by *OED* in March 2006, online consultation was available for £195 per user annually. That online version incorporated the latest revisions and augmentations of the second and third editions, making it a truly world English dictionary and signifying the advent of an era of networking and internationalization for Oxford dictionaries. Currently, over two million visits are paid monthly to the online version, and only a little over 30,000 sets (dictionary plus CD-ROM) have been sold since the second edition, which shows a diminishing market prospect for its paper edition.

Continuous effort has been going into the development of other technologies on the part of Oxford University Press to enable publishers to create

Lexicographical traditions 183

new interfaces, such as mobile phones, for consultation. Nowadays, almost all Oxford dictionaries are accessible electronically or online, which is, to a great extent, ascribable to the digitalization of the second edition and is again an indication of English dictionaries leading world lexicographical development. The likelihood of there being no more paper edition of *OED* is another testimony to the forceful impetus of electronic and online dictionaries and their huge market potentials.

Aside from Oxford dictionaries, almost all brand dictionary publishers lose no chance in getting their products electronized or online, whether they are unabridged, abridged, bilingual, learners, specialized or special-aspect dictionaries. Examples include *Longman English Dictionary Online*, *Oxford Advanced Learner's English-Chinese Dictionary*, (1995 CD-ROM) etc. *Longman English Dictionary Online* is launched on the basis of the revised CD-ROM edition of *LDCE* and covers *LDCE*, *Interactive Longman English Grammar* and *Longman Dictionary of Common Errors*. In addition to lexical information, it provides simulative situations, word grammar and language drills.

English online dictionaries may be single-brand dictionaries, such as Oxford English Dictionaries, WordBankOnline, Longman Web Dictionaries and Cambridge Dictionaries Online and composite brand dictionaries, such as dictionary.babylon.com, alphaDictionary.com, wordnet.princeton. edu, thefreedictionary.com, onelook.com, dictionary.com, yourdictionary. com and 1000dictionaries.com. As a rule, single-brand online dictionaries encompass most and even all dictionaries under their own brand and may, in some cases, include other time-tested brands as well. They intend to meet general user needs, but some may target specific user segments or cater to special needs of specialized users. Cambridge Dictionaries Online, for example, have learners of English as its targeted users, as it claims to be the most popular online dictionary and thesaurus compiled for such user groups.

Composite online dictionaries, which do not confine themselves to certain brands or types, tend to gather all useful dictionary resources under their umbrellas. For instance, alphaDictionary.com claims to "carefully select and add new dictionaries, grammars, and LANGUAGES regularly" and includes all known online dictionaries and grammars of about 300 languages with writing systems under the categories of "alphaDictionary's Most Popular Dictionaries and Glossaries" and "alphaDicitonary's Newest Dictionaries and Glossaries". (See front page of its website). Dictionary. com, which "has been helping millions of people improve their use of the English language with its free digital services" for over 20 years, claims to be "the world's leading online source for English definitions, synonyms, word origins and etymologies, audio pronunciations, example sentences, slang phrases, idioms, word games, legal and medical terms, Word of the Day and more". (See front page of its website.) Onelook.com, through its OneLook Dictionary Search, gives users access to "18,955,870 words in 1061 dictionaries indexed" and their related words (see front page of its Website).

184 *Lexicographical traditions*

Itools.com, through its OneLook Multi-Dictionary Search, enables users to "look in hundreds of general and specialized dictionaries at once. Great for obscure words or when you want to compare different dictionaries" (see front page of its website). Thefreedictionary.com, which is created by Farlex, proclaims itself to be

> the world's most comprehensive dictionary: English, Spanish, German, French, Italian, Chinese, Portuguese, Dutch, Norwegian, Greek, Arabic, Polish, Turkish, Russian, Thesaurus, Medical, Legal, and Financial Dictionaries, Thesaurus, Acronyms and Abbreviations, Idioms, Encyclopedia, a Literature Reference Library, and a Search Engine all in one.

It has "12,579,475,848 visitors served" up to January 11, 2021.

6.6 The tradition of phonetic transcription and the making of British pronouncing dictionaries in the 20th century

Of the 20th-century special-aspect dictionaries in Britain, pronouncing dictionaries should be the first category to be introduced for discussion for two reasons. One is that this category appeared relatively earlier than others, and the other is the role pronunciation plays in British social life. Speech accent is one of the major indicators that locates the British people in their social space and in regional distribution.

Although Collins and Mees (2009:179) claimed "the earliest modern types of phonetic notation have their roots in the work of Alexander J. Ellis (1814–1890) and Isaac Pitman (1813–1897)", there is solid evidence that Thomas Dysche made the first attempt to transcribe pronunciation as compiler of reference work, and his *A Guide to the English Tongue* (1707) made use of special signs for accentuation (McArthur, 1998:134). Bailey set the precedent of providing pronunciation for some headwords in the second volume of *The Universal Etymological English Dictionary* (1727). However, Ellis' studies exerted profound influence upon the 20th-century phoneticians, especially Henry Sweet, J. A. Afzelius (1753–1837) and Daniel Jones (1881–1967). In 1886, initiated by Paul Passy (1859–1940), a local association for phoneticians and English teachers was set up in France. Shortly afterwards, well-known linguists from Germany, Britain, Norway, Denmark and other countries, particularly phoneticians, became its members, and it developed into what was called The International Phonetic Association. Its significance to lexicography resides in providing a standard form of phonetic transcription that is theoretically applicable to all languages – the International Phonetic Alphabet.

Although several English pronouncing dictionaries had been published in Britain in the 19th century, the first English pronouncing dictionary in the 20th century – *A Pronouncing Dictionary of Modern English* (1909) – was compiled by J. A. Afzelius, a Swedish rather than a British

Lexicographical traditions   185

scholar. Pioneering as it was, Afzelius's dictionary did not receive its due attention. (Collins and Mees, 2009:181–183) The leading role in the field of English phonetics in the 20th century definitely went to Daniel Jones. Jones studied under the world's then-master phoneticians, such as German linguist William Tilly (1860–1935), French linguist Paul Passy (1859–1940) and British linguist Henry Sweet. He published *The Pronunciation of English* (1909), *An Outline of English Phonetics* (1918) and other important works, which laid a solid foundation for received pronunciation.

In 1913, Jones co-authored with German phonetician Herman Michaelis (1867–?) *A Phonetic Dictionary of the English Language*, which paved the way for his independent work – *An English Pronouncing Dictionary* (1917). That dictionary had 12 editions before Jones' death. In 1967, the year of Jones' death, the thirteenth edition was published. It was revised and augmented by A. C. Gimson (1917–1985). Ten years later, the fourteenth edition came out, and, in 2006, the seventeenth edition was published with CD-ROM. Reprints and new editions have been continuing up to the present day.

Subsequent to Gimson's revised edition, there appeared in Britain Gertrude M. Miller's *BBC Pronouncing Dictionary of British Names* (1971), Windsor Lewis' *The Concise Pronouncing Dictionary of British and American English* (1972), John Wells' *Longman Pronunciation Dictionary* (1990) and others. Wells' dictionary eventually superseded Jones' outdated work, and this situation was changed in the first year into the new century by *The Oxford Dictionary of Pronunciation* (2001), a work that was based on collaborative research findings by British and American scholars and jointly compiled by Clive Upton of University of Leeds, Britain and William Kretzschmar and Rafal Konopka, both of University of Georgia, USA. Its publication is a realistic reflection of the status quo of English pronunciation in the 21st century.

6.7 The changed attitude towards dialectal words and the making of British dialect dictionaries in the 20th century

The development of dialect dictionaries in Britain can be roughly divided into three stages. Before Skinner, there was basically no intentional compilation, and general dictionaries only occasionally covered dialectal words, some unmarked and some marked as "barbarous" or "vulgar". After Skinner, there was growing interest in collecting and studying dialectal words, owing to changes in the attitude towards them. Dialectal glossaries started to emerge in great numbers, and dictionaries of dialectal words also made their appearance. That accumulated large quantities of dialectal data and created necessary conditions for the compilation of large-scale dialectal dictionaries.

186   *Lexicographical traditions*

At the turn of the 19th and 20th centuries, Wright's *English Dialect Dictionary* (1898–1905) brought Britain's dialectal dictionary-making to its climax in history, which also heralded revolutionary transformations in principles and methods of English dialect research, in dialectal data collection, in techniques for description and presentation and in some other aspects. It became a trend to compile dialect dictionaries on the basis of dialect investigations and the construction of dialect corpuses. A good example was *Survey of English Dialects: the Dictionary and Grammar* (1994), which was compiled by Clive Upton, David Parry and John Widdowson and was based on *The Survey of English Dialects* conducted by University of Leeds.

The *Survey of English Dialects* lasted from 1950 to 1961 and was directed by Harold Orton (1898–1975). Its objective was to collect dialectal words in England and Wales so as to rescue dialect words that were in danger of extinction on the outskirts of urban areas and in remote regions. That survey was the most extensive English dialect investigation that was conducted in the 20th century and was the most productive so far. Apart from *Survey of English Dialects: the Dictionary and Grammar*, other important undertakings include the 13-volume *Survey of English Dialects: Basic Materials* (1962–1971), *A Word Geography of England* (1975), *The Linguistic Atlas of England* (1978) and *An Atlas of English Dialects* (1996).

Other significant dialect dictionaries in the 20th century include The Scottish National Dictionary (1931–1976), *A Dictionary of the Older Scottish Tongue from the Twelfth Century to the End of the Seventeenth* (1931–2002) and so on. In 1929, The Scottish National Dictionary Association was founded for the purpose of fostering and encouraging the Scots language, in particular by producing a standard dictionary of modern Scots. This primary objective was accomplished in 1976 with the completion and publication of the ten-volume Scottish National Dictionary, with a coverage of the language from 1700 to 1976 and materials drawn from a wide variety of written and oral sources of Lowland Scots from Shetland to Ulster, including county annals, parliamentary documents, township letters, court records, newspapers and magazines, family books, diaries and correspondences. The dictionary was produced under the editorial direction of William Grant (from 1929 to 1946) and David Murison (from 1946 to 1976). The whole project lasted for 45 years. After the completion of Scottish National Dictionary, with its supplement in 1976, the association went on to produce a wide range of smaller Scots dictionaries, including the *Concise Scots Dictionary* (1985) and *Scots Thesaurus* (1990). The association also established an ongoing Word Collection in order to create a constantly updated resource on modern Scots. It provides a panoramic view of the Scottish vocabulary and cultural life, as well as material support for researching Britain's regional language and culture.

A Dictionary of the Older Scottish Tongue consists of 12 volumes and presents a linguistic history of Scotland from the 12th century to 1700. Its compilation lasted for more than 70 years and was successively undertaken by William Craigie, A. J. Aitken (1921–1998), K. Lorna Pike, James A. C. Stevenson, Margaret G. Dareau, Henry D. Watsone and others. Its compiling principles and techniques were refined time and again for the ultimate purpose of achieving perfection and goals of deepening public understanding of the Scottish language, altering the general attitude towards it, promoting the Scottish culture and facilitating Scottish studies.

6.8 The extension of slang lexicography and the compilation of British slang dictionaries in the 20th century

English dictionaries of slangs (here jargons, cant, vulgarism and other non-standard words included) had their origins in the appendixes to historical, legal and literary literature. The purpose of providing glossaries of jargons and slangs was to help readers get an easier understanding of the text and the special terms in it. Earlier compilations also contained such terms, but their inclusion was merely an unintentional record of such words and expressions. Only few were given stylistic labels and notes of usage. Through several centuries' evolution, slang dictionaries have become a member of high cultural values and great social significance in the English dictionary family. They can roughly be classified into the following types: (1) glossaries appended to historical, legal and literary literature; (2) general collections or slang dictionaries compiled on the basis of glossaries appended to various sorts of literature and/or general dictionaries; (3) slang dictionaries compiled on the historical principles or periodical slang dictionaries; (4) slang dictionaries compiled from the sociological perspective.

Among the four types, type (1) is in most cases compiled by authors of relevant literature for the purpose of facilitating literature reading. In 1839, for instance, W. A. Miles appended Henry Brandon's *A Dictionary of the Flash or Cant Language, known to every thief and beggar* to the report submitted to the Congress – *Poverty, Mendicity, and Crime*. Types (2) and (3) are generally compiled by professionals in order to assist in research or serve consultation. Slang dictionaries mentioned previously and hereinafter basically fall into this category. Type (4) is mostly compiled by social elites, journalists and sociologists, who, in a few cases, play their part by providing relevant resources for databases. This type of slang dictionary can be of vital value to the observation and research of special social groups and the study of sociological and anthropological issues. George Orwell's *Down and Out in Paris and London* (1933) and Christina Milner and Richard Milner's *Black Players* (1973) belong to this category.

In the 20th century, the leading figure in the field of slang studies was definitely Eric Honeywood Partridge (1894–1979). He was a New Zealand-born British lexicographer and conducted extensive and profound studies of slangs in Britain, America and Australia. His research findings are covered in *Slang Today and Yesterday* (1933). In this work, he portrayed a

188 *Lexicographical traditions*

complete picture of the historical development of slang and analysed social motivations for the origins of slang, such as aspiration for differences from the public, demonstration of social or group identity, secrecy and so on. His important works include *A Dictionary of Slang and Unconventional English* (1937), *A Dictionary of Clichés* (1940), *A Dictionary of the Underworld British and American* (1949) etc. In the subtitle to *A Dictionary of Slang and Unconventional English*, Partridge claims that it contains "colloquialisms, catch phrases, fossilized jokes and puns, general nicknames, vulgarism and such Americanisms as have been naturalized", giving a fully documented account of English slang over four centuries for lovers of the English language.

The dictionary features unprecedented coverage of World English, with equal prominence given to American and British English slang, emphasis laid on post-World War II slang and unconventional English, information dated for each headword and in the tradition of Partridge and commentaries provided on the term's origins and meaning. It "presents itself as an updated version of Farmer and Henley's *Slang and its Analogues*" (1890–1904) and has "spawned a series of concise and shorter versions" (Coleman, 2009:322). A new edition came out the following year after its publication, and the third and fourth editions in 1949 and 1951, respectively. In 1961, the fifth edition appeared in two volumes. Two years later the two volumes were combined into one. New editions were published in 1967 and 1970, and the eighth edition in 1984. The latest issuance of the eighth edition was in 2002 and a concise edition in 2007. All that indicates its strong and extensive social influence and scholarly recognition.

Tom Dalzell and Terry Victor's *The Concise New Partridge Dictionary of Slang and Unconventional English* (2008) stands out among all of its remarkable offspring, which uses the eighth edition as its base and presents for the first time all the slang terms from *A Dictionary of Slang and Unconventional English* in a single volume. It details the slang and unconventional English around the English-speaking world since 1945 and through the first decade of the new millennium, with the same thorough, intense and lively scholarship that characterizes Partridge's own work, collecting over 60,000 entries, covering the language of beats, hipsters, Teddy Boys, mods and rockers, hippies, pimps, druggies, whores, punks, skinheads, ravers, surfers, Valley girls, dudes, pill-popping truck drivers, hackers, rappers and more. It provides a spectacular resource infused with humour and learning by adding a new preface noting slang trends of the last eight years, over 1,000 new entries from major English-speaking countries reflecting important developments in English language and culture, new terms from the language of social networking from a range of digital communities including texting, blogs, Facebook, Twitter and online forums, with many revised entries to include new dating and new glosses and ensure maximum accuracy of content.

A Dictionary of Cliché

is full of things better left unsaid: hackneyed phrases, idioms battered into senselessness, infuriating Gallicisms, once-familiar quotations and tags from the ancient classics. It makes a formidable list, amplified as it is with definitions, sources, and indications of the cliché, venerability in each case.

(See its advertisement)

At the end of the 20th century and the beginning of the 21st century, the Oxford University Press published two slang dictionaries – John Ayto and John. A. Simpson's *The Oxford Dictionary of Modern Slang* (1992) and Jonathon Green's *Cassell's Dictionary of Slang* (1998), as well as Green's three-volume *Green's Dictionary of Slang* in 2011. They marked a perfect conclusion to the making of British slang dictionaries in the 20th century and opened a new landscape for their development in the 21st century.

The Oxford Dictionary of Modern Slang was a highly professional compilation. Simpson once worked as chief editor of *Oxford English Dictionary*. He took full advantage of the unique resources of *Oxford English Dictionary*. He made a careful selection of over 6,000 slang words and expressions that appeared in the 20th century and were then in popular use. Each entry was provided citations and annotations of their origins and dates of first use in written form. They were collected from all possible sources of the English-speaking world, such as *abaht* from London, *zowie* from America, *dork* and *cockamamie* from North America and *Jimmy Woodser* from Australia. They unfold a colourful socio-cultural life in the English world. This dictionary was reprinted in 2005, 2008, 2009 and 2010.

Cassell's Dictionary of Slang amounted to over 1,500 pages and collected all sorts of English slangs ranging from the 18th-century underworld to the present-day homosexual language. The first edition was widely acclaimed upon its publication in 1998 and was then regarded as the world's best single-volume dictionary of English slangs. An addition of over 12,000 slangs and similar expressions was made in the second edition with greater precision of definition, etymological labelling and annotations of dates of use. However, Green did not stop at that. He continued with his efforts and devoted himself to more profound and extensive inquiries into English slang. He traced the evolutional track of English slang development, made records of their uses in real context and amassed citations from situations of actual use. Apart from over 4,000 books, he also combed through songbooks, newspapers and magazines and movie and television scripts to collect data, fill in gaps, correct mistakes and errors in dates of use and improve definition and etymological labelling. The outcome of his efforts was *Green's Dictionary of Slang* (2011).

190 *Lexicographical traditions*

Green's Dictionary of Slang is a product of his lifelong dedication to the study of English slang. It collects English slangs over the past 500 years and from all English-speaking countries and regions. Its entries reach over 53,000, and its text amounts to over 11.3 million words. It provides around 100,000 definitions and over 410,000 citations. Each headword and expression is provided with annotations of origins and actual use, which endows the dictionary with undisputable authority and incomparable scholarship. It deserves all the praises, particularly the Winner of the Dartmouth Medal.

6.9 The continuation of the etymological tradition and usage criticism and the making of British dictionaries of etymology and usage in the 20th century

At the turn of the 19th and 20th centuries, Germanic study was at its height. Scholars showed unparalleled interest in that field and produced bountiful and insightful works of long-lasting influence. That explained to a considerable extent why English etymological dictionaries developed well on this sound track. In 1899, German philologist and etymologist Friedrich Kluge (1856–1926) wrote a little book on English etymology, which was translated into English by Frederick Lutz. That put an end to the studies in English etymology in the 19th century. It is not surprising that *Etymologisches Wörterbuch der englischen Sprache* (1917), supposedly the most authoritative dictionary of English etymology in the 20th century, was completed by a German scholar called Ferdinand Holthausen (1860–1956). Unfortunately, that dictionary, which was of limited scale, did not take the place of Skeat's, as the German academics anticipated. Holthausen's other noteworthy work *Altenglisches etymologisches Wörterbuch* (1934) is the only dictionary so far compiled of Old English etymology.

Britain's local etymological dictionary – *A Dictionary of Word Origins* – was compiled by Joseph Shipley. Its compilation was interrupted from time to time during the two world wars and was not completed for publication until 1945. Other similar works include C. T. Onions' *The Oxford Dictionary of English Etymology* (1966), Ernest Klein's *A Comprehensive Etymological Dictionary of the English Language* (1966) and Eric Partridge's *A Short Etymological Dictionary of Modern English* (1958).

The notions of *use* and *usage criticism* in English may be traced back to the late 17th century and the early 18th century, when standard forms of English were established, first books of grammar and first monolingual dictionaries were written and literary masters' efforts in codifying English were still in the preliminary stage. However, disputes about whether certain usages were good or bad were surging and unsettled. In times when prescriptivism was rampant and dominant and pedagogical grammar was deeply affected by prescriptive grammar, reference works on usage were well received and extremely popular. English learners expected to produce correct English under the guidance of grammatical rules.

Lexicographical traditions 191

English reference works of usage began to appear in the 18th century, such as Robert Baker's *Reflections on the English Language* (1770). Early works may be divided into three kinds: (1) in the form of chapters with each devoted to one aspect of usage, (2) in the alphabetical arrangement of entries like in dictionaries, (3) in the form of chapters with each arranging headwords in the alphabetical sequence. What follows will mainly involve type (2), i.e. reference works of usage in the form of dictionaries. Henry W. Fowler is the first to have compiled dictionaries of usage in the alphabetical order.

Word usage has a lot to do with the knowledge of grammatical rules, the attitude towards word usage and the social status and identity of word users. From 1417, when Henry V started to employ English as a medium of official communication, issues concerning English usage standards began to surface and gradually evolved into hot topics and focal subjects among linguists. The publication of English textbooks in the 16th century and the first monolingual English dictionary at the beginning of the 17th century made headway for the writing of grammar books to standardize English usage and dictionaries to codify English usage. It further ignited discussions in that connection.

There appeared in the 18th- and 19th-century English dictionaries notes and annotations regarding word usage, especially differences between standard English and dialect and between British and American English. Those explanations added to the surging discussions mostly carried in newspapers and personal correspondences. By the end of the 19th century, Fitzedward Hall's *Modern English* (1873) and William B. Hodgson's *Errors in the Use of English* (1881) were among those few works devoted to issues of English usage. No dictionaries of English usage in the modern sense had appeared yet.

It was still quite a novelty at the beginning of the 20th century for scholars to conduct discussions concerning usage from academic or diachronic perspectives. Thomas R. Lounsbury's *The Standard of Usage in English* (1908) looked back upon previous discussions about usage and different attitudes towards it. Sterling A. Leonard's *The Doctrine of Correctness in English* 1700–1800 (1929), for the first time, made a systematic reflection of attitudes towards usage in the 18th century and their changes. Obviously, the beginning part of the 20th century was a time for academics to start their rational knowledge and understanding of English usage and grammatical issues and theoretically generalize about the making of dictionaries of English usage.

Throughout the 20th century, British scholars compiled a good number of English usage dictionaries. Henry Watson Fowler (1858–1933) and Ernest Arthur Gowers (1880–1866) are the most noteworthy compilers, and Oxford University Press is the most noteworthy publisher. The most noteworthy works include Henry W. Fowler's *The Dictionary of Modern English Usage* (1926), Henry Arthur Treble's (1877–?) and George Henry

192 *Lexicographical traditions*

Vallins' 192-page *An ABC of English Usage* (1936), Eric Partridge's *Usage and Abusage: A Guide to Good English* (1942), Ernest Gowers' *Plain Words: A Guide to the Use of English* (1948), Benjamin Ifor Evans' (1899–1982) *The Use of English* (1949), John Owen Edward Clark's (1937–) 490-page *Word Perfect* (1987), Sydney Greenbaum's and Janet Whitcut's *Longman Guide to English Usage* (1988) and George Davidson's (1949–) *Chambers Guide to Grammar and Usage* (1996).

Henry Watson Fowler received education in Oxford and worked as an English teacher until his middle age. Later on he became a lexicographer and a well-known critic of English usage. From 1906 onwards, he collaborated with his younger brother Francis George Fowler (1871–1918) in writing grammar works and compiling dictionaries. He is best remembered for *The Dictionary of Modern English Usage* and his remarkable work on *The Concise Oxford Dictionary of Current English*. *The Dictionary of Modern English Usage* was actually a revised augmentation of *The King's English* (1906), which was jointly published by him and his younger brother and was rearranged in alphabetical order so as to provide guidance in English pronunciation, usage and writing, such as the plural form, lexical discrimination, loan word usage, writing techniques etc. It advocated straightforward and forceful writing style, opposed pedantry and the use of borrowed and outdated words and resisted diction and grammar that were not in conformity with natural laws of language, such as split infinitives, ending sentences with prepositions and so on. It was a good example of integrating prescriptivism and descriptivism under one cover.

Upon its publication, *The Dictionary of Modern English Usage* received immediate public recognition and was adored as an authority in English usage. Fowler became well-known almost to every household in the English world, and users used his name to refer to his dictionary. Winston Churchill (1874–1965) was reported to have ordered his soldiers to read the book. In the first year of its publication, it had 3 reprints, and 12 more were produced before Gowers published his revised and enlarged edition *Fowler's Modern English Usage* (1965). In 1996, Robert Burchfield published his reedited third edition, *The New Fowler's Modern English Usage*. In 1999, Robert Allen published a pocket edition on the basis of the third edition and with online consultation provided. In 2004, when the third edition was reprinted, it incorporated theoretical and practical elements of corpus linguistics. In 2009, the first edition was reprinted with David Crystal's preface and the updating of some entries.

Ernest Gowers is another influential English grammarian and usage expert. He received education in Cambridge and joined the British government as civil servant in 1902. During his long career as a civil servant, he was very much involved in many of the major events in the first half of the 20th century. His final post as a civil servant was to manage civil defence in London during the Second World War. Described as Britain's "No 1 Chairman", he chaired many inquiries after the war. However, he only became

Lexicographical traditions 193

famous in 1948, when *Plain Words: A Guide to the Use of English* became an instant bestseller for Her Majesty's Stationery Offices. Edward Bridges (1892–1969), Gowers' superior, was very much impressed by his simple, smooth and succinct writing style and asked him to write a training pamphlet for the British Civil Service, including the army and the police, so as to be used as a writing guide for the avoidance of pompous and scholastic styles of expression. The result was the bestseller, which cost only two shillings then. Its continuation – The *ABC of Plain Words* came out in 1951, and the combination of the essence of the two editions – *The Complete Plain Words* was published in 1954, which was reprinted through revision by Bruce Fraser in 1973 and again by Sydney Greenbaum (1929–1996) and Janet Whitcut in 1986. That guide, through numerous reprints, became a valuable reference work aiming at linguistic simplicity and precision and became a source for the Plain English Campaign that started in 1979. From the age of 75, he engaged himself for the final ten years of his life in the revision of *Fowler's Modern English Usage*.

In addition, *Usage and Abusage: A Guide to Good English* is also a timetested influential classic reference work. Its full title is *Usage and Abusage: A Guide to Good English, an A-Z dictionary treatment*, which provides wisdom and guidance in the correct use of English and the avoidance of incorrect use. In the revised edition of 1997, Janet Whitcut added a section "Vogue Words", which provided proper suggestions and guidance in dealing with new problems in modern English use, such as the use of adverbs like *hopefully*, words relating to sexual prejudices etc. *The Use of English* had only 156 pages, but it was well received when it met its readers. Seven editions were published between 1949 and 1953. *Longman Guide to English Usage* covers over 5,000 correct uses of English words in terms of grammar, style, spelling and pronunciation etc.

As far as the 20th-century publication of dictionaries of English usage in Britain is concerned, Oxford University Press not only acts as pioneer but also makes remarkable contributions. Apart from *The Dictionary of Modern English Usage*, quite a few Oxford-branded dictionaries of English usage can still be found on office desks. Representative works include Herbert William Horwill's (1864–1952) *A Dictionary of Modern American Usage* (1935), Margaret Nicholson's *A Dictionary of American-English Usage* (1957), Michael Swan's *Practical English Usage* (1980), E. S. C. Weiner's *The Oxford Miniguide to English Usage* (1983), E. S. C. Weiner's and Andrew Delahunty's *The Oxford Guide to English Usage* (1993) and *The Little Oxford Guide to English Usage* (1994) and Bryan A. Garner's classic work *A Dictionary of Modern American Usage* (1998).

Among dictionaries of American English usage, *A Dictionary of Modern American Usage* appears to be exceptional. It is not "an adaptation but a new text" "aimed at the British market", as is described in the preface, and it is "primarily designed to assist English people who visit the United States, or who meet American friends, or who read American books and

194 *Lexicographical traditions*

magazines, or who listen to American 'talkies' ". Obviously, his dictionary differs radically from other dictionaries of American English usage in its comparison between American and British English usage. Ten years after its publication, *The Oxford Miniguide to English Usage*, through Andrew Delahunty's and Edmund Weiner's revision and augmentation, reappeared in 1993. The new edition was renamed *The Oxford Guide to English Usage*, and the following year saw the publication of its newly revised edition. This guide adopts the thematic arrangement of word formation, pronunciation, vocabulary, grammar, punctuation and so on. Under each thematic category are listed common tough problems in English writing that need practical guidance. It focuses on differences of usage between British and American English and provides a huge number of citations from the best writers with a view to demonstrating the appropriate use of English words and reflecting the changes in English objectively. Undoubtedly, it is a classic work in English usage.

Bryan A. Garner is a writer, grammarian and lexicographer. He once worked as teacher and solicitor. He spent over 30 years conducting studies in English usage and writing works on that subject. He is highly reputed as "America's Fowler". In the first edition of *A Dictionary of Modern American Usage*, each entry is devoted to discussions about word usage with illustrative citations. Entries are roughly divided into two categories: (1) word entries, which are generally short and concentrate on the uses of individual words or group words and (2) essay entries, which discuss problems of use and style, such as abbreviation, punctuation, subject-verb concord etc. and it provides genuinely authoritative guidance respecting how to avoid usage traps in American English and misuses and misreading of American English words. Only two years after the first edition, the abridged edition under the title of *The Oxford Dictionary of American Usage and Style* (2000) met its audience, followed by the second edition of *Garner's Modern American Usage* (2003). The 1998 first edition had only 723 pages, but the number exceeded 1,000 when the second edition came out, with the addition of hundreds of new words, such as *DVD*, *internet*, *webpage*, *foot-and-mouth*, *plethora*, *weaponize* etc., updating hundreds of existing entries and the introduction of citations from newspapers and magazines rather than such literary works as works of fiction, which is more in line with the features of usage dictionaries tracing and reflecting the latest developments of usage.

After the appearance of the first edition, Garner concentrated on the tracking of new changes in English usage. The third edition contains a special appendix of Garner's Language-Change Index, which shows the position of each controversial use over the spectrum ranging from "unacceptable" to "acceptable". His judgments are exclusively based on his own research findings and results of previous analyses, which is a pioneering example in usage dictionaries. Garner hired over 120 readers to assist in examining and considering manuscripts and making comments and suggestions so as to revise and improve dictionary content. This is again a pioneering example. His dictionary has become a new classic reference work for editors and general readers to seek guidance about how to write better English. It won *Choice*'s award of "Outstanding Academic Book" in 1999 and was given the title of "Outstanding Reference Source" by the American Library Association.

Practical English Usage is another work of English usage with distinctive features in the Oxford series. This work targets overseas English learners and teachers with focus on the basic description of English grammar and usage and more prominence to tough problems non-English native users often encounter. It mainly deals with British English, but special attention is paid to differences in usage and style between British and American English. In 1995, the second edition, which was completely revised, augmented and updated, came out. Ten years later, the third edition came out, which showed the latest changes in British English, especially the popularization of some American usages in British English, such as the use of *like* as conjunction. Since the first edition of 1980, its sales have amounted to more than 1.5 million, which is strong evidence of its popularity.

6.10 The studies in synonymous relations and the making of British thesauruses in the 20th century

The word "thesaurus" originated from Latin in the second half of the 16th century, a derivative of the Greek word "θησαυρός *(thēsauros)*". It originally meant "store house, treasure house" and was extended to mean "a collection of important or valuable things". Thomas Cooper's *Thesaurus Linguae Romanae et Britannicae* is most likely to be the first dictionary to have used the word in a dictionary title, though it is not a thesaurus. After Roget published his *Thesaurus*, that word got the equivalent meaning of "synonym dictionary" (Hüllen, 2009:33). Currently, the world's largest thesaurus is Christian Kay, Jane Roberts, Michael Samuels and Irené Wotherspoon's joint work – *The Historical Thesaurus of the Oxford English Dictionary* (2009).

Thesauruses have their theoretical roots in ancient Greek grammarian and historian Philo of Byblos' (also known as Hernnius Philon, c. 64–141) *On Synonyms* and Ammonius Grammaticus' *On the Differences of Synonymous Expressions*, which is a shortened version of *On Synonyms*. Philo of Byblos is also the author of the world's first reference work similar to a thesaurus, something like a categorically arranged concordance of scientific writers and works as well as proper names of cities and their well-known citizens. According to textual researches, *Onomasticon* is probably the first thesaurus compiled by the Greek grammarian Julius Pollux in the second century AD with a collection of synonyms and synonymous expressions used in ancient Athens. Its entries are arranged thematically rather than alphabetically. It consists of ten volumes and contains precious literature and information concerning ancient Greek life, drama, politics and other aspects of social life. It quotes enormously from works that are no longer

196 *Lexicographical traditions*

extant and therefore retains numerous sentences and expressions that cannot be found elsewhere. It is an important source for explorations in ancient Greek classics and culture.

The compilation of some kinds of Latin thesauruses was still going on in the 5th and 6th centuries but came to a surprisingly sudden halt. It was not resumed until the 18th century (Boulanger, 2003:448). What was closest to modern thesauruses was French grammarian Gabriel Girard's (1677–1748) *Synonymes français* (1736), which was compiled on the basis of his previous work *La justesse de la langue française* (1718). That is one of the sources of inspirations for Roget's compilation of his thesaurus (Béjoint, 2010:123).

The emergence of English thesauruses is intimately related to the tradition of treating synonyms in general reference works and defining dictionaries. Relevant literature review shows that John Trusler's (1735–1820) *Differences between Words Esteemed Synonymous in the English Language* (1766) might be the first reference book of this kind. Later on, similar works came out, such as Hester Lynch Piozzi's (1741–1821) *British Synonymy: or an Attempt to Regulate the Choice of Words in Familiar Conversation* (1794), William Taylor's (1765–1836) *English Synonyms Discriminated* (1813) and George Crabb's (1778–1851) *A Dictionary of English Synonymes* (1816). They are by nature reference books rather than synonym dictionaries compiled according to dictionary formats and styles.

The first related work that used "dictionary" in its title was William Perry's *The Synonymous, Etymological, and Pronouncing Dictionary* (1805). It is a related work because it traces word origins, classifies word classes and annotates pronunciation, as well as dealing with synonyms.

> After Dr Johnson, no alphabetical and explanatory dictionary could do without synonyms. Moreover, the books following in the wake of the Abbé Girard had greatly enhanced the techniques of synonym discrimination. It was therefore almost inevitable that, towards the end of the eighteenth century and on into the nineteenth, the production of synonym dictionaries proper would make progress. They became an important means of general linguistic reflection and education.
>
> (Hüllen, 2009:37–38)

The thesaurus with the greatest significance of linguistic reflection and education goes undoubtedly to Roget's *Thesaurus of English Words and Phrases* (1852). Obviously, Roget's work is derived from and theoretically based on the findings of analytic philosophy. It facilitated the development of historical philology and semantic studies from the late 19th century to the whole 20th century.

Roget's dictionary achieved huge success after its publication. It underwent numerous revisions, augmentations and reprints and dominated the thesaurus market in the late 19th century with almost no room being left for other similar compilations. Into the 20th century, Roget's dictionary

Lexicographical traditions   197

continued to be revised and printed. It was not until the 1970s that other competitors started their penetration into the market in close succession. Major works are Francis Andrew March's (1825–1911) *The Thesaurus Dictionary of the English Language* (1903), Marian Makins' *Collins English Thesaurus in A-Z Form* (1984), Laurence Urdang's *The Oxford Thesaurus* (1991), Elizabeth McLaren Kirkpatrick's *The Oxford Paperback Thesaurus* (1994), Betty Kirkpatrick's *The Concise Oxford Thesaurus* (1995), Maurice Waite's *The Compact Oxford Thesaurus* (1996), Patrick Hanks' *The New Oxford Thesaurus of English* (2000) and so on.

March's *The Thesaurus Dictionary of the English Language* consists of only 102 pages, provides words for precise and timely expression of specific ideas (see its cover) and "combines the principles of the dictionary and the traditional thesauruses" (foreword). Its second edition came out in 1980, and its digitalized edition was launched in 1993. Urdang's *The Oxford Thesaurus* contains about 350,000 alphabetically arranged English synonyms and antonyms, as well as thousands of regional words and idiomatic expressions. Senses are discriminated and arranged according to their frequency of use. An index of synonyms is appended to provide convenient consultation and cross-reference of about 265,000 synonyms, together with ample indicative signs and citations. It achieved great success, and its sales reached over 126,000 copies.

Kirkpatrick's *The Concise Oxford Thesaurus* collects 300,000 synonyms and antonyms as well as synonymous and antonymous expressions, which are arranged according to their frequency of use with the most commonly used ones listed first and the semantically closest ones printed in capital letters. It provides sufficient examples to assist users in choosing words and expressions for diction, coupled with over 400 explanatory boxes that contain encyclopaedic information relating to noun headwords and "word links" that provide easier access to related words and expressions. After its first edition in 1995, the dictionary underwent revision and addition by Maurice Waite in 2002 and 2007, and its size increased from 974 pages to 992 pages.

Among thesauruses that are published in Britain, some are specifically designed for foreign learners of English. For example, Tom McArthur's *Longman Lexicon of Contemporary English* (1981) and Addison Wesley Longman's *Longman Language Activator* (1993) are intended to cater to the needs of non-native learners of English. Christine A. Lindberg's *Oxford American Desk Thesaurus* (1998) mainly targets American users. This dictionary comprises only 528 pages and is made on the basis of Kirkpatrick's *The Oxford Paperback Thesaurus*. It contains over 10,000 entries and around 175,000 synonyms, inclusive of thousands of compound words and idiomatic expressions, with headwords being arranged alphabetically. It concisely explains over 30,000 common words, highlights correct uses through exemplification and offers basic guidance in writing and abundant encyclopaedic information in the back matter. In addition, there also

198 *Lexicographical traditions*

appeared a thesaurus with focus on English slangs, i.e. Jonathan Green's *The Slang Thesaurus* (1986).

At the turn of the 20th and 21st centuries, especially after the entry into the 21st century, new tendencies of thesaurus compilation began to surface. First, the development of thesauruses is gaining momentum. The number of thesauruses has been increasing rapidly, and more publishers have been involved in their making and publication. The domination solely by Oxford University Press has been broken. Collins and other dictionary publishers have joined in the competition by launching several series in order to cater to different levels of users and their writing needs. *Collins Writer's Thesaurus of the English Language* (2010) is just one of many examples.

Second, thesauruses have been growing in size and influence. *The Historical Thesaurus of the Oxford English Dictionary*, for example, is so massive and significant as to raise English thesaurus making into its peak. This thesaurus was jointly compiled by a team of lexicographers in the English Department of the University of Glasgow over a span of more than 40 years. It consists of two volumes and over 920,000 entries. Its text is categorized under themes and classified into three sections, i.e. The External World, The Mental World and The Social World. They are further divided into 354 categories, such as *food* and *drink*, *thought* and *war*, etc. All these categories are grouped from general to concrete into 236,000 subcategories and even smaller ones so as to form semantic networks that are interrelated between synonyms and their related words. Altogether, 800,000 semantic concepts are covered. All synonyms are given the dates of their first use in English, and all senses are arranged in the historical sequence with the earliest sense listed in the first place. Its comprehensive index provides nearly one million cross-referenced lexical senses. This epoch-making monumental work is the first thesaurus that covers almost all vocabulary from Old English to Modern English and is exerting extensive, far-reaching and immeasurable influence upon the development of thesaurus lexicography in the 21st century.

Third, publishers were beginning to recognize the importance of user-friendly principles and market segments of users, with special attention paid to easier accessibility of lexicographical information and competition for diversification. Entry arrangement generally adopted the alphabetical order on the basis of semantic categorization. They had in mind more specific user needs and segments. Collins, for instance, had their users targeted at the secondary level and below. Accordingly, they produced *Collins Primary Thesaurus* (2005), *Collins School Thesaurus* (2009) and the like.

Fourth, the two-in-one combination of "dictionary" and "thesaurus" had already appeared in the 20th century, though their number was quite limited. Since the entry into the 21st century, such development has been accelerating. Oxford, Cambridge, Collins, Chambers and other publishers have been bringing combinations of "dictionary and thesaurus" onto the market, for instance *The Oxford Dictionary and Thesaurus* (2007). Some target the secondary level of users and below, for instance *Collins Gem School Dictionary & Thesaurus* (2009).

Fifth, apart from the above two-in-one combinations, another mode of two-in-one combination also appeared on the market, i.e. a set of "dictionary" and "thesaurus" with each being separated as an independent part. In the wake of *The Oxford Dictionary and Thesaurus of English 2 Book Set* (2010), Collins followed suit by launching *Collins English Dictionary and Thesaurus Set* (2011). That can be a strong indication of a new mode of development for English thesauruses in the 21st century.

Finally, the media of transmission and consultation for thesauruses has changed from paper to electronic, internet and mobile interfaces, such as mobile phones, iPod and iPad, which means huge potential and prospects for their development. *The Historical Thesaurus of the Oxford English Dictionary* and *WordNet* are both large thesauruses that can operate online, while *Collins English Thesaurus Mobile Systems* and *English Dictionary & Thesaurus by Ultralingua* can be downloaded directly from the internet and applied in new-type transmission media like iPhone, iPod and iPad. No internet connection is needed for such application.

6.11 The expansion of lexicographical functions and the making of British encyclopaedic dictionaries in the 20th century

The term "encyclopaedic dictionary" originally referred to all sorts of alphabetically arranged encyclopaedic reference works but later developed to refer to specific types of reference works. It may cover different disciplines and fields (i.e. comprehensive encyclopaedic dictionary) or one specific discipline or subject (e.g. encyclopaedic dictionary of medicine, encyclopaedic dictionary of law, encyclopaedic dictionary of art etc.). They become encyclopaedic language dictionaries if macrostructural headwords cover words of language rather than just words of things. Few encyclopaedic dictionaries have been compiled in the history of British lexicography, and their overall scale and quality cannot be mentioned in the same breath as those in America. Therefore, no special attention has been deliberately paid to this dictionary genre in previous research.

In Britain, John Harris, who was a writer, priest and scientist, compiled the first alphabetically arranged encyclopaedic dictionary – *Lexicon Technicum: Or, A Universal English Dictionary of Arts and Sciences* (1704). Its theme is supposed to be mathematics, but it involves many aspects of humanities and social sciences, such as law, trade and commerce, music, heraldry etc. It is considered the forerunner of Britain's encyclopaedia making, while Robert Hunter's *The Encyclopædic Dictionary* is certainly the pioneer and example for English encyclopaedic dictionaries.

200 *Lexicographical traditions*

Throughout the 20th century, not many encyclopaedic English dictionaries were made in Britain. The most noteworthy ones are Patrick Hanks and Simon Potter's *Encyclopedic World Dictionary* (1971), Paul Procter's *Longman New Universal Dictionary* (1982), Judith Pearsall's *The Oxford Encyclopedic English Dictionary* (1991) and Robert Allen's *Chambers Encyclopedic English Dictionary: Thumb Indexed Edition* (1994). In 1988, Alan Isaacs, John Daintith, Jennifer Monk and Elizabeth Martin worked together to revise and augment the *Encyclopedic World Dictionary* and renamed it *The New Hamlyn Encyclopedic World Dictionary* with an increase in pages from 1,856 in the first edition to 1,973.

Longman New Universal Dictionary, which consists of 1,188 pages with a collection of about 90,000 headwords, is the first dictionary that was produced through joint agreement between Longman and Merriam. *The Oxford Encyclopedic English Dictionary* is a comprehensive reference work with innovations and distinctive features. It selects nearly 200,000 headwords, inclusive of nearly 10,000 personal and place names. Its definitions are concise and plain, and its explanations about grammar, usage and etymology are readily understandable. Its use of special signs and abbreviations is kept to the minimum. Nearly 15,000 encyclopaedic essays are provided to elaborate on science and technology, medicine, history, art, mythology, sports, geography, social celebrities, political affairs and so on. Over 100 pages of appendixes offer information regarding American presidents, EU legislative procedures, Indo-European languages, chemical elements, measurements, astrology, human body, world events, scientific and technological innovations etc. It is a landmark in the making of encyclopaedic dictionaries in the history of British English lexicography. *Chambers Encyclopedic English Dictionary*, a hybrid of a dictionary and encyclopaedia, consists of around 70,000 modern words and encyclopaedic terms, including place names, surnames, literary figures, organizations, artistic works, historical events etc.

6.12 The socio-cultural changes and the compilation of British dictionaries of new words

Dictionaries of new words or neologisms are a novelty in the development of British English lexicography. Their appearance is attributable to not only socio-cultural advances and developments of science and technology with each passing day but to dictionary-making itself. On the one hand, it takes quite a long time for a dictionary to be completed. Once printed, it will be in a stative form, and it will be time-consuming even if revision is done. On the other hand, with the rapid development of modern science and technology, new words pop up almost each day, and major breakthroughs in science and technology are likely to trigger an outburst of new words, which are impossible to incorporate into a paper dictionary within a short duration of time, though the case is entirely different now with online and some other multimedia dictionaries, thanks to the remarkable progress in electronic and information technologies.

Therefore, it is quite an issue to provide a timely reflection of new changes of language in dictionaries, especially new words and new uses. The workable solution is definitely the compilation of new word dictionaries that are to be geared towards this segment of market demands. John Ayto's *Longman Register of New Words* (1989–1990) and Sara Tulloch's *Oxford Dictionary of New Words: A Popular Guide to Words in the News* (1993) are among the representative works. *Oxford Dictionary of New Words* is the first dictionary that is published by Oxford University Press to be devoted exclusively to new words and new uses. It follows the tradition of *OED* supplementing and recording new words and new uses but maintaining its distinguishing features. It makes a selective collection of over 2,000 new words, new uses and new expressions that came into daily life from the 1980s and that cover such areas as politics, environmental protection, computer science, technological advances, commercial activities, sports, entertainment etc. Entries provide pronunciation, definition, etymology, examples and traces of evolution. They portray a dynamic and colourful picture of the latest socio-cultural and technological developments, and consultation of entries is like a journey through a space-time continuum from the 1980s, as its advertisement claims.

It is now no difficult task, thanks to the rapid development of electronic and online dictionaries, to record new words and uses and reflect them in dictionaries in a timely fashion. In practice, it is technically possible for compilers and users to lose no time in catching up with the latest changes and make a record of them in dictionaries through their online participation in editing. It can be safely assumed that dictionaries of new words and uses will disappear from the dictionary family in the near future and will be mentioned only as a transitional type in the history of lexicography.

6.13 The enhancement of reference function and the making of British quotation dictionaries

Britain always takes pride in its huge literary resources and has left behind a huge number of classic works for the world civilization. Their witticisms, maxims and sparkling sayings are quoted and repeated from time to time. They are pearls of wisdom and full of life philosophy. Quite a few dictionaries were produced in the 20th century to collect those witty remarks. Among such dictionaries of quotations, representative works include William Gurney Benham's (1859–1944) *Cassell's Book of Quotations* (1907), Burton Stevenson's (1872–1962) *Stevenson's Book of Quotations, Classic & Modern* (1934), R. M. Leonard's *The Oxford Dictionary of Quotations* (1941),

202 *Lexicographical traditions*

Donald Frasers' *Collins Dictionary of Quotations* (1983) and Gary Jones' *Chambers Dictionary of Quotations* (1996). *The Oxford Dictionary of Quotations* is remarkable in that it monopolized Britain's market of quotation dictionaries for most of the second half of the 20th century. It was reprinted time and again after its second edition in 1953, and the latest edition appeared in 2004.

7 English lexicography – accomplishments, developments and prospects

The 19th century witnessed the evolutional transformation and steady development of world lexicographical culture. Lexicographical paradigms continued to evolve and innovate, lexicographical information continued to be substantiated, the compiling art and craft continued to be improved, and the supporting technology and techniques continued to be ameliorated. Adventurers, travellers, priests and merchants contributed in their special ways to the progress of lexicographical culture in the world in the 19th century. Some of them worked single-handedly, made serious studies of national languages and cultures and pushed forward world dictionary-making. The interaction and integration across disciplines furnished theoretical inferences and methodological support for the progress of world lexicography. The profound impacts of historical and comparative linguistics upon diachronic lexicography and etymological explorations are good manifestations of such interaction and integration.

The 20th century was a time that marked the hardest misery and at the same time created the greatest glory in the history of mankind. In the first half of the century, the world underwent two catastrophic wars over a span of only 30 years. As a result, radical changes took place in world politics, economy, culture and military situations. The culture of world lexicography, as a part of world culture, was inevitably affected by the changes in the world political arena.

In the second half of the century, it took only 30 years or so for mankind to shift from the period of industrialization into the era dominated by internet and information technology, with innovation in science and technology, economic prosperity and cultural development reaching an unprecedented height. The application of computer science and corpus technology to dictionary-making facilitated its leap forward from manual compilation and paper medium to electronic compilation and internet medium. The gradual penetrability of electronic and information technology exerted direct and extensive impacts upon every phase of dictionary compilation, strengthened its scientificity, precision, standardization and efficiency and pushed world lexicographical culture to a new and higher level.

204 *Accomplishments, developments and prospects*

Through over 1,000 years' evolution, English lexicographic paradigms developed from its archetype characterized by coarse form, crude content and oversimplified methodology into a sign of lexicographic culture with strong modern flavour featuring structural soundness, enriched content, intricate design and theoretical rigidity, which encompassed abundant linguistic, cultural and academic sediments, as well as rich social, political, military, technological and educational accumulation.

So far in this monograph, the first six chapters, prefixed by "Introduction", have focused upon the practical aspect of British English lexicography over 1,100 years and along two major lines – the socio-cultural evolution of British society and the development of English dictionary paradigms, putting English dictionary-making under the broad context of English being employed as a medium of international communication. They have made contrastive analyses of major representative lexicographical works within a coherent system of English dictionary paradigms, establishing interactive associations of the development of English dictionaries and their paradigms with the international transmission of the English language, in addition to the rise and fall of the British nation, the ups and downs of British society, the spreading of religion and the underpinning of science and technology, thus highlighting the evolutional track of English dictionary paradigms from their archetype to prescriptive, to historical, then to descriptive and eventually to cognitive approaches. They have traced the development laws of English lexicography from the perspective of Britain's social and cultural advancement, therefore unfolding a grand spectacle of the prolonged development of British English lexicography featuring historical inheritance, paradigm continuity, theoretical innovation and systematic integrality.

In this chapter, more attention is to be paid to the theoretical explorations in English lexicography, the improvement and innovation of English dictionary paradigms against the background of various schools of linguistics in the 20th century, the breakthroughs and the latest trends of 20th-century English dictionary-making, the summing-up of experience and philosophies in English dictionary compilation and the refinement of compiling ideologies and sophisticated techniques, as well as the prospects of English lexicography in the 21st century.

7.1 Linguistic theories in the 20th century and the diversified development of English dictionary paradigms

Dictionary reviewers and critics often come up with such a view that dictionary-making always falls behind the development of linguistic theories, thus leaving a big gap between them. There would be some degree of objectivity in such comments if they were put in the second half of the 20th century, as the development of linguistic theories in the 20th century, particularly in the late part of the century, overtook any period in history, in terms of not only theoretical innovation and schools of thought but the speed and

Accomplishments, developments and prospects   205

frequency of innovation as well. Relatively speaking, there is always a cycle of dictionary-making, which may last for several years in some cases and even several decades in others, before revision, augmentation and reprinting get started and completed and repeated with new cycles like this. There must be a transitional period for the latest linguistic findings to be filtered, digested, applied and integrated into dictionary compilation.

However, an overall review of the whole picture of the development of English dictionary paradigms will put this point of view under serious question. It can even be said that English dictionary compilation played a leading role in English studies to some extent and over certain specific periods, and part of the explanation can be found in discussions in the introduction and in the previous chapter. This view will be even less convincible if we take a look at the general background of the development of world lexicography. Take Chinese lexicography for example. Fragmentary studies in dialects and etymology started around 2000 years ago between the Qin (221–206 BC) and the Han (202 BC–AD 220) dynasties, which resulted in no systematic theories, principles and methods, but an integrated and systematic analysis was made from the perspective of dictionary-making by Yang Xiong in *The Dictionary of Dialectal Words* and by Liu Xi in *The Dictionary of Chinese Characters and Terms*. With regard to researches in dialect and etymology, they both came up with ground-breaking thoughts, innovative theories and practical approaches, which are of enlightening and guiding significance even in modern times (Yong and Peng, 2008).

From the 15th century onwards, there appeared in close succession English-Latin and Latin-English dictionaries, such as *Promptorium Parvulorum, Catholicon Anglicum, Medulla Grammaticae, Ortus Vocabulorum* and so on. They almost dominated English dictionary-making in the 16th century and became the major dictionary type in the century. That predominant situation did not change until the first English monolingual dictionary appeared early in the 17th century, and English monolingual dictionary-making started to play a predominant role from Jonson's time and has continued up to the present time. In addition to the traditional types of monolingual and bilingual dictionary-making, there also appeared between the 15th and the 19th centuries encyclopedic dictionaries, special-aspect dictionaries and specialized dictionaries, though few in number. With the exception of etymological dictionaries, which became well developed in both form and content as a supplement to monolingual dictionaries, the making of other types of special-aspect and specialized dictionaries was still in its infancy.

The 20th century was a time of diversified development for English lexicography, bringing forth in a real sense new dictionary types, such as learner's dictionaries, bilingualized dictionaries, electronic dictionaries, online dictionaries, dictionary and thesaurus and so on, which were the outcome of engaging new findings of modern linguistics, latest developments of science and technology and new socio-cultural demands of modern society in

206 *Accomplishments, developments and prospects*

dictionary research and making. What follows will focus on the new dictionary types that were established in the 20th century.

Radical changes took place in compiling notions and guiding principles in 20th-century English monolingual dictionary-making, and those changes pushed it onto the track of descriptivism as a result of its breaking out of the traditional shackles of prescriptivism and the convention of diachronic approach, which was deeply rooted in Britain and on the European continent. Therefore, such transformations could hardly be possible in Britain, as the British were still indulging in the great glory and pride *OED* had created in them. However, beyond the Atlantic Ocean, Webster was adopting a brand-new approach in compiling *Webster's Third*, which was highly innovative and controversial as well. Step by step, descriptivism has become the fundamental principle for the making of general English dictionaries in modern times, and almost all types of English dictionaries in the 20th century have been imprinted to varying degrees with the spirit of descriptivism.

Among the new English dictionary types that emerged in the 20th century, the learner's dictionary is most noteworthy. It is variously known as the learner's dictionary, student dictionary, school dictionary, college (or collegiate) dictionary, pedagogical dictionary etc. Some are identified from the general type by being marked "college edition". Learner's dictionaries can be distinguished in the broad and narrow sense. The former refers to the active dictionaries that cater to the needs of general learners of certain specific languages and aims at intensifying their encoding function, for example *Collins Cobuild Dictionary of the English Language* (1987), *Webster's New Collegiate Dictionary* (sixth edition, 1949) and *The American College Dictionary* (1947), and the latter refers to the active dictionaries that cater to the special needs of only foreign or second-language learners so as to have a good command of that language, for example LDCE (1978), *The Advanced Learner's Dictionary of Current English* (1948) and *Funk & Wagnall's New College Standard Dictionary* (1958).

English learner's dictionaries can be traced back to Latin-English and English-Latin dictionaries between the 15th and the 16th centuries, but learner's dictionaries in their real sense did not appear in the English setting until the early 20th century. West and J. G. Endicott's *The New Method English Dictionary* can be reckoned as the first English learner's dictionary in the modern sense. Between the end of the 19th century and the beginning of the 20th century, linguistics underwent fundamental changes in approaches of research and in theoretical inclination, shifting gradually from prescriptivism to descriptivism. In 1911, Franz Boas published his *Handbook of American Indian Languages* (Volume 1), which signified the inception of a new school of thought and the linguistic inclination towards descriptivism.

In 1933, Leonard Bloomfield (1887–1949) published *Language*, which concentrated on descriptive theories of language and eventually became a representative work of descriptive linguistics. It was against that linguistic

Accomplishments, developments and prospects 207

background that learner's dictionaries appeared and began to prosper. The theories, such as vocabulary control, phraseology and pedagogical grammar, which aroused a great deal of attention and keen interest among language teachers and educationalists in the 1920s and 1930s and at the same time quite a lot of controversy, were the direct theoretical source of the early development of English learner's dictionaries.

The theory of vocabulary control means "the deliberate restriction of the type and number of words for pedagogical or lexicographic purposes" (Hartmann and James, 1998:154). According to the findings by McArthur, that theory originated from Britain in 1844. Sweet (1899) demonstrated the relation between vocabulary control and selection with the conclusion that, the more rigid vocabulary control, the more cautious its selection. West had his education in Oxford University with focus on pedagogy and psychology. After his graduation in 1912, he went to India to work in various educational posts. On the basis of his experience and observations in language teaching there, particularly his explorations in reading resources and competence, he proposed a series of ideas, such as the psychology of reading, the transfer of reading capabilities, the simplification of English, world English, as well as language planning schemes. His research in reading incited an intense interest in vocabulary control, and that led to his association of studies in reading methods with the theory of vocabulary control (Zhang Liwei, 1996).

There were held in New York in 1934 and in London in 1935 two conferences on the theory of vocabulary selection, which deepened theoretical explorations in vocabulary control, and their findings were put into operation. West, Lawrence Faucett and Palmer were requested to formulate a set of standards for vocabulary selection and make theoretical generalizations about vocabulary analysis, and West and Palmer compiled *A General Service List*. In 1935, *The New Method English Dictionary*, which was compiled on the basis of the theory of vocabulary control and aimed to assist non-native speakers of English in their reading comprehension, was a product of combining foreign-language classroom experience with findings from studies in foreign language or second-language acquisition and vocabulary control.

In 1936, West and Palmer published the *Interim Report on Vocabulary Selection for the Teaching of English as a Foreign Language*, which, together with *The New Method English Dictionary*, enabled West to play a leading role in the theory of vocabulary control. In 1953, he published *The General Service List of English Words*, which proved itself extraordinary in that it contained citations where necessary with focus on lexical collocations. In its subsequent augmentations, Hornby, with the help of his wife, made additions of fixed and idiomatic expressions. The theory of vocabulary control exerted important influence upon *The General Service List of English Words*, *A Grammar of English Words*, *The Idiomatic and Syntactic English Dictionary* and the making of English learner's dictionaries in the latter part of the 20th century.

208 *Accomplishments, developments and prospects*

The General Service List of English Words was an early outcome of applying phraseology to language pedagogy, as well as an initial product of integrating theories of vocabulary control and phraseology. Phraseology is "the study of phrases, idioms and multi-word expressions" (Hartmann and James, 1998:109) and has its roots in Palmer's relevant research in the 1920s. Unlike West, Palmer did not receive formal education. He did not complete even his high schooling, but that did not prevent him from setting up a language school of his own at the age of 26 or conducting research in language and language teaching. His efforts turned him into a successful English linguist, a phonetician and a pioneer in English pedagogy.

In his research, West concentrated on language comprehension, but Palmer drew comprehensive and profound inspirations from his teaching experience in Belgium and in the Institute for Research in English Teaching in Tokyo, Japan, realizing that linguistic production was more important. Consequently, he shifted his attention to issues of English grammar, lexical collocation and writing. In 1942, he published *A Grammar of Spoken English*, which provided an objective description of English in actual use. In 1933, through joint efforts with Hornby, he published the *Second Interim Report on English Collocations*. With a selection of only 3,879 lexical collocations, this report set the precedent of phraseological studies by defining fundamental concepts, principles and approaches, thus a landmark in that area of study.

Palmer believed that, for non-native learners of English, the difficulty did not lie in lexical senses but in grammatical structure and lexical collocation. In 1938, under the guidance of West's pedagogical theories, he published *A Grammar of English Words*, which resembled a writing dictionary in structure and content and was intended for linguistic output. Instead of employing the methods of defining via vocabulary control, he identified headwords into semantic varieties and demonstrated as much as possible the syntactic structure of verbs and lexical collocation by using codes and their matching appendixes and providing illustrative examples and explanatory notes. His treatment of verbs by means of codes and their appended syntactic patterns was modelled after in Hornby's dictionary.

In the initial stage of English learner's dictionary compilation, Hornby might as well have been a synthesizer, and that role was ascribable to his English teaching overseas and his involvement in West's and Palmer's research. He absorbed and digested the essentials of research findings from mutually opposing theories, which laid solid theoretical foundations for *The Idiomatic and Syntactic English Dictionary* and its derived work, *The Advanced Learner's Dictionary of Current English*. Hornby, an English grammarian and lexicographer, was also a pioneer in English pedagogy. He was educated in London University College. In 1924, two years after graduation, he went to Japan to teach English and worked together with Palmer in the Institute for Research in English Teaching in Tokyo.

Accomplishments, developments and prospects 209

From the 1930s onwards, Hornby became involved in Palmer's *The General Service List of English Words*, the *Interim Report on Vocabulary Selection for the Teaching of English as a Foreign Language*, and *Thousand-Word English*. In 1937, he collaborated with E. V. Gatenby and H. Wakefield in compiling a new type of dictionary aimed to help foreigners learn English. It was completed in 1940 and published in 1942 in Japan under the title of *The Idiomatic and Syntactic English Dictionary*, which was renamed *The Advanced Learner's Dictionary of Current English*, when it was published by The Oxford University Press in 1948. When the third edition came out, the title was prefixed for the first time with "Oxford". The dictionary was widely recognized and amazingly popular around the world and became an indispensable work of reference for English learners in all parts of the world. Indeed, it created a commercial miracle on the English dictionary market.

The tragedy of the two world wars brought English learner's dictionary-making into the doldrums, lasting for 30 years or so. With the thrilling appearance of *LDCE* in 1978, English learners dictionaries started to mushroom and flourish, which was evidently due to their being deeply rooted in linguistic and pedagogical theories, catering to the practical needs of their users and fitting in with the attributes of language acquisition and cognition. From their appearance, learner's dictionaries came under the profound influence of findings by Palmer, West, Hornby and others, and the theories generated from English teaching overseas, especially the theories of reading, vocabulary control, phraseology, teaching English as a foreign or second language etc.

In their subsequent development, compilers adopted the synchronic and descriptive approach rather than the prescriptive and diachronic approach. They incorporated the stimulus-response theory of structural behaviourism, the phrase structure marker theory of cognitivism, and the metaphor theory into their dictionary-making and turned research findings into operational systems of syntactic patterns, models and markers. Meanwhile, limits were set for the number of headwords selected in macrostructure (generally to around 1,000,000), and abundant lexical information was provided for language production, coupled with ample well-chosen illustrations. The number of defining words was kept at around 3,000 common words, and the defining language was supposed to be simple and readily intelligible. All this contributed to the miraculous success of learner's dictionaries among the 20th-century English dictionaries.

There was derived a new type of dictionaries from English learner's dictionaries – bilingualized dictionaries. In the history of Chinese lexicography, the making of bilingualized dictionaries may be traced to the earliest extant Chinese and Tangut dictionary – *A Timely Gem Dictionary Tangut-Chinese* 《番汉合时掌中珠》, inappropriately but literally translated by Chien and Creamer (1986) as *Foreign-Chinese (Glossary) As Timely As A Pearl In The Palm*, which was compiled by Gulemaocai (骨勒茂才) – an

210 *Accomplishments, developments and prospects*

ethnic of the Dangxiang nationality – and was completed in 1190. It had only 37 pages and collected 414 headwords, divided into three sections under the headings of "Heaven", "Earth" and "Man". Under each entry was listed, from right to left, the Chinese phonetic transcription of the Tangut word, the Tangut word, the Chinese translational equivalent and the Tangut phonetic transcription of the Chinese word. This glossary is most likely to be the earliest bilingualized glossary with both source and target language explanations in the world. (See Yong and Peng, 2008:377–378.)

There started in 16th-century Latin-English dictionaries the practice of adding definitions and explanations written in another language to the already existing definitions written in the target language in bilingual dictionaries to make them multilingual. For example, Veron added French definitions after English definitions in Stephanus' *Dictionariolum puerorum Latina-Gallicum* (1542) to make it a multilingual dictionary *Dictionariolum puerorum, tribus linguis, Latina, Anglica, et Gallica conscriptum* (1552). Bailey set the precedent for making a monolingual dictionary bilingualized and even multilingualized by adding definitions and explanations written in the target languages after existing definitions in *An Orthographical Dictionary* (1727), and the target languages employed involved classical and modern languages in Europe, such as Latin, French and German. Judging from the perspective of modern lexicography, it is not a bilingualized dictionary in the strict sense, but it created a new archetype for dictionary-making.

The new archetype did not get ameliorated and heightened until the 1970s. The compilers translated definitions in the monolingual dictionaries rather than employing defining techniques and inserting their translation after existing definitions so that one entry contained definitions written in two languages. Bilingualized dictionaries represent a special type in bilingual dictionaries and differ from bilingual dictionaries in that they contained definitions and explanations written in both the language of headwords and in the target language. Definitions written in the language of headwords were generally taken from the monolingual base and were written by experts and specialists of the headword language, while the target language definitions were generally the translations of the definitions in the monolingual base, though not necessarily direct translations of headwords.

As indicated previously, definitions in bilingual dictionaries are equivalents and explanations in the target language to source language headwords, while definitions in bilingualized dictionaries are intended to assist the interpretation of source language headwords and their definitions. *The Advanced Learner's Dictionary of Current English* is the first bilingualized learner's dictionary that was produced in Taiwan and Hong Kong, China in 1970 and was later introduced into mainland China. The success of its English-Chinese bilingualized edition stimulated and facilitated the bilingualization of dictionaries compiled in Japanese, Hindi, Greece, Italian, Spanish, Portuguese, Norwegian and other languages.

Accomplishments, developments and prospects   211

In the latter part of the 20th century, the wide application of computers, along with information and internet technologies, brought forth revolutionary transformations in English lexicography. The computer is blessed with huge data storage, high-speed processing, swift information retrieval and excellent display interfaces. Information and internet technologies have created reliable means of information processing, transmission and display and sound foundations for lexicographical information to be presented by digital, electronic and online means. Multimedia dictionaries are classified into electronic dictionaries and internet dictionaries (variously known as online dictionaries, e-dictionaries, web dictionaries and cyber dictionaries) according to information transmission and presentation media. They have taken shape as a result of explorations in natural language processing and machine translation that started in the 1940s and have been in popular use thanks to the wide and cheap availability of laptop computers, electronic networks and online resources.

Electronic dictionaries "utilise computers and associated technology to present information on screen", such as "spelling checkers and thesauruses built into word processors, multi-volume dictionaries and encyclopaedias on CD-ROM, multilingual terminological databanks and translation systems" (Hartmann and James, 1998:46–47). Their experiment and development started in the 1960s in the west, particularly in Britain and America, but the earliest chip dictionary, i.e. the first palm dictionary – *Alpha 8 English-German German-English Dictionary* – was brought into existence in Germany in 1983, with a selective coverage of about 4,000 headwords. The late 1980s and the early 1990s were the start of their prime period of making and publication.

According to information medium, electronic dictionaries are mainly divided into palm dictionaries (also chip dictionaries) and disc dictionaries (also CD dictionaries), and disc dictionaries are divided into CD-ROM and CD-Interactive (abbreviated as CD-I) according to modes of information storage. Owing to the advantages of novel medium, convenience to carry, quick retrieval, bulky information load, wide range of functions and strong compatibility, electronic dictionaries have radically changed the ways that lexicographical information is stored, transmitted, processed and used. The second edition of *Oxford English Dictionary* (CD-ROM edition, 1992) "made history" as "suddenly a massive, twenty-volume work that takes up four feet of shelf space and weighs 150 pounds is reduced to a slim, shiny disk that takes up virtually no space and weighs just a few ounces", and its electronic format "revolutionized the way people use the Dictionary to search and retrieve information. Complex investigations into word origins or quotations that would have been impossible to conduct using the print edition now take only a few seconds" (see oed.com). Electronic dictionaries have been gradually and quietly transforming user consultation habits and learning characteristics, as well as ways of dictionary use.

212 *Accomplishments, developments and prospects*

Internet dictionaries are classified by some into the category of "electronic dictionaries", but they display great differences. Internet dictionaries take advantage of HTML (Hyper Text Markup Language) and online facilities for their making and presentation. They are well developed in the west, especially in Britain and America, where dictionary databases have been created in large numbers, huge sizes and great varieties. There are single-website brand dictionaries, such as oed.com created by Oxford University Press and wordweb.info created by Chambers, and composite-website brand dictionaries, such as onelook.com, alphadictionary.com and yourdictionary.com. By 2020, onelook.com had 1,062 dictionaries with 19,398,235 headwords; alphadictionary.com had 1,065 English dictionaries, which users can search at once and yourdictionary.com encompasses 6,800 known languages spoken in the 200 countries of the world, among which 2,261 have writing systems (the others are only spoken) and about 300 are represented by online dictionaries. That is an ample demonstration of their immense sizes, broad ranges of function, wide involvement of species and remarkable array of languages. The parallel retrieval of information that is enabled by that composite collection of online dictionary resources has considerably expanded the scope of user knowledge of words, unlimitedly broadened the horizon of user cognition and comprehensively promoted users' capability of lexical acquisition and use. It has also revolutionized the traditional compiler–user relationship owing to its instantaneity, dynamics and interactivity and has broken away from previous compiling techniques and publishing paths of paper dictionaries in which direct revision was impossible once they were printed.

Online dictionaries are subject to new editing, augmentation, deletion, modification and updating at every point and in every conceivable aspect. In addition, dictionary users have the privilege of making comments and suggestions through designated windows of interaction and may even be directly involved in supplementation and revision. Facts prove that the changes that online dictionaries have brought about have far exceeded predictions Jones and Carr made. Their impacts have gone far beyond dictionary compilation, research and use and have made changes in ways of thinking, academic inertia and scientific development. What should be noted is that problems arise with their development, such as lack of convenience caused by their medium, lack of stability caused by technical administration and lowering of quality caused by random editing, and no solutions can be worked out instantly or overnight.

Finally, a brief introduction is made here about "dictionary and thesaurus" or "thesaurus dictionary". "Thesaurus dictionary" is actually a hybrid of a general dictionary and a synonym finder, which means allocating a special space after definitions, after a whole entry or at the bottom of the page where the entry is located to list synonyms, synonymous or related expressions with a view to expanding the scope of lexical retrieval, providing lexical selection for language production and word clues for right expressions,

Accomplishments, developments and prospects   213

such as *Collins English Dictionary and Thesaurus* (2000). To serve this end, pocket types have even been published, such as *The Pocket Oxford Dictionary and Thesaurus* (2002). A single online search via the keywords of "dictionary and thesaurus" will display over 70,000,000 results, and a great proportion of them are "dictionary and thesaurus", such as *The Sage's English Dictionary and Thesaurus*, as well as those in such famous online dictionary brands as www.merriam-webster.com/dictionary/search.

7.2 Theoretical innovations and developments in 20th-century English lexicography

Lexicography is generally defined as "the making of dictionaries". This definition has obviously taken into account the traditional aspect of English lexicography – i.e. its practical implication of dictionary-making – but overlooked its theoretical generation and development in contemporary times. In reality, it is theoretical researches in contemporary lexicography and their effective integration with modern linguistic inquiries that gave the 20th-century English lexicography a colourful, splendid and yet unique glamour and an unimaginably remarkable page in the history of world lexicography and civilization.

First, no one can tell for sure when the first language in the world originated, but it is clear that in the initial stage language always appeared in the form of speech, from which the writing system gradually evolved. The existence of written language and its use by its community became the prerequisite for dictionary-making in all languages, as the dictionary is the carrier of language in use and the reflection of language-related culture. The rationale for the dictionary to be a useful tool resides mainly in the conventional nature of language use as a fundamental precondition and the inherent value of the dictionary in revealing such conventionality by recording the actual use of language. The extent of value depends largely on what is reflected and the techniques of presentation.

Second, through prolonged exploration and practice, lexicographers have obtained well-grounded understanding and perspectives regarding basic issues of dictionary compilation, such as who dictionaries are made for, what functions they are expected to perform, what criteria should be set for lexical selection and the selection of lexical use, what information should be provided concerning such aspects and in what ways they should be presented. They have been able to, in the light of fundamental principles, user needs and their cognitive characteristics, make dictionary designs and organize contents so that the actual use of language is objectively and systematically presented according to their intentions and goals.

Third, both diachronic and descriptive approaches to dictionary-making have been nearing perfection through continuous improvement in both theory and practice as a result of lexicographers' deepening cognition of language and their profound understanding of the nature, content and function

214   *Accomplishments, developments and prospects*

of the dictionary. The diachronic approach requires collecting, sorting out and digesting linguistic data mainly from written sources so as to record, refine, explain and arrange them in the historical sequence of the appearance of lexical uses rather than merely understanding or prescribing their uses according to preferences. The synchronic approach, on the other hand, requires employing both oral and written sources, rather than merely relying on written sources such as classic works by famous authors to collect linguistic data by sociolinguistic means for the purpose of illustrating linguistic uses and making a comprehensive and objective analysis of language phenomena from multiple perspectives and dimensions. Diachronic and descriptive principles are two major theoretical breakthroughs in 19th- and 20th-century English lexicography.

Fourth, dictionaries can perform descriptive, didactic and ideological functions and can meet multi-layered demands for linguistic and cultural information on the part of users. Users have diversified, much-varied and multidimensional needs. This understanding of user demands overturned the conventional view of "one dictionary meeting universal needs". It is considered a significant discovery in 20th-century English lexicography and a starting point in modern dictionary compilation. The diversified development of English dictionaries in the 20th century was realized through continuous deepening and strenuous observation of those basic notions and guidelines.

The existence and wide employment of written language make dictionary compilation possible and necessary, and dictionary compilation and development make dictionary research indispensable. However, dictionary compilation and lexicographic theories are not usually synchronized. Serious lexicographic theories lag behind practices by thousands of years. The earliest dictionary dates back to four or five thousand years before Christ, and fragmentary researches in English dictionaries did not start until around the middle of the 19th century. According to the relevant literature, Albert Way (1805–1874) is the first British scholar to have conducted studies in dictionary-making. His research, which concentrates on the first English-Latin dictionary *Promptorium Parvulorum*, dates back to 1843. In the preface to the 1867 edition of the first English rhyming dictionary – Peter Levins' *Manipulus vocabulorum. A dictionarie of English and Latine wordes*, Henry B. Wheatley (1838–1917) made a careful study of early English and English-Latin dictionaries from a different perspective. However, those studies were fragmentary and scarce. Serious and systematic research of English dictionaries, as well as English lexicography, did not start until after the middle of the 20th century, 1960 to be exact.

Upon entry into the 20th century, numerous dictionaries came out all over the world, most notably English dictionaries launched by publishers such as Oxford, Cambridge, Collins, Longman, Webster and Macquarie. The rapid progress in dictionary-making provided precious resources and practical bases for dictionary research, which had already fallen far behind.

Accomplishments, developments and prospects 215

It became an effective propeller for coherent and integrated researches in the theory and practice of dictionary-making. In 1960, a handful of linguists and lexicographers gathered at The University of Indiana, USA to discuss a host of issues pertaining to dictionary-making and research. The major findings were carried in the fourth section of *International Journal of American Linguistics* (Volume 28, Issue No. 2, 1962), and five years later a collection of papers delivered at the conference met its readership. That is probably the first time for researches in English lexicography, and most likely for lexicography of any language in the world, to be published under one cover and in one collection.

In 1971, Ladislav Zgusta (1924–2007), American linguist and lexicographer of Czech origin, published *Manual of Lexicography*, which marked the ground-breaking of lexicography as a relatively independent discipline or branch of modern linguistics. In 1989, Franz Josef Hausmann and his co-authors brought about *An International Encyclopedia of Lexicography*, which indicated that lexicography as a relatively independent discipline had a acquired consolidated foundation and, more importantly, that it had achieved a great leap forward towards its theoretical maturity. Its publication certainly did not mean that solutions had been worked out to all problems relating to dictionary-making and research. On the contrary, it was only a good beginning and in many ways a sum-up and agglomeration of previous findings, though some parts of it contained a great deal of innovation. Many issues relating to the basics of lexicography waited to be studied, which implied that lexicography had great prospects and potential for research and development.

The Dictionary of Lexicography, which was published by R. R. K. Hartmann and Gregory James in 2000, boils lexicography down to two major aspects, i.e. dictionary research (theory) and dictionary-making (practice). The theory of lexicography includes history of dictionaries, their typology, criticism, use, structure and so on, and the practice of lexicography includes data collection, data description and information presentation. What is summed up there covers major components of lexicography but overlooks some important aspects, such as dictionary function, policy, user, cognition, terminological standardization, theoretical configuration etc. Dictionary users and their cognition of dictionaries have become heated and much-debated issues over the past few decades and have attracted more and more serious attention from lexicographers, as well as linguists and scholars of other backgrounds. Nearly ten years later, O. M. Karpova and F. I. Kartashkova's *Lexicography and Terminology: A Worldwide Outlook* (2009) discussed theoretical and practical issues concerning terminological standardization in lexicography from broader dimensions and higher academic levels.

Dictionary design is a major step and prerequisite for compilation, and studies show that English lexicography has experienced three relatively independent and yet interrelated modes of dictionary design over different

216 Accomplishments, developments and prospects

periods: the traditional mode, the transitional mode and the pedagogical mode. (See also Dubois, 1981.) The traditional mode, characterized by focus on hard words, dominated English dictionary-making for hundreds of years. The transitional mode was initiated by the publication of *Webster's Third*, which signifies the inception of descriptive lexicography, an era of language being described in dictionaries as it is. Descriptivism has been universally accepted as the fundamental principle for dictionary-making in modern times.

The pedagogical mode is characterized by focus on users, displaying a striking shift in dictionary policies and design from compiler domination to user friendliness. The appearance of *The Advanced Learner's Dictionary of Current English* can be regarded as a starting point, succeeded closely by such dictionaries as *LDCE* and *Collins Cobuild Dictionary of the English Language*. The pedagogical mode is highlighted by its inheritance of descriptivism, more attention to the representation of user needs of language and the reconstruction of cognitive modes and a greater concentration on the active use of language. The new philosophy of dictionary compilation, which is user-centred and emphasizes the objective of facilitating language teaching and learning, has won wide recognition among dictionary makers. Dictionary users and user cognition of language in their use of dictionaries has become a major aspect and a heated subject in English lexicography since the 1980s.

In terms of disciplinary construction, the foundation of lexicography has been further substantiated, and its status as a discipline has been established through systematic and comprehensive practices as well as theoretical generalization since the latter part of the 20th century. Dictionary-making involves the collection, selection, observation and description of words and expressions in one or several languages, but this is only one aspect of lexicographical activities – dictionary compilation. Just as Hausmann and Cop (1985) pointed out, lexicography also covers the description of theories and methodologies and their development, which is the foundation for lexicographical activities and a more important part of lexicography as a discipline. Some scholars use "metalexicography" for this part of lexicographical description. Only sound practices and coherent theorization can make lexicography a well-developed discipline and put it on the track of healthy development.

It can be said to some extent that language research originated with dictionary-making, and dictionary-making in turn provided substance and inspirations for linguistic and cultural studies, though they were only primitive and preliminary in the initial stage. From the 19th century, English dictionary-making absorbed beneficial elements from related and neighbouring disciplines, particularly from linguistics. The 19th century witnessed smooth and rapid development of historical and comparative linguistics. That stimulated linguists' interest in lexical changes and word histories and eventually led to the emergence of a series of English dictionaries based on

Accomplishments, developments and prospects 217

the historical principle. It has become a common practice to include etymological information at the end of the entry in English dictionaries, and that convention has continued up to the present day.

Early in the 20th century, once again, the appearance of descriptive and structural linguistics constituted steady and continuing impacts upon lexicography, and consequently the descriptive paradigm was established and put into operation. Over the past few decades, full advantage has been taken of the latest developments in linguistics and other related disciplines (i.e. electronic science, information science) in lexicographical activities. The application of electronic technologies and information science has radically transformed the landscape of dictionary research and compilation and turned lexicography into a discipline with the greatest potentials and vitality in humanities of the new century. The gradual integration of research findings of linguistics and other related disciplines into lexicography has shattered the traditional conceptualization of dictionary research and practice and lexicography as a discipline. The proposition of setting lexicography on a solid scientific footing has reached consensus among linguists and educators as well as lexicographers and has attracted concerted effort on the part of lexicographers and scholars in related fields.

All over the world, lexicographical research has been going on for the goal of attaining new heights, and works on lexicography have been published in close succession. Professional organizations for dictionary makers and researchers have been set up in different parts of the world. For example, in 1975, the Dictionary Society of North America was founded in America, followed by the European Association for Lexicography in 1983 in Britain, the Australian Association for Lexicography in 1990 in Australia, and the Lexicographical Society of China in 1992. These organizations have held conferences and workshops, published periodical journals and exchanged new developments on a regular basis. They have contributed considerably to the development and prosperity of English and world lexicography.

Aside from professional organizations, journals of lexicography have also been launched, typically the *International Journal of Lexicography*, which was started by the European Association for Lexicography in 1988 and is now published by Oxford University Press; *Dictionaries*, which was started by the Dictionary Society of North America in 1979 and *Lexicographical Studies*, which was started by the Lexicographical Society of China in 1979. The essence of lexicography resides in the improvement of dictionary quality through studies in dictionary compilation and use and in the generalization, description and assessment of theories and methods relating to lexicographical activities and advancement so as to effectively affect users' knowledge structure and ability to understand the linguistic world and integrate lexicographical theories and practices into a coherent, systematic and scientific knowledge framework.

218　*Accomplishments, developments and prospects*

John M. Sinclair (1984) once stated that it was not ripe for lexicography to become a discipline and that a disciplinary system must be reconstructed with broadened visions and reanalysis of certain issues. Only fewer than 40 years have elapsed, and lexicography has assumed an entirely different landscape. It has formed its integrated and coherent theoretical framework and has its own system of branches. What follows is a comprehensive but succinct survey of major theoretical accomplishments published in English with strong international influence in the 20th-century English lexicography, which covers theoretical and practical lexicography; general and specialized lexicography; monolingual and bilingual/multilingual lexicography; diachronic and synchronic lexicography; textual, communicative, cognitive and comparative lexicography and computational and corpus lexicography, as well as dictionary typology and dictionary criticism. Given the theoretical continuity, relevant findings in the 21st century have been touched upon from time to time.

Theoretical and practical lexicography From the perspective of research purposes, lexicography can be classified into theoretical and practical lexicography. The former studies origins and developments, fundamental principles, research methodology, typological classification, distinctive attributes, terminological standardization, structural description, functional analysis, its interactive relations to neighbouring and related disciplines and so on. The latter explores practical thoughts involved in dictionary-making, such as macro-level issues pertaining to the design, function and perspective of dictionary-making, micro-level issues regarding the art and craft and techniques that are adopted in defining words, selecting examples, annotating styles and register of lexical use and the application of lexicographical research findings to dictionary-making.

Representative works of theoretical lexicography include Ladislav Zgusta's *The Manual Of Lexicography* (1971), Henri Bejoint's *Modern Lexicography: An Introduction* (2000), Sven Tarp et al.'s *Lexicography in the 21st Century: In Honour of Henning Bergenholtz* (2009), Olga Karpova and Faina Kartashkova's *New Trends in Lexicography: Ways of Registrating and Describing Lexis* (2010), and so on. Those of practical lexicography include Bo Svensen's *Practical Lexicography: principles and methods of dictionary-making* (1993), Atkins B. T. Sue's and Michael Rundell's *The Oxford Guide to Practical Lexicography* (2008), Thierry Fontenelle's *Practical Lexicography A Reader* (2008) and so on.

General and specialized lexicography From the perspective of research areas, lexicography can be classified into general and specialized lexicography. Just as general linguistics overarches all branches of linguistics, general lexicography covers under its umbrella all branches of general lexicography and conducts general studies in lexicographical histories, concepts, theories, models, principles and methodology respecting compilation and research. Its scope is not restrained by languages, types and perspectives that dictionaries involve. It should be noted that general and theoretical

Accomplishments, developments and prospects   219

lexicography overlap to some extent in scope of study, as they share some common issues.

Representative works of general lexicography include Sidney Landau's *Dictionaries: The Art and Craft of Lexicography* (1989), Howard Jackson's *Lexicography: An Introduction* (2002), Sven Tarp's *Lexicography in the Borderland Between Knowledge and Non-knowledge: General Lexicographical Theory With Particular Focus on Learner's Lexicography* (2008), Bo Svensén's *A Handbook of Lexicography: The Theory and Practice of Dictionary-making* (2009) and so on. Specialized lexicography is considered a major theoretical and practical component of general lexicography and focuses on the theory and practice of special-subject dictionaries (i.e. dictionaries that engage specific subjects and fields) or special-aspect dictionaries (i.e. dictionaries that engage certain aspects of language). Representative works include Henning Bergenholtz and Sven Tarp's *Manual of Specialized Lexicography* (1995), Fuertes-Olivera et al.'s *Specialized Lexicography. The representation of meaning in business dictionaries* (2008), Nuria Edo Marza's *Specialized Lexicographical Approach: A Step Further in Dictionary-making* (2009) and so on.

Monolingual and bilingual/multilingual lexicography From the perspective of the number of languages involved, lexicography can be classified into monolingual and bilingual/multilingual lexicography. The former studies the historical development, typological classification, compiling principles, methodology and techniques as well as the pedagogical application of monolingual dictionaries, usually the native language dictionaries of compilers. The majority of existing monographs and articles fall into this category. Bilingual lexicography studies the historical development, typological classification, compiling principles, methodology and techniques as well as the pedagogical application of bilingual dictionaries. Representative works include Doris A. Bartholomew and Louise C. Schoenhals' *Bilingual Dictionaries for Indigenous Languages* (1983), Tadeusz Piotrowski's *Problems in Bilingual Lexicography* (1994), Martin Stark's *Bilingual Thematic Dictionaries* (2011) and so on.

Diachronic and synchronic lexicography From temporal dimensions of lexicographical research, lexicography can be classified into diachronic and synchronic lexicography. The former explores the evolution of dictionaries, either monolingual, bilingual or both, from diachronic perspectives and from general or specific aspects. General works on diachronic lexicography include Tom McArthur's *Worlds of References – lexicography, learning and language: from clay tablets to computer* (1986) and Robert L. Collison's *A History of Foreign-Language Dictionaries* (1982).

As far as the history of monolingual dictionaries is concerned, quite a number of works have been published, and those of the most extensive influence include Eva Mae Burkett's *American Dictionaries of the English Language Before 1861* (1979), De Witt T. Starnes' and Gertrude E. Noyes' *The English Dictionary from Cawdrey to Johnson 1604–1755* (1991),

220   *Accomplishments, developments and prospects*

Jonathon Green's *Chasing The Sun* (1996), Sarah Ogilvie's *The Cambridge Companion to English Dictionaries* (2020) and so on. Some monographs even focus on the historical development of only a single dictionary, such as Simon Winchester's *The Meaning of Everything: The Story of the Oxford English Dictionary* (2004), and Bill Ramson's *Lexical Images: The Story of the Australian National Dictionary* (2004). Representative works on the history of bilingual dictionaries include De Witt T. Starnes' *Renaissance Dictionaries English-Latin and Latin-English* (1954), Desmond O'Connor's *A History of Italian and English Bilingual Dictionaries* (1990) and so on. Starnes' monograph can be esteemed as a classic work of the history of bilingual dictionaries.

Synchronic lexicography studies the compilation and development of dictionaries at a specific point of time or over a limited period of time from static perspectives. The synchronic approach can be adopted for explorations in the development of a single dictionary or dictionaries compiled over the same period of time. James Sledd and Wilma R. Ebbitt's *Dictionaries and That Dictionary* (1962), for example, is a synchronic study of *Webster's Third*.

Textual, communicative, cognitive and comparative lexicography From the perspective of theories and methods involved in research, lexicography can be classified into textual lexicography (i.e. the dictionary as text), communicative lexicography (i.e. the dictionary as communication), cognitive lexicography and comparative lexicography.

The traditional view of the dictionary as reference holds that "entries in the dictionaries are looked at individually and separately and are not treated as an integrated whole" (Yong and Peng, 2007:4), thus severing relations between entries, across entries and within entries. The traditional view has dominated dictionary-making for thousands of years. It affected the ways that dictionaries were designed, compiled, used and evaluated. "A dictionary is compiled mainly for reference. This is the most primitive and most practical function of the dictionary. However, there are far more functions for dictionaries to perform than just that" (Yong and Peng, 2007:3).

It was not until the early 1980s, when user role began to draw increasing attention from dictionary makers and researchers and text linguistics appeared and prospered. "The development of text linguistics made it theoretically possible and necessary to review and assess the traditional ways of looking at the dictionary and view the dictionary from an entirely different perspective" (Yong and Peng, 2007:5), i.e. in terms of text linguistics.

A serious attempt in this connection is made by William Frawley (1989:231–248), who puts forward his straightforward proposition 'the dictionary as text' in an article under the same title. He observes the dictionary from the standpoint of text grammar, using De Beaugrande and Dressler's seven criteria for textuality (i.e. cohesion, coherence,

Accomplishments, developments and prospects 221

informativity, intentionality, acceptability, situationality and intertextuality) as the basis for his analysis.

Though Frawley tried to answer some of the questions in his paper, he nevertheless focused mainly on the information structure of lexicographical text, the prospects for reading the dictionary through the use of schemas and the semantic integration of the dictionary as text.

This view of the dictionary gives too much attention to the organizational principles of dictionary text rather than functional potentials. "Therefore, it sounds more like a structural approach than a functional one" (See Yong and Peng, 2007:6).

"It can be reasonably argued that dictionary-making is by its very nature a process of transmitting and imparting knowledge and information and that lexicography studies how this process is realized and how it affects the user's reference behavior and knowledge structure". Taking this as a starter, communicative lexicography adopts the analysis of the dictionary as reference and the dictionary as text as its base and the process school of communication studies as the fundamentals for the communicative theory of lexicography, thus "treating the dictionary as some sort of interactive system between the compiler and the user" and creating "a generally unified framework within which the theoretical foundation for lexicography is laid and both theoretical and practical issues of lexicography may be addressed". "This model generates the possibility of observing the dictionary as an entirety from three different but interdependent standpoints, i.e. from the position of *compiler*, from the position of *user*, and from the position of *context*" (Yong and Peng, 2007:7–9; emphasis in original). Representative works on communicative lexicography include *Communicative Lexicography* (Yong, 2003; revised and augmented edition, Yong and Peng, 2010) and *Bilingual Lexicography from a Communicative Perspective* (Yong and Peng, 2007).

Over the past few decades, the user demand and role in lexicographical activities have been gaining more and more prominence, and closer links of lexicographical researches have been established to socio-cultural factors and users' cognitive behaviour. With the emergence and flourishing of learners dictionaries, lexicographers have extended their studies into users' language acquisition and dictionary use so as to apply findings in language cognition to lexicographical activities. They have attempted to simulate user behaviour in linguistic cognition in dictionary design, information presentation, language needs and skills of information retrieval so that dictionaries can provide more objective reflections of the process of language acquisition, more effective assistance in consultation and more scientific improvement of functional facilitation. As far as relevant literature shows, only a few monographs of cognitive lexicography have been published, and more such findings can be found in journals and paper collections. Representative works include *Explorations in Cognitive Lexicography* (Yanchun Zhao,

222 *Accomplishments, developments and prospects*

2003) and Sylwia Wojciechowska's *Conceptual Metonymy and Lexicographic Representation* (2011).

Dictionaries can be studied from a comparative approach. Comparison can be made of different versions and editions of the same dictionary, of different dictionaries of identical and similar types, of different types of dictionaries and of dictionaries across cultures, languages and nations. In doing so, lexicographers can discover attributes dictionaries share; reveal similarities, associations and differences that exist in dictionaries of the same language and culture or different languages and cultures and eventually develop and establish more scientific notions, principles and methodology of lexicography through reference, exemplification and inspiration. That is what is meant by comparative lexicography. James David Andersen's *The Development of the English-French, French-English Bilingual Dictionaries: A Study in Comparative Lexicography* (1972) is an early representative work.

Computational and corpus lexicography From the perspective of lexicographical media, lexicography can be classified into computational and corpus lexicography. Computational lexicography studies the design, compilation, use and evaluation of electronic and online dictionaries. Its scope of study covers digitalization in major phases of dictionary-making (i.e. the selection of data from linguistic corpora, sense discrimination, on-screen text process, application of printing technology etc.), the use of machine-readable dictionaries (i.e. machine translation, natural language processing etc.), design of brand-new information retrieval systems (i.e. CD-ROM, multi-media encyclopaedia, multi-language terminology databank etc.) and so on. Quite a few works have been devoted to computational lexicography, including B. Boguraev et al.'s *Computational Lexicography for Natural Language Processing* (1988), Leo Wanner's *Lexical Functions in Lexicography and Natural Language Processing* (1996), Ferenc Kiefer et al.'s *Papers in Computational Lexicography COMPLEX'92/94/96* (1992, 1994, 1996), D. E. Walker et al.'s *Automating the Lexicon: Research and Practice in a Multilingual Environment* (1994), Maria Carmen Campoy Cubillo's *Computer-mediated Lexicography in the Foreign Language Learning Context* (2004) and Sylviane Granger and Magali Paquot's *Electronic Lexicography* (2012).

The rapid development of computer technology has made dictionary compilation more precise, comprehensive, objective and efficient. The building of corpuses has created exceptionally advantageous conditions for this trend of lexicography. Modern dictionary-making has done away with manual modes of citation collection, transcription and typewriting and moved into new modes of keyboarding, optoelectronic scanning and even phonetic transcription. All that has combined to make it possible to build large-scale corpuses. In the initial stage, corpuses were used to assist in linguistic description. Later on, more and more lexicographers realized their practical value in dictionary-making with the continuous amelioration of their technologies and functions.

Accomplishments, developments and prospects 223

In present-day dictionary-making, corpuses have become indispensable, and serious studies have been conducted concerning their application in that connection, hence the birth of corpus lexicography, which explores the development and establishment of corpuses and their significance to dictionary-making and theoretical researches of lexicography. Corpus lexicography can be of direct service to the theoretical and practical studies of lexicography in new word collection, lexical changes, citation screening, word frequency count, sense arrangement, lexical collocation, style and register labelling and many other aspects. Conferences have been held to discuss various issues and aspects from both theoretical and practical perspectives, and important works have been published, such as V. B. Y. Ooi's *Computer Corpus Lexicography* (1998) and Henning Bergenholtz et al.'s *The Internet, Digital Initiatives and Lexicography* (2011).

Dictionary typology Typological studies of dictionaries started in the 1940s. L. V. Shcherba, a former Soviet Union scholar, made a pioneering classification of dictionaries in 1940. He conducted a comparative study of dictionaries – existent and imaginary – and configured a typological framework for six contrasting sets of dictionaries with distinctive features on the basis of their most striking structural characteristics. However, his classification turns out to limited in coverage and range and therefore does not suffice to present the whole landscape of dictionaries.

About 20 years after Shcherba's classification, Yakov Malkiel, inspired by the theory of distinctive phonetic features, proposed his classification on the basis of three criteria, i.e. scope, perspective and presentation, each of which is divided into subcategories, as well as factorial analysis. Fifty years later, in his landmark *Manual of Lexicography*, Zgusta used C. C. Berg's definition of dictionaries as a starting point for his classification. He started by dividing dictionaries into encyclopaedias and language dictionaries and proceeded with his classification according to time span, scope of coverage, language presentation, dictionary function, dictionary size and so on.

Landau (1989:7–34) provided his typology based on a comprehensive survey of significant factors in dictionary classification, such as the number of languages, modes of funding, user age, dictionary size, scope of coverage, restrictions of language aspects involved, lexical unit, primary language market, span of time and so on. Comprehensive, wide-ranging and workable as it is, his classification fails to attract serious attention from linguists and lexicographers, mainly due to the fact that it is not a coherent framework that can take into consideration all existing and potential dictionary types.

Aside from the aforementioned attempts, lexicographers and linguists have conducted relevant researches from other angles. The most influential are Thomas A. Sebeok's typology based on defined features, Alain Rey's generative typology, Al-Kasimi's new typology and D. Geeraerts' framework for classification. Yong and Peng (2007) put forth their communicative

224 *Accomplishments, developments and prospects*

model of typology from three different and yet interdependent dimensions, i.e. compiler perspective, dictionary context and user perspective.

Dictionary criticism Dictionary criticism is a major component of the theoretical research of lexicography. From the perspective of historical evolution of dictionaries, the theoretical research of lexicography originated from those earliest comments and discussions, either oral or written, formal or informal. Dictionary criticism has become a significant source that generates new lexicographical theories, facilitates innovation in dictionary-making and deepens theoretical explorations in lexicography.

Owing to all that, lexicographers have given great prominence to dictionary criticism and considered it a significant part of theoretical lexicography. A great proportion of space has been devoted to articles of dictionary criticism in the *International Journal of Lexicography* and *Dictionaries. N. E.* Osselton published a collection of dictionary reviews – *Chosen Words: Past and Present Problems with Dictionary Makers* (1995), which used reviews of major dictionaries that came out from Shakespeare's time as the basis for discussions about practical issues and problems that lexicographers have encountered in making dictionaries.

Apart from the works mentioned previously, conference proceedings and collections of papers were also published by lexicographical associations, for example, R. R. K. Hartmann's *The History of Lexicography* (1986), Mary Snell-Hornby's *ZuriLEX'86 Proceedings: Papers read at the EURALEX International Congress* (1988), Mary Snell-Hornby et al.'s *Translation and Lexicography: Papers read at the EURALEX Colloquium* (1989), Braj B. Kachru and Henry Kahane's *Cultures, Ideologies, and the Dictionary: Studies in Honour of Ladislav Zgusta* (1995), Martin Gellerstam et al.'s *Euralex'96 Proceedings I-II: Papers submitted to the Seventh EURALEX International Congress on Lexicography* (1998), Julie Coleman et al.'s *Historical Dictionaries and Historical Dictionary Research: Papers from the International Conference on Historical Lexicography and Lexicology, at the University of Leicester, 2002* (2004), Arne Zettersten et al.'s *Symposium on Lexicography XI: Proceedings of the Eleventh International Symposium on Lexicography, May 2–4, 2002 at the University of Copenhagen* (2005), Ladislav Zgusta et al.'s *Lexicography Then and Now: Selected Essays* (2006) and so on. They cover various aspects of dictionary-making, use and research. They embody innovations in lexicographical practice and important breakthroughs in lexicographical research and ways of thinking about dictionary compilation. They are valuable inspirations to dictionary design, making and use.

Young though it is, lexicography is a discipline full of vitality. Its theories have not taken quite a long time in formulation, but its development is encouraging, and many existing areas await to be further explored, such as dictionary use, users, cognition, history, digitalization, application of electronic and information technologies and linguistic findings in dictionary-making and research. Many new areas await to be developed, such as

Accomplishments, developments and prospects 225

the mechanism of interaction between lexicography and culture, dictionary paradigm and user cognition, comparative studies in lexicography across languages and cultures, dictionary market and marketing strategies and so on. All those heated topics and trends of lexicography had already turned up or were beginning to gain serious attention at the turn of the 20th and the 21st centuries and will open up immense prospects and space for the amelioration of lexicography in the 21st century.

7.3 The prospect of English lexicography in the 21st century

Just as historical comparative linguistics in the 19th century paved the way for the development of English dictionaries in the 20th century, linguistic theories in the 20th century, in particular descriptive linguistics, pragmatics and cognitive linguistics, indicate the basic trend and direction for theoretical explorations and practical innovations in 21st-century English lexicography. The development of English dictionaries over the first two decades or so after entry into the 21st century is a substantial testimony to this assumption and an initial manifestation of the trend of their development. Over the past 20 years or so, theoretical studies of lexicography have continued to evolve around heated issues and keywords that appeared in the late 20th century, such as user, use, cognition, diachronism, networking, informationalization, digitalization and personalization. There is every reason to believe that theoretical breakthroughs are most probable in at least the following areas of English lexicography in the 21st century.

First, dictionary user and use will continue to be one of the research focuses. Dictionary users' linguistic cognition, especially their behaviour in vocabulary acquisition and its impacts upon dictionary-making, will become a key research area of cognitive lexicography. Theoretical accomplishments in cognitive linguistics will provide important support for breakthroughs in that area.

Second, the intimate integration of electronic and information technology and research in dictionary-making will be of vital significance to the creation of new-type multimedia and multi-interface consultation systems and platforms. Obvious progress will be made in the electronization, digitalization, informationalization and networking of dictionaries, with their levels being continuously heightened and with channels and interfaces of lexicographical information presentation and retrieval being continuously diversified. Omnipresent accessibility of lexicographical information will be a reality. Unimaginably super-scale corpuses will provide incredible technological convenience and conditions for dictionary-making and research.

Third, dictionary functions and forms will undergo fundamental transformation as a result of breakthroughs in linguistic theories and information technology. Dictionaries will retain their basic functions, but traditionally non-dictionary functions will be incorporated into them. Future dictionaries

226 *Accomplishments, developments and prospects*

are likely to become "know-all" and "help-all" tools. Additionally, the third edition of *OED* will have no more paper editions, which indicates that future dictionaries will probably bid farewell to paper editions and assume a brand-new form. Thus, future dictionaries will have to be redefined with respect to their form, content and connotation.

Fourth, future information technology will overturn traditional modes of information presentation. Traditional entry structure will be shattered and reorganized; entry information will be presented in the form of cartoon, animation, electronized illustration and other forms that will transcend existing audio-visual modes and microstructural spaces that were devoted exclusively to information consultation and retrieval are turning into real-time locations where lexical recognition, reading, drilling, teaching and simulated use are conducted. Those locations can assume an aura of actual language teaching that makes lexicographical information more intuitional, more readily intelligible and more easily acquirable and usable.

Fifth, many brand-new areas of study will be opened up and explored, such as the mechanisms of interaction between dictionary and culture, dictionary paradigms and users' cognitive characteristics, cross-language and -culture comparison, dictionary market and marketing strategies and so on. Researches in these areas will depend to a considerable extent upon the already established theoretical principles and practical foundations in fields of linguistics, cultural studies, sociology, management, marketing and other relevant disciplines, and findings from such inquiries, along with their effective integration and interaction with lexicography, will definitely bring about breakthroughs in dictionary-making and research.

Finally, owing to more in-depth explorations and deciphering of modern linguistics in socio-cultural systems and cognitive systems of the human mind, lexicography is bound to achieve more significant attainments in areas such as language cognition, lexical acquisition and cultural pervasion and interference. The interaction between lexicographical research and linguistic theories will be further strengthened so that lexicography will reach a new height in both theoretical and practical terms. From the practical perspective, it is obvious from a general survey of the development of English dictionaries in the 20th century and over the past two decades or so that dictionary compilation is assuming the following characteristics and trends of evolution, i.e. more functional elaboration, formal integration, content localization and regionalization, typological serialization, path internationalization, technological informationalization and brand diversification. These features and trends herald the paths and orientations of development in English lexicography in the 21st century.

In the 20th century, English dictionaries underwent their transition from extensive mode of development in the initial stage to elaborate mode in later stages and from single to diverse user markets so as to perform various functions and meet reference needs of different user segments and achieved a series of shifts from single function and general users to equal focus on

Accomplishments, developments and prospects   227

both general function and users and specific function and users. On the whole they gradually formed their own systems in terms of types, species and brands; their own respective series of types and species and even series of types and species within major brands, which covered both general and specific types as well as general and specific users.

While strategies of diversification and serialization were in place, the internationalization of English dictionaries was also gaining momentum. To varying degrees, major dictionary brands in Britain and America were exerting efforts on their road to internationalization and became strong players and competitors in international dictionary markets. A good example is the proportion of English dictionaries on the Chinese market. According to incomplete statistics, dictionaries from Britain and America, particularly those produced by such brands as Oxford, Cambridge, Collins, Longman, Chambers and Webster, account for nearly 70 percent of English dictionaries on China's market. They may be imported directly or compiled and bilingualized through joint effort.

In contrast to internationalization, the tendency of localization and regionalization was also strikingly noticeable in the making of English dictionaries, as a result of strengthened national identity, cultural differentiation and the tendency of independent identification and separation. *The Historical Dictionary of American English* (1936–1944) drew on international experience in English dictionary-making in order to intensify local flavour and highlight national features. It collected words and expressions that were America-specific, in popular use and of particular relevance to American history, culture and customs. It played a direct role in initiating and leading the localization of English dictionaries in Australia, Canada, New Zealand, South Africa and a few other countries. Australia, taking advantage of the trend of localization in the making of English dictionaries, produced its own national dictionaries – *The Macquarie Dictionary* and *The Australian National Dictionary*, which changed the situation in which dictionaries made in Britain and America (mainly Britain) had dominated the Australian dictionary market. Over 30 years' efforts had helped to establish a relatively complete system of Australian English dictionaries. *The Macquarie Dictionary* is widely regarded as Australia's national dictionary, "a national tie" as some call it, and it has become the pride of the Australian people. Localization has proved to be the need for lexicographical development as well as national development.

The printing technology has altered the external environment for the world lexicographical culture and contributed to the transition of dictionary-making from traditional manual transcription to printed reproduction. It became a real possibility for dictionaries to be reproduced in large quantities and for them to reach increasingly larger audiences. That expedited the transmission of world lexicographical culture. However, what electronic and information technology brought upon dictionary-making and research was a revolutionary transformation through direct involvement

228 *Accomplishments, developments and prospects*

and throughout so that the efficiency, quality and level of dictionary compilation and research were immensely heightened. Moreover, it enabled dictionaries to be accessible through new media such as internet, iPad, iPod, mobile phone and other palm devices. Lexicographical informationalization via electronic and digital technology has undoubtedly become a powerful weapon for dictionary competition in the 21st century.

Dictionaries are a cultural product. As cultural commodities, branding should be an essential marketing strategy. Branding pushed British and American dictionaries onto the road of internationalization and from one height to another and to their glamorous glory. The impacts well-known dictionary brands in Britain and America exerted have gone far beyond the role dictionaries play as reference works. Their role in cultural promotion, value enhancement and ideological pervasion is obvious, efficient and effective. Dictionaries are a linguistic tool, but they have a part to play in social, cultural and even political life. The better-known the brands are, the more pervasive their influence is, the more powerful and the more extensive. This is what commercial values and market laws bring to dictionaries. The branding of English dictionaries is basically achieved through type development with focus on specific strains.

In the early stage, English dictionaries were simple in content and type. By the Middle Ages, when bilingual dictionaries became prosperous, bidirectional dictionaries began to appear, with the dictionary text consisting of both, say, an English-Chinese and a Chinese-English dictionary, thus a two-in-one dictionary. For monolingual dictionaries, the two-in-one form means incorporating a thesaurus into a defining dictionary, thus a combination of dictionary and thesaurus. Thanks to the internet and information technology, it is commonplace for a large number of dictionaries to converge into one website and become an integrated source of lexicographical information for consultation by different means, through different media and on different interfaces. TheFreeDictionary.com, for example, integrates defining dictionaries, thesauruses, medical dictionaries, law dictionaries, financial dictionaries, dictionaries of abbreviations, dictionaries of idioms, encyclopaedias and even Wikipedia. The website goes so far as to allow users to create their own web pages through adding, deleting, using and eliminating existing contents and tag their bookmarks, weather forecast, astrological predictions etc.

It is predictable that English dictionaries in the 21st century will have a higher degree of intelligence, contextualization, autonomy and customization. They will be proceeding on the presupposed track to an improved and heightened level of functional differentiation, type serialization, path internationalization, content localization, technological digitalization, publication branding, and formal synthesization.

Bibliography

Aarsleff, Hans, 1983, *The Study of Language in England 1780–1860*, London: The Athlone Press

Aitchison, Jean, 1990, *Words in the Mind – An Introduction to the Mental Lexicon*, Oxford: Basil Blackwell

———, 1991, *Language Change: Progress or Decay?* (Second edition), Cambridge: Cambridge University Press

Alberts, Mariëtta, 2011, National Lexicography Units: Past, Present, Future, *Lexikos*, Volume 21 (AFRILEX-reeks/series 21:2011):23–52

Algeo, John and Thomas Pyles, 2009, *The Origins and Development of the English Language*, Belmont, CA: Wadsworth Publishing Company

Allen, R. E., 1986, A Concise History of the COD, in *The History of Lexicography, Papers from The Dictionary Research Centre Seminar at Exeter, March 1986*, edited by R. R. K. Hartmann, Amsterdam: John Benjamins Publishing Company

———, 1992, Usage and Usage Guidance and Criticism, in *The Oxford Companion to the English Language*, edited by T. McArthur, 1071–1078, Oxford and New York: Oxford University Press

Allen, Robert, 2009, Dictionaries of Usage, 2009, in *The Oxford History of English Lexicography* (Volume II), edited by A. P. Cowie, Oxford: Oxford University Press

Alston, R. C., 1973, *The English Dictionary* (Volume 5). *A Bibliography of the English Language*, Leeds: University of Leeds

Andersen, James David, 1972, The Development of the English-French, French-English Bilingual Dictionary: A Study in Comparative Lexicography, *Supplement to WORD* (Volume 28, No. 3), London: William Clowes & Sons Limited

Anttila, Raimo, 1989, *Historical and Comparative Linguistics*, Amsterdam: John Benjamins Publishing Company

Ayto, J., 2000, Review of the Oxford Dictionary of New Words, *International Journal of Lexicography*, Volume 13 Issue No. 1:46–50

Bailey, Richard W., 2006, "This Unique and Peerless Specimen": The Reputation of the OED, in *Lexicography and the OED, Pioneers in the Untrodden Forest*, edited by Lynda Mugglestone, Cambridge: Cambridge University Press

Barnbrook, G., 2005, Usage Notes in Johnson's Dictionary, *International Journal of Lexicography*, Volume 18 Issue No. 2:189–201

Barnhart, C. L., 1962, Problems in Editing Commercial Monolingual Dictionaries, in *Problems in Lexicography* (1967), edited by Fred W. Householder and Sol Saporta, Bloomington: Indiana University

230   Bibliography

Bartsch, Renate, 1987, *Norms of Language: Theoretical and Practical Aspects*, London: Longman Group UK Limited

Bate, Walter Jackson, 1955, *The Achievement of Samuel Johnson*, Oxford: Oxford University Press

Bately, Janet, 2009, Bilingual and Multilingual Dictionaries of the Renaissance and Early Seventeenth Century, in *The Oxford History of English Lexicography* (Volume I), edited by A. P. Cowie, Oxford: Oxford University Press

Baugh, Albert C. and Thomas Cable, 1993, *A History of the English Language*, Oxford: Routledge

———, 2001, *A History of the English Language*, Beijing: Foreign Language Teaching and Research Press in association with Routledge

Baumgartner, P. et al. (eds.), 1995, *Speaking Minds: Interviews with Twenty Eminent Cognitive Scientists*, Princeton: Princeton University Press

Bechtel, W. et al. (eds.), 1999, *A Companion to Cognitive Science: Blackwell Companions to Philosophy*, Malden: Blackwell Publishers

Béjoint, Henri, 1994, *Tradition and Innovation in Modern English Dictionaries*, Oxford: Clarendon Press

———, 2002, *Modern Lexicography: An Introduction*, Beijing: Foreign Language Teaching and Research Press

———, 2010, *The Lexicography of English from Origins to Present*, Oxford: Oxford University Press

Benson, Morton et al., 1986, *Lexicographic Description of English*, Amsterdam: John Benjamins Publishing Company

Bloom, P., 2000, *How Children Learn the Meanings of Words*, Cambridge, MA: MIT Press

Blutner, R., 1998, Lexical Pragmatics, *Journal of Semantics*, Volume 15:115–162

Boswell, James and Christopher Hibbert (eds.), 1986, *The Life of Samuel Johnson*, New York: Penguin Classics

Boulanger, J.-C., 2003, *Les inventeurs du dictionnaire. De l'eduba des scribes mésopotamiens au scriptorium des moines médiévaux*, Ottawa: Presses de l'Université d'Ottawa

Brandford, W. R. G., 1996, *Sociocultural Factors and Syntax*, Grahamstown: Rhodes University, Unpublished Manuscript

Brewer, Charlotte, 2004, The Electronification of The Oxford English Dictionary, *Dictionaries*, Volume 25:1–43, The Dictionary Society of North America

———, 2006, OED Sources, in *Lexicography and the OED-Pioneers in the Untrodden Forest*, edited by Lynda Mugglestone, Oxford: Oxford University Press

———, 2007, *Treasure-House of the Language*, New Haven and London: Yale University Press

———, 2009, The OED Supplements, in *The Oxford History of English Lexicography* (Volume I), edited by A. P. Cowie, Oxford: Oxford University Press

Brooks, Van Wyck, 1952, *The Flowering of New England*, New York: E. P. Dutton and Company

Brown, Penelope and Stephen C. Levinson, 1987, *Politeness: Some Universals in Language Usage*, Cambridge: Cambridge University Press

Burchfield, Robert, 1992, BudaLEX Presidential Debate 1988: Part 1, *International Journal of Lexicography*, Volume 5 Issue No. 4:246–251

Bibliography 231

Bussman, Hadumond, 1996, *Routledge Dictionary of Language and Linguistics*, translated and edited by Gregory P. Trauth and Kerstin Kazzazi, London: Routledge

Bynon, Theodora, 1977, *Historical Linguistics*, Cambridge: Cambridge University Press

Carr, Michael, 1997, Internet Dictionaries and Lexicography, *International Journal of Lexicography*, Volume 10 Issue No. 3, Oxford: Oxford University Press

Carruthers, P. and A. Chamberlain (eds.), 2000, *Evolution and the Human Mind: Language, Modularity and Social Cognition*, Cambridge: Cambridge University Press

Cartier, Jacques, 1534/1986, *Relations*, edited by Michael Bideaux, Bibliothèque du Nouveau Monde, Montréal: Presses de l'Université de Montréal

Cassidy, F. G., 1997, The Rise and Development of Modern Labels in English Dictionaries, *Dictionaries*, Volume 18:97–112

Cen, Qixiang, 1964, *A Synoptic History of Linguistics*, Beijing: Science Publishing House

Chambers, J. K., 1998, Canadian English: 250 Years in the Making, in *Canadian Oxford Dictionary*, edited by Katherine Barber, Toronto: Oxford University Press, pp. ix–x

Chen, Dingan, 1998, *English-Chinese Comparison and Translation*, Beijing: China Translation Publishing Company

Chen, Wei, 2008, New Dictionary Types and Digital Publication, *China Book Review*, Issue No. 10

Clifford, J. L., 1979, *Dictionary Johnson: Samuel Johnson's Middle Years*, New York: McGraw Hill

Coleman, Julie, 2009, Slang and Cant Dictionaries, in *The Oxford History of English Lexicography* (Volume II), edited by A. P. Cowie, Oxford: Oxford University Press

Collins, Beverley and Inger M. Mees, 2009, Pronouncing Dictionaries — II Mid-Nineteenth Century to the Present Day, in *The Oxford History of English Lexicography* (Volume II), edited by A. P. Cowie, Oxford: Oxford University Press

Collison, Robert L., 1982, *A History of Foreign-Language Dictionaries*, London: Andre Deutsch Limited

Congleton, J. and E. C. Congleton, 1984, *Johnson's Dictionary, Bibliographical Survey 1746–1984*, Terre Haute: Indiana State University and Dictionary Society of North America

Cormier, Monique C., 2009, Bilingual Dictionaries of the Late Seventeenth and Eighteen Centuries, in *The Oxford History of English Lexicography* (Volume I), edited by A. P. Cowie, Oxford: Oxford University Press

Cowie, A. P., 2002, *English Dictionaries for Foreign Learners: A History*, Beijing: Foreign Languages Teaching & Research Press

———— (ed.), 2009, *The Oxford History of English Lexicography*, Oxford: Oxford University Press

Crystal, David, 1985, *A Dictionary of Linguistics and Phonetics*, Oxford: Blackwell Publishing

————, 2003, *The Cambridge Encyclopedia of the English Language* (Second edition), Cambridge University Press

————, 2005, *Johnson's Dictionary: An Anthology*, London: Penguin Books Ltd

232 *Bibliography*

————, 2008, English Worldwide, in *A History of the English Language*, edited by Richard Hogg and David Denison, Cambridge: Cambridge University Press

Cummings, Louise, 2005, *Pragmatics: A Multidisciplinary Perspective*, Edinburgh: Edinburgh University Press

Cutting, J., 2002, *Pragmatics and Discourse*, London: Routledge

Davis, S. (ed.), 1991, *Pragmatics: A Reader*, Oxford: Oxford University Press

DeMaria, R., 1986, *Johnson's Dictionary and the Language of Learning*, Chapel Hill: University of North Carolina

————, 1994, *The Life of Samuel Johnson*, Oxford: Blackwell

Deng, Wenbin, 2002, *A History of Ancient Chinese Linguistics*, Chengdu: Bayou Book Company

Denison, David and Richard Hogg, 2008, Overview, in *A History of the English Language*, edited by Richard Hogg and David Denison, Cambridge: Cambridge University Press

De Schryver, Gilles-Maurice, 2003, Lexicographers' Dreams in the Electronic Dictionary Age, *International Journal of Lexicography*, Volume 16 Issue No. 2:143–199

Deverson, T. and G. D. Kennedy, 2005, *The New Zealand Oxford Dictionary*, Melbourne: Oxford University Press

Dubois, Jean, 1981, Models of the Dictionary: Evolution in Dictionary Design, *Applied Linguistics*, Volume II Issue No. 3, Oxford: Oxford University Press

Dziemianko, Anna, 2012, On the Use(fullness) of Paper and Electronic Dictionaries, in *Electronic Lexicography*, edited by Sylviane Granger and Magali Paquot, Oxford: Oxford University Press

Elmes, Simon, 2005, *Talking for Britain: A Journey through the Voices of Our Nation*, London: Penguin Books Ltd.

Farina, Donna M. T. Cr. and George Durman, 2009, Bilingual Dictionaries of English and Russian in the Eighteenth to the Twentieth Centuries, in *The Oxford History of English Lexicography* (Volume I), edited by A. P. Cowie, Oxford: Oxford University Press

Fennell, Barbara A., 2005, *A History of English – A Sociolinguistic Approach*, Beijing: Peking University Press

Finegan, Edward, 2008, English in America, in *A History of the English Language*, edited by Richard Hogg and David Denison, Cambridge: Cambridge University Press

Fodor, J., 2000, *The Mind Doesn't Work That Way*, Cambridge, MA: MIT Press

Foley, William, 1997, *Anthropological Linguistics: An Introduction*, Oxford: Blackwell

Frawley, William, 1989, *The Dictionary as Text*, International Journal of Lexicography, Oxford: Oxford University Press

Freeborn, Dennis, 1998, *From Old English to Standard English* (Second edition), New York: Macmillan

Furnivall, Frederick J., 1911, *Frederick James Furnivall: A Record*, London: Henry Frowde

Gardner, Howard, 1987, *The Mind's New Science: A History of the Cognitive Revolution*, New York: Basic Books

Gazzaniga, M. S. (ed.), 1996, *Conversations in the Cognitive Neurosciences*, New York: The MIT Press

Bibliography 233

Geeraerts, D., 1984, Dictionary Classification and the Foundations of Lexicography, *I.T.L.: Review of Applied Linguistics*, Volume 63

———, 1989, Principles of Monolingual Lexicography, in *Dictionaries: An International Encyclopedia of Lexicography*, edited by Franz Josef Hausmann et al., Berlin: Walter de Gruyter

Glucksberg, S., 2001, *Understanding Figurative Language*, Oxford: Oxford University Press

Gough, D. H., 1995, Black English in South Africa, in *English around the World: Focus on Southern Africa*, edited by V. de Klerk, Amsterdam: John Benjamins Publishing Company

Gove, Philip B., 1961, Preface to *Webster's Third New International Dictionary*, Springfield, Massachusetts: G. & C. Merriam Company

Granger, Sylviane, 2012, Introduction: Electronic Lexicography – from Challenge to Opportunity, in *Electronic Lexicography*, edited by Sylviane Granger and Magali Paquot, Oxford: Oxford University Press

Granger, Sylviane and Magali Paquot (eds.), 2010, *Elexicography in the 21st Century: New Challenges, New Applications Proceedings of eLex 2009, Louvain-la-Neuve, 22–24 October 2009*, Louvain: UCL Presses Universitaires de Louvain

———, 2012, *Electronic Lexicography*, Oxford: Oxford University Press

Green, Jonathon, 1996, *Chasing the Sun: Dictionary Makers and the Dictionaries They Made*, London: Jonathan Cape

Greene, Donald, 1989, *Samuel Johnson: Updated Edition*, Boston: Twayne Publishers

Gregg, Robert J., 1993, Canadian English Lexicography, in *Focus on Canada*, under the direction of Sandra Clarke, Amsterdam/Philadelphia, John Benjamins Publishing Company, pp. 27–44

Grice, H. P., 1989, *Studies in the Way of Words*, Cambridge, MA: Harvard University Press

Guest, Edwin, 1883, *Origines Celticae* (a Fragment) and other Contributions to the History of Britain, 2 volumes, London: Macmillan & Co.

Hanks, Patrick, 2005, Johnson and Modern Lexicography, *International Journal of Lexicography*, Volume 18 Issue No. 2:243–266

———, 2012, Corpus Evidence and Electronic Lexicography, in *Electronic Lexicography*, edited by Sylviane Granger and Magali Paquot, Oxford: Oxford University Press

Hartmann, R. R. K. (ed.), 1983, *Lexicography: Principles and Practice*, London: Academic Press

——— (ed.), 1984, *LEXeter'83 Proceedings*, Tübingen: Max Niemeyer Verlag

———, 1986, *The History of Lexicography*, Papers from The Dictionary Research Centre Seminar at Exeter, March 1986, Amsterdam: John Benjamins Publishing Company

———, 2001, *Teaching and Researching Lexicography*, Harlow: Pearson Education Ltd

Hartmann, R. R. K. and Gregory James, 1998, *Dictionary of Lexicography*, London: Routledge

Hausmann, Franz Josef, 1986, The Training and Professional Development of Lexicographers in Germany, in *Lexicography, An Emerging International Profession*, edited by Robert Ilson, Manchester: Manchester University Press

234 *Bibliography*

Hausmann, Franz Josef and Margaret Cop (eds.), 1985, A Short History of English-German Lexicography, in *Symposium on Lexicography II: Proceedings of the Second International Symposium on Lexicography* May 16–17, 1984 at the University of Copenhagen, edited by Karl Hyldgaard-Jensen and Arne Zettersten, Tübingen: Max Niemeyer Verlag

Hausmann, Franz Josef et al. (eds.), 1989, *Dictionaries: An International Encyclopedia of Lexicography*, Berlin: Walter de Gruyter

He, Jiuying, 1995, *A History of Ancient Chinese Linguistics*, Guangzhou: Guangdong Education Press

Hicks, Sheila, 2010, Firming Up the Foundations: Reflections on Verifying the Quotations in a Historical Dictionary, with Reference to A Dictionary of South African English on Historical Principles, *Lexikos*, Volume 20 (AFRILEX-reeks/series 20:2010):248–271

Hitchings, Henry, 2005, *Dr Johnson's Dictionary: The Extraordinary Story of the Book that Defined the World*, London: John Murray

Hogg, Richard and David Denison, 2008, *A History of the English Language* (First paperback edition), Cambridge: Cambridge University Press

Horgan, A. D., 1994, *Johnson on Language: An Introduction*, New York: St. Martin's Press

Hounshell, David A., 1984, *From the American System to Mass Production, 1800–1932*, Baltimore: The Johns Hopkins Press

Householder, Fred W. and Sol Saporta (eds.), 1967, *Problems in Lexicography*, Bloomington: Indiana University Press

Hu, Dewei, 2013, French vs English, France Yields to Reality, *Guangming Daily*, July 27

Hudson, R. A., 1980, *Sociolinguistics*, Cambridge: Cambridge University Press

Hudson, Richard, 1988, The Linguistic Foundations for Lexical Research and Dictionary Design, *International Journal of Lexicography*, Volume 1 Issue No. 4

Hulbert, J. R., 1955, *Dictionaries British and American* (revised by Simeon Potter, 1968), London: Andre Deutsch

Hüllen, Werner, 2006, *English Dictionaries 800–1700 – The Topical Tradition*, Oxford: Clarendon

———, 2008, *A History of Roget's Thesaurus-Origins, Development, and Design*, Oxford: Oxford University Press

———, 2009, Dictionaries of Synonyms and Thesauri, in *The Oxford History of English Lexicography* (Volume II), edited by A. P. Cowie, Oxford: Oxford University Press

Hunt, M., 1982, *The Universe Within: A New Science Explores the Human Mind*, Brighton: The Harvester Press

Hyldgaard-Jensen, Karl and Arne Zettersten (eds.), 1985, *Symposium on Lexicography II: Proceedings of the Second International Symposium on Lexicography* May 16–17, 1984 at the University of Copenhagen, Tübingen: Max Niemeyer Verlag

Ilson, Robert F., 1986, British and American Lexicography, in *Lexicography, An Emerging International Profession*, edited by Robert Ilson, Manchester: Manchester University Press

———, 2000, Review of Encarta World English Dictionary, *International Journal of Lexicography*, Volume 13 Issue No. 4:326–336

Jackson, Howard, 2002, *Lexicography: An Introduction*, New York: Routledge

Bibliography 235

Janda, Richard D. and Brian D. Joseph (eds.), 2004, *The Handbook of Historical Linguistics*, Oxford: Blackwell

Johnson, M., 1987, *The Body in the Mind: The Bodily Basis of Meaning, Imagination, and Reason*, Chicago: The University of Chicago Press

Johnson, Samuel, 1747, *The Plan of an English Dictionary*, edited by Jack Lynch

———, 1755, Preface to *A Dictionary of the English Language*, edited by Jack Lynch

———, 1952, *Letters*, edited by R. W. Chapman, Oxford: Clarendon

Kachru, Braj B. et al. (eds.), 1995, *Cultures, Ideologies, and the Dictionary: Studies in Honor of Ladislav Zgusta*, Tubingen: Max Niemeyer Verlag Gmb. H. & Co. KG

Kaster, Robert, 2009, Latin Lexicography, *The Classical Review*, Volume 59 Issue No. 1:169–171

Kinloch, A. M. and Walter Spencer Avis, 1980, *Journal of the Atlantic Provinces Linguistic Association*, Volume 2:56–59

Knowles, Elizabeth, 2009, Dictionaries of Quotations, in *The Oxford History of English Lexicography* (Volume II), edited by A. P. Cowie, Oxford: Oxford University Press

Knowles, Gerry, 1997, *A Cultural History of the English Language*, Oxon: Taylor & Francis Ltd

Kolb, G. J. and R. DeMaria (eds.), 2005, *Johnson on the English Language*, New Haven: Yale University Press

Konrad, E. F., and Ronald E. Asher (eds.), 1995, *The Concise History of the Language Sciences: From the Sumerians to the Cognitivists*, Oxford: Pergamon

Kosch, Inge, 2013, Review of G.-M. De Schryver's Oxford Bilingual School Dictionary: Northern Sotho and English (2007). *Lexikos*, Volume 23 (AFRILEX-reeks/ series 23:2013):611–627

Krache, Robert, 1975, *The Story of the Dictionary*, New York: Harcourt Brace Jovanovich

Kuhn, Thomas, 1970, *The Structure of Scientific Revolutions*, Chicago: University of Chicago Press

Lakoff, George, 1987, *Women, Fire, and Dangerous Things – What Categories Reveal about the Mind*, Chicago: University of Chicago Press

Lakoff, George and Mark Johnson, 1980, *Metaphors We Live By*, Chicago: University of Chicago Press

———, 1998, *Philosophy in the Flesh – The Embodied Mind and its Challenge to Western Thought*, New York: Basic Books

Lamb, Sydney M., 1999, *Pathways of the Brain – The Neurocognitive Basis of Language*, Amsterdam: John Benjamins Publishing Company

Lancashire, I., 2005, Johnson and Seventeenth-century English Glossographers, *International Journal of Lexicography*, Volume 18 Issue No. 2:157–171

Landau, Sidney I., 1989, *Dictionaries: The Art and Craft of Lexicography*, Cambridge: Cambridge University Press

———, 2000, Review of Encarta World English Dictionary, *Dictionaries*, Volume 21:112–124

———, 2005, Johnson's Influence on Webster and Worcester in Early American Lexicography, *International Journal of Lexicography*, Volume 18 Issue No. 2:217–219

236 Bibliography

———, 2009a, The American Collegiate Dictionaries, in *The Oxford History of English Lexicography* (Volume II), edited by A. P. Cowie, Oxford: Oxford University Press

———, 2009b, Major American Dictionaries, in *The Oxford History of English Lexicography* (Volume I), edited by A. P. Cowie, Oxford: Oxford University Press

Landes, David, 2003, *The Unbound Prometheus: Technical Change and Industrial Development in Western Europe from 1750 to the Present* (Second edition), New York: Cambridge University Press

Langacker, Ronald W., 1990, *Concept, Image and Symbol – The Cognitive Basis of Grammar*, Berlin: Mouton de Gruyter

Lee, S. and T. Kendall, 1820, *A Grammar and Vocabulary of the Language of New Zealand*, London: Church Missionary Society

Leech, Geoffrey, 1981, *Semantics: The Study of Meaning*, Harmondsworth: Penguin Books Ltd

Leith, Dick, 1983, *A Social History of English*, London: Routledge & Kegan Paul

Liberman, Anatoly, 2009, English Etymological Dictionaries, in *The Oxford History of English Lexicography* (Volume II), edited by A. P. Cowie, Oxford: Oxford University Press

Lynch, J. and A. McDermott (eds.), 2005, *Anniversary Essays on Johnson's Dictionary*, Cambridge: Cambridge University Press

Lyons, John, 1968, *Introduction to Theoretical Linguistics*, Cambridge: Cambridge University Press

Mair, Christian, 2006, *Twentieth-century English: History, Variation and Standardization*, Cambridge: Cambridge University Press

Malle, B., L. Moses and D. Baldwin (eds.), 2001, *Intentions and Intentionality: Foundations of Social Cognition*, Cambridge, MA: MIT Press

Marello, Carla, 2009, Bilingual Dictionaries of the Nineteenth and Twentieth Centuries, in *The Oxford History of English Lexicography* (Volume I), edited by A. P. Cowie, Oxford: Oxford University Press

Marshall, Fiona C., 2004, Edwin Guest: Historian, Philologist, and Founder of the Philological Society of London, in *The Henry Sweet Society for the History of Linguistic Ideas Bulletin*, edited by T. Lindström, Oxford: Jesus College

Martin, Peter, 2008, *Samuel Johnson: A Biography*, Cambridge, MA: Belknap Press

Mashamaite, Kwena J., 2001, The Compilation of Bilingual Dictionaries between African Languages in South Africa: The Case of Northern Sotho and Tshivenda, *Lexikos*, Volume 11 (AFRILEX-reeks/series 11:2001):112–121

Mathews, M. M., 1933, *A Survey of English Dictionaries*, Oxford: Oxford University Press

———, 1969, Book Review of A Dictionary of Canadianisms on Historical Principles, *Journal of English Linguistics*, Volume 3 (mars 1969):89–91

McArthur, Tom, 1986, *Worlds of References-lexicography, Learning and Language: From Clay Tablets to Computer*, Cambridge: Cambridge University Press

———, 1992, *The Oxford Companion to the English Language*, Oxford: Oxford University Press

———, 1998, *Living Words: Language, Lexicography and the Knowledge Revolution*, Exeter: Exeter University Press

McDavid Jr., Raven I., 1967, Book Review of A Dictionary of Canadianisms on Historical Principles, *Journal of Linguistics*, Volume 13:55–57

Bibliography 237

McDermott, Anne, 2005, Johnson's Definitions of Technical Terms and the Absence of Illustrations, *International Journal of Lexicography*, Oxford, Volume 18 Issue No. 2

McDermott, Anne and R. Moon, 2005, Introduction: Johnson in Context, Oxford: *International Journal of Lexicography*, Volume 18 Issue No. 2

McMahon, April, 1994, *Understanding Language Change*, Cambridge: Cambridge University Press

Meyer, C., 2002, *English Corpus Linguistics: An Introduction*, Cambridge: Cambridge University Press

Milroy, James, 1992, *Linguistic Variation and Change*, Oxford: Blackwell

Milroy, James and Lesley Milroy, 1985, *Authority in Language — Investigating Language Prescription and Standardization*, New York: Routledge and Kegan Paul Ltd.

Misra, B. G. (ed.), 1980, *Lexicography in India [Proceedings of the First National Conference on Dictionary-Making in Indian Languages Mysore, 1970]*, Manasagangotri: Central Institute of Indian Languages

Moon, R., 2004, Cawdrey's A Table Alphabeticall: A Quantitative Approach, in *Proceedings of the Eleventh EURALEX International Congress*, edited by G. Williams and S. Vessier, Vannes: Université de Bretagne Sud

Moore, B. (ed.), 2001, *Who's Centric Now? The Present State of Post-colonial Englishes*, Melbourne: Oxford University Press, pp. 59–81

Morton, Herbert C., 1994, *The Story of Webster's Third: Philip Gove's Controversial Dictionary and Its Critics*, Cambridge: Cambridge University Press

Mugglestone, Lynda, 2005, *Lost for Words: The Hidden History of the Oxford English Dictionary*, New Heaven: Yale University Press

—— (ed.), 2006, *Lexicography and the OED-Pioneers in the Untrodden Forest*, Oxford: Oxford University Press

——, 2009, The Oxford English Dictionary, in *The Oxford History of English Lexicography* (Volume I), edited by A. P. Cowie, Oxford: Oxford University Press

Murray, James A. H., 1900, *The Evolution of English Lexicography – The Romanes Lecture 1900*, London: Henry Frowde/Oxford: Clarendon Press

Murray, K. M. Elisabeth, 2001, *Caught in the Web of Words: J. A. H. Murray and the Oxford English Dictionary*, New Haven: Yale University Press

Noyes, Gertrude E., 1943, The First English Dictionary, Cawdrey's Table Alphabeticall, *Modern Language Notes*, Volume 58:600–605

Nunberg, G., 1994, The Once and Future Dictionary, Paper Presentation at The Future of the Dictionary Xerox Workshop, Uriage, France

Ogilvie, Sarah, 2020, *The Cambridge Companion to English Dictionaries*, Cambridge: Cambridge University Press

Osselton, N. E., 1983, On the History of Dictionaries – The History of English-language Dictionaries, in *Lexicography: Principles and Practice*, edited by R. R. K. Hartmann, London: Academic Press

——, 1995, *Chosen Words: Past and Present Problems for Dictionary Makers*, Exeter: University of Exeter Press

——, 2009, The Early Development of the English Monolingual Dictionary (Seventeenth and Early Eighteenth Centuries), in *The Oxford History of English Lexicography* (Volume I), edited by A. P. Cowie, Oxford: Oxford University Press

Ostler, N., 2005, *Empires of the Word*, London: HarperCollins Publishers

——, 2007, *Ad Infinitum, A Biography of Latin*, New York: Walker and Company

238 Bibliography

Peng, Jing, 2009, Studies in the History of English Lexicography: Current Situation and Reflections, *Foreign Philology*, Issue No. 3

———, 2011, A Linguistic Approach to the Evolution of English Dictionary Paradigms, *Foreign Philology*, Issue No. 5

Penhallurick, Robert, 2009, Dialect Dictionaries, in *The Oxford History of English Lexicography* (Volume II), edited by A. P. Cowie, Oxford: Oxford University Press

Peters, Robert A., 1968, Robert Cawdrey and the First English Dictionary, *Journal of English Linguistics*, Volume 2:29–42

Prinsloo, D. J., 2005, Electronic Dictionaries Viewed from South Africa, *Hermes, Journal of Linguistics*, Issue No. 34

Qin, Xiaohui, Crowdfunding in the Making of The Oxford English Dictionary – A case study of the first edition of The Oxford English Dictionary, *Lexicographical Studies*, Issue No. 4

Ramson, W. S., 2002, *Lexical Images – The Story of the Australian National Dictionary*, Oxford: Oxford University Press

Read, A. W., 2003, The Beginnings of English Lexicography, *Dictionaries*, Volume 24:187–226

Reddick, Allen, 1990/1996, *The Making of Johnson's Dictionary 1746–1773*, Cambridge: Cambridge University Press

———, 2005, *Samuel Johnson's Unpublished Revisions to the Dictionary of the English Language* (Facsimile edition), Cambridge: Cambridge University Press

———, 2009, Johnson and Richardson, in *The Oxford History of English Lexicography* (Volume I), edited by A. P. Cowie, Oxford: Oxford University Press

Richards, Jack et al., 1985, *Longman Dictionary of Applied Linguistics*, Harlow: Longman Group Limited

Riddell, James A., 1983, Some Additional Sources for Early English Dictionaries, *Huntington Library Quarterly*, Volume 46:223–235

Roach, Peter, 2004, British English: Received Pronunciation, *Journal of the International Phonetic Association*, Volume 34 Issue No. 2:239–245

Robins, R. H., 2001, *A Short History of Linguistics* (Fourth edition), Beijing: Foreign Language Teaching and Researching Press

Rollins, Richard M., 1980, *The Long Journey of Noah Webster*, Pennsylvania: The University of Pennsylvania Press

Rooney, Kathy, 1994, Book Review of The Penguin Canadian Dictionary, *International Journal of Lexicography*, volume 7 Issue No. 3 (automne 1994):254–256

Rosch, E., 1975, Cognitive Representations of Semantic Categories, *Journal of Experimental Psychology: General*, Volume 104

Rundell, Micheal, 1995, The Word on the Street: Spoken English and the BNC, *English Today Volume* 43 (July 1995)

———, 1998, Recent Trends in English Pedagogical Lexicography, *International Journal of Lexicography*, Volume 11 Issue No. 4:315–342

———, 1999, Dictionary Use in Production, *International Journal of Lexicography*, Volume 12 Issue No. 1:35–53

———, 2012, It Works in Practice but will it Work in Theory? The Uneasy Relationship between Lexicography and Matters Theoretical (Hornby Lecture), in *Proceedings of the 15th EURALEX Congress*, edited by R. V. Fjeld and J. M. Torjusen, Oslo: University of Oslo

Rundell, Micheal and Sue Atkins, 2008, *The Oxford Guide to Practical Lexicography*, Oxford: Oxford University Press

Bibliography 239

Sauer, Hans, 2009, Glosses, Glossaries, and Dictionaries in the Medieval Period, in *The Oxford History of English Lexicography* (Volume I), edited by A. P. Cowie, Oxford: Oxford University Press

Schafer, Jurgen, 1970, The Hard Word Dictionaries: A Re-Assessment, *Leeds Studies in English* [New Series], Volume 4:31–48

———, 1989, *Early Modern English Lexicography Volume 1: A Survey of Monolingual Printed Glossaries and Dictionaries 1475–1640*, Oxford: Clarendon Press

Scollon, Ronald and Suzanne Wong Scollon, 1995, *Intercultural Communication: A Discourse Approach*, Oxford: Blackwell

Sinclair, John M., 1984, Lexicography as an Academic Subject, in *LEXeter'83 Proceedings*, edited by R. R. K. Hartmann, Tübingen: Max Niemeyer Verlag

Singleton, D., 2000, *Language and the Lexicon, An Introduction*, London: Arnold

Sledd, James and Wilma R. Ebbit (eds.), 1962, *Dictionaries and That Dictionary*, Chicago: Scott Foresman and Company

Sledd, J. H. and G. J. Kolb, 1955, *Dr Johnson's Dictionary: Essays on the Bibliography of a Book*, Chicago: The University of Chicago Press

Sperber, Dan, 1996, *Explaining Culture: A Naturalistic Approach*, Oxford: Blackwell

Sperber, Dan and Deirdre Wilson, 1995, *Relevance: Communication and Cognition*, Oxford: Blackwell

Starnes, DeWitt T., 1937, English Dictionaries of the Seventeenth Century, *Texas Studies in English*, Volume 17:20–24

———, 1954, *Renaissance Dictionaries English-Latin and Latin-English*, Austin: University of Texas Press

Starnes, DeWitt T. and Gertrude E. Noyes, 1946, *The English Dictionary from Cawdrey to Johnson (1604–1755)*, Chapel Hill: University of North Carolina Press

———, 1991, *The English Dictionary from Cawdrey to Johnson* with introduction and new bibliography by G. Stein, Amsterdam: John Benjamins Publishing Company

Stathi E. Latin Lexicography // Brown K. (ed.), 2006, *Dictionary of Language and Linguistics* (Volume 6) Berlin: Elsevier Ltd., p. 723

Stein, Gabriele, 1985, English-German/German-English Lexicography: Its Early Beginnings, *Lexicographica* Issue No. 1, International Annual for Lexicography

———, 1991, Introduction, in *The English Dictionary from Cawdrey to Johnson*, edited by DeWitt T. Starnes and Gertrude E. Noyes, Amsterdam: John Benjamins Publishing Company

Stockwell, Robert P. and Donka Minkova, 2001, *English Words: History and Structure*, New York: Cambridge University Press

Svensen, Bo, 1993, *Practical Lexicography*, Oxford: Oxford University Press

Sweet, Henry, 1899, *The Practical Study of Languages – A Guide for Teachers and Learners*, Oxford: Oxford University Press

Sweetser, E., 1990, *From Etymology to Pragmatics: Metaphorical and Cultural Aspects of Semantic Structure*, Cambridge: Cambridge University Press

Taylor, J. R., 1989, *Linguistic Categorization: Prototypes in Linguistic Theory*, Oxford: Clarendon Press

Thagard, P., 2005, *Mind: Introduction to Cognitive Science* (Second edition), Cambridge, MA: The MIT Press

Thelen, Esther and Linda B. Smith, 1996, *A Dynamic Systems Approach to the Development of Cognition and Action*, Cambridge, MA: The MIT Press

240   *Bibliography*

The Philological Society, 1859, *Proposal for the Publication of a New English Dictionary*, London: Trübner and Co.

Thomas, J., 1995, *Meaning in Interaction: An Introduction to Pragmatics*, New York: Longman Group Ltd.

Travis, C., 2000, *Unshadowed Thought: Representation in Thought and Language*, Cambridge MA: Harvard University Press

Trench, Richard, 1857, *On Some Deficiencies in Our English Dictionaries; being the Substance of Two Papers Read before the Philological Society*, Nov. 5, and Nov. 19, 1857, London: John W. Parker and Son

Upton, Clive and J. D. A. Widdowson, 2006, *An Atlas of English Dialects* (Second edition), London: Routledge

Vinay, J.-P. and Pierre Daviault, 1958, Dictionnaires canadiens, I: les dictionnaires bilingues, in *Translator's Journal/Journal des traducteurs*, Volume 3 Issue No. 2 (April–June):109–113

Webb, V. N., 1996, Language Planning and Politics in South Africa, *International Journal of the Sociology of Language*, Volume 118:139–162

Wees, W. R., 1967, *Foreword to A Dictionary of Canadianisms on Historical Principles*, edited by Walter S. Avis, Toronto: W. J. Gage

Wells, John C., 1982, *Accents of English I: An Introduction*, Cambridge: Cambridge University Press

Wells, Ronald A., 1973, *Dictionaries and the Authoritarian Tradition-A Study in English Usage and Lexicography*, Paris: Mouton

Wenden, A. and J. Rubin, 1987, *Learner Strategies in Language Learning*, London: Prentice Hall International

Whiten, A. (ed.), 1991, *Natural Theories of Mind: Evolution, Development and Simulation of Everyday Mindreading*, Oxford: Blackwell

Williams, H. W., 1975, *A Dictionary of the Maori Language* (Seventh edition), Wellington: Government Printer

Williams, W., 1844, *Dictionary of the New Zealand Language*, London: Church Missionary Society

Willinsky, John, 1995, *Empire of Words: The Reign of the Oxford English Dictionary*, Princeton: Princeton University Press

Winchester, Simon, 2003, *The Meaning of Everything: The Story of the Oxford English Dictionary*, Oxford: Oxford University Press

Yong, Heming, 1997, The Aesthetic Principle in the Making of Dictionaries, *Lexicographical Studies*, Issue No. 1

———, 1999a, The Problems of Treating English Idioms in The English-Chinese Dictionary, *Foreign Language Teaching and Research*, Issue No. 4

———, 1999b, English Idioms and the Principles and Methods of Treating Them in Bilingual Dictionaries, *Lexicographical Studies*, Issue No. 2

———, 2000a, Modern Linguistics and the Making of English-Chinese Dictionaries, *Foreign Languages and Their Teaching*, Issue No. 4

———, 2000b, The Dictionary of Lexicography A Review, *Modern Linguistics*, Issue No.3

———, 2001, A Communicative Model of Lexicography, *Foreign Languages*, Issue No. 4

———, 2003, A Comparative Study of Language Needs and Reference Skills for English-Chinese Bilingual Dictionary and English Monolingual Dictionary Users, *Lexicographical Studies*, Issue No. 6

Bibliography 241

———, 2004a, Language, Dictionaries and Lexicography, *Foreign Languages and Their Teaching*, Issue No. 1

———, 2004b, A Theoretical Survey of Dictionary Typologies Overseas, *Lexicographical Studies*, Issue No. 5

———, 2004c, Thoughts about Studies in the History of Chinese Lexicography, *Lexicographical Studies*, Issue No. 2

———, 2010, *Lexicography from a Communicative Perspective* (Revised edition), Shanghai: Shanghai Lexicographical Press

Yong Heming and Jing Peng, 2007, *Bilingual Lexicography from a Communicative Perspective*, Amsterdam: John Benjamins Publishing Company

———, 2008, *Chinese Lexicography – A History from 1046 BC to AD 1911*, Oxford: Oxford University Press

———, 2010, *Lexicography from a Communicative Perspective* (Revised edition), Shanghai: Shanghai Lexicographical Press

Yule, George, 1996, *Pragmatics*, Oxford: Oxford University Press

Zgusta, L., 1971, *Manual of Lexicography*, Paris: Mouton

Zhang, Liwei, 1996, The Origin, Development and Influence of English Learners Dictionaries, *Foreign Language Teaching and Research*, Issue No. 3

Zhao, Yanchun, 2003, *Explorations in Cognitive Lexicography*, Shanghai: Shanghai Foreign Language Education Press

Major referenced websites

http://acms.sl.nsw.gov.au/item/itemDetailPaged.aspx?itemID=421143
http://adb.anu.edu.au/biography/downing-walter-hubert-10682
http://booklens.com/walter-hubert-downing/w-h-downing-s-digger-dialects
http://gutenberg.net.au/ebooks06/0600101.txt
www.ualberta.ca/~johnnewm/NZEnglish/biblio.html
http://adb.anu.edu.au/biography/baker-sidney-john-9411
www.jstor.org/discover/10.2307/486485?uid=2129&uid=2&uid=70&uid=4&s=21101159872721
www.macquarieonline.com.au/anonymous@9c9896211231/-/p/dict/index.html
www.library.uq.edu.au/services-for/about-marquarie-dictionary-and-thesaurus-online
www.historyonthenet.com/Historical_People/.htm
http://andc.anu.edu.au/node/13927
http://australiannationaldictionary.com.au/
http://trove.nla.gov.au/work/8431032?versionId=9727969
http://books.google.com.hk/books/about/Colonial_English_a_glossary_of_Australia.html?id=FS2eXwAACAAJ
http://eebo.chadwyck.com (Early English Books Online, EEBO)
http://quod.lib.umich.edu/e/eebogroup/ (Early English Books Online, EEBO)
http://homes.chass.utoronto.ca/~ian/emedd.html (Early Modern English Dictionaries Database, EMEDD, renamed Lexicons of Early Modern English, LEME)
www.onlinedictionary.co.nz/
www.ats-group.net/dictionaries/dictionary-english-new-zealand.html
http://public.oed.com/aspects-of-english/english-in-use/canadian-english/
www.oupcanada.com/reference_trade/canadian_oxford_dictionaries/dictionary_online.html

242 Bibliography

www.dico.uottawa.ca/description.en.htm
http://public.oed.com/aspects-of-english/english-in-use/south-african-english/
www.salanguages.com/dictionaries.htm
www.ru.ac.za/dsae/
www.pharos.co.za/
www.goodreads.com/author/show/4042403.Pharos_Dictionaries
www.maori.com/language
www.wikipedia.com/
http://en.wikipedia.org/wiki/
http://en.wikipedia.org/wiki/Canadian_Oxford_Dictionary
http://en.wikipedia.org/wiki/Collins_English_Dictionary
http://en.wikipedia.org/wiki/James_Hardy_Vaux
http://en.wikipedia.org/wiki/Macquarie_Dictionary
http://en.wikipedia.org/wiki/New_Zealand_English
http://en.wikipedia.org/wiki/South_African_English
http://en.wikipedia.org/wiki/New_Zealand_English
http://resources.tewhanake.maori.nz/dictionaries/maori-dictionary.html

Index

Abecedarium Anglico Latinum (Huloet) 44–45
Academia Española 59
Académie française 59, 93, 95, 97
Accademia della Crusca 59, 93
Adelung, Johann Christoph 113
Advanced Learner's Dictionary of Current English 216
Aelfric 21
Afzelius, J. A. 184–185
Ainsworth, Robert 76, 97, 113
Aitken, A. J. 187
Akkad 18
Aldhelm 21
Aleksandrov, A. 150
Al-Kasimi 223
Allen, Robert 192, 200
alphabetical order: *Bibliotheca scholastica* 47; dictionaries 23, 74–75, 78, 110, 191–192; encyclopedias in 199; glossaries 20, 27; headwords 28, 41, 43–46, 48, 52, 97, 116, 191; index 48; *Medulla* 25; *Promptorium Parvulorum* 23; Richardson's lexicon 147; semantic categorization according to 198; synonyms and antonyms organized in 196–197; vs thematic order 154, 195; *see also Table Alphabeticall* (Cawrdy)
Alphabet of Kenticisms (Pegge) 115
alphaDictionary.com 183, 212
Altieri, Ferdinando 113
Alvearie (Baret) 46
America (British colonies) 84–86
American Desk Thesaurus (Lindberg) 197
American dictionaries 108, 131, 149, 193–195; branding and internationalization of 228

American Dictionary (Oxford) 178–179, 181
American Dictionary (Webster) 148
American English 153, 159, 172, 180–181, 191; vs British English 195; *Historical Dictionary of American English* 227; slang 188
American Indian Languages (Boas) 206
Americanisms 139
American Library Association 195
American War of Independence 86–87, 117
Amiens, Treaty of 127
Ancient Human Occupation of Britain (AHOB project) 11
Andersen, James David 222
Andrews, Ethan Allen 150
Angles (nation) 11–12, 14
Anglo-Dutch wars 55
Anglo-Frisian dialect 10
Anglo-Saxon: headwords 65; language 12; invasion 11, 14–15; period 8, 20, 29, 60; proto-dictionaries 26; synonyms 21
Annandale, Charles 148–149
Apocrypha 58
Arabic 63, 69
Aramaic 38, 58
Arnauld, Antoine 93
Arnold, Theodore 113
Ash, John 112
asterisks, use of 80, 106
Augustan Age of British Literature 91
Austen, Jane 124
Australia 85, 117, 125–126, 130, 163–164; emigrants 135
Australian Association for Lexicography 217
Australian English 172; slang 187, 189

244 *Index*

Australian National Dictionary, The
  227; story of 220; see also *Macquarie
  Dictionary*
Australian Pocket Oxford Dictionary 178
Awdeley, John 48
Axon, William Edward Armytage 116
Ayto, John 189, 201

Bacon, Francis 38
Bailey, Nathan 101, 103–108,
  111–114; etymological treatments,
  explanations of 121–122; historical
  ordering found in 157; Johnson,
  influence on 97, 158; precedents set
  by 184, 210; *Universal Etymological
  English Dictionary* 114, 116, 132,
  184; user targeting by 123
Baker, Robert 191
Bale, Peter 61
Banks, James 150
Baret, John 45–46, 49–50, 74, 88
Baretti, Giuseppi 113, 133, 150
Barnes, William 151
Barnhart, Clarence 145
Barrère, Albert Marie Victor 153
Bartholomew, Dolores 219
Battaglia, Salvatore 155
Baugh, Albert C. 129, 131
Baumann, Heinrich 153
Bejoint, Henri 218
Bellows, John 150
Benbow, Timothy 175
Benham, William Gurney 201
Bergenholtz, Henning 218–219, 223
Bibliotheca scholastica (Rider) 46–47,
  73, 78
bilingual dictionary 51, 73–77; Latin
  roots of 20–27
bilingual lexicography *see* foreign
  languages and words; lexicography
Bill of Rights (British) 57
Bi Sheng 16
Bloomfield, Leonard 206
Blount, Thomas 67–69, 79, 101, 104,
  132; Philips' copyright dispute with
  69; *see also Glossographia*
Boas, Franz 206
Boccaccio, Giovanni 19, 37
Bohn, Henry George 154
Bolton, Edmund 89
Book of Common Prayer 38–39
Bopp, Franz 134–135
Boswell, James 94–95
Boulanger, J.-C. 23

Boyer, Abel 77
Boyle, Robert 59
Bradley, Henry 144–146
Brandon, Henry 187
Bridges, Edward 193
Bright, Timothy 61
British East India Company 52–53
British English *see* English (British)
British Isles 11–15, 52–54, 63, 71,
  86, 103
British monarchy, restoration of 55–56
British National Corpus 165
Brito, William 24
Brown Corpus (BC) 165
Browne, R. 67
Brown, Lesley 178
Buchanan, James 114
Buckley, Samuel 83
Bullokar, John 66–67, 88, 101, 121
Bullokar, William 61
Burchfield, Robert 174, 192
Burkett, Eva Mae 219
Burn, John 115
Buys, Egbert 77
Bysshe, Edward 115

Cable, Thomas 129, 131
Cabot, John 17
Cadell, Thomas 94
Cadena, Mariano Velázquez de la 150
Caesar, Julius 13
Calepino (Calepine, Calepinus),
  Ambrosius 19, 41, 74, 78
Cambridge Philological Society 129
Camden Society 24
Camden, William 89
Canterbury (Archbishop of) 14, 38
Canting Academy, The (Head) 70
cant (slang) 72, 96, 99; in Barrère's
  dictionary 153; in Coles'
  dictionary 70, 101
Carey, John 113
Carr, C. T. 177
Casell's Book of Quotations 201
Cassell's Dictionary of Slang see Green,
  Jonathon
Cassidy, F. 99
Catherine of Aragon 33–34
Catholic Church *see* Roman Catholic
  Church
Catholicism: Britain 56, 67–68; France 38
Catholicon Anglicum 23–24, 28, 30,
  44, 205
Cawdry, Robert 60, 64–66

Index   245

Cawdry, Thomas 64–65
Caxton, William 17
CD-ROM editions 211, 222; Jones'
  17th edition 185; *LDCE* 181, 183;
  OED 175, 182
Century Company 149
Century Dictionary and Cyclopedia 149
Chambers dictionary series 198, 212, 227
Chambers Dictionary of Quotations 202
*Chambers Encyclopedic English
  Dictionary* 200
Chambers English Dictionary 148
Chambers Etymological Dictionary 179
*Chambers Guide to Grammar and
  Usage* 192
Chambers Twentieth Century Dictionary
  179
Chambers, W. & R. 148, 198
Church of England 57–58
*Cambridge International English
  Dictionary* 181
Celts 11, 13
Charles I 54
Charles II 54, 91
Chaucer, Geoffrey 12, 16, 65, 105
Cheke, John 88
China 162; dictionary-making in 60;
  English language in 164, 210, 227;
  Lexicographical Society 217; trade
  with 17
Chinese language 11, 164, 184;
  lexicography 205, 209; phonetic
  transcriptions 210; *see also* English-
  Chinese dictionaries
Chomsky, Noam 171
Clark, John Owen Edward 192
Claudius (Emperor) 13
Cocker, Edward 102–103
Cocker's Accomplish'd School-Master 102
Cocker's English Dictionary 103
Cockeram, Henry 67, 101, 121
cognitive linguistics 168, 170, 225–226
cognitive paradigm of English
  lexicography 3–4, 204, 213; and
  comparative 218; pedagogy and
  reconstruction of 216; period of 9;
  user's needs and demands 109, 123,
  220–221
Coleman, Julie 224
Coleridge, Herbert 135, 137
Coles, Elisha 82, 75–76, 79, 101–103;
  etymology of 121; slang, dialect, and
  cant in the dictionary of 69–70
Collins, Beverly 184

*Collins Cobuild Dictionary of the
  English Language* 165, 171–172,
  180–181, 206, 216
Collins Dictionary of Quotations 202
Collins English Dictionary 179
*Collins English Dictionary and
  Thesaurus Set* 199, 213
*Collins Gem School Dictionary &
  Thesaurus* 199
Collins Primary Thesaurus 198
Collins School Thesaurus 198
Collison, Robert L. 219
Columbus, Christopher 17
Comelati, G. 150
Complete English Dictionary (Wesley) 111
comprehensiveness (in dictionary-
  making) 2, 106, 121
concordances 27
Connelly, Thomas 113
consistency: of compiling techniques 69;
  of defining words 80; in dictionaries
  and dictionary-making 2, 78–79,
  121, 174; in etymological treatments
  106, 110; of headwords 50, 109; in
  phonetic notation 114; of spelling 80,
  99; of writing systems 36
Cook, James 85–87
Coolidge, Calvin 146
Cooper, Thomas 41–45, 50, 68, 72,
  74; *Bibliotheca Eliotae* 41–42, 79;
  *Thesaurus Linguae Romanae et
  Britannicae* 42–43, 195
Coote, Edmund 61–65, 66, 71–72;
  signs and typefaces 80
Copernicus, Nicolaus 37
Cop, Margaret 216
Cotgrave, Randle 77
Cotton, Robert Bruce (Sir) 89
Crabb, George 196
Cranmer, Thomas 38
Craigie, William Alexander 142, 145–146,
  173–174, 187
Creole 130
Crystal, David 100, 192
cuneiform 18
Curme, George Oliver 168

Daily Courant, The 83
Dalzell, Tom 188
Dante 37
Dareau, Margaret G. 187
Davenport, J. 150
Davidson, George 192
da Vinci, Leonardo 37

246 *Index*

Davis, John Francis 150
Day, John 63
Defoe, B.N. 112
Defoe, Daniel 84, 90
Delahunty, Andrew 193–194
Delpino, Joseph Giral 113
DeMaria, R. 118
Descartes, René 37
descriptivism 2–3, 9, 120, 206; in
  18th-century English dictionaries
  132; historical 156; and the
  pedagogical mode 216; and
  prescriptivism in the *Dictionary of
  Modern English Usage* (Fowler) 192
diacritical marks 114
diachronic dictionaries 124–159
diachronic studies 4–6, 30; of English
  lexicography 7, 35; of Middle Ages 41
diachronism 141, 225
dialect dictionaries 185–187
dialects 12, 17, 20; Anglo-Frisian 10;
  Coote's dislike of 71; Early Modern
  English 131; English 186; European
  147; Germanic 11; and language
  standardization 89; Old English 36,
  71–72; Papuan 135; public attitude
  towards 151; regional 89, 152; study
  of 205
Dias, Bartholomeu 17
Dickens, Charles 124
Dictionaries (journal) 217
Dictionarium Anglo-Britannicum 104,
  121
*Dictionarium Linguae Latinae et
  Anglicanae* (Thomas) 43–44
dictionary criticism 224–225
dictionary functions and forms 225–226
Dictionary Society of North America 217
dictionary paradigms, evolution of 168
dictionary typology 223–224
dictionary user and use 225
Dictionnaire de l'Académie française 93
digitalization of dictionaries *see* internet
  and internet technologies
diversification of dictionaries 198,
  226–227
Donald, James 148
Drake, Francis (Sir) 34
Dryden, John 90–91, 97, 104
Du Ponceau, Peter Stephen 131
Dutch language 69; into English 17;
  etymological dictionary 116; *see also*
  English-Dutch dictionaries
Dyche (Dysche), Thomas 107, 114, 184

education in Britain, 17th century 58;
  see also language pedagogy
Edward (King of England) 15
Edwards, Jonathan 85
electronic and online dictionaries
  182–184
Eliot (Elyot), Thomas 40–42, 44–46, 49
Eliot-Cooper dictionaries 42, 78
Elizabeth I 38–39, 42, 89; British East
  India Company, charter granted by
  53; Camden's account of 89; and
  Church of England 33; death of 54,
  57; Drake's knighting by 34; English
  language spoken by 36; John Rider as
  favourite of 47
Elizabeth II 175
Elizabethan era 34, 124
Ellis, Alexander J. 131, 135, 141, 184
Elworthy, Frederick Thomas 151
encyclopedic dictionaries 199–200
Endicott, J. G. 206
England, Commonwealth of, founding
  of 55
English (British): as official language
  of Britain 16; Johnson's dictionary
  of 93–101; evolution of 11, 13,
  19, 34–35, 39, 158; lexicography
  1–6; origins and development of
  10–12; *see also* language evolution;
  lexicography
English Civil Wars 54
English Dialect Society 152
English dictionaries, humanistic and
  academic values of 117–123
English-Chinese dictionaries 118–119,
  182–183
English-Dutch dictionaries 77, 114
English-French dictionaries 150
English-German dictionaries 153
English-Latin dictionaries 9, 23–24, 26,
  29–31, 44–50; British Renaissance 38;
  departure from 40; dominating role
  of 73–79; English as headword 44;
  etymological dictionaries, influence on
  116; glossaries 29; lexicography 35;
  waning dominance of 113
English language, codification of 87–92
English Reformation 32–34, 38–39, 58
English Reformation Committee 90
English-speaking world: America and
  Australia, influence of 117; Australia,
  earliest British colonists of 86;
  British English, domination of 129;
  Johnson's dictionary, impact on 100;

and mass media 165; and *NED* 158; periphery of 162; scholars 58; slang 188–190; territories of 163; and the United States 160
Erasmus, Desiderius 88
Esquire, R. H. 90
European Association for Lexicography 217
Evans, Benjamin Ifor 192
Evelyn, John 90, 104
etymological dictionaries (British) 190–195
excise tax (example of defined word) 98, 118–119

Farmer, Stephen 153, 188
Faucett, Lawrence 207
Flaccus, Verius 20
Florio, John 47, 61
Flügel, Felix 150
Flügel, J. G. 150
Fontenelle, Thierry 218
foreign languages and words 61, 64, 116; English as 161–162, 164, 209; Oxford Dictionary 178
foreign language pedagogy *see* language pedagogy
four-letter words 106, 112
Fowler, Francis George 192
Fowler, Henry Watson 191–192
France: Battle of Trafalgar 127; British-French war 117; and Britain 16, 22, 32; Catholic 38; dictionary-making in 19; English language taught in 173; First and Second Coalition against 127
Fraser, Bruce 193
Fraser, Donald 202
Frawley, William 220–221
FreeDictionary.com 183–184, 228
Frelinghuysen, Theodore Jacobus 85
French-English dictionaries 150, 153, 210, 222
French language: as academic language 164; dictionaries 159; English language, impact on 19, 23, 37, 131; language reforms 88; Latin replaced with 87; Norman 12; multilingual dictionaries 27, 42; as upper class language 16, 130, 149; word origins 80
Freund, Wilhelm 150
Frisian *see* Anglo-Frisian dialect
Friswell, James Hain 154
Furnivall, Frederick James 135, 138–143; death of 145

Garland, John (Johannes de Garland) 22, 24
Garner, Bryan A. 193–194
Geeraerts, D. 223
Gellerstam, Martin 224
Gent, L.C. 154
Geoffrey the Grammarian 23
George III 94
George V 146
Gil, Alexander 72
Gimson, A.C. 185
Girard, Gabriel 196
Glazier, Stephen 170
Glorious Revolution 53, 56–57
glossae collectae 9, 20, 25; *see also Medulla Grammaticae*
Glossarial Index to the Printed English Literature (Coleridge) 137
glossaries (English) 1, 8–10; ancient 29; bilingual 51, 60–62, 78; characteristics and academic value of 27–30; Chinese bilingual 209–210; class 27; early English 29, 45, 50; English dialect 150–152, 185; English-Latin 47; Greek 19; hard-word 20, 63; Harman's English 48; headwords, two or modes of 28; historical 187; Latin 20; Latin-Old English 21, 23; Latin roots of 20–26; of legal terms 66; multilingual 23; of obscure words 19; Old and Middle English, as key carriers of 29; Sumerian 18
Glossographia Anglicana Nova (Anon.) 82, 104, 121
Glossographia (Blount) 67–69, 79, 101, 132
Gouldman, Francis 73–75, 79
Gove, Philip Babcock 2–3
Gowers, Ernest Arthur 191–193
Granger, Sylviane 222
Grant, William 186
Great Awakening 84–85
Great Vowel Shift 88
Greenbaum, Sydney 169, 192–193
Green, Jonathon 21, 24; *Cassell's Dictionary of Slang* 189; *Chasing the Sun* 220; *Green's Dictionary of Slang* 189–190; *Slang Thesaurus* 198
Grimm, Jakob 134–135, 155
Grose, Francis 72, 116, 153
Guest, Edwin 128, 134, 139, 158
Gutenberg printing press 51

248   *Index*

Hall, Fitzedward 191
Halliwell, James Orchard 151–152
Han dynasty 117, 205
Hanks, Patrick 179, 197, 200
Harald Hardrada (king of Norway) 15
hardwords: Coote's book of 62;
    dictionaries 52, 64–71, 216;
    glossaries 20, 51; from Homer 18;
    Old English 63; "mot difficiles"
    63; practice of collecting 27–28;
    traditions, fading of 66–72;
    traditions, termination of 82–123;
    vulgaria 27; *see also* inkhorn words
Hardy, Thomas 124
Harman, Thomas 48
Harold (king of England) 15
Harris, John 199
Harrison, Lucas 47
Harris, Roy 159
Hart, John 88
Hartmann, R.R.K. 224
Hausmann, Franz Josef 215–216
Head, Richard 70
headwords: alphabetical 28, 41, 43–46,
    48, 52, 191; Bailey 106–108, 184;
    Bullokar 101; Burchfield 174; Cawdrey
    62, 65–67, 80; Chinese 210; chip
    dictionary 211; Cockeram 101;
    cognate 50; Coles 70, 75–76; Collins
    171; Eliot 78; encyclopedic 52; Green
    190; Grose 116; Halliwell 151; internet
    dictionary 212; Johnson 97–99, 166;
    Kersey 69; Latin 21, 45; Longman 200;
    macrostructural 199, 209; Martin 109;
    noun 197; OED 146, 166; Palmer
    208; Partridge 188; Pearsall 179;
    pictorially illustrated 104; Robinet
    150; "scholarly" 52; standardizing
    orthography of 61; synonyms 22–23;
    thesauruses 197; Wright 152
Hebrew 23; Eliot's dictionary 41; "hard
    words" in 68; "inkhorn words" in
    63; Old Testament 38, 58
Henley, William Ernest 153, 188
Henry V 191
Henry VI 12, 16
Henry VIII 32–34
Henry Tudor II 17
Higgins, Thomas 113
Hilton, Walter 16
Hippocrates 19
*Historical Dictionary of American
    English* 227
historical descriptivism 156; *see also*
    descriptivism

historical dictionaries 100, 103, 128–129,
    133–135, 137; *Historical Dictionary
    of American English* 145, 227;
    Historical Thesaurus of the OED 195,
    199; *Oxford Universal Dictionary
    on Historical Principles* 178; *Shorter
    Oxford English Dictionary on
    Historical Principles* 177
historical evolution of dictionaries 224
historical linguistics 132, 134,
    153–154, 158–159, 168; 19th
    century 216, 224; and diachronic
    lexicography 203
historical ordering of dictionaries 157
historical paradigm for English
    lexicography 2, 4–5, 9, 113, 204,
    214, 217; *New English Dictionary
    on Historical Principles* 128, 141,
    144, 146
historical philology 196
historical semantics 158; *see also*
    semantics
Hitchings, Henry 98, 118
Hodgson, William B. 191
Hollyband, Claudius 47, 61
Holthausen, Ferdinand 190
Holtrop, John 114
Holyoake, Francis 73, 75, 78–79
Holyoake, Thomas 73, 75, 79
Homer 18–19
Hooke, Robert 59
Horgan, A. 100
Horman, William 60
Hornby, Albery Sydney 168, 177, 180,
    207–209
Horwill, Herbert William 193
Hotten, John Camden 153
Howell, James 77
Huloet, Richard 31, 44–45
Huloet-Higgins dictionary series 49
Hunter, Robert 147, 149, 199
Huttonus, Richardus 43

Imbs, Paul 155
India Bank of 143; British East India
    Company 52–53; British colonization
    of 83, 117; English dictionary
    published in 107; English language in
    130, 162; spice trade with 17
Indian languages 132
indigenous peoples 85–86; American
    Indians 206
Industrial Revolution 10, 33, 58; 17th
    century 162; 18th century 83; 19th
    century 126; First and Second 129–130

Index   249

informationalization 225–226, 228
information technology 226; *see also*
   electronic and online dictionaries
"inkhorn words" 63–65, 82
International Journal of Lexicography 217
International Phonetic Alphabet 184
International Phonetic Association 184
internet dictionaries 211–212; *see also*
   electronic and online dictionaries
internet and internet technologies 92,
   160–161, 163, 165; and digitalization
   of dictionaries 182–184, 199, 203,
   211; searches 158
Isaacs, Alan 200

James (king of England) 56–57; *see also*
   James I; *King James Bible*
Januensis, Joannes 24
jargon: dictionaries of 72, 111, 153, 187;
   glossary of 48
"J.K." 102–103; *see also* Kersey, John
Johnson, Samuel 1, 93–101
Johnston, William 114
Jones, Daniel 115, 131, 184–185
Jones, Gary 202
Jones, William 132–134
Junius, Franciscus 117
Jutes 11, 14

Kachru, Braj. B. 224
Kahane, Henry 224
Karpova, Olga 215, 218
Kartashkova, Faina 215, 218
Kenrick, William 114–115
Kersey, John 103
Key, Thomas Hewitt 128, 134
Kiliaen, C. 116
King's English *see* Received
   Pronunciation (RP)
King James Bible 39, 57–58
Kipchak language 23
Kirkpatrick, Betty 197
Kirkpatrick, Elizabeth McLaren 197
Klein, Ernest 190
Kluge, Friedrich 190
Konopka, Rafal 185
Kretzschmar, William 185
Kroll, Adam

Lambarde, William 71
Lancaster-Oslo/Bergen Corpus (LOB) 165
Lancelot, Claude 93
Landau, Sidney 106, 219, 223
Langland, William 16
language cognition 226

language databank 165
language evolution 109, 117, 128, 133;
   OED as record of 176; of words 156
language pedagogy 3, 8–9, 207–209;
   foreign 3, 207
Latin-English dictionaries 9, 19, 24–26,
   29, 31; 15th century 205; 16th
   century 206, 210; 17th century 45,
   73–79; 19th century 150; *Bibliotheca
   scholastica* 47, 78; bilingual 49,
   132; Blount 68; Cockeram 67;
   Coles 75; Eliot 40–41; Hutton 43;
   lexicography 35; Littleton 76; and
   national languages, revitalization
   of 50; Renaissance period 38, 40;
   Skinner 71; Veron 42; Wase 74
Latin-Old English glossaries 21, 23
learner's dictionaries 180–182
Leech, Geoffrey 169
Leibnitz, Gottfried Wilhelm 155
Leiden Glossary, The 8, 10
Leland, Charles Godfried 153
Leonard, R. M. 201
Leonard, Sterling A. 191
Levins, Peter 48
Lexicographical Society of China 217
Lexicographical Studies 217
lexicography (British) 203–228; 20th
   century theoretical developments in
   213–225; 21st century, prospect of
   225–228; bilingual 31–51; cognitive
   and comparative 220–223; culture,
   inception of 10–30; diachronic and
   synchronic 219–220; evolution
   of 4–9, 39–40, 75; general and
   specialized 218–219; Latin beginnings
   and paradigms 1–3; Latin, tradition
   of 18–20; monolingual and bilingual
   219; theoretical and practical 218
Lewis, Charlton T. 150
Lewis, Windsor 185
LDCE *see Longman Dictionary of
   Contemporary English* (LDCE)
Liddell, Henry George 157
Lindberg, Christine A. 197
Lingua Brittanica Reformata (Martin)
   108–110
linguistic theory (British) 204–213
Littleton, Adam 76, 79–80
Little, William 177
Liu Xi 157, 205
London Philological Society *see*
   Philological Society
Long, George 128, 134
Longman, Addison Wesley 197

250 *Index*

Longman Dictionary of Contemporary English (LDCE)3; CD-ROM edition 181, 183; corpus employment in 165; descriptivism of 9; first edition 171, 180, 206, 209; front matter 169; pedagogical mode represented by 216; and pragmatics 171; second edition 180; third edition 181
Lothbrok, Ragnar 15
Louis XIII (King of France) 93
Lounsbury, Thomas R. 191
Lutz, Frederick 190
Lye, Edward 117
Lynch, J. 100

Macdonnel, D. E. 115, 154
Macquarie Dictionary, The 214, 227
Makins, Marian 197
Malden, Henry 134
Malkiel, Yakov 223
Mallet, Edward 83
Mallet, Elizabeth 83
Malory, Thomas 16
Manlove, James 112
March, Francis Andrew 143, 197
Marlow, Christopher 37
Marsh, George Perkins 137
Martin, Benjamin 108, 113
Martin, Elizabeth 200
Martin, Gregory 65, 97, 108–109, 121, 123
McArthur, Tom 170, 207, 219
McDermott, Anne 96
McKean, Erin 179
Mead, Richard 113
Medulla Grammaticae 23–25, 205
Mees, Inger 184
Merriam Company 100, 200
merriam-webster.com 213
metalexicography 216
Michaelis, Herman 185
Middle Ages 22, 24, 28; bilingual dictionaries 62, 228; Latin supremacy during 36
Middle English 10–13, 16, 29; period of 23
Middle English Dictionary 24
Miège, Guy 77
Miles, W.A. 187
Miller, Gertrude M. 185
Millhouse, John 150
Milner, Christina 187
Milner, Richard 187
Milton, John 68, 97, 178
Ming dynasty 117

Minsheu (Minshew), John 47–48, 77, 116
Monck, George 56
monolingual dictionary 52–81; Cawdrey and 64–66; and hard-word traditions, fading of 66–73; making of 60–64
Monson (Lord) 24
Moore, Huge 154
Moore, Thomas 38
Morelius (Morel), Gulielmus (Guillaume) 43
Morell, Thomas 113
Mulcaster, Richard 61–63, 88–89
Müller (Mueller), Eduard 154
Murison, David 186
Murray, James 138–139, 142–146, 149, 158
Murray, John 154

national languages, rise of 59
Neckham, Alexander 21–22
Neumann, Henry 150
New and Complete Dictionary of the English Language (Ash) 112
New English Dictionary on Historical Principles (NED) 137–146, 152, 155–159
New General English Dictionary, A (Dyche/Pardon) 107–108
New Oxford English-Chinese Dictionary 118–119
New Oxford English Dictionary Project 175
Newton, Isaac (Sir) 59, 104
New Universal Etymological English Dictionary (Scott) 111–112
new word dictionaries 200–201
New World of English Words see Philips, Edward
Nicol, Henry 142
Nicholson, Margaret 193
nominales 26
Norman Conquest 12, 15–16
Norman French 12
Nowell, Laurence 71
novel *see* English novel
Noyes, Gertrude E. 25–26, 63, 65, 104–105, 112, 219

Ogilvie, George W. 149
Ogilvie, John 147–148
Ogilvie, Sarah 220
Old English 89; dictionary 71; Latin influence on 14; to Middle English 10–13, 16

onelook.com 183–184, 212
Onions, Charles Talbot 142, 144–145, 173–174, 177, 190
Onomasticon (Pollux) 195
Ooi, V.B.Y. 223
optical character recognition (OCR) 165
oriental languages 148
Origines Celticae (Guest) 128, 134
Orton, Harold 186
Ortus Vocabulorum 23, 25, 40–41, 205
Orwell, George 187
Osselton, N. E. 224
Ostler, George 177
Ostler, N. 24
overseas expansion, Britain 17–18
Oxford English-Chinese Dictionary see New Oxford English-Chinese Dictionary
Oxford English Dictionary (OED) 2, 139–146; CD-Rom edition 175, 182, 211; completion of 101; precedent for 52, 77; serializations, adaptions, new and revised editions 174–185, 189–195, 197–201; oed.com 212; pocket 213; quotations 202; slang dictionary 189; story of 220; *Supplement* 145–146, 173–175; thesaurus 197, 213

Palgrave, John 60
palm devices 228
palm dictionary 211
Palmer, Abram Smythe 152
Palmer, Harold Edward 169, 180, 207–209
Pardon, William 107, 112, 121, 123
Parenogo, Michel 150
Parker, Mathew (Archbishop) 89
Patrick, Samuel 113
Partridge, Eric Honeywood 187–188, 190, 192
Passow, Franz 156–157
Passy, Paul 184–185
Patrick, Samuel 113
Pearsall, Judith 178–179, 200
Pegge, Samuel 115
Percyvall, Richard 47
Perry, William 114, 196
Petty, William 59
Philips, Edward 67–70, 97, 101–102; *New World of English Words* 68–69, 104–105
philological dictionaries 169–170, 172; in the 20th century 173–180
Philological Society (London Philological Society) 100, 124, 136,

138, 158–159; Furnivall as secretary 138, 140–142; Murray as editor of *NED* 142–146; *OED*'s ending of connection with 139
Philological Society, New York 129
philological traditions: development of 71; European 124–159; and Johnson's dictionary 118, 132
philologist 19; Craigie 145; Freund 150; Walker 115; Wedgwood 154
philology: classical 135; comparative 132, 152–153; European 156; Germanic 154; "new" 134
phonetic: annotation 114, 120; changes 87–89; features, theory of 223; normalization of 130–131; notation 180; studies 107, 135; transcription 66, 131, 184–185, 210, 222
phonetics, discipline of 29, 135, 168, 185
phraseology 207–209
Pickering, William 147
pictorial dictionary 26
Picts 11
pidgin English 130, 153
Pike, K. Lorna 187
Pineda, Peter 113
Piotrowski, Tadeusz 219
Piozzi, Hester Lynch 196
Pitman, Isaac 184
plagiarism 73, 80
Plato 18
Pocket Dictionary, A (1753) 110–111
Pollux, Julius 195
Praeconinus, Lucius Aelius Stilo 19
prescriptivism 1–2, 204, 206; departure from 133; and diachronic approaches 209, 214; dictionary adherence to 101–112; and descriptivism192; dominance of 190; establishment of 87–92; of Johnson's dictionary 95, 100, 119–120, 132, 156; period of 9; pursuit of 82–123; tradition of 170
printing technology 16–17
Proctor, Paul 200
Promptorium Parvulorum 23–24, 28, 30, 41, 44, 214
pronunciation: annotations of 43, 111, 114; Bailey's guidance and influence on 106–108, 114, 184; changes in 36, 96, 130; Dyche/Martin's guidance regarding 110; Dyche/Pardon's special attention to 107; Dyche's attempt to transcribe 184; Grose's approach to 116; Johnson's views on and treatment of 96, 99; Kenrick's

252 Index

techniques of transcribing 115; and language standardization 89; Liu Xi's understanding of 157; *OED's* impact on 159; Perry's annotation of 196; prescriptive principles for 9; reconstruction of 2; reforms in 88; Scott's annotation of 111; and spelling 87–89, 96; stabilization of 130; *see also* Great Vowel Shift; Received Pronunciation; spelling
pronunciation system 115
pronouncing dictionaries 184–185
Protagoras 18
proverbs 22, 41, 50; Bailey's inclusion of 105; Grose's glossary of 116; Halliwell's dictionary of 151; Johnson's dropping of 107; Ray's collection of 72
Pynson, Richard 22–23
Pytheas 11

Queen's English *see* Received Pronunciation (RP)
Quirk, Randolf 165
quotation dictionaries 201–202

Ramson, William ("Bill") 220
Rask, Rasmus Kristian 134
Ray, John 70, 72, 116
Real Academia Española 93
Received Pronunciation (RP) 131, 185
Reddick, Allen 99
Reformation *see* English Reformation
Renaissance (in the United Kingdom) 37–38
Rey, Alan 223
Richard II 59
Richardson, Charles 137, 140, 147–148, 155–158
Richelieu (Cardinal) 93
Rider-Holyoake dictionary series 73–75
Rider, John 46–47, 49–50, 75–76; *see also Bibliotheca scholastica*
Roberts, Jane 195
Robinet, M. 150
Rogers, Pat 94
Roget, Peter Mark 154–155, 170, 195–196; *see also Thesaurus of English Words and Phrases* (Roget)
Roget, John Lewis 155
Roget, Samuel Romilly 155
Rolle, Richard 16
Roman Catholic Church 32–34
Rome and the Roman Empire 11–14, 18, 37; and British Empire 125;

calendar and measurements 76; classic works of 40, 134
Royal Society (Britain) 58–59, 90
Rundell, Michael 218
Ruse, Christina 177

Salesbury, William 47
Samuels, Michael 195
Sauer, Hans 19–21
Saxons 11,14
Scherren, Henry 149
Schneider, John Gottlob 157
Scottish National Dictionary 186
Scottish National Dictionary Association 186
Scots Thesaurus 186
Scott, Joseph Nichol 111
Scott, Robert 157
Sebeok, Thomas 223
semantic categorization 198
semantic classification 169
semantic composition 121
semantic fields 21; theory 170
semantic groups 155
semantic relations 45; varieties 208
semantics 2, 4, 168; diachronic 170; historical 157–158; lexical 169; studies 196
serialization: of *OED* 146, 173, 176; strategies of 227; type 228; typological 226
Sewel, Willem 77
SGML encoding 175
Shakespeare Glossary 145
Shakespeare, William 35, 37, 65; and Cawdry 65; and Cooper's dictionary 42; dictionaries from the time of 224; and Johnson 97, 105; and modern English, influence on 39, 42; and spelling 131
Shcherba, L. V. 223
Sheridan, Thomas 115
Shipley, Joseph 190
Short, Charles L. 150
Shorte Dictionarie for Yonge Begynners, A (Withals) 45–46
silent letters 88, 114
silent word endings 109
Simpson, John A. 189
Sinclair, John M. 218
Skeat, Walter W. 152, 154, 190
Skinner, Stephen 71–72, 115–117, 152; before and after 185; *Etymologicon Linguae Anglicanae* 122
slang and slang lexicography 187–190; *see also* jargon

Index 253

Sledd, James 220
Smith, A. J. 145
Smith, Thomas 88
Snell-Hornby, Mary 224
Sobral, Mateo Seoane y 150
social advancement in Europe 17, 119
social culture and lexicography 117, 161–166
social functions of dictionaries 5, 48, 50; nationalistic aspects of 73; *see also* social value of English dictionaries
social issues, language standardization as 59, 89
social life and language (British) 14; dictionary appendices focused on 66; French influence on 127; pronunciation's impact on 184; words related to 28
social motivations to change language 92; and slang 188
social networks 188
social reform 7
social status 12, 191; and dictionaries, usefulness of 64; of English language 36, 39, 62; and word usage 191
social transformation in Britain 31–32, 37, 84, 87; since the 19th century 124–125; since the 20th century 160
social value of English dictionaries 77–81
Society for Philological Inquiries 128, 134
Society for Pure English 132
Society of Antiquaries 89
Somner, William 71, 77
Song dynasty 16, 117
Sparrow, J. 112
Speght, Thomas 65
spelling; chaotic 17, 36; compilers guessing at 29; as focus of literacy education 60; inconsistencies in 80, 99; during Middle Ages 87; vs pronunciation 87–89, 96; "semi-phonetic" 114; standardizations, attempts to implement 120; traditional ways of 100; *see also* silent letters
spelling checkers 211
spelling reform 46, 88–90, 108, 130; 19th-century attempts 131; by Dyche 109
Spelling Reform Society 140
spelling system 110
Spenser, Edmund 37, 105, 178
Squarotti, Giorgio Bàrberi 155
Stanbridge, John 26–27, 60

Stark, Martin 219
Starnes, DeWitt T. 25–26, 63, 65, 104–105, 112, 219
Stein, Gabriele 45
Stephanus, Robert 42–43, 45, 50, 210
Stepney, William 61
Stevens, John 113
Stevenson, Burton 201
Stevenson, James A. C. 187
Stevenson, Robert Louis 124
Strahan, William 94–95
Sue, Atkins B.T. 218
Sumerian 18
Survey of English Dialects 186
Survey of English Usage (SEU) 165
Svensen, Bo 218
Swan, Michael 193
Sweet, Henry 135, 138, 141–142, 184–185, 207
Swift, Jonathan 90–91, 98
synonym finder 212
synonyms 22–23; Anglo-Saxon 21; Cawdrey 66; dictionaries of 147, 154–155, 170; discrimination 180; English 79, 197; etymological 77; Johnson 99, 146; Latin 24, 45; Littleton 76; Minsheu 77; Old English 29; online 183; Trench's views on 136
synonymous relations 195–199

Table Alphabeticall, A (Cawdry) 60, 62, 64–67
taboo words 106–107, 159
Tang dynasty 117
Tangut language 209–210
Tarp, Sven 218–219
Taylor, William 196
thesaurus dictionary 212–213, 228
thesauruses (British), making of 195–199
Thesaurus linguae Romanae & Britannicae (Cooper) 41–43, 78–79
Thesaurus of English Words and Phrases (Roget) 154–155, 170, 196–197
Thirlwall, Connop 128, 134
Thomas, Thomas 43–44, 65
Thomas, William 47
Thomson, John 154
Thorie, John 47
Thorndike, Edward Lee 165
Thorpe, Benjamin 134
Tilly, William 185
Tooke, John Horne 147, 158
Torriano, Giovanni 47
Trafalgar, Battle of 127

254 Index

Trebel, Henry Arthur 191
Trench, Richard Chevenix 135–137, 145, 148; dialectical words, exclusion of 152; ideal dictionary, definition of 156; and *New English Dictionary* (NED) 129, 139; and Unregistered Words Committee 135, 139–140
Trevisa, John 66
Trevithick, George 126
Trusler, John 196
Tudor dynasty 17, 31–33
Tulloch, Sara 201
Tyndale, William 36, 87

United Kingdom of Great Britain, establishment of 84
Upton, Clive 185–186
Urdang, Laurence 170, 179, 197
use and usage criticism 190–195, 225

Vallins, George Henry 191–192
Varro, Marcus Terentius 19
Verborum Latinorum cum Graecis Anglicisque (Huttonus) 43
Veron, John 42, 210
Verstegan, Richard 89
Verulam (Lord) 90
Victorian era 127–129
Victor, Terry 188
Vikings 12, 15
Vocabula (Stanbridge) 26–27, 60
"vocabularium" 20
vocabulary control, theory of 207–209
Vortigern (king of the Britons) 11
Vulgaria (Stanbridge) 26–27, 60
vulgarism 187–188
"vulgar" words 43, 67; changing attitudes to 185; dictionaries that include 72, 74, 89, 106, 153; Latin 76, 78; *see also* cant (slang); slang and slang lexicography

Waddington, Rudolph 42
Waite, Maurice 197
Walker, John 115
Ward, John 113
Wase, Christopher 73–75, 79

Washington, George 86
Watsone, Henry D. 187
Webster English dictionary series 161, 179, 227
Webster, Noah 137, 148, 180
Webster's Imperial Dictionary (Ogilvie) 149
Webster's Third 2–3, 9, 206; Sledd and Ebbitt's study of 220
Webster's University Dictionary 149
Wedgwood, Hensleigh 134–135, 154
Weiner, Edmund 175, 193–194
Wells, John 185
Wesley, John 111, 123
West, Michael Philip 180, 206–209
West Somerset Word-book (Elworthy) 151
Wheatley, Henry B. 48, 214
Wheelwright, George 142
Whitcut, Janet 192–193
Whitefield, George 85
Whittinton, Robert 60
Widdowson, John 186
Wilcocke, Samuel Hull 114
Wilkins, John 59
William III 56
William (duke) 15
William (king of England) 15
Winchester (Bishop of) 41
Winchester, Simon 220
Withals, John 45–46, 78
witticism 201
Worde, Wynkyn de 22, 24–25
word-fields 21; *see also* semantic fields
Wotherspoon, Irené 195
Wren, Christopher 59
Wright, Joseph 153, 186
Wright, Thomas 26, 151–152, 186
Wyche, Peter 90
Wycliffe, John 38
Wyld, Henry C. 179

Xun Zi 157

Yang Xiong 205
Young, William 113

Zgusta, Ladislav 215, 218, 223–224